NEW PERSPECTIVES ON AMERICAN POLITICS

NEW PERSPECTIVES ON AMERICAN POLITICS

Edited by
Lawrence C. Dodd
Calvin Jillson
University of Colorado at Boulder

A Division of Congressional Quarterly Inc.
Washington, D.C.

Copyright © 1994 Congressional Quarterly Inc.
1414 22nd Street, N.W., Washington, D.C. 20037

Printed in the United States of America.

Cover design: Debra Naylor

Library of Congress Cataloging-in-Publication Data

New perspectives on American politics / edited by Lawrence C. Dodd,
    Calvin Jillson.
        p.   cm.
    Includes bibliographical references and index.
    ISBN 0-87187-882-8 -- ISBN 0-87187-877-1 (pbk.)
    1. United States--Politics and government--20th century.
I. Dodd, Lawrence C., 1946-   II. Jillson, Calvin C., 1949-
JK261.N48   1993
306.2'0973--dc20   93-38536
                                                                                  CIP

Contents

Contributors

Edward G. Carmines is Rudy Professor and chair of the department of political science at Indiana University, Bloomington. He is the author or coauthor of numerous articles, chapters, monographs, and books including *Issue Evolution: Race and the Transformation of American Politics* (1990), winner of the American Political Science Association's 1990 Gladys M. Kammerer Award, and *Prejudice, Politics, and the American Dilemma* (1993). His research focuses on political behavior.

Lawrence C. Dodd is professor of political science and director of the Center for the Study of American Politics at the University of Colorado, Boulder. He is the author of *Coalitions in Parliamentary Government* (1976), coauthor of *Congress and the Administrative State* (1979), and coeditor of *Congress and Policy Change* (1986). He has served as president of the Southwestern Political Science Association, as a Congressional Fellow, and as a Hoover National Fellow.

Robert S. Erikson is distinguished professor of political science at the University of Houston. Prior to joining the Houston faculty in 1978, he taught at Florida State University. He is a former editor of the *American Journal of Political Science;* coauthor of *Statehouse Democracy* (1993) and *American Public Opinion* (1990); and has published numerous articles on elections and public opinion.

Thomas Ferguson is professor of political science at the University of Massachusetts, Boston. He previously taught at MIT and the University of Texas, Austin. He is the author or coauthor of many books and articles including *Right Turn: The Decline of the Democrats and the Future of American Politics* (1986).

Linda L. Fowler is professor of political science in the Maxwell School at Syracuse University. She is the coauthor of *Political Ambition: Who Decides to Run for Congress?* (1989) and author of *Candidates, Congress, and the American Democracy* (1993).

Virginia Gray is professor of political science at the University of Minnesota where she teaches courses on state politics, interest groups, and public policy. She has written books and articles on feminism, state politics, policy innovation, state economic development policy, and interest groups. From 1993 to 1994 she was a visiting professor at the

University of North Carolina, Chapel Hill, funded by the National Science Foundation's Visiting Professorship for Women Program.

Rodney Hero is a professor in the department of political science at the University of Colorado, Boulder. His primary research and teaching interests are in the areas of Latinos and urban ethnic politics in the United States. His book, *Latinos and the U.S. Political System: Two-tiered Pluralism* (1992), was the winner of the American Political Science Association's 1993 Ralph J. Bunche Award.

Calvin Jillson is associate professor of political science and director of the Keller Center for the Study of the First Amendment at the University of Colorado, Boulder. He is the author of *Constitution-Making: Conflict and Consensus in the Federal Convention of 1787* (1988) and coauthor of *Congressional Dynamics: Structure, Coordination, and Choice in the First American Congress, 1774-1789* (1994). He has served as chair of the political science department at the University of Colorado, Boulder, and as president of the Southwestern Political Science Association.

Sean Q Kelly is assistant professor of political science at East Carolina University. He is the author of several articles on congressional elections and divided government, most recently in *Polity*. In addition to divided government, his research interests include congressional party organization and party leadership in Congress. He served as an APSA Congressional Fellow from 1993 to 1994.

John W. Kingdon is professor of political science at the University of Michigan. His teaching and research concentrate on American national government, legislative process, and public policy. He is the author of *Agendas, Alternatives, and Public Policies* (1987) and *Congressmen's Voting Decisions* (1989).

Eileen L. McDonagh is an associate professor of political science at Northeastern University and a visiting scholar at the Murray Research Center at Radcliffe College. Her writings on gender and the state and on the nationalization of American public policies in the Progressive era have appeared in numerous scholarly publications. She is also the author of *From 'Pro-Choice' to 'Pro-Consent' in the Abortion Debate* (forthcoming), and is completing *Representative Democracy and the Modern American State.*

John P. McIver is associate professor of political science at the University of Colorado, Boulder. His research spans a number of areas including statistics and research methodology, public opinion, state politics, and the justice system. His work is published in the *American Political Science Review, American Journal of Political Science, Journal of Politics* as well as in other journals and books. He is the coauthor of *Unidimensional Scaling* (1981) and *Statehouse Democracy* (1993).

John F. Manley is professor of political science at Stanford University. His publications include *The Politics of Finance* (1970), *American Government and Public Policy* (1976), and *The Case Against the Constitution* (coeditor and contributor, 1987).

David R. Mayhew is the Alfred Cowles Professor of Government at Yale University. His publications include *Congress: The Electoral Connection* (1974), co-winner of the *Washington Monthly* political book award in 1974; and *Divided We Govern: Party Control, Lawmaking, and Investigations, 1946-1990* (1991), winner of the Richard E. Neustadt prize in 1992.

Bruce Nesmith is assistant professor of political science at Coe College in Cedar Rapids, Iowa. He teaches courses on American political institutions, as well as religion and U.S. politics. He is the author of *The New Republican Coalition: The Reagan Campaigns and White Evangelicals* (forthcoming).

Nelson W. Polsby is professor of political science and director of the Institute for Governmental Studies at the University of California, Berkeley. His teaching and research have focused on American political institutions and processes. He is a former editor of the *American Political Science Review* and is the author or coauthor of numerous books and articles, including *Community Power and Political Theory* (1963), *Presidential Elections* (1964), and *Consequences of Political Reform* (1983).

Paul J. Quirk is a professor in the Department of Political Science and the Institute of Government and Public Affairs at the University of Illinois at Urbana-Champaign, where he teaches courses on the presidency, political institutions, and public policy formation. He is the author of *Industry Influence in Federal Regulatory Agencies* (1981) and coauthor of *The Politics of Deregulation* (1985). He and Bruce Nesmith are currently writing a book about the presidency and public policymaking.

Bert A. Rockman is professor of political science and research professor at the University Center for International Studies at the University of Pittsburgh. He is also a nonresident senior fellow at the Brookings Institution in Washington, D.C. Most recently he has coedited *Do Institutions Matter? Government Capabilities in the United States and Abroad* (1992) and *Researching the Presidency: Vital Questions, New Approaches* (1993).

Martin Shefter is professor of government at Cornell University. His teaching and research include American political development and American urban politics. He is the author of *Political Parties and the State: The American Historical Experience* (1994) and *Political Crisis/Fiscal Crisis: The Collapse and Revival of New York City* (1992); coauthor of *Politics by Other Means: The Declining Importance of Elections in America* (1990); and editor of *Capital of the American Century: The National and International Influence of New York City* (1993).

Theda Skocpol is professor of sociology at Harvard University. She is the author of *States and Social Revolutions: A Comparative Analysis of France, Russia, and China* (1979), winner of the 1979 C. Wright Mills Award and the 1980 American Sociological Association Award for a Distinguished Contribution to Scholarship; *The Politics of Social Policy in the United States* (coedited, 1988); and *Protecting Soldiers and Mothers: The Political Origins of Social Policy in the United States* (1992), which received the J. David Greenstone Award and the 1993 Woodrow Wilson Foundation Award from the American Political Science Association and the Best Book Award of the Political Sociology Section of the American Sociological Association. For the past decade her research has focused on U.S. politics and public policies in comparative and historical perspective.

Walter J. Stone is professor of political science at the University of Colorado, Boulder. He is the author of *Republic at Risk: Self-Interest in American Politics* (1990) and coauthor of *Nomination Politics: Party Activists and Presidential Choice* (1984). He has published articles in the *American Journal of Political Science, American Political Science Review, Journal of Politics,* and other scholarly journals, and currently edits the *Political Research Quarterly.*

Gerald C. Wright is professor of political science at Indiana University. Before joining the Indiana faculty he served as program director for political science at the National Science Foundation. He is the author or coauthor of *Statehouse Democracy* (1993), *Congress and Policy Change* (1986), and *Electoral Choices in America* (1974) and has contributed articles to a wide variety of professional journals.

Foreword: On Political Change
in Modern America

One of the most obtrusive facts of modern life is the relatively fast pace of social change. Since political arrangements, themselves contingent social artifacts, must cope with social change, it is no wonder that now and again students of politics will turn their attention to the ways in which change affects the ways in which people are governed. And though Americans in their historic geographic isolation and prosperity have been protected from some of the tides that sweep through the world, an attentive reader of this book will see that political change is not one of them.

There is nothing unexpected about this. If I am right in supposing that modernity—implying technological advancement and swift communications—is a major cause of change in the social and political sphere, then as one of the world's richest, most technologically advanced, and largest societies, we would expect the United States to be in the forefront of change. Moreover, the highly modern propensity to invest in research, development, and higher education enhances the capacity of a nation organized like the United States to detect change when it occurs. What nation has so many well-trained political scientists keeping an eye on various aspects of its political life?

This does not mean that we will all agree on what the most important trends or changes are—more likely the opposite. It is precisely the diversity of judgments about important trends that makes a book about change coming from many hands especially worthwhile. And my privileged position at the head of the parade, so to speak, affords me an opportunity to give my own judgments—some of them quite speculative—about the intellectual agenda for students of American political change.

Taking as a base any year around 1940, the number and magnitude of changes in American politics and government between the base year and the present are quite overwhelming. They are all the more remarkable in that they were accomplished without the root and branch replacement of the nation's constitution or the intervention of foreign soldiers. I will list only a few examples.

Policy Outcomes

Civil Rights

Pride of place goes to the dismantling of what was an American caste system based upon the legal disabling of African Americans. Observers of contemporary communal violence in such places as India, Lebanon, and the former Yugoslavia are unlikely to doubt the depth, persistence, or destructiveness of hostilities grounded upon ethnic, racial, religious, or linguistic differences. Over the last half-century we can say with confidence that differences of this sort have not melted away in the American population; rather the reverse. Even so, the legal status of black Americans, and to a lesser but significant extent their political, social, and even economic status, has taken a sharp turn for the better.

Led by their remarkable economic achievements, the positions of Japanese Americans and Jewish Americans in the political system have also changed dramatically, to such an extent that the remaining traces of social discrimination against them are now largely seen as ludicrous. In our base year, Japanese Americans were on the verge of mass incarceration by the U.S. government and Jews were explicitly and systematically excluded from routine access to high-status occupations, private higher education, and the professions.

A nation from which the stain of legalized segregation and the systematic denial of civil rights to a significant segment of its population have been largely removed is not necessarily a nation without remaining problems. Nevertheless it is worth noting that the extension of civil rights does make a profound difference in society; the process by which that extension was accomplished constitutes political change. Important social differences of all sorts exist in the American population, but America has largely rid itself of its caste system and operates to a greater extent than any modern society on the basis of entitlements secured by legal principles rather than by status.

Welfare and the Growth of the Public Sector

When Franklin Roosevelt, in 1936, deplored the deeply depressed economic condition of "one-third of a nation" as ill-clad, ill-fed, and ill-housed, he suggested a benchmark. Today we would more properly refer to one-fifth of a nation, or less, a smaller fraction of a much more populous nation. In general, the most highly dependent parts of the population are the poor, the young, the old, and racial minorities. Of some of America's racial and ethnic minorities I have already spoken. Many members of some of these minorities remain poor; but among those no longer poor, other forms of social disability have been greatly attenuated. America's older people have grown in numbers, in health, in wealth, and in political clout. This is in part the result of a story of private-sector innovation in medicine, but only in part. The public sector played a large role in financing the rapid spread of cures for infectious diseases. And Social Security, a controversial innovation of the New Deal, is now firmly institutionalized. The post-World War II democratization of access to higher education is one significant change in public provision for the young. On the other hand, the persistent lag of the United States with respect to infant mortality is one piece of evidence inspiring reluctance to arrive too quickly at a rosy balance sheet covering the overall public provision of welfare over the last fifty years. We can say with confidence, however, that there have been many such changes. Large bureaucracies now exist with clientele among America's dependent population; a half century earlier there were none.

The Status of Women and the Family

It is somewhat harder to see how public policy has contributed to the revolution in social demography that has profoundly affected the size and configuration of the American family. For a start, however, I would point to the impact of World War II on the recruitment of women into the paid work force. And of course the effects on politics and public policy of the largely private medical revolution that gave American women—especially middle-class women—control over the timing of childbearing is immense. This has certainly facilitated the participation of women in political life and helped them to gain entry to the occupations from which political leaders are drawn. I note in passing the intimate tie between technological innovation and—as the significant mediating factor—drastic demographic change, which in turn nearly led to tidal changes in politics.

The Homogenization of the South

This causal chain running from technological change to political change via demographic changes is visible also in the social revolution that produced as its major outcome the homogenization of the American South with the rest of the country. One could begin with the spread of modern capital-intensive farming to what was once America's most rural area and the creation of World War II industries in the cities of the North. These developments respectively pushed and pulled southerners out of the South. Two later developments repopulated the South with northerners: the postwar introduction of air-conditioning and the federal highway program of the Eisenhower era.

These are the sorts of changes that, along with such public innovations as the Voting Rights Act of 1965, produced ever-stronger two-party systems in southern states, Republican electoral votes for president, and a cadre of southern Republicans in the House of Representatives that is now, fifty years on, nearly as large as the group of southern Democrats.

Constitutional Changes

All of this change in public policy outcomes and social processes scarcely precludes changes in constitutional structures and functions. I will mention only a few. The most important, I believe, has been a sharp change in the constitutional position of the presidency, a change that I believe we can refer to as the rise of a presidential branch of government. Since the late 1930s, when Congress rejected the recommendation of the Brownlow Commission to provide the president with a few staff aides with a "passion for anonymity" and killed off the National Resources Planning Board, the presidency has accumulated enormous responsibility and a lot in the way of administrative capability. This was no doubt unavoidable during World War II. What appears remarkable to a distant observer is how wartime centralization seems to have overcome resistance to the increase of presidential power.

Immediate postwar developments were, it appears, grounded in widespread anxieties about two problems: isolationism and economic depression. Both tended to empower presidents. A substantial body of opinion believed, first, that America's failure to join the League of Nations, to accept worldwide responsibilities, and to give up its traditional policies of no entangling alliances was somehow responsible for the horrors of World War I maturing into the even worse horrors of World War II, and, second, that postwar demobilization led to depression.

Not only were these beliefs widely held by American political elites, but also a widespread desire existed to do something about them. Much of what was done added to the powers of the presidents. The Employment Act of 1946, for example, in some respects made the president responsible for the operations of the business cycle, established a Council of Economic Advisers, and sanctioned activist governmental fiscal policy. In the realm of foreign affairs, there was the establishment of the Department of Defense and a permanent Central Intelligence Agency, both directly responsible to the president.

Isolationism to all intents and purposes died as a force in American party politics on the early spring day in 1952 when one hundred thousand Minnesotans wrote Dwight Eisenhower's name on presidential primary ballots. Eisenhower's Republican presidency set the agenda for the Office of Management and Budget, a presidential agency that holds the rest of government at arm's length. Career officials have a greatly diminished role in policy planning and evaluation throughout government. These activities are increasingly dominated by presidential ambassadors, who in their periodic attempts to "reinvent" government constrain career bureaucrats and reserve initiatives to themselves.

One obvious consequence of the rise of the presidential branch has been the creation of a quiet crisis among the career public servants of the executive. It is not to be expected that American senior bureaucrats will approximate the style or the power of the Prussian bureaucrats Woodrow Wilson admired so much, or even that of the mandarins of the central governments of all of the other Western-style democracies on the face of the earth. Even by far more relaxed standards, observers who care about rational, efficient government capable of performing complex tasks and responding to norms of professionalism and neutral competence are asking whether any of this can be accomplished by demoralized bureaucrats who are seldom listened to, or by agencies that cannot possibly aspire to recruit their share of the best and the brightest of each new generation, and who cannot keep senior executives from early exit.

I believe that the most significant statement that can be made about this trend is analytical, not hortatory; that it has chiefly been caused by a large set of historical trends that expanded the presidency. It lies in the hands of presidents to ameliorate the long-term effects of the trends that have harmed the capabilities of the executive branch.

A second set of significant constitutional changes has affected Congress. I have written so much about this topic—as others also have—and intend to write so much more, that it seems to me enough to give the argument in bare outline. The last fifty years has seen the transformation of both the House and the Senate. The Senate, once a body mainly responsive to sectional and devolved sentiment, has nationalized. It is now a forum where national concerns take precedence, where political leaders mobilize national interests, where national policies are initiated, incubated, and debated. This transformation was, I believe, largely mediated through changes in American party politics, notably changes in the presidential nominating process, which in turn responded to the technological stimulus embodied in the rise of television and nationalized means of communication.

The corresponding story in the House of Representatives focuses upon the pivotal role of the Democratic caucus. The caucus liberalized the House between 1960 and 1980, and continues to do so. The chief cause of this change was the drastic alteration in the composition of the caucus, mediated once again by party politics out in the country at large. Notably, the rise of the Republican party in the South deprived the Democratic caucus of Dixiecrats.

Thus it is possible to argue that air-conditioning liberalized the House of Representatives.

Changes in Mediating Structures

Enormous changes have occurred over a half century in the ways in which relations between political leaders and political followers are organized. We might speak, in a very rough way, of four main institutionalized means that connect leaders and followers: political parties, interest groups, the mass media, and direct communications, either face to face or through mail, telephone, or fax.

Parties and interest groups have at least the potential to be interactive institutions, in the sense that they both talk to and listen to political leaders, and political leaders both talk to and listen to them. It has often been observed that political parties have on the whole lost their monopoly—if they ever had one—over the control of nomination processes. In even fewer places are they essential for the mobilization of the voters. This general decline nationwide in the importance of parties as agencies of intermediation is no recent phenomenon: Since the reforms of the Progressive era—unevenly distributed among the states to be sure—parties have lost ground to other forms of intermediation.

The big winners have been the news media. Although the capacities of the news media to listen to public opinion are crude and uncertain, nobody doubts their capacities to transmit information from press room and studio outward to broad publics. This awesome technological capability has exercised enormous influence upon the formation and expression of interest-group sentiment. Arguably it has transformed the whole notion of what an interest is when, for example, stimulated by indignant radio talk show hosts, large numbers of outraged listeners create a groundswell of support for, or opposition to, policy or public figures. This phenomenon is not the same thing as politicians reaching agreements with labor leaders, or addressing Rotary clubs or church groups and hearing their concerns.

So it may be said that interest groups based upon geographic proximity or face-to-face interaction, and the sorts of demands such groups make, have to a certain degree been displaced by interest groups assembled by modern technology. Although interest groups bounded by geography may occasionally speak up out of a need for symbolic gratification, it is far easier to imagine such groups animated by traditional lunch-box concerns. The reverse is true of groups convened out of thin air by modern communications technology.

We are only beginning to learn about the consequences of communications technology for political representation, political accountability, and public policy formation and legitimization.

Causes of Change

At least three causes of political change can be identified even in a sketchy review of the evolution of the American political system over its most recent half century. We can examine first of all the results of technological change, which is to say change in the capacities of individuals to undertake work, communicate with one another, or improve their living conditions. Second, we can watch changes in the ways in which people flow over the landscape, form and dissolve nuclear families, reproduce the species, and move goods and services. Finally, we can profitably take notice of institutional adaptations more proximate to political outcomes: the effects of war on political attitudes and practices, for example, or the ways in which piecemeal adaptations of local political parties add up to sea changes in the national legislature.

Weighing the impact of factors of this sort upon political outcomes constitutes a formidable scholarly agenda. The instruction and entertainment to be derived from the pursuit of such an agenda seem to me compelling, but as attentive readers of the rest of this volume will observe, other agendas may prove equally attractive.

Nelson W. Polsby

1

Reassessing American Politics: An Introduction

Lawrence C. Dodd and Calvin Jillson

S eldom has the political world changed as dramatically and unexpectedly as it has during the early 1990s. With the end of the Cold War and of divided national government, the landscape of American politics has altered virtually overnight. After decades of obsession with national security and defense spending, the nation now debates how to reduce its military-industrial complex. After twelve years of political gridlock, during which the primary domestic focus was on restraining social spending, the combination of additional reductions in defense expenditures and united party control appears to open a window of opportunity both for deficit reduction and for the creation of a national health care system. And after a prolonged period of national hostility to politicians and government activism, the nation finds itself led by one of the quintessential "political entrepreneurs" of the twentieth century, Bill Clinton, and challenged to renew its commitment to government problem solving.

How will the nation now proceed? Will this moment of opportunity be embraced and our political processes revitalized, or will the challenges of the early 1990s overwhelm the nation? Does the passing of the Cold War solve our nation's problems and allow a new era of good feeling, or will domestic tensions and new international realities impinge upon us? Are our electoral and institutional processes sufficiently resilient to respond to the new realities of politics, or are they perpetually locked in postwar gridlock? Is there a creative potential in our political system that can stimulate national renewal, or are we likely to remain imprisoned by old ideas and orthodox agendas?

These are difficult and pressing questions, with no simple or definitive answers. We cannot expect, standing in the receding shadow of the Cold War, to discern the precise outlines of our new political world. The results of any such effort would likely be misleading. What we can hope to do, with the help of recent scholarship, is to identify the recurring factors and distinctive conditions likely to reshape contemporary politics and consider their implications for the immediate future of American politics. Less ambitious than a full-fledged prediction of the course of future developments, such a review and reassessment of our understanding of American politics is nevertheless a daunting challenge in itself and a necessary foundation for the study of contemporary politics.

1

New Perspectives on American Politics is a collection of seventeen original essays designed to facilitate understanding of contemporary American politics through an analysis of the broad historical patterns of our politics, through an examination of political developments of recent decades, and through a close analysis of the events of the early 1990s that led to the election of Bill Clinton. The collective concern of these essays is to challenge students of American politics to think in rigorous and informed ways about contemporary politics—to consider, for example, how context shapes politics and how ideas and leaders reshape context; to recognize how group tensions and competitive elections fuel political change and how institutional structures can inhibit change; to understand how broad historical forces can create the conditions for change and yet how the specific choices of citizens and politicians shape the path of change. The essays, organized in five major sections, address these and related issues and include a final assessment both of the state of scholarly understanding of contemporary politics and of the paths that American politics might take into the future.

The volume opens with a preface by Nelson Polsby, to whom we also owe credit for inspiring the book's title. Polsby sets the stage for our consideration of the opportunities and dilemmas confronting contemporary American politics by outlining the key developments of the past fifty years. Polsby suggests that among the major policy changes experienced by the nation are, first and foremost, the expansion of civil rights to African Americans and, in close tandem, the growth of the American welfare state, the greater inclusion of women in the nation's political life, and the homogenization of the American South. With these policy and societal alterations, Polsby argues, has come the rise of a presidential branch of government, a shift from regional to national politics in the U.S. Senate, and the liberalization of the U.S. House of Representatives. These developments reflect a broad shift in the "mediating structures" of our politics, particularly a decline in our political parties and a rise in the power of the news media. The deeper bases of these developments lie in the technological and societal changes the nation experienced during and following World War II.

Polsby describes the political and social forces that created our contemporary political world, but he does not speculate about the course that future change might take. It is possible, of course, that divided government and institutional paralysis will persist, with the presidency of Bill Clinton, like Jimmy Carter's before him, merely an anomaly. But dramatic shifts in American politics do occur periodically, as new political forces arise to shape a new political order.

What social pressures might lead to such a restructuring? Who might be its agents and opponents? These are some of the key questions raised in Part One. The answers to these questions most likely will be produced by the general processes that historically have characterized American politics—conflict among groups, electoral and party competition, institutional decision making, and innovation and change in policy agendas.

Part One: The Politics of Social Conduct

The structure of American politics is set largely by the shape and intensity of conflicts within society. The traditional understanding of the social bases of politics has been dominated by the pluralistic interpretations of Robert Dahl and David Truman. Pluralist theory suggests that a multiplicity of groups with widely varying concerns across the social and economic issues of the day compete to shape government policies and programs important to their well-being. Although groups may not be equal in resources, all have some resources—numbers, wealth, or leadership—that can be brought to bear in an open process of domestic policymaking. The future is shaped by the shifting nature of group conflict and no single cleavage dominates across historical eras.

The authors of the three chapters that comprise Part One present quite a different view. The authors agree that group conflict has always been an important part of American politics. However, each believes that deeper and more fundamental social cleavages underlie the group conflict that is so evident on the surface of American politics. In chapter 2, John Manley forcefully challenges the pluralist interpretation, arguing that class conflict has been the central force in American politics. According to Manley, the potential for class conflict in America was the predominant concern of the Founders as they shaped the constitutional structure of the new nation. Class conflict has produced the major turning points in our history and was the central issue of the Reagan and Bush presidencies. Manley's analysis suggests that the election of Bill Clinton may well have been one response to the growing gap between the wealthy elite and the middle class.

In chapter 3 Rodney Hero reinforces Manley's argument that pluralism provides an inadequate characterization of group politics in America. Acknowledging that American society and its politics are broadly pluralist—that is, that politics is the interplay of groups that command and wield differential resources—Hero nevertheless contends that the pluralist system has two tiers, one for the dominant society and another for minorities. In "two-tiered pluralism," formal, legal equality coexists with practices that undercut equality for most members of minority groups. Hero points to the often dramatically attenuated social, economic, and political opportunity structures that confront racial and ethnic minorities in the contemporary United States. According to Hero the procedural protection of the rights of all citizens masks substantive differences in real political power. As a result, whereas most of the political needs of the majority white community are satisfied through the normal play of the political process, the needs of the minority community are often treated as "complaints" or "demands" that must be handled outside the normal play of the process. From this standpoint, the central group conflict of the contemporary period probably will revolve around the disparities between the nation's white majority and its ethnic and racial minorities.

Finally, in chapter 4, Eileen McDonagh introduces the provocative thesis that the most intractable group disparity in American politics proceeds not from class or race but from gender. McDonagh argues that the great reform periods celebrated for expanding the rights of citizens, including the rights of the poor and of racial and ethnic minorities, actually were periods that expanded the rights of men while intensifying the exclusion of women. This is so, she argues, because the American state is premised upon a private sphere of domestic life separated from a public sphere of formal political power. Women's reproductive capacities and roles assigned them exclusively to the former, while men retained identities in both.

McDonagh illustrates her argument with a review of the major reform periods of American politics and the ways in which they advantaged men while proving regressive for women. While acknowledging that in 1992— "the year of the woman"—women officeholders registered dramatic gains, McDonagh doubts that the historical pattern has yet been broken because the basic social and economic dilemmas facing women have yet to be recognized and addressed in American politics. A reflection of this dilemma is the fact that the most visible and powerful woman in the nation, while widely acknowledged to be extraordinarily capable, derives her public visibility and power from her private role as the wife of the president.

Manley, Hero, and McDonagh suggest that the 1990s will generate more than enough social conflict to fuel a restructuring of American politics. Whether such restructuring occurs within the normal boundaries of American politics will depend heavily on the ability of our electoral politics to accommodate conflict. If it can, a transformative restructuring of American politics may occur. If it cannot, then the diffuse frustration that called forth Ross Perot will be intensified, and complex, unpredictable, and at least potentially dangerous dynamics will play themselves out.

Part Two: Issues, Candidates, and Elections

How are the social divisions discussed in Part One, and the political energy that they produce, translated into political change? Do parties and politicians respond directly to elite demands, or do they adopt issue positions that they believe are responsive to public opinion? The authors in Part Two—Edward Carmines, Walter Stone, and Thomas Ferguson— agree that elites construct and control the electoral agenda. Carmines and Stone single out party elites, whereas Ferguson points to the economic elites who stand behind them, provide the funding for their contests, and pass judgment on policy options based upon their economic interests.

In chapter 5, Carmines contends that electoral stability is a result of the salience and vividness of the central aligning issue conflicts of an era. Large-scale political change results from the passing of such issues and the search by political leaders (most obviously minority-party activists) for new issues to exploit in gaining electoral support. The possibility of dramatic political change is enhanced as new voters concerned with new issues enter the electorate and voters committed to preexisting issue alignments leave it. Political change is directed and channeled by the creativity of parties and politicians, who identify or create new issues in order to build new winning coalitions. Carmines illustrates the evolutionary process of realignment by discussing the effect of civil rights issues on the structure of political competition during the early postwar years. He also argues that in the current period social cultural issues produced a decisive shift in party alignments to the detriment of the Republican party.

Left unaddressed in Carmines's analysis is the process by which the new issues that engender new coalitions are introduced into American politics. Walter Stone begins to address this question in chapter 6. Arguing from a broad rational choice perspective, Stone contends that under normal circumstances, change is unlikely to be initiated either by citizens or by elected politicians. Citizens cannot be expected to commit sufficient resources to overcome the inertial forces in political life; elected politicians follow inherently conservative strategies in seeking to retain their positions of power. Nonetheless, Stone contends, the basic asymmetries in the incentives, resources, and benefits that politics holds out to citizens and politicians make the latter the more likely agents of change.

Stone uses the politics of the presidential nomination process to demonstrate his case. The nomination process provides powerful incentives for politicians to identify new issues and to articulate innovative positions on those issues. By being both candidate-centered, so that politicians are expected to adopt issue positions that distinguish them from their opponents, and by being divisive, so that candidates within a party are forced to emphasize different issues, the nomination process engenders extensive experimentation with the electoral salience of different issues and thus can help uncover issues that appeal to the electorate. Stone views open, candidate-centered, divisive nomination processes— often viewed as detrimental to political parties—as a central mechanism in rejuvenating political parties and in generating party realignment and fundamental political change.

Finally, Thomas Ferguson employs a detailed account of the 1992 presidential election process to illustrate his contention that patterns of campaign funding, rather than the exploration of new issues and innovative policy options, provides the deepest insight into the structure and meaning of our national politics. Stone's asymmetry argument is Ferguson's stepping-off point. To reap the benefits of holding a particular office, candidates must first win election to that office. From the candidate's perspective it is all or nothing—win and the spoils are yours, lose and you get nothing. The incentive to secure the resources necessary to win is therefore quite powerful.

Ferguson develops an "investment theory" of American electoral politics in which the pressures of time, limited information, financial constraints, and transaction costs are more burdensome to ordinary voters than classical democratic theorists have allowed. As a consequence, most voters ignore politics, leaving blocs of major investors to define the political parties. Those investors are responsible for most of the signals that parties send to the electorate and for most of the policies adopted after the election.

To understand elections and political change from Ferguson's perspective, one must look not at the issues of the campaign but at the economic interests of the organized groups that finance the campaigns. According to Ferguson, the key economic interests endowing Bill Clinton's campaign were moderate to conservative business groups supporting deficit reduction and willing to accept mildly liberal social and cultural policies in return. Clinton's promises during the fight for the nomination and later in the general election contest were ploys to gain short-term electoral advantage; his real commitments, according to Ferguson, were not to the issues he espoused but to the economic interests whose funds he accepted.

The dilemma produced by such nomination and general election strategies is that they leave candidates with little real support in the electorate. When candidates, once elected, ignore their substantive promises on issues of interest to common citizens in order to concentrate on addressing the policy needs of the major corporate interests that funded their campaign, public support inevitably declines. As support erodes, politicians become increasingly vulnerable to challenge and soon are unable even to deliver benefits to their donor constituents. Ferguson thus concludes that, in light of Clinton's nomination strategy and election, "the political system is entering a new stage of disintegration, with few parallels in American history."

Carmines, Stone, and Ferguson together argue that while the electorate cannot lead, it can respond to information and choices clearly presented by political entrepreneurs seeking to ride the electoral process to power. The question then becomes how meaningful will be the information and choices to which the electorate is asked to respond. Whereas Carmines and Stone see partisan competition as a possible means of national renewal, Ferguson sees it as a potential source of national undoing. Carmines, Stone, and Ferguson do not show how the new issues and alignments that might be generated during a campaign can alter institutional politics once a campaign turns to governance. To address these issues we turn to an assessment of institutional politics.

Part Three: Institutional Politics and Political Change

The theme of Part Three, presented forcefully by Bert Rockman, is that institutions most often foster change by inhibiting it. Group conflict in society creates a relatively constant tension that pushes the political system toward struggle and confrontation. Elections and party conflict are the avenues through which group conflicts enter mainstream politics. But as political conflict and the policy proposals meant to resolve them become part of the debate within governing institutions, they confront complex and rigid decision-making structures. These structures—created to respond to the issues of an earlier day and to maximize the career interests of powerful actors ensconced within them—pose immense obstacles to political change, obstacles reinforced by policy conflict among institutions.

The longer institutional deadlock lasts and the more severe policy conflict becomes, the greater becomes the likelihood that serious problems will engulf society, that dramatic upheavals will occur within institutions, and that a sudden rush of policy change will occur. The unresponsiveness of institutions to gradual and incremental policy adjustments thus fosters dramatic long-term political transformation. How is it that these transformations occur, and are we currently facing such a possibility in the mid-1990s? These issues are addressed in the chapters by Sean Kelly and by Paul Quirk and Bruce Nesmith.

According to Kelly, the institutions of government manage to overcome internal stalemate, cooperate with one another, and respond to societal problems through strong and united party government in pursuit of a broadly supported public agenda. When a majority party has a strong mandate to enact policy and controls the major institutions of government, policy change can occur. Without a strong party uniting government institutions, sustained and coherent policy change is unlikely. The dilemma of American politics since the 1950s, Kelly argues, is that divided party government has come to characterize both the national and state levels of government, thereby reinforcing the constitutional tensions built into our political institutions and helping to generate the severe fiscal problems that characterize contemporary government.

The end of the Cold War and the move toward united party government in Washington could help break the deadlock of modern government, resolve the nation's fiscal problems, and initiate a new period of domestic-policy activism. For this opportunity to be realized, however, the Democratic party must do more than place a minority president in the White House and maintain control of Congress. It must win the hearts and minds of the American people, becoming in the process a true majority party with broad popular support for its policy agenda and broad control of state as well as national government. While arguing that the coming of united national government under Bill Clinton will produce an increase in national policy activism, Kelly doubts that the necessary public support yet exists for strong party government in behalf of long-term and sustained policy innovation.

Kelly's conclusion—that strong party government and institutional activism require broad popular support—is reinforced by Quirk and Nesmith's analysis of the Bush presidency. Looking at four major policy arenas, the authors argue that the deadlock of American democracy results most fundamentally from uninformed public opinion. The primary obstacle to deficit reduction during the Bush years, they argue, was public resistance both to tax increases and to cuts in popular programs. The primary obstacle to health-care legislation was expected public resistance to any form of service rationing. Similarly, it was public antipathy toward banks and bankers that undermined banking reform. Only in the area of recession policy did Congress and the president oppose public opinion and resist pressures to stimulate the economy, a decision unlikely to be repeated in light of Bush's defeat in the election of 1992. Quirk and Nesmith offer little hope that public opinion will become more informed in the foreseeable future. In fact they see the increasing unwillingness of politicians, elected and appointed, to confront public prejudices as a major threat to American democracy.

Taken together, the essays by Rockman, Kelly, and Quirk and Nesmith portray the nation's political institutions as beset by severe policy problems, likely to embark on a short-term course of policy activism under united national government, yet unlikely to initiate dramatic and sustained policy innovation as long as public opinion remains as volatile, uninformed, and unfocused as it has been in the early 1990s. These bleak conclusions lead one to ask how a nation's policy agendas develop and change and to wonder why it is that a few issues capture the public imagination, gain legitimacy, and become law, whereas others do not.

Part Four: Ideas, Agendas, and Public Policy

Perhaps the central theme running through the essays in this book—from Polsby's discussion of the broad social and political changes of the postwar era to Carmines's focus on party realignments and Kelly's and Quirk and Nesmith's focus on mass public opinion—is the central role that policy agendas play in American politics. When national attention is focused on a central set of policy concerns, politics tends to take on an ordered and stable quality; as the nation shifts its policy focus, institutions and public policy eventually respond. But how is it that the nation successfully shifts its focus to a new and clearly defined set of policy concerns? Why does this shift occur differentially across time, or across states and levels of government? And what factors lead some policy movements to succeed and others to fail? The four essays in Part Four address these issues by examining both national and state policymaking and by looking at both contemporary and historical experience.

John Kingdon opens Part Four with the argument that change in policy agendas can best be seen as a sort of evolutionary selection process. In his view, "ideas float around in a 'policy primeval soup'" waiting to come to the attention of a society's policy specialists. The central issue is not whether an idea is good or bad but whether its time has come, whether a window of opportunity exists for an idea to emerge and take hold. Such windows of opportunity are generally created by decisive electoral outcomes, by focusing events such as disasters, or by technological developments that make a policy solution possible. When such a window appears, political entrepreneurs may be in a position to take advantage of it. When such entrepreneurs exist, political and policy change is likely; when they are absent, the window may close and the possibility for change be lost.

One of the most distinctive characteristics of American politics, Virginia Gray argues in chapter 12, is that our federal system of government creates numerous "windows of opportunity" for experimentation with ideas and policy approaches, so that the closing of a window at the national level or in a particular state does not automatically foreclose the possibility of agenda evolution within the political system as a whole. In point of fact, innovative policies often emerge first in states where conditions are conducive to policy experimentation (particularly large states with extensive resources) and then are adopted by other states and by the national government as word of success spreads.

Moreover, Gray contends that the processes by which innovative policies travel both horizontally (state to state) and vertically (local to state or state to nation) have become more efficient over the course of this century and particularly during the last couple of decades owing to the existence of such groups as the National Council of State Legislatures, the National Governors' Conference, and a wide range of more focused policy networks. Gray argues that President Clinton's long experience as a governor and his leadership of the Governors' Conference and other state policy organizations may make him more aware of and more comfortable with policy lessons derived from experience in the states. The Clinton case illustrates how critically important political entrepreneurship is to policy innovation and suggests that a successful experience as a state entrepreneur can set the stage for national policy innovation.

Of course, not all policy ideas spread to all states, nor do all ideas that are successful in some states spread to the national level. Reasons for this differential success of ideas and agendas are discussed in chapters 13 and 14. John McIver, Gerald Wright, and Robert Erikson argue in chapter 13 that the transmission of policy ideas from one state to another depends heavily on the ideological orientations that characterize state politics. Utilizing national polls conducted by CBS and the *New York Times,* the authors measure the opinion of state publics along a liberal/conservative dimension and then correlate the ideological orientations of the states with a wide range of state policy outputs, including state support for primary and secondary education, welfare programs, consumer protection laws, the progressivity of state income tax laws, positions on the ERA, and a large number of similar issues. More than 60 percent of the variance across the policies adopted in the states was accounted for by the differences in the ideologies of the states' citizens. Differences in the policy orientations of the states thus reflect differences in the opinions of state citizens.

As to the success of some policies nationally, Theda Skocpol argues in chapter 14 that one of the most important influences on policy success is how well the structure of the group supporting the policy movement fits with the structure of the political system. Analyzing policy change through a historical study of welfare policy, Skocpol presents the provocative argument that long before the New Deal the United States had adopted a fledgling welfare state providing mothers' pensions and veterans' benefits. The nation adopted these policies not primarily in response to economic disaster, great value shifts, or party politics, but because veterans and women's groups organized themselves in federated associations designed, perhaps serendipitiously, to place maximum political pressure on politicians throughout the nation. As a result, women's suffrage groups were able to exercise surprising political influence, at least for a short period of time, because they had formed a structure that gave them access to and influence over policymakers throughout the political system.

The four essays of Part Four, taken together, suggest that political change and policy innovation may be far more possible than analysts of national political institutions think. The key to change, in the view of these authors, lies not in the character of political institutions but in the ideas at play within society, in entrepreneurial experimentation with policy ideas across the broad array of state and national institutions, and ultimately in the effective organization of groups pursuing new policy agendas. As we saw in Part Three, the complexity and impermeability of institutions might well lead one to despair of the possibility of policy responsiveness in our democracy. Part Four, however, suggests that the role of ideas, issue agendas, and public-opinion and group politics demonstrate more clearly the creative resilience of the American political system.

What sense, then, are we to make of American politics today? Given that resilience makes political change possible, what central factors in the current political climate foster or inhibit change? These are the concerns of the three concluding essays comprising Part Five.

Part Five: Conclusions

In an essay that draws together many of the foregoing themes, Linda Fowler asks whether political entrepreneurs like Bill Clinton can bring stability and coherence to the otherwise fluid and unpredictable political system of the United States in the 1990s. Fowler believes that focusing on political activists and entrepreneurs highlights both the strengths and the weaknesses of contemporary American politics. As political parties have lost their hold on voters, politics has become more fluid and unpredictable than it was throughout the nineteenth century and well into the 1960s. While these circumstances encourage political entrepreneurs to seek their own advantage, they also open up the possibility that the successful entrepreneur might link a relatively uninformed and free floating citizenry to the formal structures and institutions of politics and governance. No alternatives seem to exist.

Fowler is convinced that political entrepreneurs, even successful ones like Bill Clinton, must ultimately fail. Although a few bold thrusts may succeed, most will break up on the sharp rocks of public ignorance and institutional fragmentation, and instability will remain the order of the day. Skillful entrepreneurship is no substitute for stable party government that can tie separate political institutions together across a diffuse federal system. As Kelly notes in chapter 9, entrepreneurs may induce change, but these achievements are likely to be displaced just as rapidly and unexpectedly as they came. A system that encourages entrepreneurial politics, while open and creative, lacks coherence and sustainability because it encourages each new entrepreneur to be just as bold as the last in challenging for positions of power.

What forces are likely to bring a new coherence to American politics? This is the question addressed by the book's final two essays. In chapter 16, Martin Shefter argues that our politics have been shaped far more extensively than we realize by international factors, including military preparedness and wars, international trade, immigration patterns, and cross-border capital flows. The Cold War, in particular, undergirded Republican dominance of the presidency following World War II because of that party's more militant defense policies. Although the Cold War is over, we remain concerned with issues such as international competitiveness, refugee and immigration policy, and the nation's role in regional conflicts. Shefter thus reminds us that although the end of the Cold War may allow the nation's political attention to shift somewhat away from national defense and military policy, international influences will continue to press upon our national policies.

With the Republican foreign-policy advantage now diminished, the Democrats have an opportunity to pursue their domestic agenda more forcefully. On the other hand, the passing of the Cold War may increase the volatility of American politics, making effective governance more difficult. Shefter suggests that voters may decide that they "need no longer select a [presidential] candidate they judge capable of leading the nation in a war with a superpower." Legislators and judges may decide, as did many legislators and at least one federal judge in the case of the president's program of military interdiction of Haitian refugees, that there is no great danger in intruding into the president's role as military commander. In fact, prior government experience may cease to be a critically important qualification for presidents, and the nation may increasingly look beyond the two political parties to an independent candidate like Ross Perot. These and similar developments could set in motion an extraordinary transformation of the American political order.

The book concludes with David Mayhew's comparative and historical discussion of popular "public politics" and resulting "policy waves" in twentieth-century America. Mayhew identifies four distinctive periods of intensive and innovative policymaking during modern American history: the Progressive era, the New Deal, the Great Society of the 1960s, and the Reagan retrenchment of the 1980s. In each case, Mayhew argues, the policy waves reflect broad temporal waves throughout the developed world. To understand the contemporary direction of American politics, Mayhew concludes, one must be sensitive to changes in policy behavior and to the possibility that such changes reflect forces that are not unique to the United States.

Mayhew's argument leads one to ask whether the recent or imminent regime changes in the United States, Canada, France, and Japan, as well as John Major's near defeat in the 1992 British general elections, represent a broad reassessment of post-Cold War politics. Does Clinton's victory set the stage for the fifth major policy wave of this century? Does the Clinton administration promise an effective new focus on a post-Cold War politics of international competitiveness and a domestic agenda concerned with education, job training, infrastructure, and health care? Intriguingly, Mayhew's reflections on contemporary change in the industrialized world lead him to suggest that the most fundamental shared concerns lie not in specific policy issues but in a broad unhappiness with existing policymaking institutions. Mayhew thus raises the possibility that the primary focus of the developed democracies, including the United States, may lie in the restructuring of our political institutions themselves.

All three concluding essays thus suggest that the 1990s may well continue to be a period of considerable upheaval and change in American politics. With united party government in Washington and the demise of the Cold War abroad, the nation has an extraordinary opportunity to re-energize its policy agenda and reinvent its political structures. Much will depend, undoubtedly, on the success of President Clinton and the Democratic Congress in addressing the nation's immediate policy problems. And yet, as these essays remind us, the structure of our democratic politics also reflects broad historical forces beyond the easy control of political entrepreneurs and party operatives. Thus, the coming decade may well prove as exciting and unpredictable a transitional juncture as any in American political history.

I. THE POLITICS OF SOCIAL CONFLICT

2

The Significance of Class in American History and Politics

John F. Manley

W hich social theory, pluralism or class analysis, best fits the United States?

Confronting the argument that class analysis, not "critical pluralism," fits best, Robert A. Dahl challenged class analysts to show the relevance of class to understanding political attitudes, ideology, and fundamental political economic institutions.[1] This article takes Dahl's challenge seriously.

There are, of course, many class-informed studies of American politics. Shefter's work on trade unions, Bridges on the creation of the American working class, Zolberg on the United States and Europe, Katznelson on urban politics, Levine on the New Deal, Gutman and Montgomery on labor history, Katznelson and Weir on education, Goodwyn and McNall on populism, Vanneman and Cannon on public opinion, and scores of other works merit attention.[2]

Merely citing such studies is unlikely to disturb pluralism's dominance in American social science. Pluralism does not deny class some importance; it denies class, especially as used by Marxists, central importance. Advancing the pluralism-class debate requires a new research approach. The one offered here follows Fenno's, in which the perceptions (and behavior) of political activists are treated as evidence of the workings of political systems.[3]

For class analysis to be compelling to those used to affirmations of the importance of groups in America and denials of the importance of classes, the evidence for class must come from unimpeachable sources: the statements and actions of leading figures in U.S. history. Because conflicting definitions of class abound, class must be defined in a way that conforms to the understanding of major participants in American politics. Only if class analysis passes these tests will it claim serious attention in the United States.

On the meaning of class, scholars generally follow Max Weber or Karl Marx. In the Weberian tradition, there are many indicators of class (income, occupation, status, education, authority); no necessary antagonism exists between classes; class analysis stresses marketable skills, mobility, and common life-chances, not exploitation of the working class and struggles for liberation; and class may be realized in the realm of consumption as well as in the mode of production.[4]

Marx roots class in how people produce the economic necessities and niceties of life, and the social relations created thereby. Under capitalism, Marx contends, one class's power over the means of production enables it to extract unpaid surplus labor from another class; class conflict is a structural imperative; and class struggle supplies the impetus for social change.[5] These propositions have been contested, defended, and amended by diverse schools of neo-Marxist thought, but for present purposes we will stick closely to Marx's definition of class. Class refers, therefore, to people who share a common place in the mode of production, and whose objective circumstances and subjective awareness put them in active opposition to another class. Marxian class analysis concentrates on four aspects of class: formation, structure, struggle, and consciousness.[6] Our main concern here is with class conflict.

Marxists and Weberians dispute, among other things, the level of class consciousness in the United States, the degree of class-based political behavior, Marx's predictions regarding the outcomes of class struggle, and why the American working class "failed" to establish socialism. Rather than join such well-worn discussions, we ask a somewhat different question: Regardless of the degree of American "exceptionalism," how have American political activists viewed class? If class considerations are nonexistent among activists, or of only slight importance, the case for class analysis would seem weak.

To set a high historical test for class analysis, we will explore the making of the U.S. Constitution, the transition from a Jeffersonian society of small independent producers to an industrial capitalist society, the movements (populism, progressivism, and the labor movement) spawned by political and economic change, the rise of the welfare state in the 1930s, and its retrenchment in the 1980s and 1990s.[7] No illusion exists that these events can be fully treated in one essay. Our objective is more modest: What role, if any, did class play in the minds of the leaders of these movements and events, and how good is the argument for class in understanding American history and politics?

James Madison and the Constitution

Contrary to what one would expect from contemporary pluralist theory, Madison's notes on the Constitutional Convention show that class lay at the heart of what the Founders did in 1787. When a delegate admitted there were classes in America but disputed the need for a strong national government because class interests did not conflict, Madison, often considered one of the founders of pluralism, took the floor in rebuttal. "In all civilized countries," Madison told the delegates, "the people fall into different classes having a real or supposed difference of interests." Of particular importance, is the distinction between rich and poor:

> An increase of population will of necessity increase the proportion of those who will labour under all the hardships of life, and secretly sigh for a more equal distribution of its blessings. These may in time outnumber those who are placed above the feelings of indigence. According to the equal laws of suffrage, the power will slide into the hands of the former. No agrarian attempts have yet been made in this country, but symptoms of a levelling spirit, as we have understood, have sufficiently appeared in a certain quarters [sic] to give notice of the future danger.[8]

Madison later admitted that the country had not reached the dangerous stage of inequality that threatened open class conflict but he predicted that as capitalism developed inequality would increase, and with it the danger of class warfare would increase.[9]

Madison's notes are the most authoritative source on what went on at the Philadelphia Convention, but he also wrote a theory of society that has lasted as long as the Constitution itself. Madisonian pluralism is often read as a rejection of class, but Madison saw groups as fractions of classes, and the multiplication of groups as the way to control class conflict, not evidence for the irrelevancy of class. As he explains in *Federalist* 10:

> The most common and durable source of faction has been the various and unequal distribution of property. Those who hold and those who are without property have ever formed distinct interests in society. Those who are creditors, and those who are debtors, fall under a like discrimination. A landed interest, a manufacturing interest, a moneyed interest, with many lesser interests, grow up of necessity in civilized nations, and divide them into different classes, actuated by different sentiments and views. The smaller the society, the fewer probably will be distinct parties and interests composing it; the fewer the distinct parties and interests, the more frequently will a majority be found of the same party.[10]

In which sense—Weberian or Marxist—did Madison think of class? Some writers stress differences between Madison and Marx,[11] but in one important respect the father of Communism and the father of the Constitution thought alike: both opposed capitalism. Madison, Franklin, Jefferson, and other Founders were acquainted with industrial capitalism in Europe, and abhorred it. Some, like Hamilton and Tench Coxe, welcomed manufactures, but the general preference in eighteenth-century America for a nation of equal, independent (white, male) citizens is well established.[12]

Madison did not distinguish sharply between class as inequality and class as structure. For him, capitalism and inequality went together, and together threatened republican America. With industrial capitalism and its dependent working class, he believed, great wealth would necessarily concentrate in few hands, the independent citizen base of republicanism would erode, and America's unique promise would be destroyed.

Although troubled by threats to property at the Constitutional Convention, Madison was a politician and, as such, was concerned about class balance. When the balance Madison sought was disturbed, he reacted strongly. In the 1790s, with Hamilton's fiscal policies enriching "stock jobbers" and speculators, a Madison few recognize today wrote a series of radical-sounding articles for Philip Freneau's *National Gazette*. Madison attacked "immoderate" accumulations of riches and endorsed redistributive taxes to "reduce extreme wealth toward a state of mediocrity, and raise extreme indigence toward a state of comfort." [13] As America went down the capitalist road, Madison warned of dangerous conflict between "wealthy capitalists and indigent laborers." [14]

Madison did not anticipate Marx by phrasing his opposition to capitalism in terms of exploitation or surplus value, but the great problem with which he struggled all his life was how to make compatible republican government, which presupposes a large degree of equality and majority rule, and capitalism, which presupposes inequality and a subordinate class. With capitalism's advance, Madison despaired of equality and republican harmony. In this, at least, he and Marx agreed.

Jeffersonian America, Capitalist America

Like Madison, Jefferson understood societies in class terms, believed a large degree of economic equality essential for democracy, and favored small, independent production over capitalism because independent citizens were the foundation of republican government.

Familiar with Europe, Jefferson frequently held industrial capitalism up as an example of what not to reproduce in the United States. Jefferson agreed with Voltaire that in Europe every man was hammer or anvil, but for Jefferson, England was the example par excellence of what America should avoid. In England, Jefferson wrote, there were three classes: the aristocracy, labor, and paupers. All rested on armed force that, ironically, depended on the exploitation of the poor. The task of the military was to keep down the laboring class by "shooting them whenever the desperation produced by the cravings of their stomachs drives them into riots." [15]

Jefferson opposed capitalism because it bred a large, unequal working class. His famous comment in *Notes On Virginia*, that America should "let our work-shops remain in Europe," was later revised when he grudgingly accepted the necessity of manufactures.[16] But industrial capitalism was only acceptable to him because U.S. workers could get a high enough price for their labor to support themselves and their families decently, and because access to the basic means of production (land) was sufficiently open so that "whenever it shall be attempted by the other classes to reduce them to the minimum of subsistence, they will quit their trade and go to laboring the earth." [17] His basic political economic premise was that "widespread poverty and concentrated wealth cannot exist side by side in a democracy" (quoted by Franklin Delano Roosevelt in a 1936 campaign speech).[18] To promote equality, he opposed primogeniture, favored progressive taxation, and proposed giving every white man a minimum of 50 acres of land (his faith in the native capacity of the people did not extend fully to blacks).

In Jefferson's day, Americans usually made what they needed themselves, bought goods from importers, or employed the services of itinerant craftsmen who owned their own tools. With the growth of cities and expansion of markets, workshops comprised of master and apprentices increasingly met the demand for goods. In time, small family enterprises and the apprentice system were displaced by merchant capitalists who "let out" production to journeymen workers. John R. Commons writes that as markets grew, and competition among capitalists intensified, the wage-bargain assumed "importance, and the employer-function comes to the front. Wages are reduced. . . . The conflict of capital and labor begins." [19]

As early as 1773, a Maryland clergyman observed that employers and the employed "no longer live together with anything like attachment . . . and the labouring classes, instead of regarding the rich as their guardians, patrons, and benefactors, now look on them as so many over-grown colossuses whom it is no demerit in them to wrong." [20] The transition to capitalism did not occur uniformly in all trades.[21] But in 1794 shoemakers in Philadelphia formed the first successful union in America. They struck against wage cuts in 1799, and when they struck again in 1805 the employers took them to court, charging them with "conspiracy to raise their wages."

In the shoemakers' view, the "master shoemakers, as they are called after the slavish style of Europe, but who are only the retailers of our labor, and who in truth live upon the work of our hands, are generally men of large property to whom the suspension of business . . . is not so great a loss as the total means of subsistence is to us who obtain our income from week to week." [22]

The shoemakers' counsel, Caesar A. Rodney, a leading Jeffersonian, quoted Adam Smith's *Wealth of Nations* on behalf of his clients: "Workmen desire to get as much, masters to give as little, as possible," with masters, aided by the law, normally having the advantage. Rodney also cited growing inequality in the shoemaking industry: A master employing 24 journeymen earned $15,000 a year compared to $600 for the average workman. Despite such pleas, the shoemakers were found guilty and fined $8 each, with costs of suit. Class conflict had come to America, and to America's courts.[23]

During the first two decades of the nineteenth century, "the emergence of distinct societies of journeymen and of masters among printers, tailors, shoemakers, carpenters, stonecutters, and other trades in every seaport indicated a new awareness of distinct class interests." [24] Workers who once prided themselves on their independence, or looked forward to the day when they would become independent, were painfully aware of capitalism's threat to their status. The shoemakers of Orange, New Jersey, years after the 1806 shoemakers case, noted the absence of common feeling between employers and workmen: "This may appear strange to some . . . that in our country, famed for the liberality of her institutions, the wisdom of her laws, the equality of her citizens, men should exist who in the very face of their country's Institutions, should endeavor to build up an aristocracy better befitting the hotbeds of Europe than the atmosphere of free America." "How can we be free," asked New York cordwainers, "while we have no control over the only commodity we have to dispose of—our labor?" [25] The first important socialist publication in America, Cornelius Blatchy's *Some Causes of Popular Poverty*, appeared in 1817, the year before Marx's birth. Works depicting labor as the source of all value, attacks on corporations for benefiting the rich, analyses of the ill effects of machines, calls for worldwide revolution, defenses of equal distribution of wealth, and predictions of class warfare all appeared in U.S. publications in the 1820s.[26]

The ideal of the artisan republic died hard.[27] Workers in individual trades formed unions, and in the late 1820s members of different trades launched a labor movement. The outstanding characteristic of the early labor movement was its involvement in party politics. Workers' parties demanding a ten-hour day, free public education, and greater equality were formed in more than sixty cities and towns in the early 1830s.

Class considerations were much in evidence. In Philadelphia, the Mechanics' Union of Trade Associations complained that workers maintain "in affluence and luxury the rich who never labour." Labor candidates attacked profits for the "idle capitalist." A workers' group in Pennsylvania pronounced the existence of "two distinct classes, the rich and poor, the oppressor and the oppressed." In New England, men of wealth were attacked as enemies of the "productive classes." Workers in Woodstock, Vermont, denounced the poverty of those who produced the nation's wealth; their colleagues in Dedham, Massachusetts, demanded a "more equitable proportion of the comforts and enjoyments resulting from their individual and joint efforts." Dorchester workers declared that the "spirit of our republican government has been perverted and its equalizing tendency thwarted by . . . the upper classes of society." When workers carried all but one ward in Troy and Albany, "terror and dismay [spread] among the aristocracy of the state of New York." [28] In 1836, printers spoke of the assimilation of the interests of employees and journeymen; in 1850 they spoke of the "perpetual antagonism between Labor and Capital . . . one side striving to sell their labor for as much, and the other striving to buy it for as little as they can." [29]

Not all workers joined unions. Nor were all or even most workers supportive of "agrarian" laws redistributing wealth. The panic of 1837, which threw thousands of workers out of work and nearly destroyed the union movement, led many workers to think about ways of becoming what once had been thought a contradiction in terms: self-respecting wage earners for life.[30] The class content of such events is, as with everything involving class in America, a source of dispute among historians.[31] Yet, by 1878 even such mainstream historians as Francis Parkman were writing: "Two enemies, unknown before, have risen like spirits of darkness on our social and political horizon, an ignorant proletariat and a half-taught plutocracy." [32] When Parkman wrote, more than 60 percent of the labor force were wage earners or salaried employees; 37 percent were self-employed.[33]

If more evidence of early class conflict is required, it may be found in abundance in the hundreds of pages of testimony gathered in 1883 by the Senate Committee on Labor and Capital. This committee, itself a notable creation in a classless society, held hearings all over the country. The overwhelming majority of witnesses denounced class conflict, but nearly all recognized it as real.[34]

Between 1800 and 1880, the revolution in the mode of economic production, as Marx emphasized, altered class relations, and people noted the change. Frank Foster, a printer, told the committee, "We are rapidly developing classes in society as well as in the industrial world, and that these classes are becoming more and more fixed." Another witness, who was asked to compare the extent of class divisions early in the century with 1880, replied "very much less." The editor of a procapitalist paper, questioned about bitterness between capital and labor, said, "We are having here a separation into classes, the one considers himself more and more as the master, and the other as the servant." This was confirmed by Samuel Gompers, who quoted the Marxian-sounding preamble to the Constitution of the forerunner to the American Federation of Labor: "Whereas a struggle is going on in the nations of the civilized world between the oppressor and the oppressed of all countries, a struggle between capital and labor, which must grow in intensity year by year, and work disastrous results to the toiling millions of all nations, if not combined for mutual protection and benefits, for the history of the wage worker of all countries is but the history of constant struggle and misery." P. J. McGuire of the Carpenters and Joiners admitted that the class feeling was less in small towns than cities, but said in cities are found "classes just as distinct as any that exist today in Europe."

Gompers and McGuire were union leaders who might have exaggerated the class threat to scare employers. It is impressive, therefore, that ministers, journalists, workers, and even capitalists all sounded the same warning. Reverend R. Heber Newton, who noted perceptively that workers who used to sell their work now sold their working, reviewed statistics on workers' income, and concluded, "The shadow of the old world proletariat is . . . stealing upon our shores." One of the largest cigar makers in the country spoke as the quintessential enlightened capitalist. "If you drive fifteen or twenty millions of people all on one side, without giving them any consideration simply because you happen to have the power, you will ultimately unite those people; and imagine the legislation which, if united, those people might indulge in as a matter of revenge!"

The committee heard calls for a progressive income tax to block socialists "who want to divide." Generally, American workers did not hold radical views, the senators were told, but the growing and ominous appeal of socialism among Chicago workers was noted. Gompers, who offered unions as the answer to calls for a revolution, quoted a Massachusetts manufacturer as an example of the kind of attitude that fueled labor upheaval: "I regard my employe's [sic] as I do a machine, to be used to my advantage, and when they are old and of no further use I cast them in the street." One senator asked if there was no hope of returning to the days of independent production. To do so, he was told, would require smashing machinery and turning back the wheels of industrial development.

Populism and Progressivism

As long as U.S. farmers could make a good living from their own labor, their families', and that of the hired help, they had no complaint against capitalism. In the 1870s, 1880s, and 1890s, however, millions of farmers saw their way of life threatened and quickly formed mass-based organizations. The so-called Populists created a vision for a new society— a "cooperative commonwealth"—based on a labor theory of value. Seeing man as alienated under the power of industrial and finance capital, they advocated basic changes in capitalism to produce more economic equality. Seeing the state as controlled by their enemies, they sought to forge ties among all "productive" workers. In short, the Populists were a class-conscious movement.

Populism's class content is easily blurred because the movement was mainly a farmers' movement, not a labor movement, and because the farmers themselves were divided by conflicts over race, strategy, and economic interest. A pioneering 1931 study of populism by Hicks, and an influential essay by Hofstadter, further blur the importance of class conflict in the movement. Hicks saw populism as a set of grievances against low agricultural prices and high production costs, noting only occasionally that the southern and northern branches of populism, for all their differences, did attempt a common class program of cooperation between the "millions who till the soil" and the "millions who consume the product of their labor." [35] Hofstadter "managed to frame his interpretation of the intellectual content of Populism without recourse to a single reference to the planks of the Omaha Platform of the People's Party or to any of the economic, political, or cultural experiences that led to the creation of those goals." [36]

An impressive body of historical literature challenges the Hicks-Hofstadter interpretation.[37] But the best witnesses are the Populists themselves. They were clear about what they stood for, who they were against, and how to remake American society.

As early as 1877, Texas farmers who formed the organization that would become the Farmers Alliance warned that the day "is rapidly approaching when all the balance of labor's products become concentrated into the hands of the few, there to constitute a power that would enslave posterity." [38] By 1886 the Farmers Alliance claimed over 100,000 members, and earned the condemnation of the Galveston *News* for being "dominated by the spirit of class legislation, class aggrandizement, class exclusiveness and class proscription." [39] By 1890 the National Farmers and Laborers' Union based its claim to speak for the mass of southern farmers on a membership of nearly one million.[40]

Outside the South, the National Farmers Alliance by 1890 claimed 130,000 members in Kansas alone, and other states were not far behind.[41] Populist senator William A. Peffer saw what was happening. Going back half a century, he wrote, people generally owned their own shops and dwellings. "The wagon-maker, the blacksmith, the carpenter, the shoemaker, the tailor, the bricklayer, the stonemason [were] all scattered about among the farmers." Now all was changed. In the cities, a regimented workforce goes to work at the ringing of a bell, and is practically as much a machine as the mechanisms they attend. A "merciless power," he wrote, makes labor a commodity. "We are steadily becoming a nation of hired men," he observed sadly—and the same fate awaited debt-ridden American farmers.[42]

Northern and southern Populists were not identical (the latter were more radical, more inclined to think in structural terms, more enamored of the "cooperative commonwealth," and less inclined toward the panacea of free silver) but they spoke the same language: class. Southern Populist Tom Watson: "What is capital and what is labor? Originally, they were the same. There was a time when there was no capital. There never was a time when there was no labor." "The men who work for wages," the *Alliance-Independent* wrote in 1894, "must earn their wages and more, that is, a profit for their employers; and if a capitalist stands behind the employer the wage earners must earn another profit for him." A Nebraska farmer: "The farmers know well that if they had got the benefit of everything they have produced since they have been farming, there would be no need for them to be in debt now. The laborer knows that if he had been paid the value of his services he could now have a home of his own." [43] A North Carolina editor: "Did the stockholder throw up the embankments? Did they make the ties, lay the rails, or string the wires?" In 1895 and 1896, the *Southern Mercury* predicted war against capital as the only way of attaining the proper distribution of wealth.[44]

Although populism was agrarian, its goal was the unification of all labor in a coalition opposing big capitalists. When the Populists met in St. Louis in 1892 to draft their political program, Ignatius Donnelly's preamble declared the meeting to be "the first great labor conference of the United States, and of the world, representing all divisions of urban and rural organized industry." Donnelly's words touched off wild support. "The urban workmen," he wrote, "are denied the right of organization for self-protection; imported pauperized labor beats down their wages; a hireling standing army [Pinkerton] unrecognized by our laws, is established to shoot them down, and they are rapidly degenerating to European conditions." Populism's basic premises, Donnelly continued, are:

> First—We declare the union of the labor forces of the United States this day accomplished permanent and perpetual. . . .
> Second—Wealth belongs to him who creates it. Every dollar taken from industry without an equivalent is robbery. . . . The interests of rural and urban labor are the same, their enemies are identical.[45]

Populists tried unsuccessfully to forge a labor alliance. Henry Demarest Lloyd, author of one of the most famous Populist books, *Wealth Against Commonwealth*, appealed to Samuel Gompers, but the head of the craft-dominated American Federation of Labor had long since abandoned his youthful socialism. Gompers branded the Populists *employing* farmers.[46] Unions were weak, the labor force divided along native and immigrant (and many other) lines, the "movement culture" that fueled populism was absent in the cities, and the 1893 depression strengthened capital's hand.

Class conflict, as illustrated by the passage in 1894 of a federal income tax and by the class-riven election of 1896, was a prominent feature of the 1890s.

The 1894 law imposed a modest 2 percent tax on incomes over $4,000, but it was passed during a time when a major plank of the People's party called for a graduated income tax to reduce the power of the plutocracy. Senator Sherman's view was not unique: "In a republic like ours, where all men are equal, this attempt to array the rich against the poor, or the poor against the rich, is socialism, communism, devilism." Justice Field, who led the Supreme Court in invalidating the law, also saw the issue in class terms. "The present assault upon capital," he warned, "is just the beginning. It will be but the stepping stone to other larger and more sweeping till our political condition will become a war of the poor against the rich; a war growing in intensity and bitterness." The New York *Sun* hailed the Supreme Court's ruling: "The wave of socialistic revolution has gone far, but it breaks at the foot of the ultimate bulwark set up for the protection of our liberties." [47]

The 1896 Democratic party platform may have adopted a mere "pseudo-populism," but the party moved far enough left to terrify prominent capitalists. The Democrats condemned the demonetization of silver in 1873 for increasing the value of gold, decreasing farm prices, and enriching the "money-lending class"; Grover Cleveland's dealings with J. P. Morgan were condemned, as was the Supreme Court's rejection of the income tax; calls were made to restrict the importation of "pauper labor," and for federal control of the railroads; and Cleveland took a second political hit for breaking the Pullman strike. True, the Democrats nominated an eastern banker and railroad director, Arthur Sewall, as William Jennings Bryan's running mate, but the People's party, which called for government ownership of the railroads, offered Tom Watson in place of Sewall.[48] All this enflamed class rhetoric in the presidential campaign.

Theodore Roosevelt, rifle at the ready, said, the "sentiment now animating a large proportion of our people can only be suppressed, as the Commune in Paris was suppressed, by taking ten or a dozen of their leaders out, standing . . . them against a wall and shooting them dead." [49] Mark Hanna, William McKinley's campaign strategist, cut short his vacation when he heard about Bryan's nomination, warning that with "this communistic spirit abroad the cry of 'free silver' will be catching." [50] McKinley warned of class conflict throughout the campaign:

> It is a cause for painful regret and solicitude that an effort is being made by those high in the counsels of the allied parties [Democratic and People's] to divide the people of this country into classes and create distinctions among us. . . . Every attempt made to array class against class, "the classes against the masses," sections against sections, labor against capital, "the poor against the rich," or interest against interest in the United States is in the highest degree reprehensible.[51]

Red-baiting was commonplace in 1896. Theodore Roosevelt was especially alarmed by the red menace. Castigating John Peter Altgeld, the Illinois governor whose review of the trial record led him to pardon those Haymarket "rioters" who had escaped the gallows, Roosevelt warned that the governor sought to substitute for the government of Washington and Lincoln a "red government of lawlessness and dishonesty as fantastic and vicious as the Paris Commune." [52] The New York *Tribune* described Bryan as a "puppet in the blood-imbued hands of Altgeld, the anarchist, and Debs the revolutionist, and other desperados of that stripe." [53] Sound Money parades in New York City, employer threats that if workers elected Bryan they need not return to work, and charges of record-setting vote fraud all marked the campaign.

Republicans were not the only ones focused on class. Democratic senator Vilas of Wisconsin thought the free coinage of silver tantamount to "the confiscation of one half of the credits of the nation for the benefit of debtors"; he warned darkly of the French Revolution, Marat, Danton, and Robespierre.[54] Bryan, who rattled conservatives by speaking of the coming struggle between the "idle holders of capital" and the "struggling masses," followed his Cross of Gold speech by opening his campaign in the heart of gold country, New York City. In Madison Square Garden he invited 20,000 people to join his campaign for "the struggling people" against "the money-owning and money-changing class." [55] Bryan rejected Republican "trickle-down" theories in no uncertain terms: "There are those who believe that, if you will only legislate to make the well-to-do prosperous, their prosperity will leak through on those below. The Democratic idea, however, has been that if you legislate to make the masses prosperous, their prosperity will find its way up through every class which rests upon them." [56] Bryan's Populist brethren were even more blunt. Senator Richard ("Silver Dick") Bland of Missouri defined the coming fight as between the "producing masses" and the "fund-owning classes." [57] "Sockless" Jerry Simpson summed up: "It is a struggle between the robbers and the robbed." [58]

McKinley and Hanna turned back the threat by just 500,000 out of 13 million votes cast. In Theodore Roosevelt's view, the fundamental cause of Bryan's defeat was fear—class fear. "Mr. Bryan's candidacy in 1896 on a free silver platform," he wrote in his autobiography, "had threatened such frightful disaster as to make businessmen, the wage-workers, and the professional classes generally, turn eagerly to the Republican party." [59]

Interpretations of the Progressive movement, like those of populism, routinely understate the importance of class. Hofstadter's landmark essay on progressivism appeared over 30 years ago, but it remains influential. "While Progressivism would have been impossible without the impetus given by certain social grievances," he writes, "it was not nearly as much the movement of any social class, or coalition of classes, against a particular class or group as it was a rather widespread and remarkably good-natured effort of the greater part of society to achieve some not very clearly specified self-reformation." [60]

Hofstadter's analysis rests on the middle-class backgrounds of Progressive leaders, on the testimony of such contemporary observers as William Allen White and Walter Lippmann, and on support for reform by certain wealthy members of the establishment. But Hofstadter ignores many contemporary analyses of progressivism that emphasize class.

"The people are beginning . . . to doubt," Louis Brandeis told the Harvard Ethical Society in 1905, "whether there is justification for the great inequalities in the distribution of wealth. . . . The people have begun to think; and they show evidence on all sides of a tendency to act." [61] In 1903 John Graham Brooks published *The Social Unrest*, predicting that reform would fail and the United States would turn toward socialism.[62] A year before, W. J. Ghent's *Mass and Class* noted that although the existence of classes in America is often indignantly denied, the "frontiers and boundaries of classes are no less frontiers and boundaries because they are traversed by certain individuals." [63] Other studies sounded similar themes, but the outstanding book of the period was Herbert Croly's *The Promise of American Life*.

Croly, a progressive Republican, argued that a fundamental change had occurred in the United States that, if left unaddressed, would destroy American democracy. A generation ago, he wrote, a man's poverty could reasonably be considered his own fault. The system gave all a fair chance. Now, with the rise of huge corporations and trusts, the "discontented poor are beginning to charge their poverty to an unjust political and economic organization." Croly blamed the chaotic individualism of Jeffersonian America for the concentration of wealth and power, and argued that the state must make "itself responsible for a morally and socially desirable distribution of wealth." Croly's book was directed primarily at Theodore Roosevelt, whom Croly regarded as a modern-day Alexander Hamilton who could adapt capitalism to a new era without repeating Hamilton's mistake of arraying capitalism against democracy.[64]

Croly knew his man. Roosevelt was one of the most class-conscious politicians in the country. Indeed, he acted as a self-appointed Paul Revere, going all over the country warning of the dangers of class conflict. He even sent messages to Congress on the subject. His 1902 opening message urged Congress "to remember that any kind of class animosity in the political world is, if possible, even more wicked, even more destructive to national welfare, than sectional, race, or religious animosity." Four years later, in an opening message entitled "Preachers of Discontent and Class Hatred," he warned Congress of men who "seek to excite a violent class hatred against all men of wealth." "The greatest and most dangerous rock in the republic," he said in 1905, "is the rock of class hatred." In a subsequent address entitled "The Spirit of Class Antagonism," Roosevelt said, "Distrust more than any other man in this Republic the man who would try to teach Americans to substitute loyalty to any class for loyalty to the whole American people." During his 1912 Progressive campaign for the presidency, having taken an assassin's bullet and shown the audience where it entered, he urged his listeners to do all they could to prevent the day when the "creed of the 'Have nots' [is] arraigned against the creed of the 'Haves,'" because when "that day comes then such incidents as this tonight will be commonplace in our history." In a 1912 article in *Outlook*, Roosevelt quoted Lincoln's words that "labor is prior to and independent of capital . . . and deserves much the higher consideration." Capital, too, had rights, but the best protection for capital was the perception that it is handled "not only in the interest of the owner, but in the interest of the whole community." [65]

Why, if class and class conflict were unimportant in American society, did Roosevelt carry on so? When the Constitution was written, Roosevelt knew, there were no giant corporations of the sort that dominated the economy in 1900. This structural change required state regulation to ensure that the benefits of capitalism flowed sufficiently to the community as a whole. Unscrupulous rich men and reactionary backers of laissez faire threatened the capitalist system, he believed, but in the long run the interests of capital and labor were the same. Writing a script Franklin D. Roosevelt would later follow, Theodore Roosevelt presented government as a neutral broker between labor and capital. Toward this end, he endorsed corporate regulation, social reform legislation, graduated taxes on incomes and inheritances, and government management of the economy. The 1912 Progressive party platform reads like a précis of the social democratic reforms then being adopted in Europe.[66]

In the late nineteenth and early twentieth centuries, when Roosevelt's views were shaped, great changes in industrial and finance capitalism were accompanied by militant and often violent labor protest. The Great Upheaval of 1877, the Haymarket riot of 1886, Homestead in 1892, the Pullman strike of 1894, a series of bloody miners' strikes, the blowing up of the *Los Angeles Times* building in 1910, the 1909-1910 garment workers strike in New York City, the 1912 Lawrence, Massachusetts, "bread and roses" strike, the 1913 strike of silk workers in Paterson, New Jersey, the 1914 Ludlow massacre, and many other clashes were discussed in class terms at the time and convinced Roosevelt and others of the dangers of class conflict. In 1912 President Taft proposed in his State of the Union address the establishment of a commission to investigate industrial relations. President Wilson appointed such a commission in 1913. On the basis of its studies, one writer dubbed 1910-1915 the "Age of Industrial Violence."[67]

Like Roosevelt, Wilson was alarmed by class conflict. Two years into his presidency, Wilson addressed a remarkable letter to William Gibbs McAdoo, his secretary of the treasury. Just a few years earlier, wrote Wilson, those who had power were "almost universally looked upon with suspicion," and in turn "seemed to distrust the people and to wish to limit their control." There was, Wilson continued, an "ominous antagonism between classes. Capital and labor were in sharp conflict without prospect of accommodation between them."[68] What had been the cause of the difficulty? Wilson's answer was a paraphrase of Marx: "Nothing is done in the country as it was done twenty years ago. We are in the presence of a new organization of society. . . . We have changed our economic condition, absolutely, from top to bottom; and, with it our economic society, the organization of our life."[69] A month before he took the oath of office as president, Wilson wrote in the *Fortnightly Review*: "The masters of the government of the United States are the combined capitalists and manufacturers of the United States."[70]

Wilson, of course, presented himself as a friend of capital and labor.[71] His New Freedom program was based on the assumption that to save capitalism, government had to limit the power of large capital, protect small businesses, and foster competition as a form of business control. All are reflected in three landmark laws passed under Wilson: the Federal Trade Commission Act, the Clayton Antitrust Act, and the Federal Reserve Act. Consistent to the end, Wilson wrote an article shortly before his death, "The Road Away from Revolution," naming capitalism as the target of the Russian Revolution and the system against which "the discontented classes everywhere draw their indictment." [72] Capitalists, he concluded, had failed to use their power for the benefit of all, had too often regarded men as mere instruments of profit, and must shoulder the blame for the present turbulence.

People like McKinley, Hanna, Bryan, Roosevelt, Wilson, and others clearly perceived the class basis of populism and progressivism and responded to it. When capitalism collapsed in 1929, overt class conflict broke out in many sectors in American society. The task of dealing with that conflict fell to Franklin D. Roosevelt.

Class Struggle and the New Deal

To some historians, the New Deal appears to be a revolutionary response to a revolutionary situation. In support of this view, Degler cites, *inter alia*, the collapse of capitalism, the abandonment of laissez faire, the "socialistic" Tennessee Valley Authority, the increased class consciousness of workers (which permitted large-scale unionization), and the words of such contemporary observers as Theodore Dreiser, who believed that Karl Marx's prediction "that Capitalism would eventually evolve into failure . . . has come true." [73]

Yet, capitalism survived. FDR was a progressive Democrat, not a socialist, and he proudly claimed credit during the 1936 campaign for saving capitalism. He took the status quo in the economic system, according to his secretary of labor, Frances Perkins, "as much for granted as his family. They were part of his life, and so was our system; he was content with it." [74] To an advisor on his left, like Rexford Guy Tugwell, the New Deal was a "mild medicine" in part because FDR's fears of frightening the middle class stopped him from saying that "capitalism no longer worked to secure the objectives of progressives." [75] "Revolution" seems too strong a word to apply to the New Deal.

Some historians detect two New Deals, the first, which favored business, emphasized economic recovery; a second emphasized reform and social welfare. Other historians see the entire New Deal as a predominantly conservative set of capitalistic reforms. Still others find the New Deal a fertile source of ideas about the relationship between the capitalist state and social classes. Little consensus exists.[76]

One reason for the lack of consensus is that social conflict in the 1930s occurred along pluralist, subclass lines as well as along class lines.

Not all capitalists were anti-New Deal. Not all labor backed FDR. Significant racial, ethnic, religious, regional, and trade divisions undermined unified class action. This said, class and class conflict were quite evident in the 1930s. The New Deal faced the normal contradictions of capitalism exacerbated by crisis; class shaped both the formation and the outcome of social and economic policies.[77]

William Leuchtenburg, author of one of the best one-volume histories of the New Deal, writes:

> As the 1936 campaign got underway, the note of class conflict sometimes reached a high pitch. At an excited night meeting at Forbes Field in Pittsburgh, a stern-faced Danton, State Senator Warren Roberts, spat out the names of the Republican oligarchs: Mellon, Grundy, Pew, Rockefeller. The crowd greeted each name with a resounding "boo." "You could almost hear the swish of the guillotine blade," wrote one reporter afterwards. . . . Then the gates opened at a far corner of the park; a motor-cycle convoy put-putted its way into the field, followed by an open car in which rode Franklin Delano Roosevelt, grinning and waving his hat, and the crowd whipped to a frenzy, roared its welcome to their champion.[78]

Of FDR's policies, Leuchtenburg writes, "Even the most precedent-breaking New Deal projects reflected capitalist thinking and deferred to businesses sensibilities. . . . Roosevelt's program rested on the assumption that a just society could be secured by imposing a welfare state on a capitalist foundation." [79]

Yet, business leaders, even as they cooperated in running the National Recovery Administration, still suspected Roosevelt. A confidential summary of discussion at the September 1933 meeting of the National Industrial Conference Board reported business leaders' perceptions that the Roosevelt Administration saw the depression as business's fault because the organization of business "has produced an inherently wrong distribution of national income and wealth." The report refers to the maldistribution of income between farm and city, and another maldistribution, more serious from the administration's point of view, between wage earners and salaried workers (who spend most of their income) and owners of property (who invest most of theirs). In a revealing comment the report says

> Those ideas . . . have a very old history. They go back farther even than Karl Marx, but they found their clearest statement in the writings of Karl Marx, whose whole theory of the inherent disease and inevitable destruction of the capitalistic order was based upon that essential idea which he gave the name of "the theory of surplus value"—the idea that the owners in industry were constantly abstracting [sic] from the product of industry too large a part of the product to permit the consumer or the worker to buy back the product of industry, and in abstracting that excessive proportion were con-

stantly digging their own grave by excessively expanding the capacity for production.[80]

According to this report, Marx's ideas had become received wisdom among young economists and were accepted by some members of Roosevelt's brain trust. None of the brain trust were, in fact, Marxists, but the report correctly states how some New Dealers understood the depression. One of FDR's closest economic advisors, Tugwell, wrote in his diary that "our troubles were made by business." As Tugwell saw it, "Businessmen have been able to take advantage of an unusual situation, arising out of the advance in productivity during the war. Costs had fallen but prices had not. Nor had wages risen." [81] Another advisor, A. A. Berle, attacked the elitism of the captains of industry, noting that behind their philosophy "is the impelling motive of greed, the desire for self-aggrandizement, the corruption of vanity." [82] FDR himself, in an article published in *Liberty* magazine just after his election, noted that the "interests of labor and industry cannot be promoted at the expense of agriculture; neither can capital reach a condition of true prosperity without at the same time offering a more legitimate share to labor." [83] Redistributive policies were a credible threat to many business leaders in the 1930s—unless economic recovery and reform could be produced another way.

Most New Dealers distinguished between capitalists who exploited labor unduly and the majority of responsible capitalists who only stooped to such practices because of unfair competition. But such distinctions did not prevent conservative attacks, some of which came from Democrats. The 1928 Democratic party nominee, Al Smith, told the Liberty League in 1936 that it was "all right with me if they want to disguise themselves as Norman Thomas or Karl Marx, or Lenin, or any of the rest of that bunch, but what I won't stand for is allowing them to march under the banner of Jefferson, Jackson and Cleveland." [84]

Revolutionary change—violent or peaceful, from the left or right— was commonly seen as a possibility in the 1930s. Raymond Moley, another member of the brain trust, was amazed that "capitalists did not understand that he [FDR] was their saviour, the only bulwark between them and revolution." [85] At the time Roosevelt took over, Representative Adolph Sabath declared on the floor of the House that there was "a well-bottomed feeling abroad the land [that] we were on the verge of revolution." [86] "People won't indefinitely endure hunger," Harold L. Ickes wrote in his diary, "and if we do not give them an opportunity to earn enough to live on, sooner or later we will run the risk of revolution." Ickes worried that it might become "a question of giving up a portion of our fortunes and saving the rest or having all of them taken away from us." [87] One of Roosevelt's closest advisors, Harry Hopkins, received field reports from Lorena Hickok saying that "vast numbers" of the unemployed in Pennsylvania were "right on the edge," and it would take little "to make

Communists out of them." She reported that Communists, who "want bloodshed," were very busy in Pennsylvania and among midwest farmers who were forcibly stopping foreclosure sales. People in South Dakota, she said, felt "sheer terror." Hickok was not the only one filing such reports. One man who toured the southern states told Hopkins in 1934 that industrialists fear "possible mob action." [88] In August 1933 FDR advised Paul Blanshard that the United States was moving toward a "new form of social structure." [89]

In 1933 and 1934, no one knew what this new structure would be. FDR had no master plan; he improvised. From the right came pressure for solutions that preserved traditional business prerogatives. From the left came pressure from Huey Long, who in 1933 wrote Roosevelt repeatedly about redistributing wealth.[90] Additional leftist pressure came from the League for Independent Political Action, formed in 1929, and headed by John Dewey. Dewey and others were mainly concerned with income distribution. Economist and future senator Paul Douglas, an ally of Dewey's, advocated workers' cooperatives along the lines of Louis Blanc and Robert Owen.[91]

Some of the most disturbing pressure came from factory workers. In 1932 about 3,000 workers marched from Detroit to Henry Ford's River Rouge plant in Dearborn. Police opened fire; four workers' bodies later lay in state under a huge red banner with Lenin's picture on it.[92] In January 1933, AFL president Green told a Senate committee that unless the bill establishing the thirty-hour week were passed, labor would resort to a general strike.[93] The National Industrial Recovery Act of 1933 affirmed labor's right to organize and bargain collectively with capital but failed to prevent violent conflicts in several states in 1934.

"Eruption" is Irving Bernstein's word for 1934. "There occurred at these times strikes and social upheavals of extraordinary importance, drama, and violence which ripped the cloak of civilized decorum from society, leaving exposed naked class conflict," he writes.[94] That year, 1,856 work stoppages involved 1,470,000 workers, workers in three cities staged social upheavals, and textile workers overcame their many divisions to shut their industry down in 20 states. In other cities, streetcar workers, aided by socialist organizers, forced a settlement of a violent strike in Milwaukee; cab drivers burned 100 cabs in Philadelphia; union electrical workers pulled the plug on Des Moines; a two-day general strike closed Terre Haute; and service workers from the Waldorf-Astoria picketed singing the "Internationale." [95]

Toledo, Ohio, in 1934 was, according to one observer, close to civil war. A socialist-led strike against the Auto-Lite company and labor troubles at Toledo Edison were marked by unusually high levels of labor solidarity. Unemployed workers refused to take the jobs of striking workers and 85 of Toledo's 103 unions voted for a general strike. There was intense street-fighting and two workers were killed.

"Minneapolis in 1934," Bernstein writes, "was ripe for class war." Eric Sevareid, who was covering the trucking-industry strike, returned home to find his father reading the paper and sputtering, "This, this is revolution!" Rich people made plans to leave town. Open battles between labor-union forces and the well-armed employers' "Citizen's Army" broke out, subsided, then broke out again. Mass marches of farmers and workers recalled failed Populist efforts to unite these two groups. On July 20 police opened fire on pickets, killing two and wounding sixty-seven. Floyd Olson, the radical Democratic Farmer-Labor governor of Minnesota ("I am not a liberal," he said in 1934, "I am a radical . . . I want a definite change in the system.") reluctantly declared martial law. The trucking strike was settled with federal intervention in August. The leaders of the strike, Bill and Ray Dunne, were both socialists, though of different persuasions. So many Communist factions vied for leadership of the strike that Minneapolis was said to be the only city in the country where socialites at cocktail parties made fine distinctions between Stalinists and Trotskyists.[96]

The third great social upheaval of 1934 was a general strike that, after two workers died on July 5 ("Bloody Thursday"), shut the city of San Francisco down. Again, labor showed unusual unity. Teamsters and others voted to join the Harry Bridges-led longshoremen in a general strike unless a settlement were reached. Archbishop Hanna said over the radio that "there should be, in the dispensation of Christ, no conflict between class and class." With ports shut down all over the Pacific coast, and with Roosevelt rejecting employer pleas to intervene, the longshoremen won a victory hailed as one of the greatest in U.S. labor history. "The class struggle," Harry Bridges said on the basis of his experience, "is here." [97]

These violent strikes, coupled with the cotton-textile strike by workers from Alabama to Maine and the famed sit-down strikes in the automobile and other industries later in the decade, defy conventional pluralist analysis. Not all workers supported the strikes, and enough strikebreakers were hired to provoke much violence, but the unity, power, and growth of unions are the outstanding characteristics of 1930s labor history. According to the National Bureau of Economic Research, union membership rose from 2,805,000 in 1933 to 8,420,000 in 1941. By 1940, 34 percent of manufacturing workers were organized in unions, as were 48 percent of the workers in transportation, communications, and public utilities; 65 percent of the building trades; 72 percent of miners; 64 percent of clothing workers; 32 percent of food, liquor, and tobacco workers; and 34 percent of leather workers. Other trades saw less union growth, but in nearly all areas unions made impressive gains. Bernstein concludes with considerable understatement that 1929-1941 was an "age of trauma" for American businessmen.[98]

Had government, as Roosevelt used to say, remained "frozen in the ice of its own indifference," the outcome for capitalism might have been different. Roosevelt's strategy for dealing with the crisis was twofold: Positive government responses to the emergency were accompanied by radical-sounding class rhetoric aimed at privileged members of society. The rhetoric vented mass discontent, delighted ordinary people, and made many of the well-to-do sputter about "that man in the White House."

FDR was masterful in his attacks on members of his own class. His 1933 inaugural address (the "money changers have fled from the high seats in the temple of our civilization") tapped popular resentments toward finance capital dating to the conflicts between Hamilton and Jefferson. He promised to restore the temple by applying "social values more noble than mere monetary profit," while his secretary of the treasury, rich, Republican banker William Woodin, relied on bankers and officials from the Hoover administration to draft emergency banking legislation.[99] When Huey Long's "Share the Wealth" program gained popularity in 1935, FDR sent his own soak-the-rich tax plan to Congress. Linking progressive taxation to the "interrelation of effort" in modern society, and citing the production of wealth not just by individuals but by "people in the mass," FDR proposed inheritance and gift taxes as a way of "encouraging a wider distribution of wealth," "very high taxes" on individual incomes to allay the "unrest and a deepening sense of unfairness [that] are dangers to our national life," and a graduated tax on corporations to enhance small capital's competitive position.[100] FDR said he was prepared to throw "to the wolves" the forty-six men with incomes over $1 million if that is what it took to save capitalism. Such attitudes led William Randolph Hearst to attribute the tax bill to a composite personality: "Stalin Delano Roosevelt." [101]

In fact, all Roosevelt wanted of Long's program was the thunder. When Congress gutted the bill, FDR put up little fight. And after Long was assassinated, little more was heard about soaking the rich.

Still, during the 1936 campaign, with at least one-third of the nation in need, FDR heated up the class rhetoric. In his opening campaign speech before the Democratic state convention in Syracuse he defended himself against charges of communism and leftism. Communism, he said, was a manifestation of social unrest that always accompanies economic distress; it was a menace that had to be faced, not merely denounced. He recalled 1933: law-abiding heads of families wondering how to get the bread in bakery windows; the rich building hideaways in the country against the impending upheaval; farmers armed with pitchforks banding together to prevent mortgage foreclosures; and the "powerful leaders of industry and banking who came to me in Washington . . . pleading to be saved." "We were against revolution," he said. "Therefore, we waged war against those conditions which make revolution—against the inequalities and resentments that breed them." This kind of liberalism, he concluded, is "the protection for the far-sighted conservative." [102]

FDR went to school on Theodore Roosevelt who, instead of crushing striking coal miners in 1902, forced the owners and no less a capitalist than J. P. Morgan to accept arbitration or face government seizure of the mines. When confronted by similarly explosive circumstances in the 1934 San Francisco general strike, FDR listened to his advisers, Louis Howe and Frances Perkins, and stayed away, thereby disappointing business leaders who wanted to use the state to spread the conflict and break the union. By showing that the state was independent enough of conservative capitalists to respond rhetorically and programmatically to labor, FDR, like his older relative, helped cool the unusually violent, frequently class-based conflict of the 1930s.

Just because capitalism did not create the means of its own destruction in a unified, radical working class does not obviate the importance of class for understanding the 1930s. All it means is that there is no inevitable, automatic outcome of the class struggle. Workers *were* moved by powerful, if temporary and imperfect, class solidarity. Even voters who were divided along many lines showed unusually high levels of class voting in the 1930s.[103]

Reaganomics

The striking aspect of Ronald Reagan's presidency is the overtness of its class politics. People on the left decried Reagan's policies from the start.[104] Supporters of Reaganomics frequently admitted the policies' class biases but defended the program as ultimately beneficial to all Americans.

Unprecedented peacetime inflation in the 1970s, coupled with high unemployment compared with the 1950s and 1960s, slow productivity growth, and the largest federal deficits since World War II, confounded neo-Keynesian theory and opened the door to "supply-side" ideas in the 1980s.[105] Reaganomics offered four ways of improving the economy's performance: (1) tax cuts favoring upper-income taxpayers; (2) spending reductions in "non-safety net" social programs; (3) continuation of Jimmy Carter's restrictive monetary policy; and (4) freeing up the economy by reducing government regulations.

Reagan's tax program included a 30 percent across-the-board cut in the marginal tax rate over three years (subsequently scaled back to 25 percent), a 20 percent reduction in the 70 percent tax on unearned income, a cut in the tax on capital gains from 28 percent to 20 percent, and more rapid depreciation deductions for corporations. By allowing people to keep more of what they earn, incentives to save and invest would increase, capital formation would grow, and greater investment would spur economic growth. To control inflation, decrease budget deficits, and increase the pressure on people to work, cuts were made in grants to state and local governments (over half of the cuts were targeted on programs assisting low-income individuals) and in direct payments to low-income individuals and families. Food stamps, child nutrition, and Aid to Families with Dependent Children accounted for 60 percent of the savings from low-income assistance programs.[106] President Reagan recorded in his diary that his goal was to undo Lyndon Johnson's Great Society war on poverty, not Franklin Roosevelt's New Deal, but there was no masking the general class direction of the new initiatives.[107]

Combining the tax and spending cuts, the Congressional Budget Office estimated that households with incomes below $10,000 would lose 1.2 percent of their income; households over $80,000 would gain 7.9 percent; and households in-between would gain lower but appreciable amounts of income.[108]

Cutting taxes across-the-board always gives more tax relief to higher-income taxpayers and offers scant benefits to those who pay little or no tax. One of the most celebrated cases of impolitic candor in the Reagan Administration was the admission by the director of the Office of Management and Budget, David Stockman, that the intention of supply-side tax cuts was to benefit higher-income people, in hopes that the benefits would in time "trickle down" to those below. "It's kind of hard to sell 'trickle down,' so the supply-side formula was the only way to get a tax policy that was really 'trickle down,' " Stockman said.[109]

Such comments earned Stockman a rebuke from the president,[110] but there was truth in the director's comments. Citing the combined effects of the 1981 tax and spending cuts, the *Wall Street Journal* reported in 1982, "The rich are getting richer and the poor are getting poorer."[111] This perception was shared by the American people. Republican pollster Richard Wirthlin recorded in February 1982 the "predominant view that Reagan's plans favor the rich." Asked who benefits from economic programs, 2 percent of respondents said poor or lower-income people, 13 percent said the middle class, 59 percent said upper-income people, and 24 percent replied all people equally.[112]

Many Republicans, but not President Reagan, conceded the redistributive effects of Reaganomics. Kevin Phillips links Reagan's policies to the "Republican party's historical role, which has been not simply to revitalize U.S. capitalism but to tilt power, policy, wealth, and income toward the richest portions of the population."[113] Conservative columnist George Will observed, "In the Reagan years, a particular social stratum has gotten a lot. . . . If Marx had been scribbling away in the Library of Congress . . . in January 1981, as Reaganites marched into Washington, he would have said: 'The class war is about to intensify.' "[114] Michael Boskin, chair of President Bush's Council of Economic Advisors, expressed in 1983 the common hope among supply-siders that Reagan's programs would in time benefit all Americans, but granted that, "unquestionably, the Reagan economic program will lead to a more unequal distribution of income than would have resulted from a continuation of previous programs."[115]

By 1990, as the perception grew that the 1980s had been especially beneficial to the rich and talk of tax increases mounted, the *Wall Street Journal* noted that "class warfare, it seems, is making a comeback." [116] The *Journal*'s conclusion rested in part on an NBC News poll showing that if a tax increase were needed, 76 percent of the American people favored raising taxes on upper-income individuals, 20 percent opposed such a move, and 4 percent did not know.

Since 1981, class has been regularly featured in national politics. To cite three examples:

- Summarizing a December 1983 ABC News/*Washington Post* poll, David Broder wrote, "America is split down the middle, on old-fashioned class and income lines, by the policy changes President Reagan and the Republicans have brought to Washington." [117]
- In 1988, Michael Dukakis stressed the issue of "fairness," and made overt class appeals toward the end of his campaign against George Bush. Lee Atwater, often credited with masterminding Bush's 1988 campaign, commented, "The way to win a presidential race against the Republicans is to develop the class warfare issue, as Dukakis did at the end. To divide up the haves and have nots and try to reinvigorate the New Deal coalition and to attack." [118]
- In 1992, a highly publicized CBO study showing that two-thirds of the growth in pretax family income from 1977 to 1989 went to the wealthiest one percent of American families drove Bill Clinton "crazy," according to his press secretary. The study "proved a point he had been trying to make for months." The *New York Times* described Bill Clinton's 1992 campaign as follows: "Pushing his new class-oriented attack that President Bush secretly plans to 'devastate America's middle class and its workers' to pay for tax cuts favoring the rich, Bill Clinton today accused the President of pursuing economic policies that would force him to gut Social Security." [119]

A Note on William Jefferson Clinton

Democrats and Republicans have long differed over trickle-down and trickle-up economics. Trickle-down features regressive taxes, government deregulation, and anti-union measures. Trickle-up favors tax cuts for the working poor and middle class, activist government, striker-replacement legislation, and the like. As William Jennings Bryan put it in 1896,

> There are those who believe that, if you will only legislate to make the well-to-do prosperous, their prosperity will leak through on those below. The Democratic idea, however, has been that if you legislate to

make the masses prosperous, their prosperity will find a way up
through every class which rests upon them.

At issue is class inequality and how best to run a capitalist economy.
Whenever anyone mentions class in America, as Gore Vidal notes in his
recent *Screening History*, a booming chorus thunders across the land denying that such a horror could ever exist in the United States. "Clinton has
gotten across the point that we are a party of growth and not redistribution," House Majority Leader Richard Gephardt told the *New York Times*
on the day Bill Clinton was elected president.

Soothing denials aside, Bill Clinton cannot escape class. Trickle-down
capitalism, also known as supply-side economics, accepts economic inequality as the price of economic growth; trickle-up capitalism tilts toward
greater equality on the theory that demand fuels growth. Both accept class
inequality as permanent; one just looks first to capital, the other to labor.

Which version of capitalism dominates America depends on the status of the cornucopia solution to class conflict. When capitalism fails to
provide an economic pie large enough to allow those seeking the American dream to do so without pulling down those who have attained it, a
failure that dogged Reagan and Bush, a new (old) formula is tried, as is
currently planned by President Clinton.

When, four years from now, Bill Clinton faces the question of
whether people are better off than they were four years ago, the answer—
and his political future—will depend on whether his version of capitalism
produces noninflationary economic growth, more jobs, and a stronger
competitive position for U.S. products in world markets.

Will trickle-up work? History suggests that it will work for a time,
but not for long. Politicians, for all their skill, have been unable to find a
permanent solution to the conflict between equality and inequality that
lies at the heart of capitalism. The metronomic quality of American politics and economics is the outstanding lesson of American history; lasting
solutions to America's contradictions are conspicuously absent from the
historical record.

Conclusion

What do pluralism and class analysis have to say about class and
inequality?

Pluralism has little to say. Mainstream political science finds many
topics interesting; class is not usually among them. Economics takes class
more seriously, and so do sociology and history. Economists are in the
forefront of national debates over Reaganomics, equality, managing or not
managing the economy, and the like. Political science is, paradoxically,
only marginally relevant to understanding some of the most important
political issues in American history and contemporary politics.

Critics of capitalism and of Reaganomics often emphasize inequality. For Marx, capitalism was objectionable not primarily because of inequality but because: (1) under capitalism, everything, including human labor, is a commodity; and (2) because capitalists, who control the means of production, extract surplus labor from those who do the actual work of production. Capital, Marx wrote, "obtains this surplus labor without an equivalent, and in essence it is always forced labor—no matter how much it may seem to result from free contractual agreement." If income inequality were Marx's main problem with capitalism, more equality would be enough to save the system. Yet, Marx argues, "in proportion as capital accumulates, the lot of the labourer, be his payment high or low, must grow worse." This is so because capitalism is a coercive system that undermines the independence and vitiates the humanity of its subjects, thus destroying any prospect for a truly democratic capitalist society.[120]

Although Marx did not base his objection to capitalism on inequality, inequality is inescapable in capitalism. Whatever else capital and labor are, they are, in normal times, not equal. As long as the economic pie expands under capitalism, so as to make credible the promise that a rising if unequal tide will lift all (or nearly all) boats, capitalism may withstand radical attacks. But when the cornucopia solution to class conflict falters, capitalism is at risk. Between systemic crises, the class struggle revolves around how much government control should be placed on the "market" in the interest of those too weak to compete effectively, and on how to protect public interests not well served by unregulated capitalism.

These issues are different from the climactic class struggle envisioned by Marx in his more exuberant moods, but they involve class conflicts fraught with significance for the maintenance of the system. Capitalism and economic inequality worried Madison, Jefferson, the workers and farmers and independent producers displaced by capitalism, McKinley, Hanna, Croly, Theodore Roosevelt, Wilson, New Deal leaders, critics of Reaganomics, and many, many others. Clearly, Marx's theory of capitalism as a volatile production system with built-in disparities of power (and rewards) is pertinent to U.S. history and politics.

Marxian class analysis is frequently dismissed on the grounds that groups, not classes, dominate American politics; that class consciousness is so weak in the United States that it is usually overwhelmed by other sources of cleavage; and that Marxism is a form of economic determinism that cannot explain the complexity of American politics.

Marx was acutely aware of divisions within classes and of beliefs that undercut class unity. He saw the lower middle class, small manufacturers, shopkeepers, and farmers struggling to save themselves as fractions of the middle class. Marx exhorted workers of all lands to unite; he worked mightily toward this end, but he continually encountered racial, ethnic, nationalistic, religious, and other barriers. The division of labor was an especially mighty force against worker unity. Group and subclass ties are best seen, from the Marxian perspective, not as evidence against the reality and the explanatory power of class but as obstacles preventing the full prosecution of class conflict.

Marx is often faulted for predicting the division of capitalist societies into two antagonistic classes, one of which, labor, was fated to overthrow capital, abolish private property, and establish socialism. This reading of Marx is widely believed and will not be dislodged easily. Yet it is based on a partial reading of Marx and rejections of Marx based on it are only weakly founded on his work.

Marx did claim (rightly) that capitalism dispossessed the many from ownership and control of the means of production, concentrated power in the hands of capitalists and their associates, and involved a structural conflict between those who buy labor power and those who sell it. But precisely how this conflict got worked out in diverse societies was a matter of history, not abstract laws. Marx went so far as to criticize David Ricardo for naively taking the antagonism of class interests as a social law of nature without considering the fact that every historical period has laws of its own.[121]

Marx first predicted proletarian revolution in 1843, when he was twenty-five; he and Engels first wrote about the proletariat being compelled to abolish private property two years later in *The Holy Family*. After the failure of the 1848-1849 revolutions, Marx was exiled to London. In 1850 he obtained a ticket to the reading room of the British Museum where he completed his mature research on capitalism. When the Paris workers' revolt was defeated in the summer of 1850, Marx concluded that, barring economic collapse, a successful immediate proletarian revolution was impossible.

The distinction between the early and later Marx is often overdone, but with respect to class polarization, there is an important difference between the early and later work. Marx's later work rejects the "immiseration of the proletariat" thesis, explains how labor's financial lot under capitalism may in absolute terms improve, and predicts the emergence of a new middle class standing between capitalists and workers.[122] Asked in 1880 by American journalist John Swinton what he saw for the future, Marx, upon reflection, answered not with the optimistic predictions of his youth but with one word: "Struggle." [123] This is one Marxian prediction amply borne out by history.

Economic inequality was, for Marx, insufficient for revolution. Revolutionary class politics required people divided into antagonistic positions in the system of production, separate class cultures, awareness of conflicting class interests, links across local and regional lines, and a well-developed political organization.[124] Marx hoped and expected that the fusion of these elements would destroy capitalism in the United States; he also thought that in the United States this might occur peacefully. Clearly, he was mistaken on both counts.

Where Marxism goes wrong when applied to the United States generates endless debate, but it is doubtful that the explanation lies in the weakness of American class consciousness. A survey of evidence shows that "Americans are amazingly clear on the shape of the American class system and their place within it." Americans recognize class divisions and have done so for many decades. Their perceptions are as clear as those of the British, who are often supposed to be especially class conscious.[125] Marx expected and hoped that workers would overcome their differences and organize along class lines. Their failure fully to do so, however, is probably best explained (1) by the fact that despite stiff resistance large numbers of workers fought for and attained middle-class incomes, and (2) by cultural values supportive of an ideology favoring capitalism. Changes in all of these, plus changes in class consciousness, would be required for a serious challenge to capitalism.

However inaccurate Marx's predictions, it would seem, on the historical evidence, that a theory of society that acknowledges the existence and importance of classes (as well as of groups) offers a more powerful explanation of America than a theory of groups that slights the importance of class. Indeed, if "Marx the heretic" [126] is ever admitted to mainstream discourse, class may prove to be as significant to understanding American history and politics as Frederick Jackson Turner once claimed for the frontier.

Notes

The staffs at the presidential libraries of Franklin D. Roosevelt, John F. Kennedy, Lyndon B. Johnson, and Ronald W. Reagan greatly assisted the research of which this article is part. I want to thank Professor Tiziano Bonazzi of the University of Bologna for a perceptive critique of an earlier version of this essay. Kathy Lynn Sharp's enthusiastic support and able research assistance were invaluable.

1. John F. Manley, "Neo-Pluralism: A Class Analysis of Pluralism I and Pluralism II," *American Political Science Review* 77 (1983): 368-383; Robert A. Dahl, "Comment on Manley," *American Political Science Review* 77 (1983): 388. For a discussion of "critical pluralism," and a strained effort at transcending the pluralism-class standoff, see Gregor McLennan, *Marxism, Pluralism and Beyond* (Cambridge, England: Polity Press, 1989).
2. Martin Shefter, "Trade Unions and Political Machines," in *Working Class Formation*, ed. Ira Katznelson and Aristide R. Zolberg (Princeton, N.J.: Princeton University Press, 1986), 197-276; Amy Bridges, "Becoming American: The Working Classes in the United States before the Civil War," in *Working Class Formation*, ed. Katznelson and Zolberg, 157-196; Aristide R. Zolberg, "How Many Exceptionalisms?" in *Working Class Formation*, ed. Katznelson and Zolberg, 397-455; Ira Katznelson, *Marxism and the City* (New York: Oxford University Press, 1992); Rhonda F. Levine, *Class Struggle and the New Deal* (Lawrence: University Press of Kansas, 1988); Herbert G. Gutman, *Power and Culture*, ed. Ira Berlin (New York: New Press, 1987); David Montgomery, *The Fall of the House of Labor* (New York: Cambridge University Press, 1989); Ira Katznelson and Margaret Weir, *Schooling for All* (New York: Basic Books, 1985);

Lawrence Goodwyn, *Democratic Promise* (New York: Oxford University Press, 1976); Scott G. McNall, *The Road to Rebellion* (Chicago: University of Chicago Press, 1988); Reeve Vanneman and Lynn Weber Cannon, *The American Perception of Class* (Philadelphia: Temple University Press, 1987).

3. Richard F. Fenno, Jr., *Congressmen in Committees* (Boston: Little, Brown, 1973).
4. Scott G. McNall, Rhonda F. Levine, and Rick Fantasia, ed., *Bringing Class Back In* (Boulder, Colo.: Westview, 1991), 2.
5. Ibid., 3.
6. Eric Olin Wright, "The Conceptual Status of Class Structure in Class Analysis," in *Bringing Class Back*, ed. McNall et al., 18. For a good discussion, see Bertell Ollman, "Marx's Use of 'Class,' " *American Journal of Sociology* 74 (1968).
7. For a treatment of these issues in the theoretical context of the American dream, see John F. Manley, "American Liberalism and the Democratic Dream," *Policy Studies Review* 10 (1990): 89-102.
8. Max Farrand, ed., *The Records of the Federal Convention of 1787* (New Haven: Yale University Press, 1937), vol. 1, pp. 397-404, 422-423.
9. Gaillard Hunt, ed., *The Writings of James Madison* (New York: Putnam, 1906), vol. 4, pp. 121-124.
10. Alexander Hamilton, James Madison, and John Jay, *The Federalist Papers* (New York: Mentor, 1961), 79.
11. Heinz Eulau, "Classes and Interests in the Early American Consciousness," in *Politische Klasse und Politische Institutionen*, ed. Hans-Dieter Klingeman et al. (Opladen, Germany: Westdeutscher Verlag, 1991).
12. Isaac Kramnick, *Republicanism and Bourgeois Radicalism* (Ithaca, N.Y.: Cornell University Press, 1990); Gordon Wood, *The Radicalism of the American Revolution* (New York: Knopf, 1992).
13. Hunt, *James Madison*, vol. 6, p. 86.
14. Marvin Meyers, ed., *The Mind of the Founder* (Indianapolis: Bobbs-Merrill, 1973), 505.
15. Andrew A. Lipscomb, ed., *The Writings of Thomas Jefferson* (Washington, D.C.: Thomas Jefferson Memorial Association, 1904), vol. 5, p. 152; vol. 14, pp. 181-182.
16. Ibid., vol. 2, p. 230.
17. Ibid., vol. 2, p. 55.
18. Kenneth Dolbeare, ed., *American Political Thought* (Monterey, Calif.: Duxbury, 1981), 513.
19. John R. Commons, ed., *A Documentary History of American Industrial Society* (Cleveland: Clark, 1910), vol. 3, pp. 19-58, quotation at p. 39.
20. Philip Foner, *History of the Labor Movement in the United States* (New York: International Publishers, 1947), vol. 1, p. 69.
21. Howard Rock, *Artisans of the New Republic* (New York: New York University Press, 1979).
22. Herbert Harris, *American Labor* (New Haven: Yale University Press, 1938), 12-13.
23. Commons, *American Industrial Society*, vol. 3, p. 151.
24. David Montgomery, "The Working Classes of the Pre-Industrial American City, 1780-1830," *Labor History* 9 (1968): 6.
25. Foner, *History of the Labor Movement*, 119.
26. David Harris, *Socialist Origins in the United States* (Amsterdam: Van Goreun, 1966); Staughton Lynd, *Intellectual Origins of American Radicalism* (Cambridge: Harvard University Press, 1982).
27. Bruce Laurie, *Artisans Into Workers* (New York: Nooday, 1989); Sean Wilentz, *Chants Democratic* (New York: Oxford University Press, 1984).
28. Commons, *American Industrial Society*, 192-193, 232-235, 292-297.

29. Nathan Ware, *The Industrial Worker: 1840-1860* (Boston: Houghton Mifflin, 1924).
30. Wilentz, *Chants*, 300.
31. Sean Wilentz, "Against Exceptionalism: Class Consciousness and the American Labor Movement," *International Labor and Working Class History* 26 (1984): 1-24. Nick Salvatore, "Response to Sean Wilentz," *International Labor and Working Class History* 26 (1984): 25-30. Steven Sapolsky, "Response to Sean Wilentz's 'Against Exceptionalism,' " *International Labor and Working Class History* 27 (1985): 35-38.
32. Alan Trachtenberg, *The Incorporation of America* (New York: Hill and Wang, 1982), 153.
33. Michael Reich, "The Development of the Wage Labor Force," in *The Capitalist System*, 2d ed., ed. Richard C. Edwards et al. (Englewood Cliffs, N.J.: Prentice-Hall, 1978), 180.
34. The quotations in the following paragraphs are drawn from the Committee's report. Senate Committee upon the Relations between Labor and Capital, *Report*, 48th Cong., vol. 1, pp. 49, 256, 288, 356, 358, 375, 376, 624; vol. 2, pp. 536, 828; vol. 3, p. 625.
35. John D. Hicks, *The Populist Revolt* (Lincoln: University of Nebraska Press, 1961), 124; Richard Hofstadter, *The Age of Reform* (New York: Vintage, 1960).
36. Lawrence Goodwyn, *The Populist Moment* (New York: Oxford University Press, 1978), 334. See also Lawrence Goodwyn, "Rethinking 'Populism,' " *Telos* 88 (Summer 1991): 37-56.
37. Norman Pollock, *The Populist Response to Industrial America* (Cambridge: Harvard University Press, 1962); M. Schwartz, *Radical Protest and Social Structure* (New York: Academic Press, 1976); Steven Hahn, *The Roots of Southern Populism* (New York: Oxford University Press, 1983); Bruce Palmer, *"Man over Money": The Southern Populist Critique of American Capitalism* (Chapel Hill: University of North Carolina Press, 1984); Alan Dawley, *Struggles for Justice* (Cambridge: Harvard University Press, 1991).
38. Goodwyn, *Democratic Promises*, 33.
39. Ibid., 82.
40. Schwartz, *Radical Protest*, chap. 6.
41. Hicks, *Populist Revolt*, 103.
42. Norman Pollock, ed., *The Populist Mind* (Indianapolis: Bobbs-Merrill, 1967), 82-87.
43. Ibid., 15, 39, 424.
44. Palmer, *"Man over Money,"* 16, 132.
45. Hicks, *Populist Revolt*, 435-437.
46. Pollock, *Populist Response*, 64.
47. Charles A. Beard, *Contemporary American History* (New York: Macmillan, 1914), 141, 154-155, 157.
48. C. Vann Woodward, *Tom Watson* (New York: Oxford University Press, 1963), 302-331, quotation at 330.
49. Ibid., 305.
50. Palolo E. Coletta, *William Jennings Bryan* (Lincoln: University of Nebraska Press, 1964), vol. 1, p. 162.
51. Beard, *Contemporary American History*, 168.
52. Matthew Josephson, *The Politicos* (New York: Harcourt, Brace, 1938), 700.
53. Beard, *Contemporary American History*, 196.
54. Ibid., 179.
55. Josephson, 689-690.
56. Ray Ginger, ed., *William Jennings Bryan: Selections* (Indianapolis: Bobbs-Merrill, 1967), 37-46.

57. Josephson, *The Politicos*, 662.
58. Hofstadter, *Age of Reform*, 64.
59. Theodore Roosevelt, *An Autobiography* (New York: Macmillan, 1913), 297.
60. Hofstadter, *Age of Reform*, 5.
61. Lawrence Herson, *The Politics of Ideas* (Homewood, Ill.: Dorsey, 1984), 176.
62. John Graham Brooks, *The Social Unrest* (New York: Macmillan, 1903).
63. W. J. Ghent, *Mass and Class* (New York: Macmillan, 1904), 53.
64. Herbert Croly, *The Promise of American Life* (New York: Macmillan, 1914), 23, 28.
65. William Griffith, ed., *The Roosevelt Policy* (New York: Kraus Reprint, 1971), 154, 190, 271, 316, 449, 752-753. Lincoln's remark may be found in his first annual message to Congress, December 3, 1861. Lincoln, who lived in the transition period from independent production to industrial capitalism, was expressing a widely held view shared by, among others, Leland Stanford, when he stressed the priority of labor. Capital had its rights, in Lincoln's view, but his preference for independent production was clear in his emphasis on the fact that a large majority of the population was neither capitalist nor wage labor. See Arthur B. Lapsley, ed., *The Writings of Abraham Lincoln* (New York: Putnam, 1906), vol. 5, pp. 406-407.
66. Kirk H. Porter and Donald B. Johnson, eds., *National Party Platforms* (Urbana: University of Illinois, 1956), 175-182.
67. Graham Adams, *The Age of Industrial Violence* (New York: Columbia University Press, 1966). See also Sharon Reitman, "The Politics of the Western Federation of Miners and the United Mine Workers," in *Bringing Class Back*, ed. McNall et al., 203-222.
68. E. David Cronon, ed., *The Political Thought of Woodrow Wilson* (Indianapolis: Bobbs-Merrill, 1965), 245.
69. John Tipple, ed., *The Capitalist Revolution* (New York: Pegasus, 1970), 11.
70. Ray S. Baker and William Dodd., eds., *The Public Papers of Woodrow Wilson* (New York: Harper, 1925-1927), vol. 1, p. 8.
71. Ibid., 144-145.
72. Woodrow Wilson, "The Road Away from Revolution," *The Atlantic Monthly* 132 (August 1923): 145-146.
73. Carl Degler, *Out of Our Past* (New York: Harper, 1959), 391.
74. Frances Perkins, *The Roosevelt I Knew* (New York: Viking, 1946), 328.
75. Rexford Guy Tugwell, *The Brains Trust* (New York: Viking, 1968), xxi.
76. One historian of the first type is Basil Rauch, *The History of the New Deal* (New York: Creative Age, 1944). Scholars of the second type include Barton Bernstein, "The Conservative Achievement of Liberal Reform," in *Towards a New Past*, ed. Barton Bernstein (New York: Vintage, 1969), 263-288; Paul Conkin, *The New Deal* (New York: Crowell, 1967); and Ron Radosh, "The Myth of the New Deal," in *A New History of Leviathan*, ed. Ron Radosh and Murray Rothbard (New York: Dutton, 1972). The third view is presented in Levine, *Class Struggle*; Theda Skocpol, "Political Response to Capitalist Crisis: Neo-Marxist Theories of the State and the Case of the New Deal," *Politics and Society* 10 (1980): 155-201; Theda Skocpol and E. Amenta, "Did Capitalists Shape Social Security?" *American Sociological Review* 4 (1985): 572-575; Theda Skocpol and Kenneth Finegold, "State Capacity and Economic Intervention in the Early New Deal," *Political Science Quarterly* 97 (1982): 255-278; Fred Block, "The Ruling Class Does Not Rule: Notes on the Marxist Theory of the State," *Socialist Revolution* 33 (1977): 6-28.
77. Levine, *Class Struggle*, 14-19.
78. William Leuchtenburg, *Franklin D. Roosevelt and the New Deal* (New York: Harper Colophon, 1963), 53-54.

79. Ibid., 165.
80. Franklin Delano Roosevelt Presidential Library, Taussing Collection, Container 32, 1933, p. 2.
81. Franklin Delano Roosevelt Presidential Library, Tugwell Collection, *Diary*, Container 15, p. 6.
82. Franklin Delano Roosevelt Presidential Library, Berle Collection, Memo Re: Secretary of the Treasury Ogden L. Mills, Container 15, p. 2.
83. Frank Freidel, *Franklin D. Roosevelt* (Boston: Little, Brown, 1973), 71.
84. Leuchtenburg, *FDR and the New Deal*, 178.
85. Raymond Moley, *After Seven Years* (New York: Harper, 1939), 313.
86. *Congressional Record*, August 1, 1935, p. 12284.
87. Harold L. Ickes, *The Secret Diary of Harold L. Ickes* (New York: Simon and Schuster, 1954), vol. 1, p. 652.
88. Franklin Delano Roosevelt Presidential Library, Harry Hopkins Papers, Containers 62, 67-68.
89. Franklin Delano Roosevelt Presidential Library, President's Personal File, No. 1848.
90. Ibid., Container 2337, 1933.
91. Drew McCoy, *Angry Voices* (Lawrence: University of Kansas, 1958); Alan Brinkley, *Voices of Protest* (New York: Knopf, 1982).
92. Arthur M. Schlesinger, Jr., *The Crisis of the Old Order* (Boston: Houghton Mifflin, 1957), 256.
93. Rauch, *History of the New Deal*, 74.
94. Irving Bernstein, *Turbulent Years* (Boston: Houghton Mifflin, 1970), 217ff. See also Frances Fox Piven and Richard Cloward, *Poor People's Movements* (New York: Pantheon, 1977). The following summary draws heavily from Bernstein.
95. Leuchtenburg, *FDR and the New Deal*, 111-112.
96. I. Bernstein, *Turbulent Years*, 229.
97. Ibid., 259.
98. Ibid., 769, 790.
99. Friedel, *Roosevelt*, 221.
100. *Public Papers and Addresses of Franklin Roosevelt* (New York: Random House, 1938), vol. 4, pp. 270-277.
101. Arthur M. Schlesinger, Jr., *The Politics of Upheaval* (Boston: Houghton Mifflin, 1966), 325-329.
102. *Public Papers and Addresses of Franklin Roosevelt*, vol. 5, 383-390.
103. J. David Greenstone, *Labor in American Politics* (New York: Knopf, 1969), 42-44; Everett C. Ladd and Charles Hadley, *Transformations of the American Party System* (New York: Norton, 1975), 66; Robert Alford, *Party and Society* (Chicago: Rand McNally, 1963); Kristi Anderson, *The Creation of a Democratic Majority* (Chicago: University of Chicago Press, 1979).
104. Frances Fox Piven and Richard Cloward, *The New Class War* (New York: Pantheon, 1982); Ira Katznelson, "A Radical Departure: Social Welfare and the Election," in *The Hidden Election*, ed. Thomas Ferguson and Joel Rogers (New York: Pantheon, 1981), 313-340.
105. Bruce Bartlett, *Reaganomics* (Westport, Conn.: Arlington House, 1981), 1-11; Martin Anderson, *Revolution* (New York: Harcourt, Brace, Jovanovich, 1988). For Congress's role see Paul Craig Roberts, *The Supply-Side Revolution* (Cambridge: Harvard University Press, 1984).
106. John L. Palmer and Isabel V. Sawhill, eds., *The Reagan Experiment* (Washington, D.C.: The Urban Institute, 1982), 468-470.
107. Ronald Reagan, *An American Life* (New York: Simon and Schuster, 1990), 316.
108. Palmer and Sawhill, *Reagan Experiment*, 474.

109. William Greider, "The Education of David Stockman," *The Atlantic Monthly*, 248 (December 1981): 47.
110. David Stockman, *The Triumph of Politics* (New York: Harper and Row, 1986), 1-5.
111. *Wall Street Journal*, "The Outlook," December 6, 1982, 1.
112. Ronald Reagan Presidential Library, Richard Wirthlin to Richard Richards, "The Reagan Economic Program," PR 015, Box 1.
113. Kevin Phillips, *The Politics of Rich and Poor* (New York: Random House, 1990), xvii.
114. Quoted in Phillips, *Politics of Rich and Poor*, 74.
115. Michael Boskin, "Distributional Effects of the Reagan Program," in *Reaganomics: A Midterm Report*, ed. William Craig Stubblebine and Thomas D. Willett (San Francisco: Institute for Contemporary Studies Press, 1983), 198. Former Reagan advisor Martin Anderson stresses, disingenuously, that real government spending rose under President Reagan, even for social welfare, but he fails to credit President Reagan's lamentation over the inability to cut spending more deeply. Anderson, *Revolution*, 178; Reagan, *American Life*, 313, 336-337. Taking credit for policies one opposed is standard politics, but questionable history.
116. *Wall Street Journal*, October 12, 1990, 1.
117. David Broder, "Election '84: A Class Struggle," *Washington Post National Edition*, January 6, 1984, 9.
118. Quoted in Phillips, *Politics of Rich and Poor*, 30.
119. L. Malkin, "Reaganites Rally 'Round the Trickle-Down Flag," *International Herald Tribune*, June 20-21, 1992, F1. Michael Kelly, "Clinton Predicts Bush Will Trim Social Security," *New York Times*, September 4, 1992, 1.
120. Karl Marx, *Capital* (New York: International Publishers, 1967), vol. 1, p. 645; vol. 3, p. 819.
121. Ibid., vol. 1, p. 14.
122. Martin Nicolaus, "Proletariat and Middle Class in Marx," in *For a New America*, ed. James Weinstein and David W. Eakins (New York: Random House, 1970), 253-283. Nicolaus's brilliant essay is unduly neglected. For additional discussions of determinism versus voluntarism in Marx, see Alvin Gouldner, *The Two Marxisms* (New York: Seabury, 1980), and especially E. P. Thompson, *The Poverty of Theory and Other Essays* (London: Merlin, 1978).
123. Richard O. Boyer and Herbert M. Morais, *Labor's Untold Story* (New York: United Electrical, Radio and Machine Workers of America, 1965), 84.
124. Robert C. Tucker, ed., *The Marx-Engels Reader*, 2d ed. (New York: Norton, 1978), 608.
125. Vanneman and Cannon, *American Perception of Class*, 283.
126. The phrase is William Appleman Williams's, *The Great Evasion* (Chicago: Quadrangle, 1964), 20.

3

Two-Tiered Pluralism: Race and Ethnicity in American Politics

Rodney Hero

Although Latinos, African Americans, and Native Americans have not received a great deal of attention in U.S. political science research, their low political and social status has led some observers to question the viability of the dominant pluralistic paradigm in American politics research and to point to a "new American dilemma." Some have even speculated that minority group inequality might be a necessary rather than an exceptional characteristic of U.S. politics and society. Whether or not this is true, the implications of persistent minority-group inequality for the pluralist interpretation have yet to be thoroughly explored.[1]

Previous work on minority politics has drawn on several broad theoretical perspectives. These include pluralism, coalitional bias/elitism, and internal colonialism.[2] At the same time, limitations in these perspectives have been identified, particularly in their applicability to Latino politics.[3] Perhaps no definitive interpretation is yet possible, but a theoretical sketch that I call two-tiered pluralism may move us toward a better understanding of minority groups in American politics.

Two-tiered pluralism as practiced in the American political system reconciles a major American dilemma, namely, that between democracy and social and political inequality. In its two-tiered variant, pluralism continues in some degree to function as commonly described and understood.[4] There are, however, two tiers, or levels, to social, political, and economic pluralism, with minority groups found very disproportionately in the second tier. The relationship between the two tiers is interdependent but unbalanced.

Essentially everyone in both tiers enjoys certain individual rights, including the right to vote, formal equal protection of the laws, and equality before the law, as well as other basic rights and freedoms. These formal rights coexist, however, with distinctive historical and structural disadvantages that tacitly undercut equality for most members of minority groups, making pluralism largely formal, or procedural, for most minority-group members.

To compensate for such structural disadvantages, groups whose initial presence in the United States was not voluntary or consensual have been afforded special protections at various times over the past 40 years. The need for such protection, however, indicates a flaw in traditional pluralism both as a description of and a prescription for American politics. Programs for protected groups smack of a "purchased" or symbolic pluralism and too often have the effect of reinforcing the subordinate status of minority groups.[5] Two-tiered pluralism, thus, has some of the same double-edged qualities as a related concept, equal opportunity, "the keystone of U.S. liberal democracy."[6]

Inequality: A Flaw in the Pluralist Design

Recent debates in American politics regarding the distribution of power and authority have explored inequality in American politics and society. Some view equal opportunity—a central tenet of pluralist theory—as the central issue in that debate. Equal opportunity, however, is a distinctly double-edged sword. Although American minorities have the opportunity for equal opportunity, opportunity is not necessarily equal in fact, because it presumes a certain minimum level of equality to begin with, as well as a certain level of awareness and understanding of social and political processes. Such awareness, understanding, and opportunity may not in fact exist to the extent or in the way that is assumed.

Pluralism, as generally understood, recognizes differences in the quantity of group resources. Two-tiered pluralism suggests that, in addition, there are substantive differences with respect to the range, the durability, and the indispensability of group resources that disadvantage minority groups in particular.[7] Moreover, because of historical and other structural factors, pluralism in the United States is marked by "coalitional bias," in which certain groups prevail consistently more often than others.[8]

Two-tiered pluralism traces its modern roots to the separate-but-equal concept enunciated by the Supreme Court in 1896. Recent programs, such as affirmative action, suggest a separate but equal, perhaps even advantageous, status for minority groups. However, the names and the language of the politics and policies have changed. The new programs are now typically referred to as special rather than avowedly separate. And they are ostensibly equalizing or compensatory—at least in terms of their stated intent—rather than equal. Indeed, critics view them as quite unfair, as reverse discrimination. The formal equality and the stated equalizing intent of these special policies have served as a kind of political and intellectual safety net in that they indicate responsiveness and the achievement of equality. At least implicitly they vindicate pluralist theory.[9] They might also be designed to maintain order and manage conflict.

For most minority groups, as distinct from white ethnic groups and other interest groups, pluralism has historically been limited. The equality of such groups has been constrained, both formally and informally. The inferior legal status of slaves and Indians was enshrined in the U.S. Constitution, for example. After the abolition of slavery, legal doctrines such as that which mandated separate but equal public facilities were controlling for many years. With the removal of formal constraints, informal mechanisms and the legacy of the formal doctrines have continued to limit minority participation in political and social life.[10]

The shift from legal segregation to de facto segregation and then to de jure pluralism can be traced through such policies as the Brown desegregation decisions, the Civil Rights Acts of 1964, voting rights legislation, and affirmative action. True pluralism, however, remains elusive, except in its two-tiered forms, which are associated with what has been referred to as institutional discrimination.[11]

Barrera contends that institutional discrimination must be understood in terms of interests; that is, that institutions are biased because particular economic, social, and political interests benefit from particular institutional arrangements and outcomes. That is not inconsistent with the theory of two-tiered pluralism. It might be added, however, that social institutions and structures also manifest a tension or dialectic between interests and ideals. Certain American ideals, such as democracy, induce institutions to respond favorably, if often inadequately, to underprivileged groups. But interests limit the nature and extent of that response. Thus, although pluralism as an ideal is achieved, it is limited, or two-tiered, partly because of the protection of interests. The interplay of the ideals and interests also shapes the nature of the ideology that is used to explain and justify the status quo. That is why conventional pluralism and various sociological deficiency theories—theories that explain inequality by claiming within-group shortcomings in minority groups—particularly the internal social structural and cultural deficiency theories, are theoretically compatible.[12]

Two-tiered pluralism is evident in specific institutional structures and practices. Studies of minority group efforts to gain voting rights have claimed that strategies to limit the impact of minority voting in local elections have changed from vote denial to dilution. In place of outright denial of minority voting rights, new, more subtle mechanisms have been used to lessen the impact of minority voters.[13] Regarding voter registration, "the current maze of laws and administrative procedures that govern voter registration suppress [overall] voter turnout in the United States by about 9 percentage points . . . [They] have their greatest suppressive effect on the turnout rates of the young, the poor, and those with few years of formal education."[14] The suppressive effect of these administrative procedures for minorities is, thus, probably greater than the 9 percent for the overall population because minorities are a disproportionately young and poor group with low educational achievement levels.

Perhaps the leading example of institutional outcomes indicative of two-tiered pluralism is found in education. In elementary and secondary education second-generation discrimination has occurred through school segregation and discrimination in the aftermath of formal desegregation.

Specific instances are the disproportionately high assignment of minority students to undesirable education programs (such as classes for the educable mentally retarded) and disproportionately low assignment to desirable classes (such as those for the gifted), differential disciplinary policies, and lower educational achievement (as expressed in higher dropout rates and lower graduation rates).[15]

Patterns suggestive of two-tiered pluralism also are apparent in higher education. Barber contends that the study of some social and political issues, such as those concerning minority politics, has been relegated to a secondary status in social science research. Those issues have been shut out of the conversation "or marginalized . . . by the establishment of academic slums and backwaters with names like Afro-American studies, or women's studies." [16]

Barber also claims that academic disciplines, including political science, "continue to reflect the inequalities and disparities of power found in the society that they seek to objectively study. He adds that the discipline of political science may be more a club than a discipline. Those excluded from the club "are without voices, and are thus disempowered in a subtle but consequential fashion. Their intellectual powerlessness in the conversations of the club mirrors the social and economic powerlessness of the groups they represent." A chief problem with political science is its "inability to achieve genuine inclusiveness." [17] The argument of two-tiered pluralism makes similar claims, and further suggests that not only do academic professions and disciplines reflect inequalities, but they also may reinforce them, however unconsciously or inadvertently.

Two-Tiered Pluralism in the U.S. Socioeconomic System

The concentration of minorities in the second tier is probably attributable to both race and class.[18] The relative importance of race/ethnicity and class is difficult to ascertain because they are highly intertwined. Stone asserts that

> for many people, race is a shorthand for class. Though it is not always done consciously, "black" is often equated with lower class and "white" with middle class. Because blacks are poor in larger proportion than whites, statistical association leads to stereotypes, and these stereotypes are hard to displace because they are convenient for making decisions in situations of incomplete information. The statistical association between race and class thus becomes fixed in mass conduct.[19]

It is important, however, that the issues of race and class be isolated. Ethnic and racial factors, along with particular historical experiences, make the minority situation distinct from that of other disadvantaged classes. For example, the political and social status of Latinos (particularly Mexican Americans and Puerto Ricans) has been formally shaped, if less visibly than for African Americans and Native Americans, through original conquest and subsequently through such actions as land rights decisions, water rights policies, arranged entrance programs (such as the Bracero program), and Mexican schools. Extensive repatriation of Mexican Americans, many of whom were U.S. citizens, to Mexico during the Great Depression, and the extent and nature of enforcement of immigration laws and policies are further examples. On the whole, the Latino situation has been shaped less formally and been less explicitly articulated in law than has the black situation. Instead, Latinos' disadvantaged status has often been linked to cultural factors, particularly language. In the context of political and socioeconomic inequality, those cultural differences have sometimes become defined and treated as cultural "deficiencies." [20]

Figure 3-1 shows how two-tiered pluralism looks and works in the broader socioeconomic and political system. The large diamond represents the Anglo/white population (comprising 70 to 80 percent of the total U.S. population) and its socioeconomic distribution—a relatively large middle class and smaller upper and lower classes.[21] The two smaller pyramids represent the African American population (of about 12 percent) and the Latino population (of about 8 to 10 percent). The pyramid shape for Latinos and African Americans suggests the socioeconomic composition of these two groups: small upper classes and sizable lower (under?) classes.

Concentrated in the second tier, Latinos and African Americans interact and compete primarily with lower-class whites and with each other for socioeconomic and political benefits.[22] The assertions and discussions of affirmative action or reverse discrimination—or, as some critics have called it, affirmative discrimination—have often been most intense at the practical political level between working- or lower-class Anglos/whites and minorities.

The figure is consistent with the standard socioeconomic status model of American politics. As one moves from the top of the diamond down, socioeconomic and political power and influence decrease. That the socioeconomic structures and size of the dominant Anglo/white group in society are somewhat different than they are for African Americans and Latinos has a variety of implications for the several groups, regarding both inter- and intragroup relations. If, as is often assumed, political leadership and activities are most likely to come from the middle class,[23] minority groups are hindered by the small size of their middle and upper classes as well as by their overall size. This can make a minority group particularly susceptible to the use of selective incentives (in return for political support), recognition politics, and cooptation.[24]

The concepts noted along the edges of Figure 3-1 link the notion of two-tiered pluralism to other theoretical frameworks. Stone's types of urban political power are juxtaposed to the socioeconomic and political

Figure 3-1 Two-Tiered Pluralism

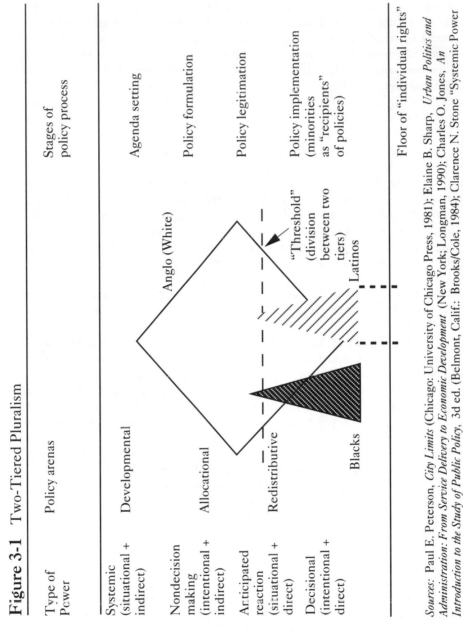

Type of Power	Policy arenas		Stages of policy process
Systemic (situational + indirect)	Developmental	Anglo (White)	Agenda setting
Nondecision making (intentional + indirect)	Allocational		Policy formulation
Anticipated reaction (situational + direct)	Redistributive	"Threshold" (division between two tiers)	Policy legitimation
		Latinos	Policy implementation (minorities as "recipients" of policies)
Decisional (intentional + direct)		Blacks	
			Floor of "individual rights"

Sources: Paul E. Peterson, *City Limits* (Chicago: University of Chicago Press, 1981); Elaine B. Sharp, *Urban Politics and Administration: From Service Delivery to Economic Development* (New York; Longman, 1990); Charles O. Jones, *An Introduction to the Study of Public Policy*, 3d ed. (Belmont, Calif.: Brooks/Cole, 1984); Clarence N. Stone "Systemic Power in Community Decision Making," *American Political Science Review* 4 (December 1980): 978-990.

distributions indicated in the figure. The implication is that minority political influence is essentially nonexistent at Stone's "systemic" level and is limited largely to the "decisional" arena of power.[25]

Peterson developed a theory of urban politics based on three types of public policy—developmental, allocational, and redistributive (see figure), with developmental policies being the overwhelming concern of—and redistributive policies shunned by—city governments because of the place of these governments in the American political economy.[26] Building on Peterson's work, Sharp puts forth the idea of bifurcated urban politics comprising two major domains, the developmental and the allocational. Decision making on allocational policy tends to have high visibility and high levels of controversy; its overall pattern of power is pluralistic. Typical participants in allocational politics are elected officials, such as mayors and city council members, public sector bureaucracies, and neighborhood organizations.[27] According to several authors, minorities have been substantially underrepresented even among the elected positions and bureaucracies in this secondary domain.[28] Peterson's later work implies that allocational politics are relatively unimportant in the big picture of city politics.[29]

Developmental policy is characterized by low visibility of decision making and the overall pattern of power tends to be elitist. Typical participants in the developmental domain are banks, developers, downtown businesses, and corporate leaders. Their socioeconomic status means that minorities are virtually absent among such participants. Another implication of Sharp's discussion is the essential absence of redistributive issues in urban politics.[30]

As illustrated in the right-hand column of Figure 3-1, minorities are seldom involved in the broadest and arguably most important stage of the policy process, agenda setting. Most commonly, minorities are primarily recipients of policies made by others.[31]

A major burden for minority groups is that their efforts at political influence seem inevitably to require explicit political activities that appear as demands or complaints. By contrast, established, mainstream groups are much more often able to practice an implicit politics that builds upon existing understandings and circumstances, to appear as run-of-the-mill distributive, developmental, promotional politics, as priorities, preferences, tastes, issues.[32] In light of their low status and resources, minority groups face a dilemma: to be ignored altogether while working and hoping for change in the long run, or to accept policies that offer recognition and even certain advantages but also signify inferior status.

The political goals and policies that minorities seek thus appear as redistributive and nonincremental; those of established groups appear as natural, normal, incremental, or just politics. There is a strong element in this of what Schattschneider called the "mobilization of bias" that works against the claims and goals of minority groups.[33] Largely for these reasons, the political and social opportunity costs of practical politics and ideological justification for minority groups are substantially higher than for other groups.[34]

The theory of two-tiered pluralism does not preclude individual or group accomplishment within any minority group. Successes and accomplishments such as the election of minorities as mayors help combat the idea that low, or "exceptional," status is a permanent or necessary characteristic of a minority. Such successes also undermine the argument that minority subordination might be a necessity in the American social and political system.

Conclusion: Race and Ethnicity in American Society and in American Political Science

Understanding and explaining minority politics is partly a matter of stress and emphasis. Which aspects or segments of the minority experience are most important? Some stress the political accomplishments that occur above the social and political "threshold" between the first and second tiers (see Figure 3-1). The area above the threshold is the one typically analyzed in conventional pluralist writing and accompanying behavioral research. Other interpretations stress the historically disadvantaged status of the mass of the Latino, African American, and Native American populations, a status that seems not to have changed despite economic expansion during the 1980s and increasing minority group electoral success. For the foreseeable future, economic and substantive inequality will continue to coexist with formal political equality and limited political success. The question is, "How peaceful will that coexistence be?"

Theorizing and research about American pluralism and democracy need to come to terms more directly, explicitly, and self-critically with the presence and persistence of ethnic/racial minority groups. African Americans and Native Americans are the leading, but not the only dilemma for the reigning descriptions and analyses of U.S. politics. Because of their in-between status in the U.S. political and social system, and because of their growing numbers in the population, Latinos, too, constitute a major challenge for pluralist theory and practice.

Two-tiered pluralism highlights the tension between liberalism and democracy in American politics and political thinking and suggests an important, and probably growing, political and theoretical dilemma.[35] It has been said that American liberal democracy has "internal weaknesses and contradictions, many of which grow more intractable as the American system ages and as its internal contradictions gradually emerge." [36] Two-tiered pluralism is better able than conventional pluralism both to recognize those contradictions, and to delineate the double-edged nature of the solutions put forth to address them.

Notes

1. Ernest Wilson III, "Why Political Scientists Don't Study Black Politics But Historians and Sociologists Do," *PS: Political Science and Politics* 18, 3 (Summer 1985): 600-606. Those who have contested the continued explanatory power of the pluralist approach include Jennifer Hochschild, *The New American Dilemma: Liberal Democracy and School Desegregation* (New Haven: Yale University Press, 1984); and Jennifer Hochschild, "The Double-edged Sword of Equal Opportunity," in *Power, Inequality and Democratic Politics*, ed. Ian Shapiro and Grant Reeher (Boulder, Colo.: Westview, 1988), 168-200. Also see, John Manley, "Neopluralism: A Class Analysis of Pluralism I and Pluralism II," *American Political Science Review* 77, 2 (June 1983): 368-383, and Robert A. Dahl, *Dilemmas of Pluralist Democracy* (New Haven: Yale University Press, 1982). A seminal statement of the race problem as an American dilemma was Gunnar Myrdal's *An American Dilemma: The Negro Problem and Modern Democracy* (New York: Harper, 1944).

2. F. Chris Garcia and Rodolfo de la Garza, *The Chicano Political Experience: Three Perspectives* (North Scituate, Mass.: Duxbury, 1977); Mario Barrera, *Race and Class in the Southwest: A Theory of Racial Inequality* (Notre Dame, Ind.: University of Notre Dame Press, 1979); Clarence N. Stone, "Race, Power, and Political Change," in *The Egalitarian City*, ed. Janet K. Boles (New York: Praeger, 1986), 200-223; Milton Morris, *The Politics of Black America* (New York: Harper and Row, 1975); Rodney E. Hero, *Latinos and the U.S. Political System: Two-Tiered Pluralism* (Philadelphia: Temple University Press, 1992); Raymond A. Rocco, "A Critical Perspective on the Study of Chicano Politics," *Western Political Quarterly* 30 (December 1977): 558-573.

3. F. Chris Garcia, Rodolfo de la Garza, and Donald J. Torres, "Introduction: Political Participation, Organizational Development and Institutional Responsiveness," in *The Mexican American Experience: An Interdisciplinary Anthology*, ed. Rodolfo O. de la Garza, Frank D. Bean, Charles M. Bonjean, Ricardo Romo, and Rodolfo Alvarez (Austin: University of Texas Press, 1985), 185-186.

4. See, for example, Robert A. Dahl, *Who Governs?* (New Haven: Yale University Press, 1961).

5. Group competition [pluralism as conventionally perceived] may not be "much of a theory if it requires constant . . . government support." Theodore Lowi, *The End of Liberalism*, 2d ed. (New York: Norton, 1979), 58.

6. Hochschild, "Double-edged Sword," 168-169, 189.

7. Stone, "Race, Power, and Political Change," 202-205.

8. Nathan Glazer, "The Political Distinctiveness of Mexican Americans," in *Mexican-Americans in Comparative Perspective*, ed. Walker Connor (Washington, D.C.: Urban Institute Press, 1985), 205-224. In "Race, Power, and Political Change" (p. 203) Stone describes a system of "coalitional bias" as one in which some groups prevail consistently, though not totally. Over time, those that prevail do so in part because they enjoy a systemic advantage and are insiders in the governmental process. Other groups lose consistently, though not totally. Over time those that lose do so in part because they suffer a systemic disadvantage and are outsiders in the governmental process.

9. Hero, *Latinos and the U.S. Political System*, chap. 10.

10. Michael Omi and Howard Winant, *Racial Formation in the United States: From the 1960s to the 1980s* (New York: Routledge & Kegan Paul, 1986).

11. Kenneth Meier, Joseph Stewart, Jr., and Robert England, *Race, Class, and Education: The Politics of Second-Generation Discrimination* (Madison: University of Wisconsin Press, 1989); Kenneth Meier and Joseph Stewart, Jr., *The Politics of Hispanic Education* (Albany: State University of New York Press, 1991); Charles S.

Bullock III and Joseph Stewart, Jr., "Incidence and Correlates of Second-Generation Discrimination," in *Race, Sex, and Policy Problems,* ed. Marian L. Palley and Michael B. Preston (Lexington, Mass.: Lexington Books, 1979): 115-129.

12. Barrera, *Race and Class in the Southwest;* also see Hero, *Latinos and the U.S. Political System,* 26-28.
13. Howard Ball, "Racial Vote Dilution: Impact of the Reagan Department of Justice and the Burger Court on the Voting Rights Act," *Publius: The Journal of Federalism* 16, 4 (Fall 1986): 29-48; Abigail Thernstrom, *Whose Votes Count? Affirmative Action and Minority Voting Rights* (Cambridge: Harvard University Press, 1987).
14. Maria Antonia Calvo and Steven J. Rosenstone, *Hispanic Political Participation* (San Antonio, Texas: Southwest Voter Research Institute, 1989), 24.
15. See Meier and Stewart, *Politics of Hispanic Education;* Meier, Stewart, and England, *Race, Class, and Education.*
16. Benjamin Barber, "The Nature of Contemporary Political Science: A Roundtable Discussion," *PS: Political Science and Politics* 23, 1 (March 1990): 40.
17. Ibid., 40, emphasis added.
18. See Hochschild, "Double-edged Sword," 188; Michael Lipsky, *Street-Level Bureaucracy* (New York: Russell Sage, 1980); Meier, Stewart, and England, *Race, Class, and Education;* Meier and Stewart, *Politics of Hispanic Education.*
19. Stone, "Race, Power, and Political Change," 204.
20. Rodolfo Acuna, *Occupied America: A History of Chicanos,* 3d ed. (New York: Harper and Row, 1988); Barrera, *Race and Class in the Southwest;* Leobardo F. Estrada, F. Chris Garcia, Reynaldo Flores Macias, and Lionel Maldonado, "Chicanos in the United States: A History of Exploitation and Resistance," in *Latinos and the Political System,* ed. F. Chris Garcia (Notre Dame, Ind.: University of Notre Dame Press, 1988), 28-64; Patricia N. Limerick, *The Legacy of Conquest: The Unbroken Past of the American West* (New York: Norton, 1987); Joan Moore and Harry Pachon, *Hispanics in the United States* (Englewood Cliffs, N.J.: Prentice-Hall, 1985); James Jennings, "The Puerto Rican Community: Its Political Background," in *Latinos and the Political System,* ed. Garcia, 65-80; Meier and Stewart, *Politics of Hispanic Education;* Morris, *Politics of Black America.*
21. Lucius J. Barker and Jesse J. McCorry, Jr., *Black Americans and the Political System* (Cambridge, Mass.: Winthrop, 1980).
22. Paula McClain and Albert K. Karnig, "Black and Hispanic Socioeconomic and Political Competition," *American Political Science Review* 84, 2 (June 1990): 535-545; Meier and Stewart, *Politics of Hispanic Education.*
23. Raymond Wolfinger, *The Politics of Progress* (Englewood Cliffs, N.J.: Prentice-Hall, 1974), 49.
24. Stone, "Race, Power, and Political Change"; Wolfinger, *Politics of Progress;* Maurilio Vigil, *Hispanics in American Politics* (Lanham, Md.: University Press of America, 1987).
25. Clarence N. Stone, "Systemic Power in Community Decision Making," *American Political Science Review* 74 (December 1990): 978-990.
26. Paul E. Peterson, *City Limits* (Chicago: University of Chicago Press, 1981).
27. Elaine B. Sharp, *Urban Politics and Administration: From Service Delivery to Economic Development* (New York: Longman, 1990).
28. McClain and Karnig, "Black and Hispanic Socioeconomic and Political Competition"; Susan Welch, "The Impact of At-Large Elections on the Representation of Blacks and Hispanics," *Journal of Politics* 52, 4 (November 1990): 1050-1076; Meier and Stewart, *Politics of Hispanic Education;* Rufus P. Browning, Dale Rogers Marshall, and David H. Tabb, *Protest Is Not Enough: The Struggle of Blacks and Hispanics for Equality in Urban Politics* (Berkeley: University of California Press, 1984).
29. Paul Peterson, Barry G. Rabe, and Kenneth K. Wong, *When Federalism Works*

(Washington, D.C.: Brookings Institution, 1986). See also Bryan D. Jones, "Public Policies and Economic Growth in the American States," *Journal of Politics* 52, 1 (February 1990): 219-233.

30. Sharp, *Urban Politics*. Moreover, substantial evidence concerning the lack of Latino political influence in state and national politics (see, for example, Hero, *Latinos and the U.S. Poltical System*, chaps. 5 and 6) indicates little if any modification of that political weakness at the local level. Finally, redistributive policies at the national level are dominated by "power elites," not ethnic/racial minorities, according to Theodore Lowi and Benjamin Ginsberg, *American Government: Freedom and Power* (New York: Norton, 1990), 634.

31. Charles O. Jones, *An Introduction to the Study of Public Policy*, 3d ed. (Belmont, Calif.: Brooks/Cole, 1984).

32. Robert B. Albritton, "Social Services: Welfare and Health," in *Politics in the American States: A Comparative Analysis*, 5th ed., ed. Virginia Gray, Herbert Jacob, and Robert B. Albritton (Glenview, Ill.: Scott Foresman, 1990), 442; Lowi and Ginsberg, *American Government*, 616.

33. E. E. Schattschneider, *The Semisovereign People* (Hinsdale, Ill.: Dryden Press, 1975).

34. Stone, "Race, Power, and Political Change."

35. Hochschild, *New American Dilemma;* Barber, "Contemporary Political Science," 40.

36. Barber, "Contemporary Political Science."

4

Gender Politics and Political Change

Eileen L. McDonagh

Introduction

The presidential elections of 1992 will be remembered in many ways, not least of all as the "Year of the Woman." Five women were elected to the Senate, four of them as freshman members, while the number of women in the House doubled to more than forty. Before we wax too enthusiastic over these gains, however, we must remember their context. Women still constitute a mere 6 percent of the Senate and just under 10 percent of the House.

Even more striking, however, as we settle into the Clinton administration, is the reality that the woman many would acknowledge as wielding the most political power is none other than the president's wife, Hillary Rodham Clinton. Even after the "Year of the Woman," therefore, the world's oldest constitutional democracy lags behind India, Israel, Pakistan, the Philippines, Iceland, and several countries of Europe in elevating women to formal positions of political power.

Why is this so? This question and its answer draw attention to the way the liberal heritage of the American political system sets parameters for political change affecting gender within and across major dimensions of political development. As we shall see, reform periods celebrated for expanding the political rights of men have tended to be exactly the same periods in which the political exclusion of women intensified.

Viewing American political reform through the lens of sex and gender adds to our understanding of how principles of liberal democracy affect American state development and of how we assess the relative salience of race, class, and gender for that development. Prominent scholars have argued that race is the essential "American dilemma." Others, equally prominent, have focused on class relationships to explain American political reform.[1] The analysis presented here suggests another ordering. American political development illustrates how gender often transcends race and class as a criterion producing exclusion from public rights.

Feminist scholars point to the creation of the liberal state itself as the source of obdurate political discrimination against women. Because kinship and political power were linked in feudal social, economic, and political forms, sex and gender competed with class for political relevance. In royal and noble families, women shared rule with men and often served as head of state.[2]

By contrast, the liberal state at its founding split off the private sphere of familial relationships from the public sphere of political rule and assigned women solely to the family sphere based on their reproductive capacities and roles. Within that sphere, men, in principle equal to each other as citizens in the public sphere, ruled over women and children as head of household. Over time, as inequalities among men became the subject of concern, debate, and political action, private inequalities between men and women by contrast often were dismissed as being necessary for the operation of a democratic state.[3]

Women's quest for full participation as citizens in the American state, therefore, has been a saga not only of their political mobility within the public sphere, but also of the struggle to emerge from the private sphere of the family into that public sphere. Scholars have long studied the problem of how inequalities among men in the public sphere drive political change, but only recently have other scholars begun to examine what may be a more intractable inequality between the private and public spheres.[4]

The difficulty of improving political conditions for women becomes clear when we look at patterns of inclusion and exclusion during key periods of political reform. I will argue in the balance of this chapter that women's political segregation was institutionalized at the inception of the American nation, democratized during the Jacksonian period, legalized after the Civil War, and funded by the government in the Progressive era. It is this heritage that underlies 1992 as the "Year of the Woman," explaining why we rejoice at the recent gains, even while recognizing how far there is yet to go.

The American Revolution: Institutionalizing Women's Exclusion

During the Revolutionary era the Founders engineered the structures that defined formal political power in the new American democracy.[5] Women established nationwide organizations to support the war effort. One Philadelphia canvass, for example, collected $300,000 from more than 1,600 persons, a considerable financial feat for its time. Equally impressive were the economic boycotts implemented by the women's organizations and the more homely production of homemade goods as import substitutes. The war also hit women close to home as they experienced the turmoil and fighting of the war. Every movement of "troops through the American countryside brought a corresponding flight of refugees, an invasion of epidemic disease, the expropriation of foodstuffs, firewood, and livestock, widespread plundering or destruction of personal property" and "a specific terror to American women: the fear and/or the fact of rape."[6]

Participation in the war effort did not improve women's access to the public sphere, however. In some ways, women in the new American republic had fewer political rights than those enjoyed by women in the monarchies from which the new American republic had sought to distance itself. Whereas women of noble birth wielded political power, even sovereign power, in monarchical political systems, women of comparable status in the new American republic could not even cast votes as citizens.[7]

One of the most important outcomes of the Constitutional Convention, of course, was a government controlled by the people. Although it is easy in hindsight to criticize the Founders' limited idea of who comprised the people, one must remember that the principle of full suffrage still lay in the future. Government "by the people" must be contrasted with aristocratic traditions in which political authority was based on inherited kinship ties.

What distinguished the American system as a great political experiment, therefore, was the selection of political leaders by means of elections, not the breadth of who qualified to vote in those elections.[8] For women, however, the transition from the English monarchical regime to the American democratic republic was regressive in at least one way.

Slavery and Marriage

Those engaged in building the new American institutions following the war for independence were sensitive about what we might today term the "political correctness" of the institutions forming the new nation. In the case of slavery, this sensitivity generated voluminous debate, with proponents and opponents alike conceding that this "nefarious" institution was antithetical to the liberal and republican principles of the inchoate regime. The solution for some was to forgo republican government. Others, however, acceded to the infamous "compromise" under which slaves were counted as three-fifths of a person for purposes of determining state representation in the House of Representatives.[9]

Slavery, though surely the severest example, was by no means the only institution fundamentally at odds with principles of a republican regime. Marriage in colonial America was based on the English common law doctrine of coverture, in which husband and wife became one upon marriage, that one being the husband. Married women were femes covert and civilly dead. They could not in their own right sue or be sued, make contracts, draft wills, or buy or sell property. They had no right to their own property and no right to earnings from their own employment, since the property and earnings of married women legally belonged to their husbands. Further, if they "owned property prior to marriage, any personal estate went fully into their husbands' hands and any real estate came under their spouses' sole supervision . . . [and] the children of the marriage fell entirely within the custody of the father."[10]

Though it may seem farfetched to compare coverture marriage and chattel slavery, some scholars map their "legal symmetry." [11] A married woman, civilly "dead in law," was under the absolute control of a husband who "could collect and spend [her] wages and . . . beat her, although 'with a stick no bigger than a judge's thumb.' " The "husband owned the wife's person. Should she be injured in an industrial accident, he could sue for damages for loss of services. Should she rebel and run away, he could collect damages from whoever sheltered her." [12] Another scholar, rebutting the argument that women (unlike slaves) were free to abstain from the marriage contract, has taken issue with the quality of that freedom.[13]

How could the Founders, so sensitive to republican institutional correctness, have ignored the negation of women's civil rights as a direct institutional effect stemming from the coverture basis of marriage? Although delegates to the Constitutional Convention voiced extraordinary concern about the evil effects on human beings of tyranny and the institutional arrangements that caused it, they ignored Abigail Adams's plea, penned in a famous 1776 letter to her husband, to "remember the ladies." Since "all Men would be Tyrants if they could," reasoned John Adams's wife, "why then, not put it out of the power for the vicious and lawless to use us with cruelty and indignity with impunity?" [14]

Institutionalizing Republican Motherhood

Women's exclusion from political life was institutionalized early in the nation's history through the doctrine of "republican motherhood," according to which women fulfill roles in the private sphere viewed as necessary for the operation of the public sphere. As depicted by Linda Kerber, republican motherhood was a distinctly American creation; motherhood was viewed almost as a "fourth branch of government." The "Republican Mother's life was dedicated to the service of civic virtue: she educated her sons for it, she condemned and corrected her husband's lapses from it." A republican mother had "political purpose and . . . her domestic behavior had a direct political function in the Republic." [15]

Women with no formal political rights could be "political actors" in the public sphere precisely on the basis of their formal exclusion from that sphere, denoted by their maternal identity in the private sphere. In Linda Kerber's view, the American invention of republican motherhood was a revolutionary doctrine because it elevated the value of women's informal participation in the civic culture as a substitute for, rather than supplement to, formal political participation. Susan Okin has pointed out the irony of socializing citizens into their public and political roles within an institution (marriage and the family) founded upon illiberal principles.[16]

At the nation's inception, therefore, women's formal exclusion from the public sphere became entrenched on normative grounds. Women's citizenship was defined in terms of their maternal roles, and women were not accorded even the most basic political rights in the nascent liberal state.

Defining women's citizenship in terms of their dependence upon men had a particularly negative consequence for women in a nation that emphasized independence as a primary requisite for full status as a citizen. Whereas feudal systems were hierarchically structured on principles defining the mutual dependence and obligations of groups, that notion was rejected by the founders of the American state. As Nancy Fraser and Linda Gordon note, women's continuing dependence on men acquired a new, pejorative status that stigmatized women and contributed to their formal exclusion from the public sphere.[17]

The establishment of republican democracy, therefore, normatively elevated sex, a biological principle of group differentiation, and, gender, culturally prescribed roles and norms associated with sex, as absolute principles of political discrimination, overriding all other group identities, including class and race. And this was just the beginning.

Jacksonian Democracy: Democratizing Women's Exclusion

Democratizing the Public Sphere

Conventional wisdom portrays Jacksonian democracy as a golden age of American political reform, an age that saw the "elimination of traditional institutions and practices . . . which deviated from liberal-democratic values," with the significant exception of slavery.[18]

A major political accomplishment of the early nineteenth century was the universal enfranchisement of white males. As a complement, in 1828 the United States elected its first "common man" as president. Andrew Jackson was a westerner and the antithesis of the class-based eastern elite that had, until then, held the presidency.

Democratization of the franchise for unpropertied white males by the 1830s has been heralded as an indicator of American "exceptionalism," one that set the parameters for subsequent political development. Early establishment of white male suffrage, it is argued, diffused class conflict and helped detach class ideology from party organization. The result was partisan conflict based on patronage politics, not class. This, in turn, suppressed the development of a strong, centralized administrative state capable of launching the sort of comprehensive welfare policies that came to characterize the nations of Western Europe.[19]

Women did not share in the dramatic democratization of voting rights in Jacksonian democracy, however. As Ellen Carol DuBois notes, "the rise in popular political passions in the Jacksonian period was accompanied by a rise in the obstacles to the political inclusion of women." [20] Women's exclusion from political rights was broadened by means of the "cult of

true womanhood," an early nineteenth century cultural ideal that democratized the private sphere for white women in a way that paralleled the
democratization of the public sphere for white men, even as it retained
the separation between the two.

As Nancy Cott so lucidly argues, Americans created a unique, democratic concept of "the lady" based no longer on kinship inheritance but on
biological status as a female. Any woman, and all women, in principle,
could be the American "ladies," eligible to participate in the cult of true
womanhood.[21] In this sense, the American lady is the private sphere's
analog to the public sphere's Horatio Alger.

Women's sole destiny in the cult of true womanhood was marriage.
The adolescent girl "spent much time preparing for a 'good' marriage,"
following "a life of self-sacrifice and right thinking," in the belief that by
"some kind of divine justice . . . a successful and kind husband" would be
the result. Other options for women, such as education and work, were
subordinated to the goal of marriage. The original purpose of women's
colleges, for example, was to make a woman "a better helpmeet to the
American man." Similarly, mill girls at Lowell were "widely reported to be
among the truest women in New England . . . their adolescent purity [nec-
essary for marriage] was maintained by rigorous supervision of hours, required church attendance, and a schedule of self-improvement lectures." [22]

Thus, as Gerda Lerner argues, the period between 1800 to 1840 was
decisive for changing the social and economic status of American women,
but not their political status. Idealized maternal norms for women dominated the culture, undercutting recognition of the changing realities affecting women's lives, such as the growing numbers of factories and the
sharpening of class interests. As a result, the "society lady and the mill
girl" had in common only their membership in the "largest disenfran-
chised group in the nation's history." [23]

Marriage, though now ennobled by myth as the proper goal of all
"true" women in the early nineteenth century, nonetheless retained its
antiliberal features. A married women was still, for the most part, "dead
in law." The husband continued to exercise absolute control over the
children and his wife's property, a condition that did not begin to change
until the passage in the mid-nineteenth century of married property laws
in some states.

If anything, the legal status of married women deteriorated in the
early nineteenth century. A series of "obscure, but effective, state-court
decisions," later buttressed by Supreme Court decisions, undermined
dower rights for women. As a result, the "legal and cultural fiction that
the interests of husband and wife were one masked . . . [the] enormous
loss of property and potential economic influence of early republican
wives and mothers." [24]

At the same time, however, in the struggle against slavery the seeds
of the women's rights movement were planted, as sex discrimination ex-

perienced by women in the course of their abolitionist efforts led to the first organized women's rights movement, marked by the Seneca Falls convention in 1848.[25]

To what extent did women share directly in the progressive reforms of the Jacksonian era? Women did not share in the democratic advances made by comparable groups of men. Instead, their confinement within the private sphere intensified with the promulgation of the myth of true womanhood. The cultural diffusion of private-sphere norms prescribing maternal roles for women in lieu of political rights reached new heights, thereby reinforcing, rather than challenging, political sex discrimination. While the right to vote was democratized for white men in the Jacksonian era, impediments to that right were democratized for women.

The Civil War: Legalizing Women's Exclusion

The Civil War rivals the War of Independence as a dramatic turning point in American political history. In recent years, it has seized the attention of the general public and is the subject of renewed academic scholarship by political scientists.[26]

Women's War Contributions

Women distinguished themselves in "the first modern war" in a wide range of capacities. All over the North women plunged into hospital and relief work. They were found in the battlefield and in field hospitals, engaged in everything from emergency services to writing letters for the wounded and dying. Women proved to be expert administrators when charged with supervising nursing services in the army's general hospitals. Some pioneered new positions, such as that of "matron," and were responsible for organizing new hospitals. In major cities women's auxiliaries organized a network of county and village relief societies to raise funds and collect hospital supplies for the war effort. Women organized the Chicago Sanitary Fair of 1863, for example, which raised more funds than any other event of the entire war and was used all over the North as a fundraising example.[27]

Suffrage leaders supported the war effort, gathering hundreds of thousands of signatures on petitions to Congress demanding passage of the Thirteenth Amendment, which ultimately abolished slavery. Julia Ward Howe contributed the war's anthem, "The Battle Hymn of the Republic," a powerful symbol that focused northern morale.[28]

Adding the Word "Male" to the Constitution

Nevertheless, when we look at the political consequences of the Civil War through the lens of sex and gender, we see regression, not progress, in women's political rights. Two civil rights amendments to the Constitution passed in the aftermath of the war legitimized the political discrimination of women more explicitly than had henceforth been the case. The Fourteenth Amendment, which in 1868 enjoined the states to provide equal protection of the law to all citizens, added the word "male" to the Constitution for the first time in spelling out sanctions against states that deprived male citizens of the right to vote.[29] As a corollary, the Fifteenth Amendment (1870) guaranteed that "no state shall deprive a person of the right to vote on the basis of race, color, or previous condition of servitude" but failed to preclude sex as a discriminator, thereby necessitating a separate amendment for women's suffrage that would take another fifty years to accomplish. Meanwhile, by omitting sex from federal voting guarantees, Congress legalized the exemption of women from the formal protection of law.

Republicans in Congress, while pushing for the Thirteenth Amendment, had "declared again and again that suffrage was a natural right that belonged to every citizen . . . [and] that the ballot was the only weapon by which one class could protect itself against the aggressions of another." [30] Some contemporaneous critics failed to see progress in purging the Constitution of invidious distinctions as to color while concomitantly creating new restrictions on the basis of sex.[31]

That women were not drawn along in the democratic expansion of political rights after the war testifies to the weight of sex and gender in the American political system.[32] In one senator's view, the "immediate triumph" of African-American male suffrage would "weaken," should it be coupled with woman suffrage. He contended that proposals for women's suffrage were "not for the enfranchisement of woman, but against the enfranchisement of the black man." [33] It is notable that the inclusion of women in the electorate was still viewed as a greater threat to the American polity after the Civil War than the inclusion of previously excluded groups of men. At a time justly celebrated for breaking down historically institutionalized racial barriers for men, therefore, new ones were legislated for women.

The United States as Laggard

After the Civil War, the irony of women's political status in the United States was evident to some. One senator pointed out that the "exercise of political power by women is by no means an experiment. There is hardly a country in Europe . . . that has not at some time of its history been governed by a woman, and many of them very well governed too." He went on to list the achievements of the empresses of Russia, the leadership of Elizabeth, Anne, and Victoria of England, Queen Isabella's support of Columbus's discoveries, the effective rulership of Anne of Austria, and the "great and glorious" governance of Marie Theresa. For contemporary examples he observed that a woman [Queen Victoria] then served as the "high admiral of the most powerful fleet that rests upon the seas." "Shall we say that a woman may properly command an army," he asked, "and yet can not vote for a common Councilman?" [34]

Northerners and southerners alike countered these views by applauding women's domestic contribution to the public sphere and vigorously denying that these activities had any bearing on their enfranchisement. As one senator put it, "To have intelligent voters we must have intelligent mothers. . . . The voter from this source receives his moral and intellectual training. Woman makes the voter, and should not descend from her lofty sphere to engage in the angry contests of her creatures." [35]

Although some associate women's suffrage solely with white, middle-class interests,[36] prominent African-American women also voiced deep concern. As ex-slave and woman's suffrage leader Sojourner Truth told a meeting of the American Equal Rights Association in 1867, "I feel that if I have to answer for the deeds done in my body just as much as a man, I have a right to have just as much as a man. There is a great stir about colored men getting their rights, but not a word about the colored women." [37]

Sojourner Truth also pointed out the serious consequences of not extending to African-American women the basic political right of the vote:

> If colored men get their rights, and not colored women theirs, you see the colored men will be masters over the women, and it will be just as bad as it was before . . . [colored women] go out washing . . . and their men go about idle, strutting up and down; and when the women come home, they ask for their money and take it all, and then scold because there is no food. . . . I want women to have their rights.[38]

The Progressive Era: Funding Women's Exclusion

Expansion of Public Power

The Progressive era of the early twentieth century is significant for its use of public power to mitigate at least some of the most glaring excesses of unregulated market capitalism. The term "poverty," denoting economic hardship for which the individual is not responsible, emerged during the period, replacing "pauperism," a term that implied individual responsibility for economic hardship.[39]

During the Progressive era, state and federal administrations passed economic welfare measures affecting mothers' pensions, public health programs, child labor restrictions, an eight hour day for railroad workers, unemployment insurance, wages, prison labor restrictions, support for strikes, railroad rates, violations of antitrust laws, food labeling regulations, interstate commerce, and workmen's compensation.

In the words of Ellen Carol DuBois,

> Where were women in all this? . . . The importance of women in the Progressive Era has gained notice, but there remains a tendency to concentrate on their roles with respect to social reform . . . [resulting] in the tendency to minimize, even to omit, the woman suffrage movement from the general literature on the Progressive Era.[40]

To what degree did the innovative use of government in the Progressive era translate into a reconceptualization of women as citizens possessing full formal political rights?

Reinforcing Republican Motherhood

In general terms, the Progressive era seems to have increased, not decreased, women's distance from full participation in the public sphere. The longstanding cultural tradition of republican motherhood was powerfully bolstered in this period and reached a historical high. Mothers' pensions legislation, the innovative precursor of Aid to Families with Dependent Children, passed like wildfire at the state level in the Progressive era. By 1920, forty states had authorized direct payments to widowed women and their orphans, the first example in American history of government funding of women's maternal capacities.[41] Courts countered the reality of women in the workforce with even more explicit support for their nurturing, maternal roles. The landmark Supreme Court case in 1908, *Muller v. Oregon*, established the constitutionality of protective labor legislation for women, justified on maternalist grounds. Similar legislation for men had earlier been voided.[42]

Although other nations politicized maternity as being essential to the good functioning of the public sphere and the survival of the state,[43] the American version is remarkable for its exceptionally tenacious hold, especially during periods of change in major principles and practices of government. Some scholars see the prominence of the concept of republican motherhood in the United States as a major cause of the unique two-track system of welfare in this country. Theda Skocpol has contrasted the dismal failure of attempts to establish a paternalistic welfare state in the Progressive era attending to the needs of male workers with the success of voteless women in obtaining maternalist welfare legislation to meet the economic needs of working class wives and mothers.[44]

Johanna Brenner and Barbara Laslett link women's success in the private sphere during the Progressive era to later setbacks in the New Deal era. They argue that "the reorganization of social reproduction, developing from the late nineteenth century but completed during the 1920s" cleared the way for state legislation and the establishment of welfare programs that "encoded and reinforced gender difference, [and] most crucially, women's dependence" on the basis of the "assumption that men were or should be breadwinners while women were or should be non-earning mothers." One disastrous result was that, during the 1930s, "married women came under pervasive attack for wage work outside the home despite their increased participation in the labor force." [45]

The Nineteenth Amendment, ratified in 1920, guaranteed women the right to vote. Ironically, this first acquisition of formal political rights at the national level by women may be the exception that proves the rule. Some scholars believe that full suffrage did not mark a departure from defining women's citizenship in terms of maternal roles but was attained precisely because those roles held such powerful sway. [46]

In the debates over the amendment, legislators argued that women had earned the right to vote by virtue of their maternal merits. Their nurturing contributions through the Red Cross and other organizations during World War I were highlighted, as were their contributions as the mothers of the soldiers who had fought in the war. [47] Justifying the women's suffrage amendment in terms of women's maternal roles undercut its full potential for fostering women's political equality.

Conclusion: The Paradoxical Pattern of Political Reform and Voting Rights

Until the twentieth century women did not benefit from political reforms targeted for disadvantaged groups of men. Too often women's formal political rights actually deteriorated at the time of the advances made by men. Looking at political reform in American history through the lens of sex and gender, it is possible to see how each reform period reinforced the exclusion of women from the electorate, an exclusionary pattern that remained fixed until as late as 1920.

This analysis of American political reform reveals the endurance of sex and gender as principles of political exclusion in American political history. Although women are by no means unified in all ways, all women shared the same political discrimination throughout much of American history regardless of their class or race.

Whereas gender functioned to exclude women from political participation, it functioned as a principle of inclusion for men. The Founders saw all men, including unpropertied men and slaves, as potentially having claims to political rights. That it took decades to actualize those claims composes part of the story of American political development. In contrast, however, at the time of the nation's birth, few saw women as having claims to formal political rights, and the ensuing progress for disadvantaged men only reinforced the political exclusion of women.

The American case illustrates, therefore, how the creation of a republican democracy was particularly exclusionary for women. In substituting an electoral mechanism for the selection of political leaders for one based on kinship, many more men were included as formal participants in the public sphere than had been the case before. The situation of those men excluded on the basis of class or race was at least recognized and debated, a decided improvement over a monarchical system in which their status as political aspirants would have no meaning whatsoever.

Women, however, lost ground. Whereas the monarchical system had provided some women with opportunities to exercise political power, the new democracy denied all women the right to vote and to hold elective office. Even more telling, the political status of women received none of the attention devoted to the political exclusion of groups of men.

A parallel problem exists with respect to the differential attention accorded the problems of slavery and coverture marriage. Whereas slavery was recognized at the outset of the nation's history as an institution seriously at odds with the liberal principles underlying the American state, the same concern was not directed toward coverture marriage. Although slavery was abolished by the Thirteenth Amendment in 1865, remnants of coverture principles are still embedded in the legal institution of marriage, where they constitute a continuing source of sex discrimination that subverts women's civil rights.[48]

As we have seen, women's exclusion from formal political power rivals in its intractability the cleavages of race and class precisely because principles of universal equality are premised in tandem with assumptions about sex differentiation that reflect (or mask) new conceptualizations of the private and public spheres.

The apparent ease in overlooking how "gender has mattered" in the American political system testifies to the problem. Gunnar Myrdal, for example, when developing his landmark analysis of race in the United States, *The American Dilemma*, "found the barrier against blacks much stronger than that against women in America." His wife, Alva, however, disagreed. Women, she said, faced obstacles "more intractable, in the long run, than that of racial discrimination" in part because there was "no evidence yet of a dilemma in people's hearts concerning [women's] treatment."[49]

It is the "lack of discomfort" about the political exclusion of women in the liberal American state that stands in contrast to the discomfort evident for the exclusion of groups of men on the basis of race or class. By identifying the inverse political pattern characterizing political reform eras, in which political progress for men was accompanied by regression for women, we gain a better understanding of how sex and gender have been elevated to private-sphere principles of political discrimination in the American state, a legacy that illuminates the past as surely as it portends continuing influence for the future.

Notes

The author thanks Nancy Cott, Laura Frader, Evelyn Glenn, Barbara Hobson, Christopher Howard, Jane Jenson, Mary Katzenstein, Debra Kaufman, Seth Koven, Sonya Michel, Ann Orloff, Frances Fox Piven, Theda Skocpol, and Ann Tickner for their advice; Jane Mansbridge for a particularly helpful critique; and Rachel Harris, Olwen Huxley, and Susan Lee for research assistance.

This research was supported by National Science Foundation grant R11-880499 and by the Henry A. Murray Research Center of Radcliffe College. Acknowledgment is extended to the Inter-university Consortium for Political and Social Research for providing some of the data used in this research; the original source, collectors of the data, and the Consortium bear no responsibility for the analyses or interpretations presented here.

1. The literature is vast, but two classic examples are Gunnar Myrdal, *An American Dilemma: The Negro Problem and American Democracy* (New York: Harper and Row, 1944) and Sombert Werner, *Why Is There No Socialism in the United States?* (New York: M. E. Sharpe, 1976).
2. Alison Jaggar, *Feminist Politics and Human Nature* (Totowa, N.J.: Rowman and Allanheld, 1983); Susan Moller Okin, *Justice, Gender, and the Family* (New York: Basic Books, 1989); Carole Pateman, *The Sexual Contract* (Stanford, Calif.: Stanford University Press, 1988); Carole Pateman, *The Disorder of Women: Democracy, Feminism, and Political Theory* (Stanford, Calif.: Stanford University Press, 1989); Joan Kelly, "Did Women Have a Renaissance?" in *Women, History, and Theory: The Essays of Joan Kelly* (Chicago: University of Chicago Press, 1984).
3. Theorists advancing the view that domestic institutions, though subordinating women, nevertheless are normatively of value to the well-being of a democratic society include among their ranks Alexis de Tocqueville. For a critique of his views and others, see Jean Bethke Elshtain, *Public Man, Private Women* (Princeton, N.J.: Princeton University Press, 1981), chap. 3. For an analysis of how this view developed into the cultural norm of "republican motherhood," see Linda Kerber, *Women of the Republic* (Chapel Hill: University of North Carolina Press, 1980).
4. For example, see Pateman, *Sexual Contract*, and Okin, *Justice, Gender, and the Family.*
5. Clinton Rossiter, *The Political Thought of the American Revolution* (New York: Harcourt, Brace, 1963); Gordon S. Wood, *The Radicalism of the American Revolution: How a Revolution Transformed a Monarchical Society into a Democratic One Unlike Any that Had Ever Existed* (New York: Alfred A. Knopf, 1992).
6. Mary Beth Norton, *Liberty's Daughters: The Revolutionary Experience of American Women, 1750-1800* (Boston: Little, Brown, 1980), 155, 160-181, 195, 202.
7. One exception was New Jersey, where women were granted the constitutional right to vote in 1776, though this was revoked thirty-one years later. Joan Hoff attributes this anomaly to Quaker and colonial custom, neither of which survived "postrevolutionary republican attitudes about women for very long." Joan Hoff, *Law, Gender, and Justice: A Legal History of U.S. Women* (New York: New York University Press, 1991), 98-99.
8. It is debatable whether England at this time was a feudal monarchy or a modernizing democracy, but from the vantage point of those designing the new American government, it was the principle of inherited political power that was the anathema, not the degree to which this principle might be mixed with other methods of selection of political rulers.
9. Max Farrand, ed., *The Records of the Federal Convention of 1787*, vols. 1-4, supple-

ment (New Haven: Yale University Press, 1966), vol. 3, p. 256.

10. Norton, *Liberty's Daughters*, 45-46.
11. Amy Dru Stanley, "Conjugal Bonds and Wage Labor: Rights of Contract in the Age of Emancipation," *The Journal of American History* 75 (September 1988): 471-500.
12. William J. Crotty, *Political Reform and the American Experiment* (New York: Crowell, 1977), 20, emphasis in text.
13. Pateman, *The Sexual Contract.*
14. Norton, *Liberty's Daughters*, 50.
15. Linda K. Kerber, *Women of the Republic: Intellect and Ideology in Revolutionary America* (Chapel Hill: University of North Carolina Press, 1980), 200, 229, emphasis added.
16. Okin, *Justice, Gender, and the Family.*
17. Nancy Fraser and Linda Gordon, "Decoding 'Dependency': Inscriptions of Power in a Keyword of the Welfare State," manuscript, 1991. See also Joan Gundersen, "Independence, Citizenship, and the American Revolution," *Signs* 13 (Autumn 1987): 59-77.
18. Samuel P. Huntington, *American Politics: The Promise of Disharmony* (Cambridge: Harvard University Press, 1981), 224.
19. Terrence J. McDonald, "The Burden of Urban History: The Theory of the State in Recent American Social History," in *Studies of American Political Development*, vol. 3, ed. Karen Orren and Stephen Skowronek (New Haven: Yale University Press, 1989), 7; Theda Skocpol and John Ikenberry, "The Political Formation of the American Welfare State in Historical and Comparative Perspective," *Comparative Social Research* 6 (1983): 92-93.
20. Ellen Carol DuBois, "Outgrowing the Compact of the Fathers: Equal Rights, Woman Suffrage, and the United States Constitution, 1820-1878," *The Journal of American History* 74 (December 1987): 838.
21. Nancy F. Cott, *The Bonds of Womanhood: "Woman's Sphere" in New England, 1780-1835* (New Haven: Yale University Press, 1977).
22. Barbara Welter, *Dimity Convictions: The American Woman in the Nineteenth Century* (Athens: Ohio University Press, 1976), 8, 10, 15.
23. Gerda Lerner, "The Lady and the Mill Girl: Changes in the Status of Women in the Age of Jackson," *American Studies* 10 (Spring 1969): 5-15.
24. Joan Hoff, *Law, Gender, and Justice*, 107, 109-115.
25. Eleanor Flexner, *Century of Struggle: The Woman's Rights Movement in the United States* (Cambridge: Harvard University Press, 1975). Sarah and Angelina Grimké provide a classic example. The sisters, from a slave-owning plantation family in South Carolina, had detested slavery from earliest childhood. Renouncing life in the South, they moved to Philadelphia as young women and joined with abolitionist Quakers. In 1836 they delivered abolitionist speeches in Boston and New York City to public audiences composed of men and women. To their consternation, their audacity as women assuming "the place and tone of man as a public reformer" far overshadowed their abolitionist messages. (pp. 45-46)
26. Barry R. Weingast,"The Political Economy of Slavery: Credible Commitments and the Preservation of the Union, 1800-1860" (Paper delivered at the annual meeting of the American Political Science Association, Washington, D.C., 1991); Richard Franklin Bensel, *Yankee Leviathan: The Origins of Central State Authority in America, 1859-1877* (Cambridge: Cambridge University Press, 1990); Richard M. Valelly, "Party and Bureaucracy in the Two Reconstructions of the South's Electoral Politics" (Paper delivered at the annual meeting of the American Political Science Association, Washington, D.C., 1991). Drew Gilpin Faust, "Altars of Sacrifice: Confederate Women and the Narratives of War," *The Journal of American History* 76 (March 1990): 1200.

27. Janet Wilson James, "Introduction," in *Notable American Women*, vol. 1, ed. Edward T. James, Janet Wilson James, and Paul S. Boyer (Cambridge: Harvard University Press, 1971), xxiii-xxiv.
28. James David Barber and Barbara Kellerman, *Women Leaders in American Politics* (Englewood Cliffs, N.J.: Prentice-Hall, 1986), 205.
29. Section 2. Representatives shall be apportioned among the several States according to their respective numbers, counting the whole number of persons in each State excluding Indians not taxed. But when the right to vote in any election for the choice of electors for President and Vice President of the United States, Representatives in Congress, the Executive and Judicial officers of a State, or the members of the Legislature thereof, is denied to any of the male inhabitants of such State, being twenty-one years of age, and citizens of the United States, or in any way abridged, except for participation in rebellion, or other crime, the basis of representation therein shall be reduced in the proportion which the number of such *male* citizens shall bear to the whole number of male citizens twenty-one years of age in such state. (Emphasis added.)
30. Elizabeth Cady Stanton, Susan B. Anthony, Matilda Joslyn Gage, *History of Woman Suffrage*, vol. 2 (Salem, N.H.: Ayer, 1882), 95.
31. Ibid.
32. Christopher Howard, Theda Skocpol, Susan Lehmann, Marjorie Abend-Wein, "Government Institutions, Women's Associations, and the Enactment of Mothers' Pensions in the United States, 1910-1930" (Paper delivered at the annual convention of the American Political Science Association, Washington, D.C., 1991).
33. Stanton, *History of Woman Suffrage*, 130.
34. Ibid., 108.
35. *The Congressional Globe*, U.S. Government Documents, 39th Cong., Senate, 952.
36. Judith N. Shklar, *American Citizenship: The Quest for Inclusion* (Cambridge: Harvard University Press, 1991).
37. Stanton, *History of Woman Suffrage*, 193.
38. Ibid.
39. Norman Furniss and Timothy Tilton, *The Case for the Welfare State: From Social Security to Social Equality* (Bloomington: Indiana University Press, 1979); see also Fraser and Gordon, "Decoding 'Dependency.'"
40. Ellen Carol DuBois, "Working Women, Class Relations, and Suffrage Militance: Harriot Stanton Blatch and the New York Woman Suffrage Movement, 1894-1909," *The Journal of American History* 74 (June 1987): 34.
41. Theda Skocpol, *Protecting Soldiers and Mothers: The Politics of Social Provision in the United States, 1870s-1920s* (Cambridge: Harvard University Press, 1992); Theda Skocpol, "State Formation, Group Capacities, and the Origins of American Social Policies" (Paper prepared for the Conference on the Dynamics of American Politics, Department of Political Science, University of Colorado, Boulder, February, 1992), 11; Theda Skocpol, "Gender and the Origins of Modern Social Policies in Britain and the United States," *Studies in American Political Development* 5 (Spring 1991): 36-93.
42. *Lochner v. New York*, 198 U.S. 45 (1905).
43. Sonya Michel and Seth Koven, "Womanly Duties: Maternalist Politics and the Origins of the Welfare State in France, Germany, Great Britain and the United States, 1880-1920," *American Historical Review* 95 (October 1990): 1076-1108.
44. Skocpol, *Protecting Soldiers and Mothers*, 2. Some argue that women's voteless activities in the public sphere "domesticated politics." See Paula Baker, "The Domestication of Politics: Women and American Political Society, 1780-1920," *American Historical Review* 89 (June 1984): 620-647.
45. Johanna Brenner and Barbara Laslett, "Gender, Social Reproduction and the State" (Paper delivered at the Social Science History Association, Washington,

D.C., 1989); see revised paper, "Gender, Social Reproduction and Women's Self-Organization," *Gender and Society* 5 (September 1991): 311-333.

46. Steven M. Buechler, *The Transformation of the Woman Suffrage Movement: The Case of Illinois, 1850-1920* (New Brunswick, N.J.: Rutgers University Press, 1986); Skocpol, *Protecting Soldiers and Mothers,* 340.

47. U.S. Congress, House, *Congressional Record,* 66th Cong., May 21, 1919, 80.

48. Linda K. Kerber, "The Paradox of Women's Citizenship in the Early Republic," *American Historical Review* 97 (April 1992): 349-378.

49. Gunnar Myrdal, *The American Dilemma: The Negro Problem and Modern Democracy* (New York: Harper and Row, 1944); Sissela Bok, *Alva Myrdal: A Daughter's Memoir* (New York: Addison-Wesley, 1991), 140.

II. ISSUES, CANDIDATES, AND ELECTIONS

5

Political Issues, Party Alignments, Spatial Models, and the Post-New Deal Party System

Edward G. Carmines

The purpose of this essay is to outline a dynamic spatial model of party alignments and to examine the transformation of the New Deal party system within this model. We argue that party alignments undergo a three-stage evolutionary process. In the first stage the alignment becomes organized around some central issue that is sufficiently salient to unite and motivate the majority party's winning coalition. The second stage results in the institutionalization of the alignment, allowing it to persist. Finally, in the third stage, an alignment is transformed when a second dimension of issue conflict emerges and eventually alters the existing political coalitions. From this theoretical perspective, a *party re-alignment* is merely the transformation of an existing alignment caused by the introduction of a new dimension of conflict.[1]

The essay is divided into three sections. The first section outlines an abstract model of the rise and decline of party alignments, reflecting the dominant issues in society. The second section shows that this evolutionary model of party alignments can be given a meaningful spatial representation. Finally, the third section examines two changes in the New Deal party system to illustrate the utility of the model.

The Development of Party Alignments

A party alignment, as we have suggested, is a situation in which different groups in society have relatively enduring attachments to the various political parties. As Cavanagh and Sundquist observe, "the *alignment* of the party system reflects the composition of the strength of each competing party in terms of identifiable groups—demographic, occupational, religious, ethnic, ideological, or whatever—to which individuals belong."[2] A basic premise of the model proposed here is that newly formed party alignments become more stable over time as parties' sources of electoral support in the electorate become established and regularized.

Initially parties may be too weak and undeveloped as institutions to perform major representative functions. As individual parties and the party system as a whole become firmly mapped onto the underlying cleavage structures in the society (for example, classes, regions, and religions) and become the major mechanism for representing group interests in the political arena the resulting party alignment becomes an enduring feature of the political system. There are at least three major factors that lead to the formation of stable party alignments.

Vividness of Party Alignment for the Founding Generation

The first factor is the vividness of the alignment to the founding generation. That is, for the generation that participated in the formation of the new alignment, the personalities, conflicts and experiences surrounding the alignment are likely to be highly salient to them throughout their lives. Thus, for example, the New Deal is likely to be a continuing political reference point for those citizens who came to political maturity during the 1930s and early 1940s.[3] For these citizens the New Deal was a vivid, personal, pervasive experience that permanently shaped their political identities. They are likely to cling tenaciously to their strong partisan identifications throughout their lifetimes.

Salience and Stability of the Issue Agenda

The second factor leading to the development of stable party alignments is closely related to the first. Since a newly formed party alignment is most consequential to the generation that participated in its founding, its issue basis also is likely to be especially salient to these voters, and *ceteris paribus*, likely to dominate all other issue concerns. All alignments embody and reflect a dimension of political conflict—a set of political issues—that gives them both symbolic and substantive meaning.[4] The New Deal party alignment, for example, was based on two related sets of core issues: the extent to which the government should intervene in and manage the economy and the degree to which the national government should provide for the social welfare of its citizens. New Deal Democrats believed that the government should act to protect people against the defects, instabilities, and hardships of the market economy, whereas the Republicans believed in the efficacy of private markets and opposed the development of the modern welfare state.[5]

New issues will no doubt be proposed during the early stages of an alignment, but the political environment is inhospitable to their development. The new issues represent a potential source of political conflict—a potential that is largely unrealized under these highly unfavorable circumstances. No new lines of political cleavage are likely to develop as long as the issues embodied in the existing alignment remain predominant. On the contrary, new, cross-cutting issues are likely to be easily overridden by the prevailing issues as long as the latter are embedded in a strong and still dominant partisan alignment. As a consequence, new issues remain almost entirely subordinate to the policy interests represented in the existing party system. The original aligning issues—and their logical descendants—dominate political debate during this period.

Constraints on Politicians

The final force contributing to stable party alignments is a logical outgrowth of the previous two factors. Losing parties and politicians, who naturally turn to new issues to improve their political situation, are severely constrained in a political system in which the existing alignment is pervasive and its issue basis salient. In such a situation political discussion is likely to revolve around the existing issue agenda no matter how much some political entrepreneurs would like to change it. The dominance of the existing party alignment, together with the all-encompassing nature of its issue agenda, provide little or no opportunity for losing politicians to employ new issues to drive a wedge into the winning party's electoral coalition unless external circumstances change. The result is predictable: rational politicians find other means for advancing their causes (and careers) if new issue proposals seem likely to fall on deaf ears. In a sense all politicians—ritualistically and by instinct if not by conscious, deliberate choice—tend to focus on the same dominant, overriding political issues. Because there is little likelihood of altering the issue agenda in this situation, rational politicians contribute in their own way to the development of stable party alignments.

Republican candidates in the immediate aftermath of the New Deal provide a good example of the futile attempt to bring new issues into the political arena. After failing to succeed running against the New Deal (and FDR) or as a paler version thereof, Dwight Eisenhower found the winning formula: to disregard issues almost completely and concentrate on the personal attributes of a former war hero. This is not an isolated example. When new issues do not provide an effective vehicle for undermining the political status quo, rational politicians will find other means to win elections.[6]

As the Eisenhower case demonstrates, however, the opposition gains only a temporary victory as long as the underlying alignment has not been challenged or altered. Deviating—not realigning—elections are the likely product of such nonissue-oriented electoral strategies.[7]

In sum, there are three basic, related forces that contribute to the formation of stable party alignments: the vividness of the alignment for the founding generation; the salience of the alignment's issue agenda; and the constraints these factors impose on losing but rational politicians.

The Institutionalization of Party Alignments

If these factors lead to the initial development of stable party alignments, what accounts for their persistence over an entire generation or more? The fundamental answer to this question has to do with those forces that led to the formation of stable alignments in the first place. The multifaceted process that leads to the emergence of party alignments is likely to change only over an extended period of time. The inertia built into party alignments makes it unlikely that their decline will be either immediate or precipitous—only inevitable. Alignments are strengthened initially through the gradual process of normal population replacement, which produces regular variations in the composition of the electorate. This institutionalization comes about when older citizens, who are least likely to have been affected by the new alignment due to their well-established prior partisan commitments, leave the electorate through death and are replaced by newly eligible young voters whose weakly formed political views are easily influenced by the new alignment. As Philip Converse observes, "new voters are flexible, unstable, and much more responsive to new events than are older voting cohorts." [8] During a period of rapid partisan alignment, therefore, younger cohorts should be more fully and quickly socialized into the alignment than older cohorts.[9] The newly acquired partisanship of these younger voters, moreover, should be further strengthened as they move through the life cycle.[10]

The replacement effect, moreover, can continue over a considerable period of time, certainly beyond the aligning generation. The complex process that makes this possible not only includes normal population replacement and the strengthening of partisan loyalties with age for young voters but also the successful intergenerational transfer of partisanship.[11] Without the latter, partisan alignments would be extremely short-lived irrespective of their initial strength. But the very forces that contribute to the development of party alignments outlined earlier also make it quite likely that partisanship will be passed on successfully from parents to offspring during the intermediate stage of partisan alignments.[12] The children of the founding generation should be relatively well socialized into their parents' partisanship precisely because they are only one generation removed from the alignment itself. Their parents were members of the founding generation who directly experienced the intense political conflicts associated with the birth of the alignments. As a consequence, as Beck argues, "the 'children of realignment' are presumed to possess at least some attachment to their inherited party system, as a consequence of parental socialization if nothing else." [13]

Converse has formalized the process by which partisan stability is strengthened in a simple but elegant model based on individual learning and intergenerational transmission of partisanship. His model predicts that as a party system ages, the proportion of the electorate expressing partisan attachments increases, reaching an equilibrium point of about 72 percent by the second or third generation. A mature party system, according to Converse, is characterized by a high and stable level of partisanship, presumably reflecting the original lines of political cleavage. His model suggests that over time party alignments not only persist but become increasingly institutionalized.[14]

The Transformation of Party Alignments

Do party alignments have the capacity to sustain themselves indefinitely? That seems to be the logic of Converse's model and of Lipset and Rokkan's more historical analysis.[15] Our model, by contrast, presumes that realignment is the natural outcome of a party alignment. The same forces that account for the development and maturing of party alignments also explain—by their declining influence and eventual absence—the transformation of aging alignments. Viewed from this perspective, the development and institutionalization of a party alignment as well as its transformation are stages of the same evolutionary process driven by the same dynamic forces.[16] Having considered those forces that lead to the development and persistence of stable party alignments, let us now examine those factors that undermine and eventually transform aging alignments.

New Voters

Let us begin with the factor that proved so crucial in the formation and development of party alignments: normal population replacement and its effects on the changing composition of the electorate. At first this process strengthens the emerging alignment because it leads to the progressive replacement of older voters (who were least likely to be affected by the alignment) with younger voters (who are most susceptible to forces of partisan change). Projected over a longer period of time population replacement has just the opposite effect because the salience of the alignment gradually but inevitably declines and, as a consequence, its influence over mass partisanship weakens as well. The major influence of the alignment is now concentrated among older voters—those whose partisanship was formed during the heat of the political conflicts that gave rise to the alignment in the first place. Younger voters, not having directly experienced the alignment, are least likely to be polarized by it.[17]

The fragility of intergenerational partisan socialization also contributes to the progressive decline of the existing alignment. As noted above, it is plausible to presume that the children of the aligning generation will be relatively well socialized into their parents' partisanship. But beginning with the next generation, this is no longer likely to be the case. These newer voters did not experience the intense political conflicts that gave rise to the alignment, nor were they socialized by those who played a prominent role in its formation. Instead, their connection to the existing alignment is purely inherited and "since they are two generations removed from the realignment even their political socialization into the prevailing party system must be incomplete." Subsequent generations are likely to have even more enfeebled partisan loyalties as a result of their greater psychological and temporal distance from the alignment.[18]

Both the changing composition of the electorate and the fragility of intergenerational partisan socialization lead to a party system containing many members who are only weakly and indirectly connected to the underlying alignment. New, incompletely socialized voters represent a primary threat to the continuation of any party alignment, as we shall see below.[19]

Not all new voters result from generational replacement. There are several distinct sources of older new voters. The steady extension of the franchise in the United States during the nineteenth century swelled the ranks of the voting universe with a large pool of older but politically inexperienced citizens.[20] Similarly, waves of immigration during the twentieth century have created a large pool of new voters.[21] Finally, as long as electoral participation is incomplete, the ranks of potential new voters include older citizens with low levels of political participation and weak commitments to the existing alignment. New voters, in short, may include not only the young but a diverse group of older citizens who have in common the fact that they are less than fully socialized into the current party alignment. These incompletely socialized and weakly aligned citizens represent groups that can be mobilized to overturn the existing party alignment and thus are likely to be on the cutting edge of partisan change.

Realigning Issues

Although unaligned and weakly aligned citizens play an important role in transforming the existing party alignment by creating a pool of potentially mobilizable voters, their presence alone is not sufficient to bring about partisan change. A second and equally significant factor is the changing issue agenda. As we said, during the formation and development of a party alignment, the issues embodied in the alignment are likely to be predominant. Over time, the vividness of the original policy agenda gradually declines, providing an opportunity for the introduction of new issues.[22]

The declining salience of "old" issues is not difficult to understand. The events that brought these issues into prominence are located in the increasingly distant past, and as these events fade in public memory the issues associated with them lose their salience. The fragility of intergenerational socialization also contributes to the declining salience of the aligning issues. When the issue rationale for a party alignment is inherited, not experienced, it lacks emotion and fails for that reason to maintain its grip on public opinion. Moreover, it is well known that issue preferences are less successfully transmitted from parents to offspring than are partisan preferences.[23] This differential pattern of intergenerational socialization means that over time new members of the electorate will possess increasingly enfeebled partisan attachments, since their partisan preferences will lack a reinforcing infrastructure of attitudes and perceptions about politics. An aging party alignment is thus vulnerable to disruption by new issues even among those voters who maintain a nominal commitment to the existing party alignment. The potential impact of new issues is greater still among those citizens who are not even weakly socialized into the current alignment.

Not all new issues, of course, have the capacity to disrupt, much less transform, the existing party alignment. I have argued elsewhere that realigning issues possess three key characteristics. First, they cut across the line of development of the existing party alignment. Realigning issues emerge from the old environment, but once having emerged they introduce fundamental tensions into the party system and are inconsistent with the continued stability of old patterns. Second, realigning issues are not temporary but relatively long lasting. Clearly, they last beyond a single presidential election and likely are salient over several election cycles. Realigning issues are distinctive, finally, in their degree of salience for they not only affect individual voting decisions but can shape the partisan loyalties of new voters and possibly alter the partisanship of established voters. Realigning issues, in sum, are long-term, salient, and cross-cutting to the existing alignment.[24]

Incentives of Parties and Politicians

The emergence of salient, cross-cutting, enduring issues and the existence of unaligned citizens are fundamental elements in the transformation of party alignments. New issues create the opportunity for partisan change; unaligned citizens are its most likely agents. But these factors, although perhaps necessary, are not sufficient conditions for generating partisan realignment. For the current alignment to be transformed parties and politicians must have incentives for inventing and championing new issues and so possibly setting in motion the realignment process. After all, voters themselves have little capacity for creating new issue alternatives. However, new issue proposals are typically forthcoming in great profusion, and the reason is not difficult to understand. Dissatisfied political losers always have an incentive to unseat the governing status quo, and new, cross-cutting issues are the natural vehicle for this purpose.[25] New issues—if they can split the majority coalition and are sufficiently attractive to the electorate—can convert old losers into new winners (and old winners into new losers). They are thus the stock-in-trade of successful parties and politicians.

This does not mean, of course, that all new issues have this effect. On the contrary, the vast majority of new issue proposals are bound to fail, striking an unresponsive chord in the electorate and leaving the current majority party's coalition intact. This may leave political losers in an even more disadvantageous position than they occupied before they introduced the proposal. Be this as it may, sponsoring new issue proposals is one of the few strategies that losers have for permanently improving their political fortunes. On those rare occasions when losing politicians provide exactly what the public is seeking, the public responds and, as Riker observes, the issues "flourish, even to the point of completely reshaping the environment in which they arose." [26] Moreover, these occasions become increasingly less rare as party alignments age and their issue rationale declines in salience. Issue proposals that failed to make a dent in the majority party's electoral coalition during the developmental and institutional stages of the alignment become a source of strain and disruption as the alignment ages. In other words, over time the coalition assembled by the majority party becomes increasingly vulnerable to the issue appeals of the opposition.

Given the logic of this situation, it is not surprising that parties usually compete with each other not by taking opposite sides of the same issue but by emphasizing their positions on different issues. All successful politicians instinctively understand which issues benefit them and their party and which do not. The trick is to politicize the former and depoliticize the latter. The majority party has an obvious incentive to keep winning; the equally obvious strategy for doing so is to emphasize the original aligning issues and their logical descendants. By contrast, the minority party, as we have seen, has a strong incentive to deemphasize issues associated with the current alignment and instead raise new, potentially disruptive issues in order to dislodge the majority party's winning coalition.[27]

Finally, it would seem that the losing party's activists rather than its leaders should provide the main impetus for political change. Party leaders, even if they are part of the minority, receive a variety of material and symbolic benefits not available to party activists. Thus, ideologically motivated activists are more disadvantaged under the current party alignment and have more to gain by dislodging the current winner. Disaffected policy entrepreneurs, in short, should be in the vanguard in efforts to break up the old coalition and replace it with one of their own.

Spatial Models of Party Alignments

The evolutionary model of party alignments outlined above can be usefully represented within a simple spatial configuration. There is some irony in this, of course, because the logic of spatial voting would seem to preclude the existence of any party alignment. Spatial voting is based on the idea that voters are able to measure the distance between themselves and the parties on an issue and that each voter will vote for the nearest party. Hotelling first suggested and Downs later demonstrated that in the one-dimensional spatial model, assuming voters' single-peaked utility curves and simple majority rule, there is a clearly defined equilibrium: the ideal point of the median voter.[28] Because no other position in the issue space can defeat this alternative, both parties should converge to this location and there should be no party difference on policy.

But plainly parties regularly do differ over policy. One way to account for this is to recognize that parties not only appeal to the tastes of mass electorates but also to the preferences of their own activists. Typically party activists have more extreme positions than ordinary voters, and thus parties are drawn away from the positions of the median voter in the electorate and toward the medians of their respective party activists. Indeed, one crucial test of political leaders is whether they can successfully mediate between these divergent political demands.[29]

In any case, a modified version of the Downsian model can readily accommodate party differentiation as well as party convergence and thus is consistent with the existence and stability of party alignments. For purposes of illustration, consider a hypothetical figure in which two parties, the Democrats and Republicans, differ over the traditional issue of social welfare policy. If more voters were closer to the Democratic party position than the Republican party position in this unidimensional space, the Democrats would have a stable majority as long as voters took into consideration only the parties' positions on this issue. The American party system during the New Deal period corresponded approximately to this model, and the Democrats enjoyed a majority coalition.

The minority Republicans were not without strategic opportunities during this time, however. As we mentioned earlier, one strategy was to deemphasize policy differences and to focus attention on nonpolicy characteristics of presidential candidates. Such a strategy could sever the link between parties and issue dimensions and provide an opportunity for the minority party to win elections—on nonpolicy grounds.

A second strategy, one that has been explored by Riker, is to attempt to modify individual preferences, thereby shifting voters' ideal points closer to the minority party position. Riker has examined the way in which political actors use rhetoric to change the opinions of voters, thus possibly altering political outcomes. Applied to the New Deal, the Republican strategy would have been to persuade voters that the taxes required to build a more elaborate welfare state would deprive them of needed private expenditures or that the welfare state would eventually bankrupt the country. Giving voters reasons to reconsider their original position opens up the possibility that persuasion may alter those tastes and the party alignment that resulted from them. Thus, the spatial model can highlight the logic of maneuvers by politicians even when political competition is restricted to a single dimension of conflict.[30]

But the power of the spatial model becomes especially striking when a new dimension of conflict is added to the issue space. As Riker observes, "one of the great virtues of the spatial model is that, by using it, the importance and pervasiveness of changing dimensions is readily recognized." [31] Prospective losers, as we have argued, have a strong incentive to introduce new issues into the political debate, hoping thereby to capitalize on them. Within a one-dimensional space, the minority party is confined to a losing status; its basic strategy is to change voters' preferences, obviously a very difficult undertaking. But as soon as a second issue dimension is introduced, not only does a real-world equilibrium become unlikely, but, perhaps more importantly for political competition, there is a distinct possibility that the new division of voters will benefit the formerly minority party.[32] It should not be surprising, therefore, that the heresthetical device of raising new issue dimensions is a fundamental strategy of losing politicians and lies at the very core of politics.

It is difficult, if not impossible, to predict the exact outcome of political competition once a second dimension is added to the issue space. It depends, of course, on the distribution of voters' ideal points relative to party positions in the two-dimensional space. But the spatial model can highlight two basic features of this multidimensional competition. The first is the salience of the issues to the voters. Salience can be represented within the spatial model by the length of the axes: if the new issue dimension is substantially less salient than the original dimension, then the latter is stretched out relative to the former. In this case, the new issue dimension is shorter than the original dimension. Hence, voters' ideal points on the new dimension are greatly restricted relative to their spread on the original dimension. This means that the new issue has less probability of altering the party preference of voters based on the original issue and thus less capacity to upset the distribution of mass support. More generally, the implications of a shift in the salience of issues to voters is highly significant for, as Johnston notes, it implies that "realignment can occur even if no party and no voting bloc shifts its position." [33]

The second feature of this multidimensional competition relates not to the salience of the issues to voters but rather to the competition between parties. In other words, the effect of the new issue will depend in part on the extent to which it shapes party competition relative to the original issue. Figure 5-1 shows two issue dimensions—social cultural issues and social welfare issues—arranged across the vertical and horizontal axes, respectively. Social cultural issues focus on matters of life style and include attitudes toward abortion, school prayer, women's roles, and homosexual rights. The slope of the competitive axis reflects the relative importance, or salience, of the dimensions in the election. If social cultural issues and social welfare issues were equally important to the competition between the parties, then the competitive axis would fall exactly between the two issue dimensions (competitive axis A). On the other

Figure 5-1   Spatial Model of Party Competition with Different
Levels of Salience for the Social Welfare and
Social Cultural Issue Dimensions

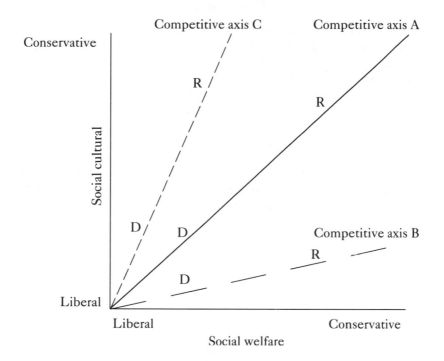

Note: D is for Democratic party and R is for Republican party.

hand, if social welfare issues were more important to the party competition, then the competitive axis would lie closer to the horizontal axis
(competitive axis B). Finally, if party competition was determined primarily by social cultural issues, then the competitive axis would be closer to
the vertical axis (competitive axis C).[34]

In sum, the spatial model can be used to illustrate the salience of
issues to voters as well as to parties and thus can help clarify how adding a
new issue to the policy space can alter party competition in the election
and ultimately transform the party alignment itself.

The underlying logic of party alignments and realignments has been
appreciated only very recently. Party coalitions are inherently unstable
because the groups making up the coalition—although they may agree on
the original aligning issue (or set of issues)—are unlikely to agree on a
variety of potential new issues. If the minority party—through conscious
design or trial-and-error strategy—can raise an issue that is salient with
the public and divides the majority coalition, it has an opportunity to gain
an advantage. Even if the new issue does not lead to a new majority party

coalition, it may still be to the loser's advantage to introduce a degree of uncertainty and instability into the political competition.

Two Examples

We can illustrate the utility of the realignment model outlined above by examining two episodes in the evolution of the New Deal party system. The first episode was a genuine realignment of the party system that resulted from the introduction of the civil rights issue into political competition. The second episode concerns a potential realignment that could occur if social cultural issues become a focus of political competition.

Civil Rights and the New Deal Party System

Roosevelt's New Deal Democratic coalition has typically been viewed as a coalition of overlapping social groups, including a majority of Catholics, Jews, industrial workers, urban residents, the poor, northern blacks, and southern whites. These groups were brought together under Roosevelt's leadership, primarily in response to the Great Depression. The Republican coalition during the New Deal was essentially the mirror image of the Democratic coalition, composed of upper- and upper-middle-income earners, whites, nonunion families, Protestants, nonsoutherners, and nonurban residents. As mentioned earlier, the issues of the New Deal alignment divided the parties along a broad social welfare dimension. Presumably the groups composing the Democratic coalition agreed that the national government had a substantial responsibility for the citizenry's social welfare whereas Republican coalition groups opposed the development of the American welfare state.

The New Deal party system was a stable alignment and had a stable winner. Democrats were the winning party as long as elections were fought over New Deal social welfare issues. But civil rights for black Americans posed a severe challenge to the Democratic majority coalition because the party included two groups, blacks and southern whites, that had diametrically opposed preferences on civil rights. Thus, when the race issue became increasingly salient during the 1950s and 1960s, there was little chance that the Democratic coalition would remain intact.[35]

Figure 5-2 presents a visual picture of the strains in the Democratic coalition caused by the introduction of civil rights. It uses data from the 1956 National Election Study (NES) to plot the mean position of black Democrats and southern white Democrats on the issues of social welfare and civil rights. The means for the entire sample on the two issue dimensions are drawn through the plots; higher scores on both dimensions indicate greater conservatism.

The horizontal axis shows that southern white Democrats were slightly to the left of the entire sample on social welfare issues, whereas

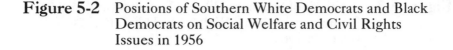

Figure 5-2   Positions of Southern White Democrats and Black
Democrats on Social Welfare and Civil Rights
Issues in 1956

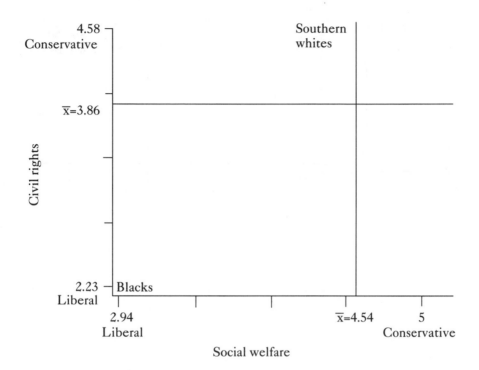

black Democrats were decidedly on the left. Because both groups were to the left of the total electorate's mean position, an election fought only on social welfare may have led members of both groups to remain part of the Democratic coalition.

The vertical axis indicates the complication for Democratic unity of introducing civil rights into political competition. Not surprisingly, black Democrats had extremely liberal positions on civil rights issues. In contrast, southern white Democrats had markedly conservative positions on civil rights, being not only far more conservative than black Democrats but also more conservative than the electorate as a whole. It is clear, then, that civil rights posed a powerful challenge to Democratic hegemony for it sharply divided two of the coalition's principal groups.

Figure 5-3 brings the story forward to the 1964 presidential election when southern Democrats split decisively from the Democratic presidential coalition. Once the region of the country most loyal to the Democratic party, the 1964 election saw five Deep South states vote for the Republican senator Barry Goldwater and substantial GOP support among white voters in the peripheral South. Again, black Democrats were quite liberal on both

Figure 5-3   Positions of Southern White Democrats and Black
Democrats on Social Welfare and Civil Rights
Issues in 1964

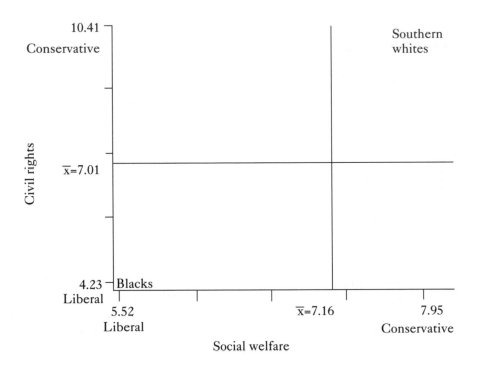

race and social welfare in 1964 whereas southern white Democrats were
somewhat to the right of the total electorate on social welfare and very much
to the right on civil rights. Figure 5-3 shows clearly why the introduction of
the race issue into political debate and eventually into party competition
was incompatible with the continuation of the New Deal party alignment.

Social Cultural Issues and the Republican Coalition

The second example focuses on the Republican party and examines
what *could* happen to the Republican coalition if social cultural issues
become a salient concern to voters and an active dimension of competition
between the parties.

After racial issues were brought into political competition during the
1964 presidential election, it became clear that a Republican majority
would have to be formed among whites. The black vote, greatly expanded
by the 1965 Voting Rights Act, was overwhelmingly Democratic.[36] But
could Republicans muster a majority composed only of whites, and what
issues would unite this Republican white majority?

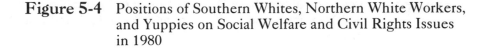

Figure 5-4   Positions of Southern Whites, Northern White Workers, and Yuppies on Social Welfare and Civil Rights Issues in 1980

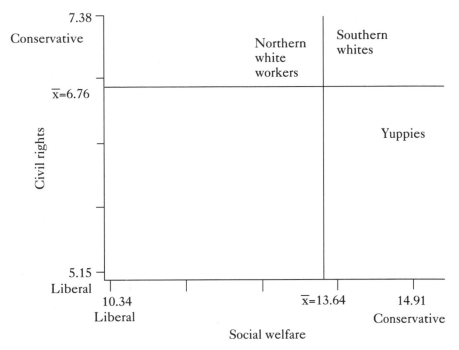

Figure 5-4 shows the positions of three key groups of white voters—southerners, northern workers, and yuppies—on welfare and racial issues in 1980, at the beginning of the Reagan presidency.[37] Yuppies are young, educated professionals with above-average incomes. If majorities of these groups could be combined with traditional sources of Republican support in the electorate, then a Republican majority was virtually assured. The figure clearly indicates the overall agreement among these three groups on the issues of social welfare and race. Looking at the social welfare issue dimension, white yuppies and southern whites are somewhat to the right of the electorate's mean position, whereas northern white workers are just to the left of this mean. Similarly, on racial issues, although yuppies are slightly more liberal than southern whites and northern white workers, it is the overall similarity of the positions of the three groups that is most notable. In short, if party competition could be restricted to social welfare and civil rights issues, then there was a strong possibility that Republicans could gain substantial support among all three groups and perhaps build a majority coalition among white voters.

Figure 5-5 shows, however, how social cultural issues drive a wedge directly into this Republican coalition. Southern whites and northern

Figure 5-5   Positions of Southern Whites, Northern White Workers, and Yuppies on Social Welfare and Social Cultural Issues in 1980

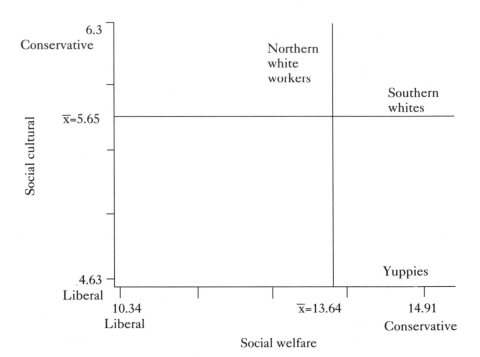

white workers have similar positions on cultural issues: both groups are more conservative than the average voter. But yuppies are at the opposite end of the scale, being extremely liberal on this issue dimension. Thus, although Republicans won a major presidential victory in 1980, social issues posed a clear and present danger to their presidential majority.

Figure 5-6 brings the story forward to 1988 and focuses only on voters identifying themselves as Republicans. (In this way, tensions within the Republican party can be highlighted.) Republicans in all three groups (southern whites, northern white workers, and yuppies) have similar positions on social welfare and civil rights issues: they are all more conservative than the average voter on both dimensions. But, as Figure 5-6 shows, the situation fundamentally changes when social issues become part of the policy space. Yuppies—even Republican Yuppies—are liberal on social issues and thus have issue preferences on this issue very much unlike their northern worker and southern counterparts. An emphasis on social issues thus has a real potential to drive yuppies out of the Republican party and jeopardize any future majority party aspirations of the GOP.

This seems to be exactly what happened in the 1992 presidential

Figure 5-6 Positions of Southern White Republicans, Northern White Working Republicans, and Yuppy Republicans on Social Welfare and Social Cultural Issues in 1988

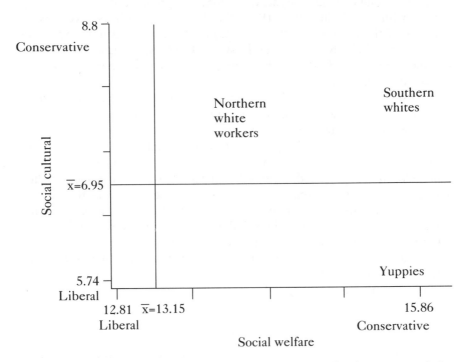

election. With the economy no longer working to their advantage and the communist menace greatly reduced by the collapse of the Soviet Union, Republican strategists turned to social issues to sustain their string of presidential victories. This strategy, at least in the abstract, may have seemed an adroit one, for it seemed to provide an opportunity not only for the GOP to consolidate its conservative base but also to appeal to socially conservative southerners and northern workers. These groups were often seen as providing the margin of victory for recent GOP presidential triumphs, and so it was crucial to retain their electoral support. If the economy and foreign policy could no longer be counted upon to keep them in the Republican column, then perhaps an appeal based on "family values" would do the trick.

In a narrow sense the strategy appeared to work, but in the end it proved disastrous. The GOP did consolidate its conservative base: Independent conservatives and Republican conservatives voted overwhelmingly for Bush, giving him support equal to that which he enjoyed in 1988. And white born-again Christians gave him nearly three-quarters of their two-party vote, down only slightly from the 80 percent level of support he received in 1988. Bush also retained a plurality of the white southern vote, although at a reduced level from 1988. But yuppie voters of various descriptions turned decisively away from the GOP in 1992. For example, whereas Bush enjoyed a 25-percentage-point advantage over Dukakis among college graduates in 1988, this group split its vote evenly between Bush and Clinton in 1992. Similarly, young voters gave Bush a majority of their votes in 1988 but among this group Clinton had a 10-percentage-point advantage over Bush in 1992. Suburban and middle-income voters also followed the same route away from the GOP and toward the Democrats in 1992.

In sum, even as the GOP strategy allowed it to unite and consolidate its support among the social and cultural right, it simultaneously alienated the broad middle, most especially yuppie voters, who felt most threatened by the GOP's strident and aggressive tone on social issues. Such was the bitter fruit on which the GOP choked when it attempted in 1992 to build a presidential victory on the discordant basis of an extreme social-issues agenda. There is some irony in this, of course, because it was the Democratic party that for a quarter century before 1992 had paid a heavy political price for becoming too identified with the "lifestyle Left." But in 1992 Clinton steered a more moderate course on social issues, emphasizing social responsibilities as much as individual rights. In any case, in 1992 the country seemed more interested in pursuing a program of economic renewal than in being led into cultural wars.

Conclusion

All party alignments reflect central issues in the electorate that favor some groups at the expense of others. Party alignments are stable in that they persist through time, but this stability is guaranteed only when a single issue dimension dominates politics. As soon as a second issue dimension is introduced into party competition equilibrium becomes very unlikely and the advantage enjoyed by the majority party is likely to disappear. Prospective losers therefore have an incentive to introduce new issues into political competition in the hopes of upsetting the winning party's majority coalition. Because many new issues can have this disruptive impact, this strategy is fundamental to politics and political competition. As we have seen, this simple logic—displayed in the form of a dynamic spatial model of party alignment—casts a revealing light on the evolution of the New Deal party system.

Notes

This essay has benefited from discussion with my colleagues Michael McGinnis, Burt Monroe, and John Williams. As always James Woods provided excellent research assistance.

1. For an elaboration of the evolutionary model of party alignments outlined here

see Edward G. Carmines, "The Logic of Party Alignments," *Journal of Theoretical Politics* 3 (January 1991): 65-80. The nature and changes in party alignments have a long research tradition. The classic work is S. M. Lipset and Stein Rokkan, "Cleavage Structures, Party Systems, and Voter Alignments: An Introduction," in *Party·Systems and Voter Alignments*, ed. S. M. Lipset and Stein Rokkan (New York: Free Press, 1967), 1-64. Most recently see Stefano Bartolini and Peter Mair, *Identity, Competition, and Electoral Availability* (New York: Cambridge University Press, 1990).

2. Thomas E. Cavanagh and James L. Sundquist, "The New Two-Party System," in *The New Direction in American Politics*, ed. John E. Chubb and Paul E. Peterson (Washington, D.C.: Brookings Institution, 1985), 35.

3. Paul Abramson, *Generational Change in American Politics* (Lexington, Mass.: D. C. Heath, 1975).

4. E. E. Schattschneider, *The Semi-Sovereign People* (New York: Holt, Rinehart and Winston, 1960).

5. For an excellent account of the issue basis of the New Deal party system see James L. Sundquist, *Dynamics of the Party System: Alignment and Realignment of Political Parties in the United States*, rev. ed. (Washington, D.C.: Brookings Institution, 1983), 198-239.

6. Ibid., 332-351.

7. For a discussion of the different types of presidential elections see Angus Campbell, "A Classification of the Presidential Elections," in *Elections and the Political Order*, ed. Angus Campbell, Philip Converse, Warren E. Miller, and Donald E. Stokes (New York: Wiley, 1966).

8. Philip E. Converse, "Of Time and Partisan Stability," *Comparative Political Studies* 2 (July 1969): 43.

9. Ronald Inglehart and Abram Hochstein, "Alignment and Realignment of the Electorate in France and the United States," *Comparative Political Studies* 5 (October 1972): 343-372; Edward G. Carmines and James A. Stimson, "Issue Evolution, Population Replacement, and Normal Partisan Change," *American Political Science Review* 75 (March 1981): 107-118.

10. Adam Przeworski, "Institutionalization of Voting Patterns, or Is Mobilization the Source of Decay?" *American Political Science Review* 69 (March 1975): 49-67.

11. Converse, "Of Time and Partisan Stability," 139-171.

12. Paul A. Beck and M. Kent Jennings, "Parents as 'Middlepersons' in Political Socialization," *Journal of Politics* 37 (February 1975): 83-107; Edward G. Carmines, John P. McIver, and James A. Stimson, "Unrealized Partisanship: A Theory of Dealignment," *Journal of Politics* 49 (May 1987): 376-400; Robert C. Luskin, John P. McIver, and Edward G. Carmines, "Issues and the Transmission of Partisanship," *American Journal of Political Science* 33 (May 1989): 440-458.

13. Paul A. Beck, "The Electoral Cycle and Patterns of American Politics," *British Journal of Political Science* 9 (April 1979): 131.

14. Converse, "Of Time and Partisan Stability," 139-171.

15. Ibid.; Lipset and Rokkan, "Cleavage Structures."

16. For an elaboration of this point see Carmines, "The Logic of Party Alignments."

17. Edward G. Carmines and James A. Stimson, "The Dynamics of Issue Evolution: The United States," in *Electoral Change in Advanced Industrial Democracies*, ed. Russell J. Dalton, Scott Flanagan, and Paul Allen Beck (Princeton, N.J.: Princeton University Press, 1984), 134-158.

18. Beck, "The Electoral Cycle and Patterns of American Politics," 131, and Paul A. Beck, "A Socialization Theory of Partisan Realignment," in *The Politics of Future Citizens*, ed. Richard G. Niemi et al. (San Francisco: Jossey-Bass, 1974), 199-219.

19. Przeworski, "Institutionalization of Voting Patterns, or Is Mobilization the Source of Decay?"; Beck, "A Socialization Theory of Partisan Realignment"; Beck, "The

Electoral Cycle and Patterns of American Politics"; Paul A. Beck, "Realignment Begins?" *American Politics Quarterly* 10 (October 1982): 421-437; Carmines and Stimson, "Issue Evolution"; and Kristi Anderson, *Creation of a Democratic Majority, 1928-1936* (Chicago: University of Chicago Press, 1979).

20. Converse, "Of Time and Partisan Stability."

21. Anderson, *Democratic Majority*. Also see Robert H. Salisbury and Michael MacKuen, "On the Study of Party Realignment," *Journal of Politics* 43 (May 1981): 523-530.

22. Edward G. Carmines and James A. Stimson, *Issue Evolution: Race and the Transformation of American Politics* (Princeton, N.J.: Princeton University Press, 1989).

23. M. Kent Jennings and Richard Niemi, *Generation and Politics* (Princeton, N.J.: Princeton University Press, 1981).

24. Carmines, "The Logic of Party Alignments," 72-74 and Carmines and Stimson, *Issue Evolution*, 9-12.

25. William Riker, *Liberalism Against Populism* (San Francisco: Freeman, 1982), chaps. 8 and 9.

26. Ibid., 210.

27. For two different perspectives on this point see Ian Budge and Donald Farlie, "Party Competition—Selective Emphasis on Direct Confrontation? An Alternative View with Data," in *Western European Party Systems*, ed. Hans Daalder and Peter Mair (Beverly Hills, Calif.: Sage, 1983), 267-306, and John R. Petrocik, "Divided Government: Is It All in the Campaigns?" in *The Politics of Divided Government*, ed. Gary W. Cox and Samuel Kernell (Boulder, Colo.: Westview, 1991), 17-24.

28. Harold Hotelling, "Stability in Competition," *Economic Journal* 39 (March 1929): 41-57, and Anthony Downs, *An Economic Theory of Democracy* (New York: Harper, 1957). The connection between party alignments (and realignments) and spatial models is examined in Sundquist, *Dynamics of the Party System*, and Stuart Elaine Macdonald and George Rabinowitz, "The Dynamics of Structural Realignment," *American Political Science Review* 81 (September 1987): 775-796.

29. The role of party activists in spatial models of elections is explored in John H. Aldrich, "A Spatial Model with Party Activists: Implications for Electoral Dynamics," *Public Choice* 41 (1983): 63-100; John H. Aldrich, "A Downsian Spatial Model with Party Activism," *American Political Science Review* 77 (December 1983): 974-990; and Richard Johnston, "Issues and Party Alignments: A Review with Canadian Examples," unpublished paper.

30. William H. Riker, "Heresthetic and Rhetoric in the Spatial Model," in *Advances in the Spatial Theory of Voting*, ed. James M. Enslow and Melvin J. Hinich (New York: Cambridge University Press, 1990), 45-65.

31. Ibid., 51.

32. Theoretically, the equilibrium in the multidimensional space is again the median voter. But the spatial arrangements resulting in a multidimensional median are extremely restrictive, indicating that real-world equilibriums are very unlikely in more than one dimension. See Charles Plott, "A Notion of Equilibrium and Its Possibility under Majority Rule," *American Economic Review* 57 (September 1967): 787-806.

33. Johnston, "Issues and Party Alignments," 6.

34. This paragraph draws heavily on MacDonald and Rabinowitz, "The Dynamics of Structural Realignment," 776.

35. For an account of how racial issues affected the New Deal party system see Carmines and Stimson, *Issue Evolution*. For a more popular treatment see Thomas Edsall with Mary Edsall, *Chain Reaction* (New York: Norton, 1991).

36. For a treatment of the Voting Rights Act from this strategic perspective see Edward G. Carmines and Robert Huckfeldt, "Party Politics in the Wake of the

Voting Rights Act," in *Controversies in Minority Voting*, ed. Bernard Grofman and Chandler Davidson (Washington, D.C.: Brookings Institution, 1992), 117-134.
37. These data are again from the National Election Studies of the appropriate year. Northern workers are those respondents who answer "skilled workers" or "workers" on the NES occupation question. Yuppies are defined as young respondents (born since 1944) who have at least attended college and earn above the median income. Social cultural issues include abortion, school prayer, women's rights, and homosexual rights (in 1988 only).

6

Asymmetries in the Electoral Bases of Representation, Nomination Politics, and Partisan Change

Walter J. Stone

This policy of supplying by opposite and rival interests, the defect of better motives, might be traced through the whole system of human affairs, private as well as public. We see it particularly displayed in all the subordinate distributions of power; where the constant aim is to divide and arrange the several offices in such a manner as that each may be a check on the other; that the private interest of every individual, may be a sentinel over the public rights.

—James Madison
Federalist 51

Madison's comment is optimistic about representative government. While lamenting the "defect of better motives," Madison claims that selfish interests can be channeled productively to achieve the public good—that self-interest "may be a sentinel over the public rights." Can a system be constructed in which everyone—leaders as well as followers—pursues his or her self-interest, yet the public good is still protected? Neoclassical economic theory, according to which producers and consumers seek to maximize their own personal gain, is built upon this principle, and the economic system as a whole is deemed to achieve something like the "public good." A similar argument can be extracted from Madison's writings, although the theory depends heavily upon institutions, rather than unbridled self-interest in an unconstrained market. Even in the context of the limited argument in *Federalist* 51, Madison emphasizes the importance of separation of powers, federalism, bicameralism, and representation. Ambition will not automatically check ambition; "ambition must be *made* to counteract ambition." Republican government, where the "scheme of representation" ties the self-interest of the representative to the self-interest of the represented, is the linchpin of Madison's argument about how to protect "the public rights." [1]

Madison is not alone in linking self-interested behavior to representative government. Anthony Downs and his utilitarian progenitors argue that self-interested behavior on the part of leaders and followers produces representative government. Downs puts it bluntly: "We assume that every individual, though rational, is also selfish." Voters compare the utilities associated with the policy streams promised by competing political parties (or candidates). Voters-as-consumers choose between or among competing vendors based upon product differentiation. Parties and candidates offer policy streams, voters choose from among the offered products based on which will maximize their utility. Citizens have no intrinsic interest in which party governs; their only concern is with maximizing their own self-interest. Parties likewise have no intrinsic interest in "helping" voters or in solving problems for the common good (providing more efficiency, fair distribution of wealth, or national defense). Downs states explicitly that party members seek only to win access to power to satisfy their own selfish desires:

> We assume that they act solely in order to attain the income, prestige, and power which comes from being in office. Thus politicians in our model never seek office as a means of carrying out particular policies; their only goal is to reap the rewards of holding office per se. They treat policies purely as means to the attainment of their private ends, which they can reach only by being elected.[2]

In this view, representative government results from individual pursuit of self-interest. The electoral bargain between voters and politicians is simple. From the voters' point of view, it is: "Provide the policies we seek and we will vote for you." Because voters think that way, politicians must promise to provide such policies (and deliver on their promises) in order to enjoy the preferments of power. No one (certainly not politicians) has an interest in representative government or in being representative for its own sake. Both sets of actors are pursuing selfish ends. Yet, out of this bargain comes government that is reasonably responsive to voter interests.

The simplicity of the electoral bargain is appealing to theorists looking for the key to modern democracy. In fairness to Downs, his book is replete with complicating issues such as problems associated with information costs, rational abstention, and the like. Nonetheless, the core argument apparently stands as a kind of working hypothesis to explain modern representative democracies: The division of labor between politicians and citizens is bridged by an electoral connection linking the self-interest of voters to the interests of officeholders and prospective officeholders. One commentator on Downs's work recently summarized the hypothesis as follows: "Voters are preference revealers; politicians are vote maximizers. The assumption of vote maximization means that the role for political leadership is highly circumscribed, with the policy positions of leaders being completely dependent on the distribution of voter preferences." [3] This summary is consistent with Madison's optimistic belief that the "private interest [is] a sentinel over the public rights."

Despite the simple elegance of rational-choice models, however, questions can be raised about their optimistic interpretation of the electoral bargain. I have two goals in this chapter. First, I suggest that the Downsian assumptions in fact lead to a much more pessimistic conclusion about the electoral connection. Powerful and enduring asymmetries between elites and citizens that follow from the Downsian assumptions about what motivates both groups undermine the electoral connection. The literature pointing out the asymmetries is well known, and in discussing the problem I will briefly evaluate some of the mechanisms suggested as being capable of reestablishing the efficacy of the electoral connection. My second goal is to consider implications of the asymmetry hypothesis for processes of change. I do so in the context of an analysis of the contemporary presidential selection process and its consequences for the American party system. I argue that the asymmetry hypothesis has some underappreciated consequences for understanding party change. Despite a prevailing tendency among party scholars to make the nomination process their whipping boy, that process helps promote party responsiveness to change and thereby overcomes some of the negative implications of the asymmetry hypothesis.

The Asymmetry Hypothesis

The presence of asymmetries between political elites and citizens is well known. Political elites are likely to be much better informed about public affairs than ordinary citizens, much more politically active, more consistent in their thinking about politics and in linking general value premises to specific attitudes and beliefs, and more partisan in attitude and behavior.[4] These differences are linked to differences in levels of information about politics and in quantitative and qualitative differences in political participation. On the elite side of the electoral bargain, we find professional politicians who immerse themselves in politics. They are conversant with the subtleties of a wide range of issues, they are likely to have organizing cognitive frameworks that enable them to evaluate information quickly, and they participate literally as professionals. On the citizen side of the bargain, three generations of survey researchers have shown that information levels are often astonishingly low, that there is little evidence of organizing frameworks for sorting through and retaining the information that is available, and that levels of involvement in electoral campaigns are low. Even voter turnout, a heavily subsidized activity on which the bargain turns, hovers around 50 percent in presidential elections. Elites invest very heavily in gathering information about politics and in political activity; citizens invest almost nothing.

The reasons citizens invest so little are well understood, even by Downs himself. The problem is that the utility the individual citizen derives from political outcomes is almost always directly tied to the production of collective goods. As Mancur Olson pointed out, rational utility-maximizers will not invest in the production of collective goods. Instead, they "free ride," hoping that others will bear the costs of producing the goods. This free-rider strategy is rational for the individual even if his or her preferences for the collective outcome are strong, so long as the collectivity is reasonably large and incentives to induce participation are absent.[5]

For the ordinary voter, an election outcome, along with the policy stream associated with a particular party's or candidate's victory, is a collective good. All citizens, whether they voted or not, and whether they voted for the winning party or for a loser, share the benefit. Moreover, the individual voter's contribution to the production of the victory is negligible. Knowing this, the rational citizen does not bear even the minimal costs associated with voting. She wishes other like-minded citizens well in their attempts to win electoral victory, but free rides on their efforts.

The prediction that rational citizens will not vote is obviously problematic, and has caused a storm of controversy in the literature.[6] More useful (and much less controversial) is the expectation that citizens will not bear significant information costs.[7] Most citizens pick up information only as a byproduct of their other activities, and their information store about politics (including electoral choices) is incomplete and haphazard. In sum, many citizens do not vote and many more refrain from engaging in more costly forms of electoral activities. Many of those who vote do so without much information about the choices they face, the differences between promised policy streams, or the likely policy outcomes associated with election results. In short, the citizen is a remarkably passive party to the electoral bargain.

Several qualifications to the argument as it applies to citizens are probably in order. First, there are substantial amounts of "free" information available, especially in a national election campaign. One function of a campaign is to make it costly to *avoid* receiving information, so that even passive citizens become informed about the choice they face. In addition, the adversarial nature of campaigns means that the information flow may be balanced (although it need not be).

Second, some models of voting presume very low levels of information in order to enforce the "bargain." Retrospective voting, for example, requires only that the citizen knows whether things (such as the economy) are going well and which party controls government.[8] If things are going well, the voter rewards the incumbent; if things are going poorly, the citizen casts a negative vote. In this model, the average voter need not understand the differences between the candidates or parties in order to create an incentive for politicians to solve the problems that matter to most voters. The biggest problem with the retrospective voting model is that in the American constitutional system, and in the absence of strong national parties, it is often difficult or impossible to know whom to blame.

Third, while collective goods are theoretically available to all citizens, governmental policy affects citizens differentially. National defense is a collective good, but some citizens benefit from "private" goods associated with national defense policy such as contracts to build weapons systems. Even an election victory benefits some more than others. For example, a winning presidential campaign can offer patronage positions to thousands, benefit its retinue of campaign consultants with enhanced income and reputation, and enable its candidate to ascend to the Oval Office. Indeed, it is precisely this differential effect of collective benefits that defines the "elite" side of the asymmetry hypothesis.

If Downs is correct, citizens and elites (party leaders, candidates) pursue qualitatively different benefits through political action. Citizens seek a policy stream that, for most individuals most of the time, looks very much like collective benefits. As a result, the relationship between the costs of producing the benefit (which amount to the costs of participation and of becoming informed) and the actual enjoyment of the benefit are severed. Elites, however, seek private benefits. There is a close relationship between the amount of resources expended in pursuit of these benefits and the probability of actually enjoying them. Citizens have no incentive to bear information costs or participation costs, and so we are not amazed to find that most are not well informed and that levels of participation beyond voting are very low. Indeed, we may be more confounded to find that the average citizen has as much information as she does and that voting rates are as high as they are. Doubtless a commitment to the political process accounts for much of this effort. On the other side of the bargain, politicians expend tremendous amounts of time, energy, effort, and money to achieve high office. I do not think we can account for all of this activity by arguing that they have proportionally higher levels of interest in the political process, or that they are that much more committed to the production of public policy. Politicians are compensated instead by attaining the "income, prestige, and power which come from being in office." [9] These are selective, not collective, benefits.

This asymmetry between the collective payoffs from citizen participation versus the private benefits associated with elite involvement accounts for the vast differences in resources committed. Without a personal expenditure of resources, the chances of a politician enjoying the benefits are nil. With such an expenditure, the chances are significantly improved, if still far short of certain. For citizens, the expenditure of personal resources is not directly tied to receiving the benefits associated with the electoral bargain. As a result, effort is sporadic and low.

Implications of the Asymmetry Hypothesis

The most important implication of the asymmetry hypothesis is that citizens are relatively passive participants in the electoral bargain. This is hardly news, but it does create difficulties for theories of representation that implicitly or explicitly assume an active role for the citizen. Most close observers of electoral politics have agreed that citizens react to elite behavior rather than actively eliciting elite responsiveness, although many authors have still held out hope for democratic control. E. E. Schattschneider expresses little patience with the "pedagogues" who set unrealistic standards for an informed electorate and then chastise the public for failing to measure up. For Schattschneider, the electorate has great power because it can grant or withhold assent, but it can "speak only when spoken to." V. O. Key's metaphor of the echo chamber is apt because it suggests that, although the public has limited control over the agenda, it can react meaningfully to electoral choice. Douglas Arnold goes further in suggesting an "audit" metaphor that compels decision makers to anticipate the reactions of inattentive publics. In this way, the public has a kind of indirect influence over the agenda. Others have argued that the "principal-agent" problem in economics offers a way to conceptualize the problems surrounding the relationship between the electorate and officeholders.[10]

At the same time, the asymmetry hypothesis opens the door to much more pessimistic interpretations of the electoral bargain. If we assume politicians are out to win the "preferments" of power, we ought not to be surprised if they deviate from the prescribed path of providing policy representation in order to do so. Downs's model leads him to be optimistic about competing politicians responding to the "median voter" in elections; but what if there are cheaper and surer methods of winning election and reelection? The literature on the "incumbency effect" in Congress is a case in point. In various ways members of Congress manipulate the electoral process in order to reduce the level of competition and increase the likelihood of winning reelection. Campaign finance laws are stacked in favor of incumbents and against challengers; members vote themselves resources not available to challengers; and they exploit their access to the policy process to assure a favorable distribution of particularized benefits.[11] These activities more or less distort the electoral bargain. Voters choose between competing candidates without necessarily pushing governmental institutions closer to providing policy consistent with their interests.

Other intriguing implications are consistent with the hypothesis. One is that levels of conflict between elites, institutions, and parties may be significantly lower than those expected by theorists from Madison to Schattschneider and Riker. The potential for conflict is generated because representatives from different constituencies are linked to different interests, to constituencies demanding different and competing streams of public policy. Yet various forms of collusion may be possible between officeholders sharing a common interest in "preferments" even if their electoral bargains push them toward competition. Examples abound, from

Mayhew's norm of universalism to the literature on "iron triangles." [12] Political corruption—where the exchange of private goods is direct—is an extreme (if not uncommon) example of elite collusion.

Despite these unsavory consequences of the asymmetry problem, there is reason to believe that parties are in a unique position to overcome some of its implications for representative government. Competition between parties on a national scale can be highly visible. It provides cheap and useful information to an inattentive electorate, and alerts citizens to the stake they have in public affairs. Party conflict, for all of its side shows, ambiguities, posturing, and symbolism, also is about competing views of how to promote collective interests. This is why studies of party elites regularly show distinct ideological and issue differences between the parties, even in the American case. Strong party organizations also provide regularized and predictable pathways to the preferments of power and high office. Those who would specialize in the pursuit of such benefits must pursue party careers. Finally, parties hold the potential for providing collective responsibility. As institutions their interests transcend particular individuals' careers. Individuals compete to hold office, but the basis of competition is a highly public debate about how well they perform there.

The problem with party as an institutional solution to the asymmetry problem is that American parties tend to be weak. At the highest levels of national office, they appear to have been in prolonged decline with little or no chance of organizing electoral conflict, providing collective responsibility, or commanding the loyalties of citizens or elites.[13] The constitutional deck has always been stacked against strong national parties, and now the electoral arena in which they must compete is especially inhospitable to their existence. The 1992 independent candidacy of H. Ross Perot, which attracted almost 20 percent of the popular vote, seems to underline the claim that the American parties are in decline.

At the same time, parties are remarkably resilient and adaptive institutions. They exist because of natural pressures toward differences and conflict in society, and because achieving their goal—control of public office—requires sustained cooperative effort. Because the presidency is the grandest prize in American politics, and because nominating candidates is the defining function of political parties, the presidential nomination process is a place where the electoral bargain may be reexamined. Moreover, the contemporary presidential nomination process is commonly seen as high on the list of antiparty features of our national politics. But there is reason to be optimistic about the parties in today's nomination process, especially when viewed through the lens of party and electoral change. This analysis suggests some of the ways the presidential nominations help overcome the negative consequences of the asymmetry hypothesis for the electoral bargain and representative government.

Presidential Nominations and Party Change

In their pathbreaking work on party change, Carmines and Stimson put the matter succinctly: "As agent of change the mass public will not do." [14] The electorate by itself cannot stimulate or guide political change, although it may play its part. Initiating change in public policy or in the agenda of political conflict requires a tremendous commitment of energy. Likewise, Carmines and Stimson are not optimistic about officeholders, for they have too much to lose by being entrepreneurs of change. In this view, the bargain between politicians and voters leads to a static form of representative government. (Indeed, one criticism of Downs's analysis is that it does not accommodate or explain change.)

Carmines and Stimson's answer to the problem of stasis is that electoral change is stimulated by campaign activists. Theirs is a variant of the opinion-leader hypothesis, in which ordinary citizens typically have little interest in politics and low levels of information, in contrast to opinion leaders scattered throughout the electorate who are interested and well informed. In their contacts with others through ordinary social interactions (and some overtly political interactions), opinion leaders disseminate their perceptions and opinions (though probably not their information). In Carmines and Stimson's argument, such activists provide the dynamic in electoral change because they come and go, not because their own opinions are subject to change. In fact, as individuals their political attitudes are probably more crystallized than those of ordinary citizens, but they are "occasional" in that they circulate in and out of a loosely defined activist stratum, and it is this circulation that provides the potential for change. Popular perceptions of the candidates and parties respond to the cues provided by activists. If an ideological candidate captures the fancy of youthful campaign workers, the ripple effects through the electorate may be substantial. Carmines and Stimson do not trace in detail the processes their argument suggests, but they do present intriguing aggregate and time-series data consistent with the argument.

Carmines and Stimson do not directly confront the implications of asymmetries between citizens and elites. I build on their argument to suggest that the contemporary presidential nomination process is an underrecognized source of electoral change. In making this case, I also argue that some of the positive consequences of the nomination process help resolve difficulties for the electoral bargain posed by the asymmetry hypothesis. The argument proceeds in four steps:

1. a description of the open and highly visible nature of contemporary presidential nomination campaigns;
2. a reconsideration of the "candidate-centered" and "divisive" qualities of these campaigns;
3. a review of evidence on candidate choice; and

4. a summary of the positive "carryover" and "spillover" effects associated with nomination campaigns.

Nomination campaigns do not resolve all of the difficulties associated with the asymmetry problem. However, they are an important arena of representation, their contemporary configuration works to promote party responsiveness, and they are an engine of long-term party and electoral change. In time, the positive consequences of the process as it has evolved may be a basis for a resurgence of the national parties in the United States.

The Postreform Nomination Process

Following the debacle of the 1968 Democratic National Convention, the national party set out to reform its nomination process in order to promote more participation in the selection of party nominees, ensure greater representation of various constituencies within the party, and enhance the legitimacy of the party and its nominee. The reforms certainly achieved the first goal. Participation in nomination campaigns in primary elections, local caucuses, county and state conventions, and in the campaigns themselves soared.[15] Whereas the nomination process prior to 1968 was dominated by local party interests often out of the view of the press and the public, the postreform process is, perhaps to a fault, open to the mass media, participatory, and national.[16] Although the process remains formally organized on a state-by-state basis, campaigns in Iowa, New Hampshire, and even South Dakota and Vermont play to a national audience. The "Super Tuesday" innovation, in which states band together to hold their primary elections, also pushes us toward a national process. Nationalization of the nomination process further increases participation because of the visibility of campaigns, polling, and debates.

If the reforms increased rates of participation, it is not at all clear they made the process more representative. Critics have argued that nominations encourage participation by activists and primary voters who are more ideologically extreme than the November electorate and more committed to narrow issues or group agendas, and who are demographically unrepresentative. The representativeness of the process is also subject to question because such atypical states as Iowa and New Hampshire play a role far out of proportion to their population or to the interests in those states. Polsby has argued that the multicandidate nature of many nomination campaigns further distorts the process because candidates can carve up the party's nomination constituency into relatively narrow and atypical factions whose preferences need not conform with the rest of the party, to say nothing of the November electorate. More recently, John Geer and Barbara Norrander have shown that primary electorates as a whole are actually quite representative of the general electorate.[17]

Assessing the legitimacy of the nomination process is difficult, but implicit in many critiques is the claim that the party has not benefitted from the reforms. Intraparty factionalism is more visible to the general public, and the candidates selected often have been viewed as beholden to narrow interests within their party. Furthermore, some have concluded that the Democrats' difficulties winning the White House were linked to their reform of the process of nominating their candidate.[18]

Candidate-Centered and Divisive?

The short answer is, yes, the nomination process is candidate-centered and divisive. But how can it be otherwise? A nomination campaign must necessarily focus on individual candidates because the party is at some remove from the fight. The contest is over who shall represent the party in the fall, and although party leaders of various kinds may express a preference, the party is the object of the conflict, not a participant in it. Because individual candidates are the contestants and only one can win the nomination, it is also no surprise that evidence of "divisiveness" abounds. Candidates attract their following by identifying a constituency based upon some combination of ideological, issue, group, and personal appeals. They can focus on the foibles of the opposition party, but inevitably they must also compare themselves with the competition within their own party.

It is, in short, entirely appropriate to characterize nomination campaigns as candidate-centered and divisive. Moreover, their highly public character—coupled with the frenetic schedule of campaign visits, debates, fundraising affairs, media consultations, and polling—may enhance both the personal and divisive nature of nomination campaigns. But what are we to make of these characteristics? The most common claim is that the divisive, personal quality of today's nominations invades the general election process and the process of governance beyond the November election. Kenney and Rice place the blame for a party's difficulties in November squarely on the "divisive primary" that occurs in the spring. Their evidence from the twentieth century suggests that a candidate who experiences a primary fight for the nomination suffers measurable losses in the general election. They quote Jimmy Carter, a victim of Sen. Edward M. Kennedy's spirited challenge to the incumbent president: "The result of his protracted effort was that Fritz [Vice President Walter Mondale] and I were required to spend an enormous amount of time and resources after the convention in winning Democratic voters back to our side. Many of them were alienated permanently." [19] Lowi traces many of the problems associated with the "personal presidency" to the lack of party control over the nomination process:

Because of the absence of party leaders, state party units, and an institution in which meaningful bargains can take place, the ultimate nominee of the so-called party does not possess a coalition, does not represent a coalition, and does not contribute in the quest for the nomination to the formation of a coalition.[20]

There is certainly truth in the proposition that candidates in the general election face difficulties assembling a broad coalition, but it is far from certain that nomination campaigns add to their problems. The nomination and general election stages are parts of a complex process that defines the party and electoral systems. The critics noted above, viewing nominations in isolation, have inferred negative consequences from the personalized factionalism and intraparty divisiveness that they see as characterizing nomination campaigns. For example, it is surely true that Carter's troubles in the 1980 general election did not begin with Senator Kennedy's challenge for the nomination or the factionalism surrounding the nomination fight. Rather, Carter's weaknesses attracted Kennedy's challenge and these same weaknesses contributed to his defeat in November.

More generally, divisive nomination fights are at least as much a consequence of factional conflicts within the party as they are a cause of such conflict. E. E. Schattschneider reminds us that an important function of political parties is to expand the "scope of conflict" by alerting citizens to the stakes involved in politics and mobilizing them into the electoral arena. Whatever their unintended consequences, the reforms expanded the scope of conflict surrounding nomination politics. Some of this occurred simply because the rules mandated more widespread participation, publicly announced meeting times for caucuses, and the like. But some of the expanded participation is also due to the conflict itself; due, that is, to the divisive and public character of the fight among candidates and factions for control of the party. Surely the changes in rules encouraged the insurgent appeals of candidates as varied as George McGovern, Jimmy Carter, Ronald Reagan (in 1976), Edward Kennedy, Gary Hart, Jesse Jackson, and Pat Robertson. These candidacies, moreover, themselves contributed to a highly visible form of conflict that drew into the parties constituencies as diverse as young antiwar activists, blacks and other minority groups, and the religious right.

The reforms make intraparty conflict more public, but critics of the post-1968 process have almost surely overstated the degree to which the reforms increased intraparty divisiveness. Were the contests between the Taft and Eisenhower, the Kennedy and Johnson, or the Rockefeller and Goldwater wings of their respective parties less divisive merely because they were not as public? Jillson describes the strategic and ideological intraparty factionalism that arose in the pre-Civil War years.[21] Intraparty factions have always fought with one another, and they always will. The real question is not whether the nomination fights are more contentious in the contemporary period than in the past, but whether conflicts are more likely to invade the general election and weaken the party.

An effect of the candidate-centered and divisive quality of today's campaigns has been to draw into the nomination process a diverse set of interests attached to the various candidates who have contended for their party's nomination. These constituencies can be defined by the ideologies, candidate preferences, and campaign activities of their activist members, whose opinions are quite stable over time.[22] But as those activists circulate in and out of presidential campaign politics, they help give definition to the parties. If we focus only on their activities in the nomination campaign itself, we can readily observe the conflict and diversity among them. But we may miss the implications of their presence for political representation and long-term patterns of change in the party system. To sketch those effects, we must explore how activists make their candidate choices and the short- and long-term implications of their participation in the nomination process.

Nomination Choice

The explanations of candidate choice in nomination campaigns that immediately followed the initial reforms built upon James Q. Wilson's notion of the "amateur." [23] In this view, nomination activists supported candidates based on their own ideological and issue preferences and without regard for the larger interests of the party or the November electorate. This work made it easy to view the process as divisive and candidate-centered because it portrayed participants as concerned only with their own ideological interests, which were pursued primarily through attachment to candidates of like views. The process was thought to compel candidates to adhere to commitments to nomination constituencies even if such commitments interfered with the candidate's ability to broaden his appeal to the November electorate.

Evidence I have gathered in collaboration with Ronald B. Rapoport and Alan I. Abramowitz supports the claim that activists are strongly committed to their ideological and issue preferences, preferences that probably push them to participate in the first place.[24] For the same reason, the presidential selection process compels them to give heavy weight to their candidate's chances in the general election campaign. To back a candidate who represents personal preferences but has little or no chance to win in November does little to further one's ideological interests. The candidate who best combines policy affinity with the ability to win in November is the candidate most participants will choose to support.[25]

Concern over the candidates' electability produces a kind of representation. And, like the traditional formulation of the electoral bargain between citizens and politicians, this representation arises out of nothing more than the self-interests of the participants. Activists are not concerned about electability out of some abstract commitment to the public's interests. Rather, they know that winning the nomination is but the first step in furthering their interests. If they are to succeed, they must see their interests represented by the occupant of the White House. Moreover, most activists do not labor under the illusion that their own ideological interests conform neatly with those of the general electorate. When asked to place themselves on a left-right continuum, Democrats locate themselves to the left of center and Republicans place themselves distinctly to the right of center. They also place their own party and that of the opposition clearly off center. When asked to locate the average American voter, however, activists in both parties place the electorate just a shade to the right of center—almost exactly at the point of the average voter self-placement in recent National Election Study surveys.

The result is that we find greater ideological variance within candidate factions than would be expected if candidate choice were motivated by ideological proximity alone. At the same time, because ideology figures prominently in activists' choice there is a very strong *aggregate* relationship between mean factional preferences and the actual location of candidates on the left-right continuum. For example, candidate factions differentiated themselves on the ideological scale in ways that matched the differences among the candidates themselves in 1988. However, candidate electability, not ideological proximity, is the more powerful predictor of individual respondents' candidate choice across these same thirteen candidates.[26]

As candidates of differing ideologies come and go, new and different cohorts of activists are drawn into the nomination process. The more different a contender is from his or her party (McGovern in 1972; Reagan in 1976 and 1980; Jackson in 1984; Robertson in 1988) the greater the potential for ideological and issue conflict within the activist ranks. What happens to this conflict and what is its potential for promoting party change?

Carryover Effects of Nomination Participation

Priscilla Southwell and others have suggested that divisions aroused in the nomination campaign invade the general election campaign by alienating supporters of losing candidates. This "negative carryover" from the nomination to the general election is a centerpiece of the argument against the postreform nomination process.[27]

It is true that those who preferred nomination-round losers participate at lower rates in the fall than those who backed a winner. It is also true, however, that the greater the mobilization on behalf of nomination candidates—whether the preferred candidate wins or loses his party's nomination—the greater the tendency to participate for the presidential ticket in the fall. This relationship is strongly positive and remains robust in the face of controls for activists' assessments of the general election choice confronting them and for their predispositions toward party activity. This "positive carryover" effect is probably due to the socializing consequences of nomination activity. Activists drawn to a candidate during a nomination campaign are socialized to more general partisan activity. Even newcomers drawn to insurgent candidacies like Jesse Jackson's in 1984 and Pat Robertson's in 1988 remained active on behalf of their party's nominee in the general election. Overall, the positive carryover effect associated with nomination participation is much stronger than the negative effects.[28]

The Nomination Process and Party Change

Much of the literature on presidential nominations is skeptical about the normative effects of opening the process to greater participation from the base of the party. A reassessment now under way suggests that the post-1968 reforms had positive consequences for the parties and for the political system.[29] The reforms can also be seen as part of a historical trend toward greater democratization of presidential nominations, which have been moving out of the "smoke-filled room" for two centuries, from the congressional caucus to the party convention, from the national convention to a "mixed" system involving the direct primary following the Progressive reforms, and finally to the current system dominated by the direct primary.

The putatively undesirable characteristics of further democratization include greater participation by amateurs whose motivations for participation and candidate support undermine the party's interests, increased divisiveness in the nomination and general election stages, candidate-centered quality of contemporary campaigns, and the generally unrepresentative character of nomination outcomes. Evidence now suggests, however, that these conclusions were too quickly drawn. Democratizing the nomination process has positive consequences for party responsiveness. Scholars such as Geer and Ware have argued that opening the process creates incentives and opportunities for the parties to respond to shifting popular sentiment. Geer and Shere offer the innovative argument that the intraparty competition fostered by the direct primary prevents elite collusion of the sort that might be expected by the asymmetry hypothesis. The result is a process that compels parties to be sensitive to changing popular interests.[30]

A democratic nomination process open to participation by a wide variety of interests makes the party a tempting target for candidates who engage in the risky and expensive business of contending for their party's nomination. Many, like John Connally, Alexander Haig, Bruce Babbitt, and Pat Robertson do not last long. Others run viable, if not necessarily successful, campaigns. More than just a conflict of personalities, the conflict among candidates generates interest and participation and is a proving ground for competing ideas and interests within the party. For the activist it is a serious conflict over competing ideological positions and the agenda that will define the party in the general election and beyond. Sometimes the conflict takes the form of an ideological debate; at other times it occurs between ideologically compatible candidates over the issues that should define the party's agenda.

The campaign between and among candidates brings into the nomination campaign cadres of activists who share the policy goals of their champions. Even if the contest has a zero sum outcome for candidates, the "losing" activists do not lose all. It is *their* party that the candidates are fighting over, and many remain active in it long after the nomination fight is done.[31] Those who are attracted to party activity for the first time because of nomination campaigns tend to stick around. The give and take, coming and going, and successes and failures among candidates give rise to participatory patterns among rank and file activists throughout the party, in campaigns other than that for the presidency, and in years other than the one that provided the initial stimulation. The activist party is a constantly evolving result of such interactions. As Carmines and Stimson note, the experience of the party in the electorate at large is not merely the result of a particular candidate's campaign as represented in debates, commercials, and appearances. That experience is shaped by the complex web of social interactions with hundreds of thousands of "occasional" activists who themselves move in and out of party activity over time.

The mobilization (and creation) of campaign activists in recent presidential nominations may have the power to stimulate a regeneration of the parties. While the process has made the parties appear more vulnerable to internal conflict and division, it has given vast numbers of people political experience. The genesis of Ronald Reagan's successful campaign in 1988 was the Goldwater debacle of 1964; the Clinton campaign of 1992 was rooted in the antiwar campaigns of 1968 and 1972. In much the same way, the Perot movement of 1992 benefitted from a large class of activists schooled in past nomination campaigns. Even as these examples find their beginnings in the past, they also give rise to new directions in the party system. Surely the Reagan legacy will remain with the Republican party for some time to come. Whatever the impact of Clinton's presidency, the generational and ideological shifts embodied in his 1992 campaign will structure partisan conflict into the next century. And Perot demonstrated that nomination campaigns are not the only arenas available to candidates intent on identifying an agenda and mobilizing a constituency.

The extraordinarily vital nature of presidential nomination politics is due to its open and democratic character. A process that invites participation from constituencies as diverse as those embraced by the two American parties is bound to stimulate an added measure of conflict. But those who focus only on the conflict in nomination campaigns miss the potential of conflict for strengthening the electoral bargain in national politics.

The impediments to electoral representation described by the asymmetry hypothesis are not trivial or easily overcome. But the postreform nomination process offers cause for optimism. Nomination participants, acting out of their own perceived interests, promote substantive debate over their party's direction. Although the candidates who bear the risks associated with a run for the presidency also stand to gain substantial private benefit, they are carriers of conflicting views of party direction and agenda. Insurgent candidates are especially likely to generate party change. Because successful candidates must appeal to voters' interests, candidates and activists alike must consider likely voter response to competing appeals. Contemporary nominations join candidates, activists, and the electorate in a process that channels and directs change as it promotes party response to changing electoral interests.

Conclusion

A central theme of this volume is the study of political change. Different authors attack different subjects with different approaches. The approach to the study of change in this chapter is most firmly rooted in the behavioral tradition. Yet critics of the behavioral approach to the study of politics have raised three significant objections:

First, the behavioral approach has not been very good at addressing questions of change because conducting behavioral research over extended periods of time is extremely expensive. Moreover, scholars in the behavioral tradition have had difficulty deciding what data to collect. In this they are like their colleagues working with other approaches: they have difficulty formulating the most productive questions. The National Election Studies at the University of Michigan now has an impressive series of data on the national electorate since 1952 that is being mined by behavioral scholars addressing questions of change. Without more such sustained data collection efforts on a variety of questions, however, behavioral scholars will be constrained by the limits of their data. Long-term data collection efforts must be mounted and sustained.

Second, the behavioral tradition lacks a coherent theoretical basis, and much behavioral work lacks any serious theoretical ambition. It is fair to say that much behavioral research is overly descriptive and inductive, although the rational-choice tradition provides an important source of theoretical guidance for much behavioral research. Likewise, behavioral research provides a crucial empirical referent for rational-choice modelers. Certainly the two traditions are drawn to similar questions, and the dialogue between them promises to be very productive. That dialogue (among others) can and should expressly include problems related to political change.

Third, the behavioral tradition is wedded to "methodological individualism" in its focus on individuals as research subjects. (So, for that matter, is the rational-choice approach.) This is almost always true of work in the behavioral tradition, and it may ultimately prove to be a serious liability. But I am not convinced by this critique. It is very clear, for example, that "institutions matter" by shaping individual incentives and behaviors. Perhaps scholars working on individual-level problems have been slow to recognize the independent effects of institutions in large part because institutional variation is difficult or impossible to capture within most survey designs. I would like to believe that, in the spirit of James Madison, the behavioral approach can be theoretically grounded, sensitive to the institutional context shaping individual incentives, perceptions, and behaviors, and capable of addressing large questions of political change.

Whatever the approach taken, the claim that selfish interests can produce representative government remains a tantalizing one because it does not require us to assume that unusual or heroic people are necessary to make government function in a desirable way. It is also attractive because of its simplicity. Citizens and politicians, in pursuit of easily identifiable goals, behave in predictable ways. Properly organized in political institutions, ordinary behavior in response to selfish goals produces good government. The American penchant for tinkering with institutions of government is probably a manifestation of this faith in political engineering. A favorite place for this tinkering is the presidential nomination process, especially of late.

Presidential nominations work the way they do because of self-interest. Candidates and prospective candidates calculate their chances for success, and decide whether to commit the massive resources necessary to make a run. Activists of various kinds survey the field of candidates and latch on to the one whom they believe can best further their interests. Some do so out of purely "selfish" concern for selective benefits such as a job in the campaign or a chance to meet the candidate personally. Many are motivated by the social benefits they derive from working with like-minded citizens in the highly charged atmosphere of a national campaign. Most simply derive utility from attempting to further their policy goals and partisan objectives. Meanwhile, many millions of citizens "free ride" on the process by sitting on the sidelines, watching with only sporadic interest. They do not attend caucuses or conventions, contribute money to campaigns, canvass neighborhoods or telephone on behalf of a candidate, or vote in a primary election. But the contemporary nomination campaign resolves some of the serious impediments to representation described by the asymmetry hypothesis. That candidates, activists, and ordinary citizens can be understood as responding to their self-interests in a process that encourages participation and promotes responsiveness to change by the parties bodes well for the hopes of theorists from Madison to Downs.

Do nomination campaigns organize all of this self-interested activity to further the "public rights"? If political parties are necessary for representative government, and if nominations contribute to the responsiveness and health of the national parties, then the answer is optimistic. But these are big "ifs." Certainly the claim that today's nomination process promotes the party and encourages responsiveness is controversial. As usual, what we find depends on where we look and what our question is. To settle the controversy, perhaps it is time to look more closely at presidential nominations with a new set of questions.

Notes

I would like to thank John Geer and Cal Jillson for helpful comments on an earlier draft of this essay.

1. Walter J. Stone, *Republic at Risk: Self-Interest in American Politics* (Pacific Grove, Calif.: Brooks/Cole, 1990).
2. Anthony Downs, *An Economic Theory of Democracy* (New York: Harper, 1957); James Mill, *An Essay on Government* (New York: Cambridge University Press, 1937), quotations at pp. 27, 28.
3. Bryan D. Jones, "Causation, Constraint, and Political Leadership," in *Leadership and Politics*, ed. Bryan D. Jones (Lawrence: University Press of Kansas, 1989).
4. The literature is extensive. Prominent examples of studies demonstrating these asymmetries include Philip E. Converse, "The Nature of Belief Systems in Mass Publics," in *Ideology and Discontent*, ed. David Apter (New York: Free Press, 1964); Robert D. Putnam, *The Comparative Study of Political Elites* (Englewood Cliffs, N.J.: Prentice-Hall, 1976); and Warren E. Miller and M. Kent Jennings, *Parties in Transition* (New York: Russell Sage, 1986).
5. Mancur Olson, *The Logic of Collective Action* (Cambridge: Harvard University Press, 1965).
6. A good place to start is John A. Ferejohn and Morris P. Fiorina, "The Paradox of Not Voting: A Decision-Theoretic Analysis," *American Political Science Review* 68 (1974): 525-536.
7. Recent treatments include John Ferejohn and James Kuklinski, eds., *Information and Democratic Processes* (Urbana: University of Illinois Press, 1990); and Samuel Popkin, *The Reasoning Voter* (Chicago: University of Chicago Press, 1991).
8. Morris P. Fiorina, *Retrospective Voting in American National Elections* (New Haven: Yale University Press, 1981).
9. Downs, *Economic Theory*, 28.
10. "Who, after all, are these self-appointed censors who assume that they are in a position to flunk the whole human race? Their attitude would be less presumptuous if they could come up with a list of things that people must know. ... The whole theory of knowledge underlying these assumptions is pedantic." E. E. Schattschneider, *The Semisovereign People* (Hinsdale, Ill.: Dryden Press, 1975), 132; V. O. Key, Jr., *The Responsible Electorate* (Cambridge: Harvard University Press, 1966); Douglas Arnold, *The Logic of Congressional Action* (New Haven: Yale University Press, 1990). The principal-agent (P/A) problem applied to the question of political representation is complicated by several issues. In the first place, the principal—the constituency—is not a single actor, but a collectivity. As a result, various options are open to the agent to enhance discretion. Useful discussions are provided by John Ferejohn, "Incumbent Performance and Electoral

Control," *Public Choice* 50 (January 1986): 5-25; Morris P. Fiorina and Kenneth A. Shepsle, "Formal Theories of Leadership: Agents, Agenda Setters and Entrepreneurs," in *Leadership and Politics*, ed. B. Jones; and Joseph E. Stiglitz, "Principal and Agent," in *Allocation, Information, and Markets*, ed. John Eatwell et al. (New York: Norton, 1989). The P/A problem in economics, for all of the asymmetries attending the division of labor on which the problem turns, nonetheless involves an exchange of private goods. Insofar as I am aware no one has grappled with the asymmetry problem in a context where the agent delivers collective goods.

11. The classic statement is David Mayhew, *Congress: The Electoral Connection* (New Haven: Yale University Press, 1974).

12. Ibid. On "iron triangles" see Douglass Cater, *Power in Washington* (New York: Vintage, 1964).

13. See Martin P. Wattenberg, *The Rise of Candidate-Centered Politics* (Cambridge: Harvard University Press, 1991).

14. Edward G. Carmines and James A. Stimson, *Issue Evolution: Race and the Transformation of American Politics* (Princeton, N.J.: Princeton University Press, 1989).

15. Nelson W. Polsby, *Consequences of Party Reform* (New York: Oxford University Press, 1983).

16. Gary Orren and Nelson Polsby, eds., *Media and Momentum* (Chatham, N.J.: Chatham, 1987).

17. Peverill Squire, ed., *The Iowa Caucuses and the Presidential Nominating Process* (Boulder, Colo.: Westview, 1989); Polsby, *Consequences of Reform*; John G. Geer, *Nominating Presidents: An Evaluation of Voters and Primaries* (New York: Greenwood, 1989); Barbara Norrander, "Ideological Representativeness of Presidential Primary Voters," *American Journal of Political Science* 33 (August 1989): 570-587.

18. Thomas Edsall, *The Politics of Inequality* (New York: Norton, 1984).

19. Patrick J. Kenney and Tom W. Rice, "The Relationship between Divisive Primaries and General Election Outcomes," *American Journal of Political Science* 31 (February 1987): 31-44.

20. Theodore J. Lowi, *The Personal President* (Ithaca, N.Y.: Cornell University Press, 1985), 112.

21. Calvin Jillson, "Patterns of Periodicity in American National Politics," in *The Dynamics of American Politics: Approaches and Interpretations*, ed. Lawrence Dodd and Calvin Jillson (Boulder, Colo.: Westview, 1993).

22. Walter J. Stone, "On Party Switching among Presidential Activists: What Do We Know?" *American Journal of Political Science* 35 (August 1991): 598-607.

23. James Q. Wilson, *The Amateur Democrat* (Chicago: University of Chicago Press, 1962). An example (among many) of an application to presidential activists is Thomas H. Roback, "Amateurs and Professionals: Delegates to the 1972 Republican National Convention," *Journal of Politics* 37 (May 1980): 436-468.

24. I will summarize the findings and conclusions of the "Active Minority" project without detailed citations to work in progress or in print. For a recent statement on candidate choice, see Walter J. Stone, Ronald B. Rapoport, and Alan I. Abramowitz, "Candidate Support in Presidential Nomination Campaigns," *Journal of Politics* 54 (November 1992): 1074-1097. For an analysis of the positive and negative carryover effects of nomination participation, see Walter J. Stone, Lonna Rae Atkeson, and Ronald B. Rapoport, "Turning On or Turning Off: Mobilization and Demobilization Effects of Participation in Nomination Campaigns," *American Journal of Political Science* 36 (August 1992): 665-691.

25. Compare Paul R. Abramson, John H. Aldrich, Phil Paolino, and David Rohde, " 'Sophisticated' Voting in the 1988 Presidential Primaries," *American Political Science Review* 86 (March 1992): 55-69; and Stone et al., "Candidate Support."

26. Walter J. Stone, Ronald B. Rapoport, and Lonna Rae Atkeson, "A Computer

Simulation of Nomination Choice," unpublished manuscript, Department of Political Science, University of Colorado.

27. See Donald B. Johnson and James R. Gibson, "The Divisive Primary Revisited: Activists in Iowa," *American Political Science Review* 68 (March 1974): 67-77; Priscilla L. Southwell, "The Politics of Disgruntlement: Nonvoting and Defection among Supporters of Nomination Losers, 1968-1984," *Political Behavior* 8 (March 1986): 81-95; Walter J. Stone, "The Carryover Effect in Presidential Elections," *American Political Science Review* 80 (March 1986): 270-279.

28. Stone, Atkeson, Rapoport, "Turning On or Turning Off?"

29. Highly suggestive arguments are made by Alan Ware, *The Logic of Party Democracy* (New York: St. Martin's, 1979); and John G. Geer and Mark E. Shere, "Party Competition and the Prisoner's Dilemma: An Argument for the Direct Primary," *Journal of Politics* 54 (August 1992): 741-761.

30. Geer and Shere, "Party Competition."

31. It is zero sum for candidates only in the limited context of the nomination race itself. Witness George Bush's nomination to the vice presidency in 1980 and Jack Kemp's cabinet status in 1988. Jesse Jackson lost only in a narrow sense, and even John Anderson got to run an independent campaign in 1980 and then stayed pretty busy on the college lecture circuit. Because most of the rewards for party activism are not selective benefits, activity is generally sporadic, with lots of coming and going. Much of this circulation in and out of party activity does not appear to be systematic but is probably tied to perceived opportunity, personal inclinations and energy level, and the like. Note also that our ability to explain why activists participate in the extraordinary ways they do is still fairly primitive. For example, I doubt most nomination activists are convinced their personal support significantly affects the chances of a nomination candidate's victory. The best explanation is probably that they are extraordinarily committed to their ideological and policy goals, and to their political party as the means for achieving them. See John Aldrich, "A Downsian Spatial Model with Party Activism," *American Political Science Review* 77 (December 1983): 974-990.

7

"Organized Capitalism," Fiscal Policy, and the 1992 Democratic Campaign

Thomas Ferguson

All through last year's marathon race to the White House, candidate Bill Clinton and his surrogates kept chanting one word like a mantra: "change." The morning after the election, however, signals switched dramatically. Suddenly the president-elect and his spokespersons began warning that bringing about real change would be a long and difficult process.

Over the next few weeks, the bond market rallied euphorically while the man who promised that his cabinet would "look like America" announced an economic team that looked like Wall Street, a foreign policy team that resembled Jimmy Carter's, and a raft of other appointments that looked, if not exactly like the Business Council (still a white male bastion), then perhaps like the affluent clientele of an exclusive spa or ski resort.

At the celebrated two-day economic summit in Little Rock in December, more strange new signals started flashing. Clinton advisors encouraged John White, who originally had put together Ross Perot's deficit plan before defecting to the Arkansas governor, to repackage data that *they had possessed for months* to emphasize the impression that the deficit was growing faster than anyone suspected. The president and his advisors also made a public commitment to a strong dollar.[1]

In mid-February, after embarrassing missteps over appointments and the question of gays in the military, the president at last unveiled his economic plan. In a society already filled with forebodings about the future of its economy and political system, the president's stark portrayal of the available policy alternatives touched off a riot of speculation and criticism. But while all the subsequent commentary has undoubtedly heightened many Americans' sense of apprehension, it has done little to clarify what all the shouting is really about.

At first glance, everything appears very simple. As William Kristol and many other Republicans have charged, the rise in income taxes in the highest brackets and the increase in corporation tax rates suggests an abrupt declaration of "class war" on the rich by the traditional party of lower-income Americans.

As so often happens in American politics, appearance and reality diverge. From the standpoint of social equity, it can scarcely be doubted that the Clinton fiscal program differs drastically from anything ever contemplated by Presidents Reagan or Bush. Still, the notion that the plan amounts to class war is absurd on its face. Sometimes one picture is worth a thousand words. Such was the case with the televison shots of Federal Reserve chairman Alan Greenspan and Apple Computer CEO John Sculley sitting next to Hillary Rodham Clinton during the president's speech to Congress. It is no easier to imagine Greenspan and Sculley as class warriors than it is to picture Lloyd Bentsen, Robert Rubin, or Roger Altman in the role of Lenin or Trotsky. And it is impossible to forget the millions of dollars in soft money that flowed to the Democrats in 1992 or the less than convincing plan put forward by the president to curb the influence of lobbyists and political money.

For all the wailing in the upper brackets, the plain fact is that the proposed tax-rate changes are modest indeed. In addition, the plan's own projections show that once the regressive energy tax is fully phased in, it and the extension of the gas tax will provide virtually as much new revenue as the higher income taxes on the wealthy. Furthermore, a plenary share of the proposed new spending is destined directly or indirectly for business, including a variety of subsidies masked, sometimes, by such labels as "defense conversion" or "research." To say this is not to condemn the program—from an equity perspective, it is probably the best we are likely to see. But much more is going on here than anyone has suggested in public.[2]

One more yellow caution flag is in order. In the presidential campaign, candidate Clinton repeatedly objected that Ross Perot's "cold turkey" approach to cutting the deficit would crash the economy by fatally constricting total demand. He was correct. Perot, however, did have a partial answer. The economic simulations that were run to check out his plan's overall impact assumed a substantial devaluation of the dollar. A rise in exports as government spending contracted would have partially compensated for the fall in total demand.[3]

Now, however, the Clinton administration has taken over much of Perot's deficit plan, but not his devaluation. Instead it is trying to persuade the Japanese to boost the value of the yen by 20 percent, a proposal that runs flatly against the current needs of the depressed Japanese economy while bypassing the equally compelling problem of the smaller Asian tigers, which, year after year, run huge export surpluses with the United States.

A year or so down the road, the likely outcome is unpleasant indeed: continued austerity, as exports fail to rise enough to offset the reductions in aggregate demand occasioned by a shrinking budget deficit, with the trade deficit shrinking as the United States grows more slowly than other parts of the world.

This policy package is precisely what the millions of Americans who elected Clinton voted *against*, and what they believe they are avoiding by supporting his plan to reduce the deficit. It is not difficult to imagine their reactions as they discover over the next several years that they were wrong. With their hopes dashed for recovering the "American dream," many are likely to turn to Ross Perot or a Republican supply-sider.

Such reflections may serve to remind us that Hollywood's easy access to the Clinton White House does not guarantee a happy ending to the current imbroglio. Whatever impelled the president to become a born-again deficit hawk in the first place? Could his belated metamorphosis have been predicted by a careful observer of the 1992 campaign? Why, with unemployment so high, is the proposed economic stimulus so feeble? Who is the sizeable investment component of the administration's program designed to help? And why is the administration so concerned with the level of the dollar?

This essay cannot deal in detail with all of these questions. But it can lay some essential groundwork for answering them by carefully retracing the steps by which the Democratic coalition was assembled in the 1992 campaign. Relying on the "investment approach" to party politics I have developed elsewhere, this chapter analyzes the 1992 Democratic campaign. Although the discussion is necessarily somewhat summary, I believe it is fair to say that after one has analyzed the business base of the Clinton campaign, little mystery remains about how or why the deficit supplanted growth in the thinking of the new administration.[4]

A Very Exclusive Party

Any serious analysis of the 1992 Democratic campaign or the new Clinton administration has to begin by acknowledging that the Democratic reconquest of the White House in 1992 represents a culminating moment in a process that stretches back over a decade: the effort by center-right business groups to remake the party in the wake of the triumph of Reaganism. Though the first stirrings of this effort trace back to the Carter years, the most striking shifts occurred after the 1980 debacle.[5]

At that time—and subsequently, for this "right turn" had to be reconfirmed at every election—Democratic leaders could have tried to rally the millions of middle class and poor Americans who were about to suffer the economic reverses that the party—in a vastly different context—was at last willing to discuss in the 1992 campaign. They could have tried, for example, to explain to voters what Reaganomics was really all about: to talk about the years of high interest rates and austerity that the president's plan would entail; the massive export of American jobs that loomed; the steady deterioration of schools, roads, and services that would ensue; the demoralization, crime, and drugs that would mushroom in big cities and, eventually, in whole regions; the true costs of deregulating not only S&Ls but airlines and the banking system; or the swelling tide of money that would corrupt all levels of government and overwhelm other forms of political participation.

For the most part Democratic party leaders did not even try to sound these warnings. Instead, contemplating the real estate boom around Washington and the skyrocketing compensation of America's corporate managers, they decided to compete with the Republicans for funds. Amid much flatulent oratory about finding a "third way" between New Deal and Great Society liberalism—whose programs and formulas certainly needed updating—and what was then a newly self-confident Republican conservatism, the entire spectrum of respectable discussion in the party lurched to the right.[6]

In 1984 and 1988, the party's strategy for the presidential race turned on the pursuit of investor blocs disenchanted by one or another feature of Reaganomics. In 1984 party support among top investors was pretty well limited to investment bankers (led, among others, by two New Yorkers named Robert Rubin and Roger Altman, who flew to Minnesota to press Mondale on the deficit issue shortly before his ill-fated pledge to raise voters' taxes) and urban real estate interests (centered mostly in the Northeast and Midwest). The latter helped smother efforts to have Mondale endorse tax simplification, which would have cost them many of their most important tax breaks. They also strongly championed "fairness," that is, continuing federal aid for mass transit and infrastructure, which automatically put them at loggerheads with the Pentagon for a share of the budget.[7]

In 1988, this conservative, business-led coalition widened appreciably as the investment bankers and real estate interests were joined by many high-tech and other businesses that favored free trade but were increasingly edgy about administration policies that allowed the Japanese to run massive trade surpluses year after year.[8]

At the same time, the party restructured its relations with its (former) mass base. The most critical of these efforts involved its ties with organized labor. In the early 1980s, Democratic National Committee (DNC) chair Charles Manatt worked out an understanding with the AFL-CIO that guaranteed labor representation within the DNC apparatus. Despite criticism from some business elements in the party, the arrangement survived. In due course there came another momentous shift. Congressional Democrats, with timely bipartisan assistance from influential Republicans, applied an old tactic—business and government subsidies to amiably inclined elements of the labor movement—on a grandiose scale. Through the National Endowment for Democracy and other government agencies, enormous subsidies flowed to union leaders for foreign activities associated with the Cold War. By the mid-1980s, the AFL-CIO was spending over $40 million a year on foreign activities—a sum almost equal to its total domestic budget. Approximately 90 percent of this money came from the U.S. government. Revenues on this scale virtually ensure that, in sharp contrast to the 1930s, when declines in dues encouraged several union leaders to split from the moribund and corrupt AFL and organize the CIO, AFL-CIO membership losses can now continue for decades before the leadership will have to face the problem.[9]

The Democratic party leadership also confirmed a longstanding pattern of trying to organize other potential mass political constituents—African Americans, Hispanics and Latinos, women, even environmentalists—along almost Balkan lines. An earlier coauthored work traced in some detail how, in the late 1970s, these emerging social movements restructured in response to the combined pressures of financial exigency, selective press coverage, and political patronage. What had started out as grassroots social movements were now developing more complex organizational structures. At the top were legally incorporated, hierarchically organized institutions dependent for their functioning on expensive lawyers, foundation grants, and steady political patronage. Increasingly tending to define the very real problems of their constituencies in conservative, market-oriented terms, the leaders of most of these institutions rarely considered strategies such as attempting to raise the incomes of the vast majority of underpaid African Americans, Latinos, or women by unionizing them. Instead they sought to function as junior partners, and often as paid advisors, to businesses and the Democratic party. At the same time they refrained from condemning the party's commitment to economic austerity.[10]

Given the party's decision to pursue money, there was no chance of developing a message that would excite a mass audience. The formally organized constituency groups, accordingly, were of immense value to the party. By selectively doing business with their leaders, the Democrats could practice a sort of symbolic mass politics. By drawing on the energies of their core members, the party would acquire a sort of ersatz mass base to replace the millions of voters it was abandoning.

There was a downside. Because the leaders of these groups refrained from criticizing the party's conservative macroeconomic policies, their own demands for access and position could easily be made to look purely self-interested (which, when divorced from any critical stance on common problems, they often were). In the money-driven American political system, direct public exchanges between rival financial groups partake of the logic of a nuclear exchange between superpowers. They are rare; "proxy" wars, or symbolic political struggles between the respective "mass" clientele groups, fill most of the political universe. As a consequence, Republicans and right-wing Democrats, by talking as though it were the clientele groups, rather than the party, that were breaking all records for fundraising and that had pushed Walter Mondale to promise to raise taxes, could fan immense resentment. Also, to the extent that any of these groups preserved any real links with their base, they remained a potential obstacle that could, on occasion, prove startlingly inconvenient. Still a party had at least to look like it wanted a mass base, and these groups were all the Democrats had. Organizing new groups—even promoting voter registration, as opposed to drives to get out the vote of the already registered—risked putting control of the party into the hands of voters again.

In the wake of the 1984 election, many of the party's business interests reckoned that the cost of dealing with several of these groups—notably organized labor (whose pre-primary endorsement of Walter Mondale upset many conservatives), Jesse Jackson's "rainbow coalition," and various defense and foreign policy groups (including some that intermittently claimed strong business support)—was still too high. Accordingly, they organized a new group to push the party even further to the right. Calling itself the Democratic Leadership Council (DLC), the group was led in public mostly by southern politicians. No one, however, should be fooled: it was financed extensively from New York—not least by investment houses—and by defense concerns and utilities.[11]

As the 1988 race demonstrated, there were few, if any, real conflicts of interest between the national party and the DLC. Not only had the national party long been self-consciously moving right, but in the mid-1980s, the wonderful world of so-called soft money opened up for it, pushing it even further to the right. Soft money—donations given nominally to state and local parties for purposes unconnected to federal races but in fact closely connected to national parties and particularly to presidential campaigns—was completely unregulated at the federal level until 1991, when the Federal Election Commission (FEC) decided that whatever was spent had to be reported. State regulation was, as ever, minimal. Not surprisingly, affluent Americans and corporations quickly seized on this loophole to eviscerate laws regulating the size of campaign contributions. Contributions of $100,000 or more were common. The result was evident in the 1988 election. Michael Dukakis selected as his running mate Texas senator Lloyd Bentsen, whose fundraising prowess qualified him as the Six Million Dollar Man of American politics, and ran essentially even with the fabled Bush money machine in total funds raised.

Preparing for '92

Following the 1988 loss, Ron Brown took over the DNC. Dissolving the doubts of skeptics, who initially suspected the Patton, Boggs & Blow partner of sharing Jesse Jackson's goals, Brown worked closely with congressional Democratic leaders and business groups to help raise millions of dollars for the party, and many millions more in soft money.[12]

These efforts coincided with a series of economic changes—the collapse of real estate values in some parts of the country, the increasingly hopeless condition of many major cities, and the lagged effects of the 1986 Tax Act, which eliminated several important real estate tax breaks—that had major effects on one of the Democrats' core constituencies in the 1980s. Amid signals by the Bush administration that it might be open to restoring some of the tax breaks and moves by leading American developers into Europe (which assuredly changes their calculation regarding the potential role of military force and the U.S. budget), major real estate interests began backing out of the party. As those interests were the heart of the Democrats "fairness" coalition, all mention of that virtue vanished from the vocabulary of the Democratic party along with most references to the poor and the cities.[13]

Though an almost invisible seam remained in regard to organized labor, by 1992 the biggest remaining difference between the DNC and the DLC may well have been the middle initials. Brown had an easy time (and many allies) in persuading Jesse Jackson not to run. No one in the party rose to rebuke him after his harsh attacks on Jerry Brown's criticisms of money's role in American politics. On at least some occasions, the party appears also to have sought to charge poor farm groups for the right to address the Democratic platform committee![14]

The collapse of the real estate constituency within the Party—I mean interests on the order of the *Forbes* 400 list of richest Americans; smaller fry are of course scattered everywhere among the FEC contributor lists—explains why the truly sophisticated response to Nebraska senator Bob Kerrey's celebrated retort in the primaries to Jerry Brown ("Are you saying that I am bought and paid for?") might well be, in the end: "No, and so much the worse for your campaign."

Of all the Democratic primary candidates, Kerrey's pattern of contributions from the sample of top business figures I analyzed most resembles Mondale's and Dukakis's: knots of urban real estate magnates, investment bankers (including, according to one newspaper account, Paul Volcker, now at J. D. Wolfensohn & Co.), a handful of oilmen, plus some Hollywood money. There just were not enough of these types, however, to float a mild center-left campaign with a serious thrust on health care—an issue guaranteed to bring down on the head of anyone who raised it a mass of well-financed objurgation. As a consequence, Kerrey looked around hastily for other issues to emphasize and made the fatal choice of international trade. While also popular with voters, who in some polls favor restricting imports of foreign consumer products by a margin of 71 to 22 percent (with 7 percent having no answer or no opinion), the issue was a core concern of multinational industry and finance in both parties.[15] After another fusillade of bad press notices, Kerrey began flailing. On some days he dramatized himself as a quasi-protectionist hockey goalie; on another, a free trader (who lets the puck go by?), and so on. Almost inevitably, the campaign collapsed, leaving behind a large debt.

Senator Tom Harkin's campaign was another that suffered from the collapse of the realtors' bloc within the party. In the very earliest stages of the race, prominent developers within the party touted his candidacy. Their support, however, never materialized. (One initially vocal developer whose contributions I made a special effort to trace turned up as a contributor to Tsongas and Clinton, raising the question of whether the true aim of the early talk about Harkin was to weaken Cuomo by bringing another perceived liberal into the race.)

Harkin compounded his difficulty by making two grave mistakes. First, as some critics promptly noted, while the Iowa-based head of one of the largest insurance companies in the United States and other insurance industry executives contributed to his campaign, Harkin dodged the health care issue that Senator Kerrey had so bravely raised.

Second, the candidate and his staff confused running a campaign with holding a seance. In 1992, it was not enough to invoke the shade of Franklin D. Roosevelt (or more precisely, of "traditional Democratic values") or to assure voters that, save perhaps on insurance-related issues, the Iowa liberal was indeed "on the side of" average Americans. To reach an increasingly jaundiced electorate requires not indirect discourse and symbols, but plain speaking on the handful of major issues that really matter to people—issues that Jerry Brown, Paul Tsongas, and Ross Perot addressed in different ways.

Harkin instead usually confined himself to an inside game increasingly dependent on the official union movement, which is now widely unpopular with its own members. The political-action-committee (PAC) support that Tsongas criticized him for in the early primaries never amounted to much, so that Harkin had almost no money to use to transmit his unstable and somewhat Aesopian message. (It cannot have helped that the first primary outside of his home state occurred in New Hampshire, one of the most strongly anti-union states in the country.) Around the time he withdrew, 75 percent of the population was telling pollsters that they did not know enough about him to have an opinion.[16]

Running out of money, by contrast, was one problem that Bill Clinton never had to face. Like Michael Dukakis four years before, but unlike Walter Mondale, the Arkansas governor began the race with strong support from businesses in his own state, including Tyson Foods, Murphy Oil, Wal-Mart (where his wife Hillary sat on the board and whose owners, the Walton family, were almost all campaign contributors); giant Beverly Enterprises, a large private provider of health care; and the investment banking, oil, and gas interests associated with the Stephens family.

It may be sheer coincidence that back in 1976 the latter were also close to Jimmy Carter as he began his run for the White House. But the Clinton campaign assuredly bore a striking resemblance to the earlier Carter effort—in which a moderately conservative (former) member of the Trilateral Commission with some well disciplined center-left humanitarian impulses ran from the periphery of America supported by internationally oriented investment bankers and their allies in Wall Street, Washington, and the press.

In 1992, however, most of American business was far more conservative than it was in 1976, when, it should be recalled, the much **more** liberal Morris Udall could find important business supporters in addition to his labor backing. As a consequence, Clinton's candidacy centered far more on investment bankers than Carter's did.

Partners from giant Goldman, Sachs, for example, which, with the cloud that settled over Salomon Brothers, now ranks as probably the strongest of all the investment houses, were among the earliest to begin raising funds for Clinton. Members of the firm—whose leading figure, Robert Rubin, once compared the Glass-Steagall Act to the Magna Carta, only half in jest—contributed far more than $100,000 to the campaign and raised many times that amount. Another early fundraiser among investment bankers was Roger Altman, vice chair of the Blackstone Group, who had known Clinton in college and who is reported to have renewed ties after encountering Hillary Clinton on the board of the Children's Television Workshop, producer of the highly acclaimed "Sesame Street." Peter Peterson, Blackstone's chair and husband of Joan Cooney, chair of the executive committee of the Children's Television Workshop, was another early contributor. So were many other prominent investment bankers from Greenwich Capital Resources and other large houses.[17]

With the obvious though very important exception of Glass-Steagall and related financial regulatory legislation, such interests differ only marginally from the internationalists at the core of the Bush coalition with respect to foreign and domestic policy. More than a few—including Goldman and Blackstone—have Japanese partners (though Sumitomo, Goldman's partner, has only a minority stake). Together with the myriads of Washington lobbyists for U.S. and foreign multinationals who contributed heavily to the campaign (and who honeycombed the campaign organization), they virtually guaranteed what in any case rapidly became obvious: that the Clinton campaign accepted free trade and an open world economy as its fundamental strategic premise.

The campaign also fully accepted what the foreign policy community likes to call the "responsibilities" of being the world's only superpower, although only someone aware of Senator Sam Nunn's early endorsement of Clinton or a person paying close attention to the very striking contributions rolling in from aircraft and other defense producers could have been sure of that fact at the time.[18] By convention time, the Clinton camp was actually leapfrogging the Republicans on the need to bear the superpower's burden, with volleys of neo-Wilsonian rhetoric suggesting that the Bush administration (which averaged an armed intervention every twelve months in office) was not aggressive enough in promoting freedom, human rights, and democracy around the world.

The Clinton Difference

What, then, distinguished the Clinton effort from the multinationally oriented Bush administration? At first glance, the response is, not much.

Table 7-1   Party and Industry in the 1992 Election ($N=948$)

Industries significantly above the mean in support of Clinton	Percentage contributing	Significance level
Tobacco ($N=4$)	50	.20[a]
Oil and gas ($N=65$)	28	.18
Capital intensive exporters ($N=7$)	43	.17[a]
Aircraft ($N=13$)	54	.00[a]
Computers ($N=16$)	38	.12[a]
Transportation ($N=33$)	33	.08
Investment banking ($N=50$)	46	.00

Source: Calculated from FEC data, which includes individual contributions, soft money, and PAC donations through the last week of October 1992.

Note: Percentage of firms ($N=948$) contributing to the Bush campaign was 55 percent and the percentage of firms contributing to the Clinton campaign was 21 percent.
   The text cautions about the utilities industry (not shown above).

[a] Expected value of cell in chi-square is less than five. Warning of low power. Significance levels reported in such cases are results of Fisher's Exact Test.

But this is too clever by half. The data presented in Table 7-1 show the sectors that contributed disproportionately to the Clinton campaign. In the light of the campaign's rhetoric and proposed policy initiatives, those data reveal an interesting pattern. With one exception, the sectors that backed Clinton disproportionately appear to share several characteristics. On one hand, like the mainline multinationals that dominated the Bush coalition, they support an open world economy. On the other hand, in contrast to the "borderless world" celebrants on the Republican side, they all have some direct, crucial tie that links them closely to the American state. The aircraft companies clearly depend on the government in an almost unique way. The ties to government of the investment houses (whose Glass-Steagall privileges are currently up for grabs in the GATT negotiations over foreign banking rights) are equally clear, as are those of the oil and gas industry, transportation, and tobacco.[19]

   One might well ask about the utilities industry, which is not listed in the table but which certainly has a peculiarly strong dependence on the state. Here reality may be sending a message: By conventional standards, the results for utilities (29 percent and $N=31$, with a .28 level of significance) just miss qualifying for the table. This is one industry that may in fact be affected by the data in the FEC's final report, which will not be available until late in 1993. As a practical matter, I have reckoned it as a part of Clinton's coalition at least since he added Al Gore to the ticket. In my 1988 study, support for Gore's presidential bid from this sector was strong, and the Tennessee senator has long been identified with technological issues of concern to telecommunications and utilities.

The one instance where the condition of dependency on the state appears to break down, referred to in the table as "capital intensive exporters" (a portmanteau term for an industry that includes Xerox, Honeywell, Kodak, and similar firms), is an exception that proves the rule. These are firms that in several cases (Xerox, Kodak) have made strenuous and sometimes noisy efforts to reinvent themselves in the face of foreign (usually Japanese) competitors. They are looking for an ally in the Clinton administration to help with subsidies and market penetration.

All of this is to say that the Clinton coalition is exactly what several of the executives of these firms have said in public: a bloc of businesses that are prepared to countenance the public rejection of laissez faire because they need the American state to work. Given the exceptional dependence of their businesses upon that state, they cannot simply go elsewhere if the decline of the United States in the current world economy continues unabated.[20]

In the best known cases of industrial support for Clinton, calculations along these lines were clearly operative. Because Table 7-1 refers to large firms and relies on sectoral assignments derived from the Commerce Department's Standard Industrial Classification series, it does not contain an entry for "high technology." Thus no statistics in the table directly reflect the collective endorsement of Clinton by John Young of Hewlett-Packard, John Sculley of Apple Computer, and other leading figures in the industry. (The entry for computers assures us that we are not seeing ghosts, but the fit is not perfect.) These business executives expressly rejected claims by critics in and out of the Bush administration that all would be well if everything were left to the invisible hand. Indeed, in the mid-1980s, after the Reagan administration had declined to press ahead on recommendations for a more active role for the government in what has come to be known as industrial policy, Young complained. (Young chaired the President's Commission on Industrial Competitiveness.) When the administration still declined to move, Young and like-minded CEOs established their own privately funded Council on Competitiveness to promote their ideas for change in business-government relations. One of the consultants they hired was Ira Magaziner, viewed by most of the business community as a virtual Jacobin and a prominent supporter of Bill Clinton for president. Eventually, of course, a large section of the high-tech industry came noisily over to the cause of the Arkansas governor.[21]

The Clinton campaign's now celebrated interest in "managed trade"

clearly derives from similar pressures. Certain parts of the computer industry are thoroughly transnational, to the point of agitating against national actions in favor of the industry. But other sections of it and of
related industries, including portions of semiconductors and most of the
software industry, have concerns that only action on a truly large scale can
relieve. Many firms, for example, view themselves as pitted against "Japan, Inc." Up against what they perceive as the resources of an entire
country, these producers strongly champion the view that laissez faire is
obsolete. Many, in addition, believe that timely government action—for
example, on education—would also assist their industries by widening
their markets or improving the skills of their workforce. Software producers, in addition, are acutely aware that the position of English as a worldwide second language (and thus the world's premier software language) is
bound up with the long-term position of the United States in the world
economy.

In sharp contrast to firms in older industries such as steel or textiles,
however, most of these firms import components. Often they also sell
abroad, so that they continue to distrust high-tariff policies. At the Little
Rock economic summit in December 1992, for example, Apple's John
Sculley, a strong promoter of both Clinton and "competitiveness" initiatives, flatly ruled out protectionism. But with the continuing growth of the
Japanese trade surplus and the persisting overvaluation of the dollar relative to the rest of Asia, these firms and many others increasingly have
come to accept the practical necessity for managing trade with the export
oriented economies of that region, especially Japan. They also want what
the Clinton campaign promised to give them and what his proposed budget, if enacted, will deliver: substantial programs of government subsidies
through existing cabinet departments and a civilian counterpart to the
Defense Department's Advanced Research Projects Agency (DARPA).[22]

As far back as 1984, carefully superintended programs along these
lines were winning acceptance from prominent Democratic investment
bankers. By now, on the top rungs of American business, as well as in the
military, few dispute that economics is as vital to national security as any
defense treaty or military base. Within the part of the business community
that was sympathetic to Clinton (and a few other candidates, such as
Tsongas and Perot, who raised similar issues), there is also curiosity about
the advantages of "organized capitalism" on what is imagined to be the
German or Japanese model. To these groups, Clinton's promise of an
"economic security council" (as the new National Economic Council was
referred to during the campaign) on par with the National Security Council appeared about as dangerously radical as the program to restructure
the U.S. military advanced by Clinton's early champion, Georgia senator
Sam Nunn. And the celebrated Clinton tax proposals, calling for a very
small rise in their taxes, looked more like political cover for new programs
that would benefit them, first and foremost.

Few Americans, however, are familiar with the strong, top-down state structures evolved by foreign business groups to catch up with their more advanced rivals in the Anglo-Saxon countries. As a consequence, all many Americans could see in these and similar proposals was the break with laissez faire.

To hard-pressed voters, who knew little and understood even less about Alan Greenspan, the Federal Reserve, or exchange rate policy, but who were increasingly anxious about the maddeningly slow pace of the economic recovery and saw all around them signs that the United States was declining in the world economy, all this meant only one thing: relief, something at last that would benefit an average person.

This perception the Clinton campaign fanned assiduously by all sorts of devices. It put out front not Rubin or Altman, but a flock of liberal former Vietnam-era protesters destined for second-tier slots in the administration (or no positions at all). For a long time the Clinton camp also talked around the fact that the candidate had flatly rejected a proposal advanced by more than a hundred economists for a temporary two-year job creation bill, while excitedly promising that he would boost economic growth in the long run by increasing public investment in education, infrastructure, and the environment. Eventually, as even some bond traders began calling for a modest stimulus, Clinton relented. The issue was used with telling effect against Bush. After the election, it was scaled back to a vanishing point and then defeated in Congress.[23]

The candidate and his economic advisors advanced an economic plan filled with optimistic figures suggesting that Clinton could halve the deficit in his first term while implementing a tax cut for the middle class. They also promised somehow to reform the health care system, while, almost uniquely among the Democratic candidates, collecting substantial campaign contributions from parts of it.[24] And, very quietly, the Clinton campaign lined up with trial attorneys, whose campaign to stop tort reform is now running in high gear.

This mix of appeals was probably the most brazen conflation of electoral *Dichtung* and investor bloc *Wahrheit* since "read my lips," but it worked. In the beginning, when he trailed far behind others, including Jerry Brown, in the polls, Clinton was built up massively by the press—which is, after all, yet another mostly multinationally oriented industry for which the continued economic decline of the United States spells unique problems. (The *New York Times* may eventually flee New York for Connecticut. But even free trade with Mexico will not afford it a major share of the market south of the border.)

In Clinton's one moment of maximum danger—the Gennifer Flowers scandal—the combination of money and favorable press coverage, along with the Clintons' own television performance, saved the day. With their candidate on the ropes, investment bankers from Goldman and other houses organized a gigantic dinner at the Sheraton in New York only a few days before the New Hampshire primary. The affair raised more than $750,000. No less importantly, as one investment banker observed, "that dinner signaled to a lot of people that some very smart money was behind him. It was critical to Clinton's campaign." [25] In sharp contrast to the treatment meted out to Gary Hart, all but the yellow press put the story behind it, while proclaiming that a second-place finish would keep Clinton viable.

Clinton's strategy for winning the Democratic primaries ultimately came down to a financial counterpart of the Russian strategy that turned back Napoleon: Keep spending until your opponents run out of money.

Sometimes, the resulting irony was almost painful. Massachusetts senator Paul Tsongas, for example, entered the race as a self-declared "probusiness liberal." If one wanted a tag line for his effort, the "Route 128 view" of American politics might do. Both the campaign's definition of America's economic problems and the most controversial parts of its proposed solutions (along with much of its early money that was not raised from ethnic Greek businesses) originated from around the famous high-technology highway.

Tsongas himself had served as a director of a number of major New England concerns. Among these were Boston Edison and several high-tech firms, including Wang Labs and a subsidiary of the highly regarded Thermo Electron, founded by George Hatsapoulos, a Greek-American MIT graduate who was then serving as vice chair of the American Business Conference.

Hatsapoulos has produced a stream of papers (some coauthored with Lawrence Summers, an economist from Harvard who now serves as undersecretary of the Treasury for international affairs, and Paul Krugman of MIT) on the cost of capital as a factor in U.S. economic growth. In the campaign, the senator often said that he took the capital problem very seriously. A capital gains tax cut for long-term holdings was the remedy he proposed, along with a further tilt by government in the direction of business, a sharp reduction of the federal deficit, and sweeping education reforms.

By the usual standards of American politics all this should have resulted in a shower of money for his campaign. But it did not, for the simple reason that Clinton had already cornered the market. After what was usually said to be a surprise victory in New Hampshire (although Tsongas had been campaigning in the state for almost a year and, by concentrating his funds on a neighboring state where he was already well known, was not badly outspent), his campaign coffers were almost empty. Though some money streamed in, he had to scramble to line up television time in the multistate media buyouts in the South and Midwest. Clinton, in the meantime, with most party organizations already behind him, deployed his mighty bankroll. As his affluent backers looked the other way, he denounced Tsongas in almost populist tones as unsympathetic to ordinary Americans, an enemy of social security, and an advocate of a regressive gas tax. Tsongas's efforts collapsed, and turnout generally declined, while blue-collar workers, African Americans, and lower-income voters who did vote cast ballots for their "champion." [26]

That left only Jerry Brown. To the amazement of virtually everyone, Brown, whose refusal to take donations larger than $100 was driving party leaders to distraction, gamely hung on. In Michigan, the leadership of the United Auto Workers Union (though not all locals) lined up behind Clinton, who favored the North American Free Trade Agreement that the union opposed. Brown, who opposed the pact, pointed up the hollowness of Clinton's populism and did well. In Connecticut, he briefly panicked the establishments of both parties by winning.

The showdown came in the New York primary. Here Clinton's money afforded him almost complete domination of the airwaves. This turned out to be decisive when Brown began promoting a regressive "flat tax" plan that he appears to have hoped would win him plaudits on the right. Instead, Clinton focused his attack on the plan, thus positioning himself once again to Brown's left. The media played along. By the time the *New York Times* eventually gave Brown's plan some serious notice, the primary had passed. Before the primary, however, the *Times* had virtually nothing good to say—indeed, it had surely been many years since the *New York Times* had been so solicitous about the progressivity of income taxes.

Clinton's victory in New York effectively clinched the nomination. Almost up to convention time, however, rumors ran rife that one or another Democrat was considering an eleventh-hour challenge. In the end, however, none took the plunge.

Shapes of Things to Come

As a political coalition, the new Clinton administration resembles the Seattle Space Needle. At the top are well-appointed quarters nominally open to all but in fact occupied by those who can afford them. (The Associated Press claims that there are more millionaires among Clinton's top advisors than among Reagan's or Bush's.)[27]

The supporting structure, however, is thin indeed. Within the business community, it consists essentially of the relatively small group of firms that really want the American state to work and that are prepared to pay very modestly to make it happen. Alongside these firms—whose personnel directly control most of the levers of economic policy in the administration—are grouped the remnants of the now heavily subsidized official labor movement and the various constituency organizations that the Democrats have cultivated over the last couple of decades. The electoral base, as many have noted, is exiguous: Clinton was elected with just 43 percent of the total vote—the third lowest winning total since 1828, when something like a modern system of presidential selection began evolving. Another way of putting the point is even more revealing. In terms of the winning candidate's percentage of the total potential electorate (including nonvoters), 1992 ranks with the election of 1912 at the very bottom.[28]

Historically, closing budget deficits is among the most perilous acts a regime can undertake. While there is, as yet, no reason to expect that the tumescent American deficit will have the explosive consequences of the red ink that preceded the French Revolution or the collapse of the Second Empire, there is little doubt that the Clinton plan represents the existing American political system's last chance.

As this essay goes to press, President Clinton has announced the appointment of a special panel, chaired by his wife, Hillary Rodham Clinton, to address the health care question. While it deliberates, the United States appears likely to become involved in several more armed interventions around the globe, besides its current actions in Somalia and Iraq.

With the former Soviet Union reeling from its encounter with "free enterprise" in laboratory pure form, and, in the distance, faint rumblings coming once again from Mexico, the Clinton administration appears to be walking a tightrope between domestic and foreign affairs, and between the hopes of its exultant voters and the demands of its investors.

Will the rope snap? The barometer suggests the approach of political winds of hurricane force. Investment banker Peter Peterson and former senators Tsongas and Rudman are sounding the trumpets for their Concord Coalition, a lobbying group for swifter balancing of the budget. New Republican groups are stirring. Ross Perot is organizing United We Stand and has endorsed the balanced budget amendment he formerly derided. Though some of these organizers sometimes say nice things about Clinton's budget plan, all appear to be determined to force much larger budget cuts. The inner meaning of all this activity is clear: as the crisis deepens, various business groups are reaching out to organize portions of the middle classes most sympathetic to spending cuts and budgetary restriction.

No similar mobilization of labor or other groups is underway, and one may doubt that the business groups that now dominate the Democratic Party will be any more keen to mobilize them in the 1990s than they were in the 1980s. Accordingly, as the next wave of well-funded "populist" appeals crashes over the U.S. political system, two facts seem clear. First, the political system is entering a new stage of disintegration, with few parallels in American history. Second, as huge areas of the world reintegrate into the world economy they left in 1917 or 1945, pressures on the average American's living standards are likely to grow rapidly while the Clinton administration's programs will work at best incrementally. As a consequence, in the next few years the United States faces an economic crisis of major proportions, in which the demands of investors for austerity and of voters for relief will collide head on. The Clinton fiscal program expresses precisely this tension.

Notes

For very helpful discussions I am grateful to James Galbraith, David Hale, Robert Johnson, Alain Parguez, and the editors of this volume. I should also like to thank Walter Dean Burnham for showing me a draft of his own manuscript on the 1992 election; the members of seminars at York University (Toronto) and Swarthmore College, who patiently endured early versions of the paper, and Benjamin Page, who quickly read a draft. I am also grateful to the John W. McCormack Institute of the University of Massachusetts, Boston, for assistance in defraying computer costs and to Goresh Hosangady for invaluable help with the statistics. The staff of the Federal Election Commission, as ever, was unfailingly helpful, as were Ellen Miller and the staff of the Center for Responsive Politics. Max Holland and Jeri Scofield also supplied valuable material.

1. On the fact that Clinton and his aides were well aware of the problem during the campaign, see the *Boston Globe*, January 10, 1993, and the *New York Times*, of the same day. On the dollar, see the *Financial Times*, December 16, 1992. Note that against many European currencies, the U.S. dollar might well be slightly under-valued (as of February 1993).

2. For the projections, see Office of the President of the United States, *A Vision of Change For America*, February 17, 1993, 139. While the oil industry is almost certainly exaggerating the amount of money the energy taxes will raise, it would not be surprising if the administration turns out to have underestimated their yield. This would tend to make the plan more regressive.

   Note that the discussion of the Clinton fiscal plan refers to his original pro-posal. This will no doubt be modified in the course of passage. If I understand the bargaining strategy, virtually all the changes will be in a more conservative direc-tion. These will detract still more from the program's fiscal thrust and emphasize the essentially conservative nature of the plan.

3. This information comes directly from a distinguished economist who went over the plan before it became public. On the general problem of reducing the deficit, see Robert Blecker, *Beyond the 'Twin Deficits'* (Armonk, N.Y.: M. E. Sharpe, 1992).

4. See Thomas Ferguson, "Party Competition and Industrial Structure: The Invest-ment Theory of Political Parties in Historical Perspective," in *Research in Political Economy*, ed. Paul Zarembka, vol. 6 (Greenwich, Conn.: JAI Press, 1983); Fergu-son, "Industrial Structure and Party Competition in the New Deal," *Sociological Perspectives* 34 (Winter 1991): 496-498, and my "Deduced and Abandoned: Ra-tional Expectations, the Investment Theory of Political Parties and the Myth of the Median Voter," in William Crotty, ed., *Political Parties in an Age of Change* (Washington, D.C.: Political Organizations and Parties Section, American Politi-cal Science Assocation, in press).

5. See, among many sources, Thomas Ferguson and Joel Rogers, *Right Turn: The Decline of the Democrats and the Future of American Politics* (New York: Hill and Wang, 1986).

6. Ibid.

7. See Ferguson and Rogers, *Right Turn*, 150 and the appendix, which uses statisti-cal evidence to rule out some alternative hypotheses about the real estate in-vestors.

8. See Ferguson, "An Unbearable Lightness of Being—Party and Industry in the 1988 Democratic Primary," in *Do Elections Matter?* 2d ed., ed. Benjamin Ginsberg and Alan Stone (Armonk, N.Y.: M. E. Sharpe, 1991), 237-254. This shows that Democratic primary candidates who received disproportionately high rates of do-nations from real estate interests received disproportionately low rates of dona-tions from aircraft companies and vice versa—a striking finding.

I lack the space to analyze the direct responses of voters in 1984 or 1988. Though many critics of the investment approach seem to believe that it implies passive voters, in fact it does not. On the contrary, I essentially accept the analysis of voters' reasons for casting their ballots developed in Stanley Kelley, Jr., *Interpreting Elections* (Princeton: Princeton University Press, 1983) or John Geer, who has continued Kelley's work in a notable series of recent papers. See his "The Electorate's Partisan Evaluations: Evidence of a Continuing Democratic Edge," *Public Opinion Quarterly* 55 (Summer 1991): 218-231, and "New Deal Issues and the American Electorate, 1952-88," *Political Behavior* 14 (1992): 45-65. Geer's "What Do Open Ended Questions Measure?" *Public Opinion Quarterly* 52 (1988): 365-371 and "Do Open-Ended Questions Measure 'Salient' Issues?" *Public Opinion Quarterly* 55 (1991): 360-370, are important replies to some common criticisms of the method.

The interpretation of their findings, however, might alter somewhat. For example, both Kelley and Geer emphasize how badly the Democrats were hurt by the loss of their identification as the party of prosperity. From an investment standpoint, what needs explaining is why the party kept offering only conservative economic messages—which the voters kept rejecting. (Note that Mondale in 1984 offered little but a tax rise, while Reagan at least talked about growth and was riding a huge political business cycle.) That some voters are influenced by racial or religious considerations is also no point against the investment approach—such issues became significant in these elections in no small part because conservative Democratic elites blocked cross-cutting economic appeals.

I would also emphasize the social character of voters' perceptions and "theories" about candidates and elections. Recognizing more explicitly that these are the result of processes of social discussion somewhat alters the interpretation that comes most readily to mind when reading Kelley or Geer. In particular, one perhaps can understand that it is not at all contradictory to agree with them that voters had "good reasons" individually for voting as they did in 1992, but that viewed as a whole, the 1992 transit from Reagan-Bush to Clinton also represents a broad move from illusion to fantasy. To see this, however, no amount of individual inquiries will suffice. One must also characterize the collective deliberative processes. Interesting starts in this regard are Donald Granberg and Soren Holmberg, *The Political System Matters* (New York: Cambridge University Press, 1988) and Lance Bennett *The Governing Crisis* (New York: St. Martin's, 1992).

In regard to 1992, what was on most voters' minds seems clear enough. This essay goes to press before the National Election Survey for 1992 is released. The consortium of polls that banded together to conduct election day exit polls also appears to be notably slow in releasing data (while they make their findings available to those who can afford to pay for them). But Gary Langer, "Clinton Reclaims the Center—But It Remains Wary," ABC News Briefing Paper: The 1992 Exit Poll," November 18, 1992 (updating a paper of November 6) reports that 42 percent of voters identified the economy as the most important issue in their vote. The next two choices named by large numbers of voters, the deficit (named by 21 percent) and health care (20 percent), are obviously economic in a broad sense. From an electoral standpoint, Bill Clinton did not win the election; George Bush lost it.

9. See the discussion in Ferguson and Rogers, *Right Turn*, 63-66, chap. V, and 198-200. See also Ferguson and Rogers, "Corporate Coalitions in the 1980 Campaign," in *The Hidden Election*, ed. Ferguson and Rogers (New York: Pantheon, 1981), 21-24.

Note that a few days after the 1992 election, two major unions, the United Auto Workers and the American Federation of State, County, and Municipal Employees, effectively pulled the rug out from under the coalition for single payer ("Canadian style") health insurance—a step that both common sense and well connected insiders indicated was related to the ascent of the new chief executive. See the editorial in the *Nation*, December 7, 1992, 1. Along with its highly touted program of subsidies to high-tech industries (discussed below), the new administration has also announced special programs to aid very highly unionized sectors: automobiles and construction. See the *Frankfurter Allgemeine Zeitung*, February 24, 1993, 15.

10. Ferguson and Rogers, *Right Turn*, 53-57, 70-73. I fear that most of those writing on "new social movements" in both the United States and Europe do not understand that the willingness of such groups not to agitate against austerity is a major factor in accounting for their acceptability within the establishments of various countries.

11. A good study of the DLC is William Crotty, "Who Needs Two Republican Parties?" in *The Democrats Must Lead*, ed. James M. Burns, William Crotty, Lois L. Duke, and Lawrence D. Longley (Boulder, Colo.: Westview, 1992), 66-70. On the Northern financing, see, *inter alia*, Paul Starobin, "An Affair to Remember?" *National Journal*, January 16, 1993, 120-122.

12. See Lawrence Longley, "The National Democratic Party Can Lead," in *Democrats Must Lead*, ed. Burns et. al., 29-55.

13. Compare the percentages for 1984 in Ferguson and Rogers, *Right Turn*, appendix, and Ferguson, "Unbearable Lightness," 243, with the nonentry for real estate in Table 7-1 of this chapter. As explained below (note 19), the real estate entries in the table relate to individuals, and all come from the *Forbes* 400 lists. They may, accordingly, be compared directly.

In chapter 9 of his *The Power Elite and the State* (New York: Aldine de Gruyter, 1990), G. William Domhoff claimed that an analysis of campaign contributions in the 1936 election by one of his students ran counter to my work on the New Deal. He also argued that *Right Turn*'s analysis of 1984 data, according to which real estate and investment banks disproportionately supported the Democrats, confounded ethnic and economic factors. In both these sectors, he suggested, Jewish Americans were represented in large numbers, and these tend to favor Democrats.

My "Industrial Structure and Party Competition in the New Deal" showed in detail that his claims about my New Deal work were untenable and that the campaign finance data for 1936 strongly confirm my earlier conclusions. In regard to the 1984 case, his analysis of individual contribution slipped past our point that our conclusions rested upon an analysis of both individual and PAC contributions; the latter cannot possibly be written off as purely individual, or, accordingly, ethnically based.

The real estate results for 1992, in addition, are powerful, and quite devastate views that the industry was ethnically driven. The Bush administration's relations with American Jews were rocky indeed—far more so than Reagan's. Yet real estate fell out altogether from the ranks of industries disproportionately supporting the Democrats. While I am sure the industry changed between 1988 and 1992, no plausible "circulation of elites" can account for this; the industry really changed its politics.

While I think these new results are dispositive for the cases at issue, there is no reason why weak ethnic effects, along the lines of the second order regional effects my New Deal study identified, should not also sometimes be present. But, as the varying percentages of industry contributions across elections and candidates should caution us, slow-changing factors like ethnicity are unlikely to drive free enterprise economies. They are more likely to register strongly in the mass electorate, though even there I believe most voting analysts underestimate the influence of economics because they so rarely test directly for economic influences other than social class.

    The most obvious place for regional effects to show in the 1992 data is in the contributions to Clinton. I therefore tested for South/non-South differences, and found none at all. This underscores the point made earlier about northern support for the DLC.

14. Credible representatives of such groups have made this claim privately.

15. See, for example, the breakdown in the *New York Times* poll of June 17-20, 1992, for the import question. The *Times* poll of July 8-11 indicates that 55 percent of the respondents described the trade agreement with Mexico as a "bad idea," versus 27 percent who thought it was a "good idea."

    For what follows on the primary (aside from the discussion of Clinton), see my "The Democrats Deal for Dollars," *The Nation*, April 13, 1992, 475-478. The newspaper account linking Paul Volcker (and Warren Buffett) to Senator Bob Kerrey's campaign comes from the *Boston Globe*, February 16, 1992. Note that Kerrey, in response to his critics, took pains to say that he generally favored an open economy.

    As explained in note 19, the statistical results reported in Table 7-1 are for the Clinton-Bush race only, *not* the primaries.

16. For Harkin, including the poll figure, see my "Democrats Deal for Dollars."

17. For Altman, Hillary Clinton, and the Children's Television Workshop, see *Boston Globe*, January 10, 1993. The Glass-Steagall Act, incidentally, passed early in Franklin Roosevelt's first term. It separated investment from commercial banking.

18. For Nunn's early endorsement, see Starobin, "An Affair," 121.

19. See my "By Invitation Only: Party Competition and Industrial Structure in the 1988 Election," *Socialist Review* 19 (October-December 1989): 73-103. See also William Greider, *Who Will Tell The People?* (New York: Simon and Schuster, 1992), chap. 12, for an extension of this analysis, with much useful supporting detail. On the multinationals and Bush in the 1992 election specifically, see Ferguson, "Money and Destiny in the 1992 Election: Who Bought Your Candidate and Why," *The Nation*, April 6, 1992, 442-443.

    Table 7-1 has been compiled along the lines of Ferguson, "Industrial Structure and Party Competition in the New Deal," the appendix to *Right Turn*, and my two studies of 1988 mentioned above. Like the 1988 statistical study, however, the sample size is vastly larger than that for *Right Turn*. It includes 1,945 individual entries from 948 "firms" (when that term includes large individual investors, as explained in "Industrial Structure and Party Competition"). Although readers seeking detailed discussions of why the sample is constructed the way it is will want to refer to these studies (and my essay on "Money and Politics" in Godfrey Hodgson, ed., *Handbooks to the Modern World--The United States*, vol. 2 (New York: Facts on File, 1992), 1060-1084, which describes the limitations of existing data on campaign finance), the general ideas are these: In sharp contrast to virtually all other election studies, my research includes individual contributions and soft money as well as PAC contributions (which for Bush and Clinton in 1992 were relevant only as sources of soft money channeled through the parties, since both candidates made the grand but empty gesture of refusing PAC donations to their formal campaign accounts). The general procedure is to compile a systematic sample of top officers of firms at the apex of the American economic pyramid—the largest 200 *Fortune* industrials, the top 20 commercial banks, the 15 largest insurance firms, and so on, from the *Fortune* service list, but also the largest firms on Wall Street, which do not necessarily appear on these other lists, and the *Forbes* 400 list of the richest Americans for the year preceding the election. Then, by hand—the only way it can really be done—the individual and soft money contributions are pulled out of the Federal Election Commission files, along with contributions from their firms.

This data is then analyzed. Typically the procedure is to identify industries (or other groupings, including sets of firms) that aid various candidates disproportionately. The typical test involves chi-square tests in which particular industries are tested against the others for a statistically significant difference in the rates of contribution to a particular candidate. As discussed in my "Industrial Structure and Party Competition in the New Deal," these procedures need to be carefully interpreted; in particular, I would call attention to two facts. First, non-contributors are left in to avoid an impression of inflated (primarily Democratic) totals. Second, some firms give to both sides.

At the time this paper goes to press, the Federal Election Commission has not released its final report for the 1992 election. Accordingly, Table 7-1 refers to individual, soft-money, and PAC contributions from the individuals and firms in my sample to the Bush and Clinton campaigns (including soft money given to the parties in Clinton's case after March 21, 1992, when he was incontestably the most likely nominee; and in Bush's case, all GOP soft money) through late October, 1992. This is the great bulk of all the money taken in by the two chief candidates; thus the table is unlikely to require major revision. Note, however, that the table does not record contributions to the other primary candidates. My discussion below does draw on a survey of early money I prepared in the spring of 1992, but aside from the principal candidates, small numbers of contributions make statistical generalizations hazardous. Accordingly, I have not sought to present a statistical treatment of the primaries now, and the remarks in the text about the primaries (other than for Bush and Clinton) should be interpreted as preliminary.

One last point requires mention. My 1984 and 1988 studies reported results for individuals within industries. As explained in "Industrial Structure and Party Competition in the New Deal," this procedure makes sense where there is reason to believe that corporations have an incentive to spread donations among more than one individual, as they did when the FEC limits to contributions still meant something. The enormous growth of soft money, however, has rendered this point moot. This was not a problem in 1984, and, after checking, I believe my 1988 results do not require significant correction. By 1992, however, the raising of soft money was formalized and endemic, incorporated into everyone's political strategies, and reported to the FEC. Accordingly, I revert to the practice of reporting results by firms, as in my study of 1936. This has one bad consequence: by reducing cases, it decreases reliability. Because I use 2 x 2 chi-square tests, whenever the expected values in any of the cells goes below five, I report the results of Fisher's Exact Test for the level of significance and identify it accordingly to call attention to it in Table 7-1. (Here I follow K. H. Jarausch and K. A. Hardy, *Quantitative Methods for Historians* (Chapel Hill: University of North Carolina Press, 1991), 109).

20. In late October, 1992, the "Nightly Business Report" of the Public Broadcasting System carried a special five-part report on campaign finance in the 1992 election. Several of these programs included some striking interviews with various chief executives of major corporations about their (new) views of the state. I analyze these in a forthcoming study.

Note that Clinton's Texas campaign managers were openly promoting "clean burning" natural gas, and he himself had a long record on this point.

21. For high technology in general, see *Washington Post*, September 17, 1992; for specific quotations and a discussion of the high-tech executives' meetings with Clinton, see the *New York Times*, October 29, 1992 (note that Sculley said he still thought of himself as Republican); for Magaziner and the Council on Competitiveness, *Boston Globe*, November 15, 1992, which adds more details.

22. For Sculley, see *New York Times*, December 15, 1992. Note that the administration may be tempted to drop its request for a yen revaluation in exchange for a Japanese fiscal stimulus and promises of market openings. This may produce some strong tensions within the investment banking community in the United States along very predictable lines.

23. See the excellent discussion of how big the stimulus should have been by Paul Davidson in "Clinton's Economic Plan: Putting Caution First," *The Nation*, March 1, 1993, 260-262. Robert Eisner has critiqued the plan from a broadly similiar viewpoint, and I am grateful to him for sending me an early copy.

   The new spending in the Clinton fiscal package adds up to an intertemporal version of the well known "balanced budget multiplier" theorem of Keynesian theory, save that its net effects on national income, because of the cuts, will be deflationary.

24. A study I undertook as part of the research for this essay suggests that most of the industry was solidly Republican. Democratic contributions were concentrated in several specific parts of the health care industry: nursing homes, long-term health care, research and training hospitals, some HMOs, and many so-called "nonphysician providers." The limited sample and numerous categories, however, caution against resting too much on these conclusions, although they appear to make economic sense and offer a good guide to the apparent politics of the Clinton program.

25. Starobin, "An Affair," 123.

26. Rough analyses of the social composition of the electoral coalitions in the various primaries are contained in the various *New York Times* polls for the elections concerned. Note that turnouts in most of the Democratic primaries were low.

27. *Boston Globe*, January 27, 1993.

28. Walter Dean Burnham, private communication.

III. INSTITUTIONAL POLITICS AND POLITICAL CHANGE

8

The New Institutionalism and the Old Institutions
Bert A. Rockman

Institutions and the Dynamics of Politics

As a perspective for studying politics, institutionalism is about stasis, not dynamics. At least that is so in the short run. If things are stable in the short run, they must change over the long. The institutionalist perspective in the study of politics is roughly analogous to the geologist's perspective on the evolution of the Earth's surfaces. Everything looks unchangeable in the short run. But in the long, everything changes. Similarly, the periods of stable equilibrium often seem permanent to the observer. When there is a stable equilibrium, our attention is on how individuals adapt. But underlying contradictions nevertheless exist and eventually destabilize any equilibrium.

"The problematics of attention" are crucial[1]—the extent to which preoccupation with present problems precludes attention to signals of change in the short run. In the longer, however, adaptation requires evolution. The subcommittee bill of rights (1973) in the House of Representatives, for example, reflected an adaptation of the chamber to the rank-and-file Democratic members' dissatisfaction with the power of full committee chairs. It was also an adaptation to demands for more influence and authority on the part of members sufficiently senior to occupy subcommittee chairs while insufficiently senior to occupy full committee chairs. By cutting more than two-fifths of the majority members directly into the action, the payoff was substantial. When the Speaker's prerogatives were strengthened later in the 1970s, this represented an adaptation to some of the excesses created by this diffusion of authority. Because institutional rules cannot provide equal payoffs to all institutional participants, pressure mounts for reform. Typically, reform efforts are directed at the effects of earlier reforms. Thus, there is always a potential for endogenously generated change, though it is easy to underestimate when we look at institutions over narrow timespans.

Changes in meaning and values exogenous to an institution are the more obvious determinants. It is easy to conjure up historical images that once seemed part and parcel of an unchanging social reality. The seemingly timeless racial segregation of the American South or, for that matter, of South Africa (now in the process of change) is illustrative. The grim faces atop the Kremlin peering down at the military might on parade during the Bolshevik anniversary of the now defunct Soviet Union was another such image. What seemed more closed and durable than the Communist *nomenklatura?* The demise of all of these seemingly permanent institutions has complex and therefore debatable causes. Whatever the root causes, though, once pressures for change become strong, we no longer look at institutions in the same way. We see them as vulnerable, in the process of either adaptation or extinction.

Leadership is an agent of change. Institutions, by definition, tend to resist change. Leaders must therefore be ambivalent about institutionalization. If we can assume that leaders wish to maximize their discretion, they are likely to resist institutionalization because, by providing for regularity and predictability, institutions circumscribe discretion. No leader desires to be restricted by rules designed to seal in the past.

Conversely, while leaders resist being bound by institutional constraints, they generally prefer to bind others. By this logic, the durability of leadership is marked by the institutionalization of its policies, meaning, therefore, the lessened capability of succeeding leaders to alter them. The social insurance and regulatory state of the New Deal became imbedded. So has the structural budget deficit generated by the Reaganomics of the 1980s. All of these matters—social entitlements and budget constraints—define the contemporary political and policy struggle in the United States.

Policy institutionalization will continue to shadow new leaders promising a new day. The smart money is on institutions grinding down nonincremental leadership, and political scientists have an unerring instinct for betting with, rather than against, the odds.[2] The question is whether leaders are shrewd enough to make the smart money look foolish. Reagan was.

What, then, is the relationship between institutions and leadership? In its simplest form, institutions circumscribe, and leaders circumvent.

The Revival of Institutionalism

Why has institutionalist study experienced a boom over the past decade and a half? In truth, it never went into eclipse. But the behavioral focus in political science tended to microanalyze individual members of institutions qua individuals. A consequence of this was to treat institutions as arenas for the behavioral predilections of members. One of the classics of early behavioralism in legislative politics, for example, the Wahlke, Eulau, Buchanan, and Ferguson study of legislators in four states, focuses almost entirely on the attributes and attitudinal dispositions of the members.[3] Its major contribution was to generate a set of role types likely to characterize the behavior of members in the legislature. The role types themselves were constructed from attitudes as though the legislatures occupied by the individual members had no institutional meaning at all.

I surely do not mean to fault behavioral studies such as that just cited. *The Legislative System* was a pathbreaking study of its time. Rather, I just want to note that the then youthful pioneers of the behavioral movement in political science found inspiration in the emergent behavioral sciences that were nourished during and immediately after World War II. They produced the massive behavioral studies of the American military, resulting in *The American Soldier*.[4] The motivating message of the pioneers was to find out what was really going on underneath the formal overlay of traditional public law studies.

The pioneers of behavioralism in political science were undoubtedly struck by the juxtaposition of formalized structures defining what was supposed to happen and the lively informality of social settings that frequently defined what did happen. The studies of the American soldier by Samuel Stouffer and his colleagues illustrated the virtues (and not as yet the problems) of survey research, of finding out what individuals reported they did that was at odds sometimes with the formal expectation of what they were supposed to do. The importance of social psychological concepts such as identity (in *The American Soldier*, for example) was stressed as a determinant of both individual and collective behavior. Of course, these studies had antecedents in the observations of industrial psychologists who earlier observed work groups in plants and, among other things, noted such practices as the tendency of such groups to norm workloads and punish ratebusters.

Similarly, studies of authoritarianism by Adorno, Frenkel-Brunswick, Levinson, and Sanford undertaken in the post-World War II environment brought forth an array of psychological tests and provided a basis for a subsequent literature on authoritarianism, alienation, and disaffection.[5] Implicitly, a causal connection was made between the authoritarianism of individuals and the fascism that engulfed Germany and Italy. Equally implicit, the basis for the individualistic fallacy was being constructed, that is, institutions are the sum of individual propensities.

A common concern with the behavioral methodologies of individualism was that they lacked a theory of political equilibrium and, equally, a theory of political change. Viewed from a political cosmologist's perspective, behavioralism as a methodology seemed incapable by itself of telling us why we are where we are. That question, in turn, became pivotal as political scientists became increasingly interested in policy studies, especially comparisons of policymaking in different political settings. That further yielded an interest in the evolution of policy and, with that, the way in which institutions repeat existing interpretations,[6] and also the ways in which meanings are altered and opportunities arise.[7]

It would be a feckless exercise to try to explain why there has been a renewal in the study of political institutions. Obviously, a great many factors arrive at a point of coincidence. In my view, the combination of a shift in the agenda of questions being asked (from individual behavior to political and policy relevance), the inability of behavioral methodology qua political psychology to address those questions, and the emergence of approaches emphasizing, albeit very differently, the shaping of collective choice account for the revival in the study of institutions. It is, to be sure, a more theoretical enterprise than it had been before the onset of behavioral political science. However differently focused, the unifying creed of the institutionalist revival is that the architecture of institutions counts, the rules by which they do business matter, and the meanings vested in procedures are consequential. How much these count is a question, vital as it is, that must be left open for now. Clearly, if William Riker is correct that there can be no stable general equilibrium in politics,[8] then they do not count for much. Alternatively, if institutions provide the stuff of political meaning and define the range of acceptable behaviors, then they are apt to count for a lot.

Neoinstitutionalist Modalities

While the return to institutions has flourished, it has done so in distinctive ways. One stream of neoinstitutionalist work emphasizes policymaking as the focus, utilizing the method of historical and comparative case analysis. A second stream emphasizes the cognitive boundaries of organizational decision making and derives from the conjunction of cognitive psychology and organizational theory. A third stream focuses on the evolution of institutional behavior and its logic through rational choice, deriving from ideas located in microeconomic theory. For purposes of labeling, I will call these, in order, the historical-comparative approach, the bounded rationality approach, and the rational choice approach.

The Historical-Comparative Approach

Although no discrete work of scholarship demarcates an entire era, students of American politics would not be amiss if they singled out one that refocused our attention on the relationship between institutions and the governance of the polity. That piece of work would be Theodore Lowi's *The End of Liberalism*, first published in 1969 and revised and reissued a decade later.[9] It struck the loudest chord, if not necessarily the first notes, in heralding the return of institutions and law to the study of American politics and public policy.

Lowi's book generated big and hence debatable questions for political science. He harkened back both to the founders of the American political science profession as well as the country's political institutions by prescribing an organizational structure for governance and the legal underpinnings of public policy. For Lowi, law is the basis of universality, and discretionary authority the basis of corruption and favoritism. So long as particularistic and fragmented authority prevailed, justice, in Lowi's view, was impossible.

The institutional history vein has been mined deeply since Lowi's book initially appeared. Lowi's student, Stephen Skowronek, in the early 1980s published what has since become a staple in the literature on the development of American political institutions, and it coincided with a broader movement to reconsider the state's role.[10] Skowronek's book, *Building a New American State*, identifies the importance of the past in shaping adjustments to U.S. efforts to forge a modern administrative apparatus and military force. Those struggles continue to shape responses to the present. According to Skowronek, the U.S modernization process multiplied the problems of political control, accountability, and policy direction. Coming from a rational choice perspective on institutions, Terry Moe would concur and, in turn, has generated a logic of institutional choice predicated on the conflicting imperatives of interest groups, Congress and the bureaucracy, and the president.[11]

The interest in the historic development of institutions has recently spawned a new annual volume called *Studies in American Political Development*—a sign no doubt of the appeal of this stream of institutional work. In the first volume (1986), editors Karen Orren and Stephen Skowronek stipulate the rationale of a historic perspective on institutions: "History provides the dimension necessary for understanding institutions as they operate under varying conditions. Beyond that it is also a natural proving ground for the claim that institutions have an independent and formative influence on politics." [12] Similarly, the editors of another important collection of papers on social policy in the United States argue that,

> a macroscopic and historical perspective that highlights political institutions and processes in relation to the regional, economic, and racial diversity of American society allows us to understand past policies and their effects. . . . Such a perspective not only improves our understanding of the implications of these experiences for the present but also helps us wisely examine alternative possible futures for social provision in America.[13]

The historical approach to the role of institutions in policymaking tends to lie outside the orbit of positivist methodologies, which seek to operationalize variables, quantify them, and formalize an explanatory structure through a process of analytic decomposition. By way of contrast, the historical approach seeks not to decompose but to recompose—to intertwine the play of societal forces with institutional structures and processes, rather than dissect them. Policy-making patterns over time suggest to us the range of feasible options for the future. Positivists looking for a causal structure are apt to find it largely unspecified. From the perspective of neoinstitutionalists fishing in the historical stream, however, the searching for precise and decomposable causal structures is likely to be regarded as a misplaced effort. The logic used by the actors in place is seen as more compelling than the reconstructed logic generated through positivist analyses.

Time provides one dimension of comparison. Space provides another. The two can be joined. Indeed, the rationale for their intersection is persuasive. Cross-national studies over time hint at how tensile or malleable institutions are and how different institutions both filter and structure external social forces.

The study of social policy outcomes as measured by aggregate data indicates little institutional effect.[14] This, of course, has something to do with the unsubtle measures of both the dependent policy variables (usually expenditures) and the independent institutional variables (usually the political ideology of the government). Aggregate expenditures, of course, are notoriously unresponsive to changes in political leadership because they are typically locked into spending formulas and driven greatly by demography.

A great deal of valuable literature exists on how institutions in different systems make policy. Much of the best of this literature compares various European systems.[15] An outstanding study of the organizational structure of politics on social welfare policy compared Canada and the United States—two federal systems with different regime structures at each level of government.[16] The study focused on welfare backlash and concluded that federalism was a relatively negligible factor. Yet the differences between a Westminster-style system (Canada) and a separation-of-powers system (the United States) were important. The greater accessibility of legislators in the separation of powers system made them more susceptible to popular contagions, whereas in the Westminster system the networks between federal and provincial elites were narrower, more structured, and more insular.

The inclination of so many scholars to attribute numerous U.S. policy dysfunctions to the structure of the country's political institutions sparked my interest and that of Kent Weaver. With the help of a veritable army of scholars, we evaluated the relationship between institutions and governing capabilities[17] by comparing policy-making processes and outcomes in the United States with other industrialized democratic polities. The United States provided a constant point of comparison, while the other countries (at least two for any policy-making case) depended on the expertise of the contributing scholars.

The primary question of this exercise was whether parliamentary systems and the U.S. separation-of-powers system differed in their policy capabilities. But, to answer this, further questions and additional institutional differentiation were required. Thus, a second question asked, to what extent do parliamentary systems differ among themselves? This required probing at a second level of institutional difference focused on the electoral rules by which governments are formed and different regime types produced. We could distinguish at least three parliamentary systems: (1) majority party, Westminster-style systems; (2) multiparty coalition governments; and (3) single party dominant governments. Hence, a third question relates to the import of these institutional considerations for policy capabilities. Are they less important than a system's other institutional features that have little to do with the fusion or separation of executive and legislative power? Some of these features may be constitutional, for example, federalism, judicial review, or bicameralism. Others may be a matter of rules, for example, the existence of open or closed votes in the legislature. A fourth question was whether any of these institutional factors was more consistently important for predicting policy capabilities than noninstitutional considerations, such as the existence of stable majorities, social homogeneity, and the like.

Institutions, we conclude, matter in that they contribute to or impede particular policy capabilities. We cannot conclude, however, that any set of structural arrangements is necessarily more decisive than exogenous political conditions. Rather, institutional arrangements make opportunities more or less available and increase or decrease the risks of acting.

As a stream of work, the case study historical-comparative approach is heavily inductive and carries with it only modest theoretical baggage. Whether that is regarded as a virtue or a liability clearly depends on one's research epistemology. Historical study, however, is empirical rather than theoretical. It is a story-telling, not an axiomatic, discipline. The stories enable us to see a web of factors at work in policymaking. One story, however, may not necessarily tell us much about another.

The Bounded Rationality Approach

The bounded rationality stream of institutionalist study has more evident theoretical antecedents. It joins together theories about individuals as information processors with ideas about organizations as information processors. The two levels of analysis are intimately connected. The theoretical base line is that individuals, like organizations, are cognitive misers. The pioneering work of Herbert Simon showed our inclination to arrive at satisfactory rather than optimal solutions because we have not the wits (nor time or energy) to optimize.[18]

Putting aside for the moment complications arising from operationally distinguishing between a satisfactory and an optimal decision process, Simon's powerful insight organized a great deal of thinking about organizations as institutions. Attention is a commodity, and it has costs. The supply of information in organizations exceeds their capacity to assimilate it. Therefore, boundaries filter both the supply and the nature of the demand.

Boundaries are arrived at structurally through jurisdiction and function. They are fortified by routines, rules, norms, and so-called organizational memory. These latter characteristics institutionalize organizations. They provide the cognitive shorthand for coping with the environment and the buzz of stimuli demanding attention.

Among the implications of surplus information are these: (1) inertial states dominate by providing the shorthand and frame of reference for cognizing new stimuli (jurisdiction, routine, and precedent define the face of the problem); (2) surplus information sometimes winds up as solutions to as yet ill-defined problems; and, consequently, (3) when windows of opportunity arise, solutions are available.

Because organizations through their elites have limited attention spans, problems tend to be treated sequentially instead of being defined strategically.[19] Rather, they come to an organization in a sequence defined by the environment. The metaphor of "the garbage can" is the operative image of how organizations deal with their environment. Problems come to organizations in a quasi-random sequence much like the layers of garbage set out for disposal.[20] Complexity, however, mitigates against simple responses. The rootedness of organizational subcultures, the existence of organizational rules and constraints, and the dependencies of the governing elites within organizations make unlikely a definitive resolution of issues. As Cyert and March put it, problems reach quasi resolution, but not resolution.[21] In plainer English, this means that compromise is the likely outcome of complex processes, and this in turn promotes ambiguity. Ambiguity, then, provides the basis for future contradictions, which thus provide a basis for endogenously generated institutional change.

Organizations tend to do what they have done in the past not because it is the best of all possible worlds, but because it is the known and, therefore, comprehensible world. The past is in more than one sense prelude to the future. What has been done can be done. We feel a need to simplify a complex and frequently threatening world according to the cognitive miser psychology that underlies the organizational concept of bounded rationality. Hence, this is also what organizations are predisposed to do.

As life becomes more institutionalized, it also inevitably becomes more predictable. Equally, as with individuals, institutions develop routines to cope with external uncertainties. The routines become part of the lore of an institutionalized organization. The lore, being passed on, becomes a central component of organizational memory. The lore helps define norms of appropriate behavior, and thus becomes a central component of organizational memory.[22] Organizational memory is what we commonly mean by the word *experience*.

For any agenda of institutional reform, however, it is exceedingly important to comprehend just precisely what organizational memory is. What, in other words, is learned over time by successive individuals occupying similar roles? Obviously, what is learned most completely are the routines that decrease transaction costs—that is, the organizational shorthand. It is far less clear that more complex lessons about decision making are understood over time until they get reduced to formulas (Munich comes to mind). If this hypothesis is true, then learning is unlikely to be institutionalized beyond the routines and shorthand of organizational life. The logic for this, I believe, is clear from the cognitive miser underpinnings of bounded rationality. By implication, then, the institutional learning that we like to think constitutes experience and seasoning in decision making is largely a function of the experiences of the individuals occupying crucial organizational roles. When these experiences are lost to an organization or to a political body virtually all but the routines are lost to the organization. Putting this in a slightly different way, the learning of subtleties is not a supraindividualistic phenomenon. But rules and norms about processes are the stuff of institutions, and these, especially the former, are more easily conveyed.

The Rational Choice Approach

In the long tradition of rational (strategic) choice, rules and processes have been central. Agenda orders, individual preference orderings, and collective decision rules have been the basic stuff of rational choice theory.[23] In contrast to the bounded rationality approach to institutions, whereby individual preferences are regarded as incomplete and influenced both by the sequencing of problems and institutionally defined meanings, rational choice approaches are apt to emphasize fixed preference schedules based on individual interest. Institutional structures take on importance to the extent that (1) they shape the incentives for individual behavior; (2) these incentives have collective consequences; and (3) the institutions structure conflicts (or collaborations) of interest and, thus, define the terms under which bargaining takes place.

As with any broad stream of inquiry, there are numerous tributaries. Justice cannot be done to them all here, so I want to focus on two of particular importance. One emphasizes the development of institutional features, particularly legislative committees, as mechanisms to induce and maintain cooperative behavior.[24] The other emphasizes the institutional bases of conflicting interests.

Shepsle and also Shepsle and Weingast tie central elements of rational choice theory together with anthropological notions of institutions as a set of inherited meanings.[25] Shepsle's argument is that institutions develop practices in response to cooperation problems and thus reduce the transaction costs associated with individual negotiations. Institutionalized practices make it much more difficult for deals to get unstuck by providing an enforcement mechanism. These practices are rational in that they respond to the cooperation problems induced by the structure and organization of authority. Committees meet individual member needs by disproportionately representing those who have reason to be interested in the subjects of the committee's jurisdiction. The investment of members' careers in committees follows from the power of committees to propose but also to have, through the mechanism of the conference committee, ex post veto power as well. The institutional practice, therefore, can be summarized as reciprocal deference. Such a practice is unlikely to be established in the legislatures of cabinet system governments because in these systems bargaining power tends to be concentrated in the cabinet.[26]

Those familiar with Samuel Huntington's discussion about Congress (an institution where the norm of reciprocity among specialists prevails) will hardly be startled by Shepsle's conclusion.[27] Indeed, Shepsle largely repeats the prevailing literature of congressional texts. If the conclusions are not so novel, though, the logic linking individual interests, institutional structures and practices, and committee power is. Especially interesting is that, from a rational choice perspective, institutional practices are posited to have a stable equilibrium and are not merely the product of prevailing majority policy preferences. Thus, we have the notion of a structure-induced equilibrium.

The logic underpinning Shepsle's formulation that committee power provides a stable basis for generating cooperative behavior and reducing the underlying transaction costs rests on two key assumptions. One is that committees are "preference outliers," and the other is that committees have established and nonoverlapping jurisdictions.[28] The first assumes that committees are distinct from and more important than chamber or party majorities. The second assumes that committees in each chamber will be powerful in promoting reciprocal deference because they hold nearly exclusive jurisdictional claims. Otherwise, there will be conflict between entrepreneurs to stake out territorial claims over legislation and agency behavior rather than deference to specialists. If these assumptions fail, the logic used to explain the cooperative basis for committee power would need at least some modification.

A different rational choice slant on institutions is reflected in the work of Terry Moe, which emphasizes that congressional and presidential behaviors are driven by different forces. The logic of congressional behavior is interest group-based particularism, while that of the president is universalism. Only the president sits where all the expenditure grids come together. Moe's assumption is that Congress will seek to implant interest group definitions of policy into its administration. This gives Congress leverage over a critical policy resource and impedes presidential control over policy. Because Congress writes the laws, it can define standards for implementation. Presidents respond by trying to control the bureaucracy, which they do by politicizing it and centralizing as much authority as possible in the White House. This is designed to channel administrative responsiveness directly to the presidency.[29]

The logic of institutional conflict is overpowering and is inherent in the separation of legislative and presidential power. Presidents politicize the bureaucracy in their own self-defense—an entirely rational response, just as it is rational for Congress to do what is expedient for the interest groups that can help them.

Several interesting and highly debatable assumptions are floating around these formulations. The first is that presidents are not affected by interest group politics as is Congress (which in any case is far more than a mere agent of dominant interests).[30] An instructive example is provided by a White House operative interviewed by Hugh Heclo in his study of political layering at the Office of Management and Budget (OMB) during the Nixon administration. While discussing the professional (but presumably politically disinterested) civil servants at the old Bureau of the Budget (OMB's predecessor agency), this individual claimed that they "could make a one-term president out of anybody." [31] One might infer from this that presidents are also keenly aware of the political implications of what they do, or is done, in their name. Pleasing (or at least not displeasing) interest groups in their support coalition figures into their calculations. A second reservation centers around the assumption that differences from president to president are not as great as the similarities of the institutional forces at work on all presidencies. These forces, it is asserted, push presidents to seek central control over the bureaucracy to ensure its compliance with White House preferences. This supposition, however attractive it seems to be, is a matter to be empirically evaluated. Not all presidents are equally inclined to grab for the executive gusto. In fact, only a few may be, and even they may do so quite selectively, the logic of how they *should* behave notwithstanding. A third contestable assumption is that presidents have expansive energies to generate control over agencies when, in fact, even if they did care, this is but one corner of a set of matters competing for presidential attention, most of which are more compelling for a president's self-interest than tending the bureaucracy. Finally, it is questionable as to whether presidents have completely formed preferences (or even any at all) on matters that only marginally affect their presidencies and in respect to programs about which they are likely to care little and know less.

In sum, rational choice is an approach to institutions that begins with a logic of interest. That logic begins at the individual level, but in politics must usually be expressed through institutions. Institutional interests are presumed to exist on the basis of the interests of their individual members and the logic of institutional behavior is based on structural inducements. Precisely what constitutes self-interest, however, is both debatable and inherently untestable because it is not observable. Mostly, individual self-interests are posited as following the logic of one's role. So members of Congress are presumed to have interests in reelection and thus tend constituencies, while presidents are compelled to see the whole picture.

They need, therefore, to gain control over wayward bureaucrats and their congressional and interest group sponsors. From this neat formulation, we have a theory of institutional conflict based on differing institutional imperatives.

Yet Shepsle's (and Weingast's) analyses posit that institutions do not necessarily stem directly from individual self-interest. Institutions serve to reduce transaction costs even when they frustrate majority preferences. Shepsle's formulation is fascinating because he has conjoined political anthropology (the study of how ritual is maintained) with political economy (the logic of individual self-interest in relation to the structure of choice).

Each of the three streams of inquiry—historical-comparative case method, bounded rationality, and rational choice—gives us a different take on institutions. They range in order of presentation from the highly inductive to the axiomatic. Equally, their foci are, in the same order, likely to range from the macroscopic to the microscopic. Each has granted us special insights, although the latter two have a more distinctive theoretical edge to them. All three, I suspect, will continue to flourish in their own vineyards. Rational choice, to repeat an argument I set forth elsewhere, provides a compelling logic for getting at the problem of dynamics.[32] The logic of incentives is powerful but usually insufficient by itself to specify the conditions under which a stable equilibrium is established or those under which change is likely to be induced. That is where assumption comes into play. It is here that rational choice, with its need for Spartan assumptions, frequently diverges from the other streams of neoinstitutionalism.

Studying the Old Institutions

The years following World War II saw significant organizational developments in both the Congress and the presidency. Legislative reorganization redefined standing committees in both chambers and developed the rudiments of committee staffing behind them. The National Security Act set up the National Security Council in the executive branch and provided the basis for further staffing ornamentations. The Full Employment Act generated the Council of Economic Advisers to the president. These developments have often led observers to conclude that both the White House and the modern presidency evince the characteristics of an institution. In my view, that observation is about half-right. Congress has developed institutional habits, the presidency less so. That is largely because Congress has a collective decision-making problem that requires procedures to diminish conflict. The presidency has acquired, as has Congress, lots of support agencies and staff, but, in the end, the president needs no one's consent within the executive branch.

The design of American political organization probably made this asymmetry inevitable. It might have been avoided had a collective executive been agreed on in Philadelphia. That, like most European cabinets, would have required some procedures for arriving at executive agreement. But that did not happen, and, so, while the presidency as an organization has become more complex and expansive, it is less clear that it has developed into an institution as fully as Congress has. Of course, as Dodd has pointed out, Congress has gone through cycles of development.[33] Although stable in the short run, it has changed a great deal over the long run.

Both the Congress and the presidency have undoubtedly mushroomed in their staffing and organization. Signs of bureaucracy surround each. Alphabet soup agencies such as the General Accounting Office (GAO), Office of Technology Assessment (OTA), and Congressional Budget Office (CBO) are congressional agents. Committee staffs likewise have grown dramatically, though they are more susceptible to short-run electoral change in their composition. Similarly, a president has, in theory, a set of units and even agencies designed to serve the office, but which are more likely to be responsive mostly to its incumbent (the only operational definition of the office). The Office of Management and Budget, Office of Personnel Management (OPM), and the Executive Office of the President (EOP) provide support for the president. And, obviously, so too does the White House staff.

From the standpoint of professionalization, an impressive legion of experts are available to serve their principals. Whether or not these staff organizations serve the purpose of institutionalizing experience is a different matter. On the whole, congressional agencies and committee staffs appear to have greater continuity than do most presidential ones. After all, one party has had continuous control of the House of Representatives for nearly forty years, a tenure that has been equalled in the Senate but for the interregnum of the 1981-1987 period of Republican control.

As with the presidency, it may be that much of the organizational apparatus exists to serve not the institution, per se, but its majorities. Obviously, there is much to that, and were one or both congressional chambers to swing back and forth more frequently, we might see how unstable its institutional apparatus actually might be. Nonetheless, congressional procedures and etiquette have formed over a long period of time to reflect institutional evolution and the creation of norms. Without a center for bargaining in the executive (that is, a cabinet of peers), the separation of powers led to the emergence of legislative committees as a way of dealing with the problem of collective action. It also meant that the early development of congressional committees would create turf battles over the executive branch between Congress and the president.[34]

The chambers, of course, differ. Although larger, the House has more efficient procedures for working through the collective action problem. The rules of the Senate in theory enhance its deliberative powers and weaken its ability to legislate. That is to say, the House gives little leverage to minorities, whereas the Senate continues to defer to its minorities, making the chamber into a notoriously inefficient legislating body. Which of these is the more institutionalized? In theory, the House has more rules, and rules tend to circumscribe the latitude of individuals. Alternatively, the Senate gives more leeway to minorities and, in this respect, is likely to change less with a shift in its majorities than the House might.

In any event, despite the sizable organizational growth and professionalization of both the Congress and the Presidency in recent decades, only one of these branches is faced with the coordination problem around which rules and norms must be worked out. The president's staff and his means of organizing them tend to be tied to his interests as he and his entourage understand them. The president needs no one's cooperation to run the presidency. He alone has the authority. The cabinet members serve at his pleasure and rarely represent independent sources of political authority to be bargained with. There is little reason for any new president to follow in the organizational footsteps of his predecessor. Indeed, politically there are powerful reasons to do just the opposite. That hardly bespeaks institutionalization in spite of staff development.[35]

Policy Institutionalization

As I earlier commented, the goal of leaders is to have their policy preferences institutionalized. That is power. Equally, it is the goal of leaders to inherit a blank slate. But because that cannot happen, leaders seek to deinstitutionalize the status quo when they want to change it. Put differently, most individuals in leadership roles most of the time want to maximize their discretion. Institutionalization impedes that.

The condition of divided government in the midst of massive budget deficits prompted interesting responses to mutually constrain both the Congress and the president and to make a defection on the part of either costly. It is clear that neither branch trusts the other nor wishes to grant it discretionary authority. Each side wants to constrain the other. By itself, that is nothing new, just the traditional bargaining game between the branches. But the magnitude and scope of the constraint have changed. The seeds of this change began with the Congressional Budget and Impoundment Act of 1974 and its reconciliation provisions. The enormous structural deficits generated during the Reagan presidency then led to the Gramm-Rudman-Hollings legislation of 1985, which specified target dates for deficit reduction. Although the day of deficit reduction never arrived and the targets were adjusted from time to time, the effect of the law was to make government respond to, if not in fact meet, the targets. When the sequestration provisions of the Gramm-Rudman legislation looked in 1990 as though they would have powerfully disruptive effects on the government for the following fiscal year, it was evident that

Gramm-Rudman had at least to be partially replaced. The new model was the 1990 budget deal that provided for spending caps across separate expenditure categories, thus sealing each off from the other.

Although the budget compromise of 1990 was a five-year deal with shorter provisions for reevaluation, the effect is to constrain room for maneuver in the budget. For the most part, that also means constraint on new program expenditures.

Maneuver, of course, is the stuff of politics. Riker could be right.[36] The deal might hold only until its costs (for very different reasons) become too evident to continue it. But the price for breaking the deal also has potential political costs. An institutionalized status quo raises costs for those seeking to displace it.

The irony, then, is that crisis tends to produce negotiated solutions designed to increase the costs of defection. These also decrease, therefore, the costs of decision making by reducing the number of decisions. To a degree, members of Congress can play the game both ways. The institutionalization of policy allows politicians to create "solutions"—at least maintaining the present equilibrium—without having to make decisions. At the same time, they can rail against the deal that constrains them.

Divided government in the midst of a severe long-term problem provided the conditions for an institutionalized truce. Truces, however, settle little. They provide only the means for reducing sanguinary conflict while deeply conflictual decisions are deferred. The institutional legacy of the budget deficits that mounted in the 1980s was to place the budget in a web of constraints and targets, effectively lessening the impact of subsequent political choice. No deal is forever, perhaps not even a fiscal year. For now, though, political discretion has been circumscribed, and the long-term effects of the budget deficit are likely to continue to result in efforts to limit choices that might otherwise reflect majority preferences. This is among the legacies of the politics of budget deficits and divided government.

Institutions and Policy Change

Stephen Krasner's metaphor to describe long periods of equilibrium interrupted by a flurry of change is that of *punctuated equilibrium*.[37] Unless we are living in the midst of one of these flurries, stability and resistance to dramatic change appear to be dominant.

For the first time in twelve years, the election of 1992 brought an end to party-divided government, in which at least one congressional chamber had a majority led by a party other than the one occupying the White House. It did not, of course, alter the constitutional status of the legislative body of the United States as an entity independent of the executive and, therefore, subject to political forces at least somewhat at variance with those influencing the White House and the executive branch. In sum, the political change of 1992 was more topical than fundamental. It changed the agenda around which the country's political conversation was constructed, but it by no means ensures that much of that agenda will come to fruition as public policy. Despite the existence of party-unified government, the fundamental characteristics of a political system designed to check majorities continue to prevail.

Although an unusually large number of new members entered the 103d Congress, little has changed in how the chambers go about their business. The House continues to be reasonably sensitive to majority preferences where they exist, whereas the Senate continues to be more sensitive to strong minorities. Complex legislation (such as health care) runs great risks in a system containing so many hurdles and veto points. For while it is relatively easy to find majorities preferring a change in the status quo, it is difficult to rally those majorities behind any given option to alter the status quo.

Despite Riker's admonition that the characteristic feature of politics is disequilibrium, political scientists tend to cling to the conventional wisdom, which is to see more obstacles in the path of change than possibilities for it. Yet, even the long run can be radically foreshortened. In 1963, a precursor to Medicare proposed by the Kennedy administration suffered a narrow defeat in the Senate. Three years later, it passed overwhelmingly, for reasons that had less to do with institutions than with preferences: Democrats had won an enormous victory in the 1964 election.

In some fashion or other, a national system of health care has been on the agenda since at least 1948. Within the next decade, a national health-care insurance system is likely to be established in response to growing social and economic pressures. At the same time, such a system is unlikely in the immediate future despite the emergence of a plan and nominal party majorities because institutions and political arrangements make it difficult to settle on a particular option.

Observers of politics, whether political scientists, journalists, or simply ordinary citizens, concentrate disproportionately, if understandably, on the seeming paralysis of the here and now. But what is now may not be here for very long.

Conclusion

What explains existing equilibria? Is it pure preference or otherwise? If it is otherwise, what structures and processes buffer against changes in preference? How did they arise? What holds them together? What internal contradictions are built into them? How susceptible are they to endogenous or exogenous change? These are hardly new questions. They are in fact the hardy perennials of political science.

We need history and comparison to understand why policy problems tend to get defined as they do, why they bump into similar obstacles and occasional opportunities. We need both history and comparison to evaluate the impact of institutional architecture on politics and to see how politics can differently configure the same basic architecture. We also need theory to guide us toward explaining why people do what they do. And here there is fundamental though perhaps not irretrievable divergence. I assume for whatever it is worth that we are all self-interested. I further assume that knowing that is of little value in specifying behavior. Like the bounded rationalists, I assume that all people are guided by habit and inertia and will do less rather than more if less is sufficient. But like rational choice theorists, I assume that conditions of consistently negative payoff are not likely to be sustained. So, presumably the norms and rules and structures associated with institutional behavior must be beneficial over time. Rational choice helps us understand the difficulties of institutional change even when things turn sour by pointing to the costs attached to cooperation under conditions of uncertainty.[38]

Normally in the American system, Congress provides stability while the president introduces a dynamic element. The natural conflict between the two has been exacerbated during much of the recent period of divided government by the different policy preferences expressed by congressional majorities and the president. With the advent of the Clinton administration, the condition of divided government has at least temporarily subsided. But the institutionalized policy legacies that contribute to the large budget deficit and subsequent efforts to grapple with it continue to circumscribe present choices. In economics, the starting point of wisdom is that there are no free lunches. In politics, it is that there are no free agents. Our present condition proves both.

Notes

1. James G. March and Johan P. Olsen, *Rediscovering Institutions: The Organizational Basis of Politics* (New York: Free Press, 1989), 93.
2. See Bert A. Rockman, "What Didn't We Know and Should We Forget It? Political Science and the Reagan Presidency," *Polity* 21 (Summer 1989): 777-792.
3. John C. Wahlke, Heinz Eulau, William Buchanan, and LeRoy C. Ferguson, *The Legislative System; Explorations in Legislative Behavior* (New York: Wiley, 1962).
4. Samuel A. Stouffer, Carl I. Homan, and Robert K. Merton, *The American Soldier* (Princeton, N.J.: Princeton University Press, 1949), vols. 1 and 2.
5. Theodor Adorno, Else Frenkel-Brunswick, Daniel J. Levinson, and R. Nevitt Sanford, *The Authoritarian Personality* (New York: Harper and Brothers, 1950).
6. Douglas E. Ashford, *The Emergence of the Welfare State* (Oxford: Basil Blackwell, 1988).
7. For example, see Hugh Heclo, *Modern Social Politics in Britain and Sweden* (New Haven, Conn.: Yale University Press, 1974), and John W. Kingdon, *Alternatives, Agendas, and Public Policies* (Boston: Little, Brown, 1984).
8. William H. Riker, "Implications from the Disequilibrium of Majority Rule for the Study of Institutions," *American Political Science Review* 74 (June 1980): 432-446.

9. Theodore J. Lowi, *The End of Liberalism* (New York: Norton, 1969).

10. Stephen Skowronek, *Building A New American State: The Expansion of National Administrative Capacities 1877-1920* (Cambridge: Cambridge University Press, 1982). Peter Evans, Dietrich Reuschemeyer, and Theda Skocpol, eds., *Bringing the State Back In* (New York: Cambridge University Press, 1985).

11. In a series of impressively argued essays, Terry Moe claims that an institutionalist perspective on politics emphasizes the use of law and organization in the struggle for long-term policy control. From this perspective, winners seek to seal in their preferences, while losers try to slacken legal and organizational boundaries. The logic, of course, is that winners would like to institutionalize their preferences while losers seek to avoid that. See, *inter alia,* Terry M. Moe, "The Politics of Bureaucratic Structure," in *Can the Government Govern?* ed. John E. Chubb and Paul E. Peterson (Washington, D.C.: Brookings Institution, 1989), 267-329; Terry M. Moe, "The Politics of Structural Choice: Toward a Theory of Public Bureaucracy," in *Organization Theory: From Chester Barnard to the Present and Beyond,* ed. Oliver E. Williamson (New York: Oxford University Press, 1990); and Terry M. Moe, "Presidents, Institutions, and Theory," in *Researching the Presidency: Vital Questions, New Approaches,* ed. George C. Edwards III, John H. Kessel, and Bert A. Rockman (Pittsburgh: University of Pittsburgh Press, 1993).

12. Karen Orren and Stephen Skowronek, eds., *Studies in American Political Development: An Annual* (New Haven: Yale University Press, 1986), vol. 1, vii.

13. Margaret Weir, Ann Shola Orloff, and Theda Skocpol, *The Politics of Social Policy in the United States* (Princeton, N.J.: Princeton University Press, 1988), xi.

14. Harold L. Wilensky, *The Welfare State and Equality: Structural and Ideological Roots of Public Expenditures* (Berkley and Los Angeles: University of California Press, 1975).

15. For example, see Heclo, *Modern Social Politics;* Ashford, *The Emergence of the Welfare States;* and Peter J. Katzenstein, *Small States in World Markets* (Ithaca, N.Y.: Cornell University Press, 1985).

16. Christopher Leman, *The Collapse of Welfare Reform: Political Institutions, Policy, and the Poor in Canada and the United States* (Cambridge: MIT Press, 1980).

17. The study in question is R. Kent Weaver and Bert A. Rockman, eds., *Do Institutions Matter? Government Capabilities in the United States and Abroad* (Washington, D.C.: Brookings Institution, 1993). Among the critics of the American governmental institutions who helped spark our interest were Lloyd N. Cutler and James L. Sundquist. See, for example, Lloyd N. Cutler, "To Form a Government," *Foreign Affairs* 59 (Fall 1980): 126-143, and James L. Sundquist, *Constitutional Reform and Effective Government,* rev. ed. (Washington, D.C.: Brookings Institution, 1992).

18. Herbert A. Simon, *Administrative Behavior: A Study of Decision-Making Processes in Administrative Organization,* 3d ed. (New York: Free Press, 1975). The original publication date of this book was 1947.

19. Richard M. Cyert and James G. March, *A Behavioral Theory of the Firm* (Englewood Cliffs, N.J.: Prentice-Hall, 1963).

20. See Michael D. Cohen, James G. March, and Johan P. Olsen, "A Garbage Can Model of Organizational Choice," *Administrative Science Quarterly* 17 (March 1972): 1-25.

21. Cyert and March, *Behavioral Theory of the Firm.*

22. March and Olsen, *Rediscovering Institutions.*

23. For discussions of the classic works of Condorcet and Borda, for example, see Duncan Black, *The Theory of Committees and Elections* (Cambridge: Cambridge University Press, 1958).

24. For example, see Kenneth A. Shepsle, "Institutional Equilibrium and Equilibrium Institutions," in *Political Science: The Science of Politics,* ed. Herbert F.

Weisberg (New York: Agathon Press, 1986), 51-81, and Kenneth A. Shepsle and Barry R. Weingast, "The Institutional Foundations of Committee Power," *American Political Science Review* 81 (March 1987): 85-104.

25. See Shepsle, "Institutional Equilibrium," and Shepsle and Weingast, "Institutional Foundation." On institutions as a set of inherited meanings, see March and Olsen, *Rediscovering Institutions.*

26. Shepsle and Weingast, "Institutional Foundations."

27. Samuel P. Huntington, "Congressional Responses to the Twentieth Century," in *The Congress and America's Future*, ed. David B. Truman (Englewood Cliffs, N.J.: Prentice-Hall, 1965), 5-31.

28. Krehbiel attacks the notion of committees as "preference outliers" on a different set of collective action grounds. Committees diminish transaction costs for the plenary chamber by gaining information that the chamber otherwise could not. Krehbiel's median legislator hypothesis, therefore, is that "legislative choices in salient policy domains [committees] are median choices." See Keith Krehbiel, *Information and Legislative Organization* (Ann Arbor: University of Michigan Press, 1992), 263. The multiplication of subcommittees with uncertain jurisdictions was earlier noted by Dodd and Schott. See Lawrence C. Dodd and Richard L. Schott, *Congress and the Administrative State* (New York: Wiley, 1979). On the role of multiple referrals that has accompanied jurisdictional uncertainty, see Melissa P. Collie and Joseph P. Cooper, "Multiple Referral and the 'New' Committee System in the House of Representatives," in *Congress Reconsidered*, ed. Lawrence C. Dodd and Bruce L. Oppenheimer, 4th ed. (Washington, D.C.: CQ Press, 1989), 245-272.

29. For example, see Moe, "Politics of Bureaucratic Structure," "Politics of Structural Choice," and "Presidents, Institutions, and Theory."

30. For example, Arnold claims that congressional responsiveness to articulated constituency demands is overstated. See R. Douglas Arnold, *The Logic of Congressional Action* (New Haven, Conn.: Yale University Press, 1990).

31. Hugh Heclo, "OMB and the Presidency—the Problem of 'Neutral Competence'," *Public Interest* 38 (Winter 1975): 80-98, 97.

32. Bert A. Rockman, "Minding the State or a State of Mind? Issues in the Comparative Conceptualization of the State," *Comparative Political Studies* 23 (April 1990): 25-55.

33. See Lawrence C. Dodd, "Congress, the President, and the Cycles of Power," in *The Post-Imperial Presidency*, ed. Vincent Davis (New Brunswick, N.J.: Transaction, 1980), 71-100, and Lawrence C. Dodd, "The Cycles of Legislative Change: Building a Dynamic Theory," in *Political Science: The Science of Politics*, ed. Herbert F. Weisberg, 82-104.

34. James Sterling Young, *The Washington Community: 1800-1828* (New York: Harcourt Brace Jovanovich, 1966).

35. Samuel Kernell, "The Evolution of the White House Staff," in *Can the Government Govern?*, ed. Chubb and Peterson, 185-237.

36. Riker, "Disequilibrium of Majority Rule."

37. Stephen D. Krasner, "Approaches to the State: Alternative Conceptions and Historical Dynamics," *Comparative Politics* 16 (January 1984): 223-246.

38. Gary J. Miller, "Formal Theory," in *Researching the Presidency*, ed. Edwards, Kessel, and Rockman.

9

Punctuated Change and the Era of Divided Government

Sean Q Kelly

D
ivided partisan control of American political institutions has been the defining characteristic of American politics since the 1950s. Congress and the presidency have been controlled by different political parties for twenty-six of the last forty-one years. The Reagan-Bush era represents the longest sustained period of divided government in U.S. history: twelve years of divided government. Preceding the inauguration of Bill Clinton in January 1993, the Republican party seemed to have a lock on the White House; it had won seven of ten presidential elections, and controlled the presidency for twenty-eight of the preceding forty years. The Democratic party, for its part, had demonstrated a knack for controlling the Congress. Since 1955 the Democrats have had a monopoly on the House, and their dominance of the Senate was only briefly interrupted in the early 1980s. The elections of 1992 did little to weaken their hold over Congress; the Democrats broke even in the Senate and maintained a significant majority in the House.

Similarly, since the 1950s many of the American states have experienced divided government. A number of states have seen their executive controlled by one party and part or all of their legislature controlled by the other. On average more than half the states experience divided government in any given year. Following the 1992 elections, more than half have divided government.

This persistent and pervasive pattern of divided government is unique in American political history. American politics has generally been characterized by sustained one-party control of government, resulting in focused and coherent policy agendas.[1] This custom helped to establish a central role for parties in American politics. Indeed, partisan control of political institutions has become the defining characteristic of American political eras. Realignment theory, developed to explain and predict the operation of the prevailing system, has proved to be a useful analytical paradigm for several decades. The realignment perspective lends us little insight, however, into the era of divided government. This leads one to question the usefulness of realignment for understanding American political history.[2]

I suggest that we consider an alternative to the realignment perspective based on a theory of punctuated change. From this new perspective

American political history is marked by relatively static political eras with well-defined electoral characteristics and policy agendas, punctuated by compressed periods of rapid transformation and subsequent stasis. The era of divided government is the result of a "punctuated change" in American politics. It displays unique institutional and policy dynamics that distinguish it from other periods in American political history. The purpose of this essay is to describe and explain this change.

Patterns and Explanations

The era of divided government is unique in American political history in several respects. First, before the 1950s divided government usually occurred as a result of midterm elections and was resolved in the following presidential election, in which the electorate restored united government. In the era of divided government, split control is initiated during presidential election years and is not corrected in subsequent elections.

Second, episodes of divided government from the 1860s to 1913 were often caused when the Democratic party controlled the House and the presidency, and the Republican party controlled the Senate. Prior to the adoption of the Seventeenth Amendment, members of the Senate were chosen by the state legislatures, the majority of which were controlled by the GOP. This resulted in frequent Republican majorities in the Senate even when national electoral tides swept the Democrats into the House and the presidency.[3] After the adoption of the Seventeenth Amendment, Senate elections consistently followed national trends.

Third, divided government at the national level has consistently posed a Democratic Congress against a Republican president, which suggests that the phenomenon is not the result of random electoral forces.[4] If it were the result of chance, partisan control of political institutions would also be random; this has not been the case. The era of divided government has displayed a distinctive pattern of institutional control.

Finally, divided government has emerged as a dominant pattern in state governments. Since the mid-1950s more than half of all nonsouthern state governments, in any given year, have experienced divided government. Mirroring divided government at the national level, the modal pattern in the states juxtaposes a Democratic legislature against a Republican executive.[5]

These observations suggest that the period since the 1950s constitutes a distinct political era and marks an important departure from past patterns of institutional control. Divided government represents a new organizing principle of governing in the United States.

Several explanations for the emergence of divided government have been advanced. Gary Jacobson argues that divided government is the result of a classic collective action problem. Voters prefer the benefits of the modern service state (Social Security, Medicare/Medicaid and the like) yet seek to avoid the costs of these services. Thus, a politically relevant minority of voters split their ticket, favoring Democratic candidates for Congress who promise to protect social programs and Republican presidential candidates who promise to cut, or "hold the line," on taxes.[6]

Similarly, John Petrocik demonstrates that the Democratic and Republican parties have captured issues that appeal to different electoral constituencies. The Republicans have captured foreign policy and economic management issues, which are more "presidential," while the Democrats have captured distributional issues that comport with the local nature of congressional constituencies. Individual electoral choices, according to Petrocik, are based on two different sets of criteria: managerial issues, which favor the Republicans at the presidential level, and distributional issues, which benefit the Democrats at the legislative level.[7]

Martin Wattenberg takes another tack, laying the blame for divided government on the doorstep of the Democrats' presidential nomination process. He contends that the McGovern-Fraser reforms in the wake of the 1968 election created an intractable and divisive nomination process that puts the Democratic nominee at a disadvantage in the general election. Wattenberg demonstrates that the more divisive the nomination, the less likely the nominee is to win the general election. Because the Democratic party's nomination process encourages divisiveness, the Democrats have been largely unable to capture the White House. The result is divided government.[8]

Finally, Morris Fiorina has advanced a theory of "policy balancing" to explain the emergence of divided government. He argues that voters have a fundamental understanding of American political institutions and perceive the Democratic and Republican parties as polarized. A politically significant minority of voters therefore chooses to divide control of political institutions between the parties on the assumption that divided control will result in more moderate policy outcomes.[9]

Any complete explanation of the causes of divided government would take into account elements of each of these theories and the historical dynamics that undergird them. For instance, each of these explanations relies on the decline of political parties as a cognitive link between political institutions and, thus, a decoupling of congressional and presidential election outcomes. In addition, some of these explanations (Jacobson, Petrocik, and Fiorina) require that the individual voter's conception of the American state has been transformed. The pre-New Deal American state was minimalist, and individual expectations of the state were equally minimal; citizens expected the production of public goods to be at a relatively low level. However, the emergence of the modern service state led individuals to *expect* that the state would provide a relatively high level of services, and in turn extract the costs of those services in the form of taxes. Thus, any theory predicated on some sort of policy balance, such as Fiorina or Jacobson, must acknowledge the unique historical, as well as partisan, electoral and institutional circumstances that condition individual voters' perceptions and choices.

Punctuated Change and Political Eras

The Theory of Punctuated Change

The term *punctuated change* has begun to gain some currency in the lexicon of political science.[10] Developed by paleontologists Niles Eldredge and Stephen Jay Gould, it refers to a sudden, transformative change in an otherwise stable system. The theory of punctuated change was developed as a means for explaining the gap between evolutionary theory and the fossil record. Evolution implies a linear and incremental process, "a stately unfolding." [11] Through the interpretive lens of the theory of evolution "the fossil record for the origin of a new species should consist of a long sequence of continuous, insensibly graded intermediate forms linking ancestor and descendant." [12] The fossil record, however, reveals breaks in this process; long periods of stasis followed by the rapid transformation of a species.

Students of evolution often dismiss the lack of evidence for gradual change and attribute breaks in the fossil record to catastrophic events that erased the record of gradual change in the various species represented. Eldredge and Gould suggest that breaks in the fossil record represent important elements of the story of evolution rather than technical nuisances. They posit that these breaks represent sudden, transformative change in a previously stable system. In other words, natural history is marked by periods of stasis, *punctuated* by periods of intense change: "The history of evolution is not one of stately unfolding, but a story of homeostatic equilibria, disturbed only 'rarely' (that is, rather often in the fullness of time) by rapid and episodic events of speciation." [13]

The concept of punctuated change may be fruitfully employed to explain change in the American political system. As we look back through political time we recognize periods of relative stasis punctuated by periods of important, system transforming change. Authors differ in their names for these periods; some speak of electoral realignments, some of "party systems," others of constitutional eras, and still others of "mood cycles." [14] There is a haunting similarity in the timing of these periods of change that has been noted by several scholars. Each interpretation of. American political history, whether from the perspective of realignments or mood cycles, suggests a dimension of transformative political change. However, no single one of these explanations is completely convincing. The confluence of these different periods in political time suggests that they identify distinct dimensions of significant transformations in American politics.[15]

Burnham contends that periods of *punctuated political change* "are 'moments,' or compressed event sequences, that differ not only in degree but to a considerable extent in kind from natural phenomenon found within chronological party systems." There are two criteria for identifying such periods. First, "politically decisive minorities of the politically relevant population of any given time stop doing what they have traditionally been doing in politics (including participation or nonparticipation) and rather suddenly begin doing something very different; and thereafter, for many years keep on doing it." Second, "there are exceptionally important and enduring consequences for the organization of the political system." [16] Electoral behavior changes, political parties alter electoral strategies, relationships between political institutions are transformed, and policy agendas shift; the political system is remade in light of a new political reality.

The study of punctuated change thus requires that the analyst be comfortable with the uncertainty and contingency of American political history, and the precise interpretation and explication of that history. As Stephen Jay Gould has stated regarding the study of natural history: "the 'pageant' of evolution [is] a staggeringly improbable series of events, sensible enough in retrospect and subject to rigorous explanation, but utterly unpredictable and quite unrepeatable." [17]

Punctuated change provides a broader framework within which political change, and political eras, may be interpreted. Punctuated change removes the blinders from the political analysts who seek regularity colored by a theory of realignment, mood cycles, or constitutional eras. These approaches dictate a search for repetition of historical patterns and regularities in timing; if regularities are not found, the theory is discarded. The theory of punctuated change requires that one search for new patterns that are enduring.

Punctuated change proceeds from a confluence of political forces, which alters the trajectory of political development. Political change from this perspective is produced by a web of causation that is not necessarily replicable. In addition, change will not always follow the same causal path over time and space. Some elements of this causal web will exhibit linear and incremental characteristics, others may be nonlinear; the way these forces converge is what creates sharp and enduring systemic change. And change both reflects and results in a transformation in the shared understanding of the functioning of the political system. [18]

From the punctuated change perspective, political eras are defined by two criteria: broad and sustained changes in the behavior of the electorate, and subsequent changes in the behavior of government. Have voters changed their conception of the role of political parties, elections, and institutions? Have governmental outputs changed in a significant fashion? These criteria provide a method for distinguishing a period of punctuated change from change that is more limited in scope. Punctuated political change is marked by an enduring, qualitative shift in the structure and outputs of a political system, in this case the American system.

Periods of Punctuated Political Change

From the punctuated change perspective there are five distinct and identifiable political eras in American politics. The *Revolutionary period* (1775) was marked by the relative lack of influence of political parties, although an embryonic party system began to emerge in Congress despite the antiparty tenor of the Founding period.[19] Congressional elections were very competitive, resulting in high turnover. Presidents were not popularly elected and, lacking a mass electoral base, were institutionally weak relative to the Congress. By and large, debate over national policy revolved around the definition of the American nation-state, national goals, and values.[20] Minimalist expectations about the American state were firmly established during this period. Electoral activity and policy demands, to the extent that they existed, were focused at the state level.

The *Jacksonian period* (1824) is characterized by the emergence of the Democratic party as the dominant political party in the electorate. This era is characterized by a politics of participation in the form of universal white male suffrage. Although the states continued to be the dominant focus in electoral politics, the presidency established a national electoral base that would serve as a foundation for the future accumulation of institutional power. However, the presidency remained a weak institution relative to the Congress. Minimal expectations about the national government fostered the expansion of an agrarian-based economy, accompanied by a rudimentary industrial economy in the North. The dominant policy agenda reflected the increasing tension between the power of the national government and the state governments, marked primarily by accommodation on the issue of slavery.

The *Civil War period* (1854) was characterized by the dominance of the Republican party at the national level. Following the Civil War the issue of national versus state power was largely resolved, and the supremacy of the national government was firmly established. An emergent national and international economy thrust the power of the federal government into the spotlight, and the national government expanded its role vis-à-vis civil rights and the economy. Thus, elections for national office became increasingly important. Although the Lincoln presidency had hinted at the potential institutional power of the presidency based on a national electoral following, a series of weak presidents ensured that the Congress would remain the dominant institution in American politics. The agenda revolved around the power of the national government. Newly found governing power was used to lay the foundation for an emerging national and international industrial economy.

The *Progressive era* (1894) reestablished the dominance of the Republican party at the national level. Reform of what was perceived as a corrupt political system assumed center stage, and mainly targeted political parties and the electoral process itself. In a series of reforms aimed at cleaning up government, links between political parties and the electorate were severed. Progressive reforms sought to reduce political patronage, further insulate government bureaucracy from partisan influence, and destroy the urban political machines.

Equally, if not more, important, the electoral mechanism for divided government was established. Adoption of the Australian ballot allowed individuals to split their votes at the national level, encouraging the decline in the influence of parties in the electoral process.[21] In addition, the strong appeals of presidents such as Theodore Roosevelt and Woodrow Wilson were harbingers of a changing presidency, although a complete transformation of the office was several decades away. Congress remained strong but became increasingly willing to transfer key powers to the presidency. By and large the policy debate during this period revolved around the appropriate role of the national government in an industrial economy.[22]

Finally, the *New Deal period* (1930/1932) witnessed the reemergence of the Democratic party at the national level, temporarily stemming the tide of partisan decay initiated by the Progressive reformers.[23] The election of Franklin D. Roosevelt, and the policies he pursued, transformed public perceptions of the national government and popular expectations of the presidency. In the post-FDR period the presidency has emerged as the central focus of electoral politics, and the public has come to expect the president to fulfill many roles, from economic manager to foreign policy manager.[24] Institutional power continued to be transferred from Congress to the president at a breakneck pace, reinforcing public perceptions of a strong presidency and severely diminishing public perceptions of Congress. The policy agenda of the New Deal instituted an activist government committed to the regulation of the industrial-capitalist system, the erection of a social "safety net," and the delivery of particularized benefits to more and more beneficiaries.

The Era of Divided Government

Each period described above is characterized by a relatively sudden shift in the role of political parties and the behavior of a sizable number of voters, usually resulting in new and stable partisan alignments and a solid governing majority. Each period is also marked by a change in the organizing principles of government, and a resulting alteration in the patterns of governing and the policy agenda.

To this periodization, I contend, we should add a sixth: the era of divided government (1952-present). This era has been widely considered one of "dealignment," "drift," "party decomposition," and so forth. I contend that this period represents a distinct political regime in and of itself:

Figure 9-1   Percentage of Districts with Split House/Presidential Outcomes, 1900-1988

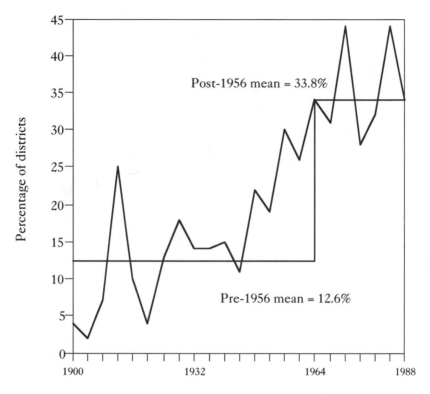

We are currently experiencing the consequences of a period of punctuated change. As in other periods of punctuated change we find enduring change both in the behavior of voters and in the performance of the American political system. In this section I describe the scope of this change.

The percentage of districts voting for divided government from 1900 through 1988 are shown in Figure 9-1. Although the district congressional vote has increasingly gone one way and the presidential vote the other, the average from 1900 to 1952 was just over 12.5 percent, while the average beginning with the election of 1956 is almost 34 percent. This jump represents a significant shift in voting behavior. In the past voters were highly partisan; since the mid-1950s parties have deteriorated as a link between voting for members of Congress and the president.

The percentage of House seats controlled by the Democratic party and the percentage of the two-party presidential vote garnered by the Democratic candidate are shown in Figure 9-2. Democratic representation in the Senate is shown in Figure 9-3. Both figures indicate a *decoupling* of congressional and presidential elections in the post-New Deal era. Until 1932 the two series track each other closely; after 1932 a

Figure 9-2   Democratic Representation in the House,
                  1868-1992

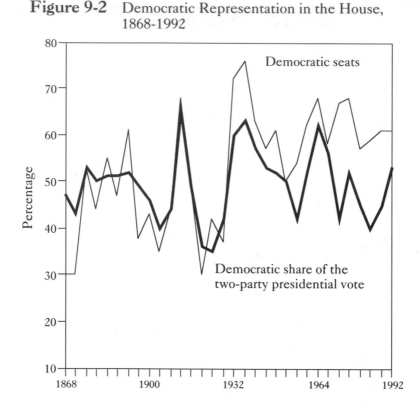

significant gap appears between the series in each figure. Before the election of 1932 this gap averaged -1.3 percent for the House series and -4.2 percent for the Senate series, indicating that Democratic presidential candidates did slightly better at the national level than did their party brethren in Congress. After 1932, however, this gap exploded to $+11.1$ percent for the House series and $+8.6$ percent for the Senate series. This pattern illustrates nicely the increasing independence of national electoral outcomes in the post-1932 period.

If these figures show change in the aggregate behavior of voters, Figure 9-4 illustrates the effects of this change. Divided government was present during only 6.6 percent of the period between 1920 and 1940 (the exception being a result of the midterm elections of 1930).[25] Yet 60 percent of the period from 1950 to the present has been characterized by divided government, nearly a tenfold increase.

The extent of this sea change is represented in Figure 9-5, which illustrates the tremendous explosion of divided government at the state level. At roughly the same time that divided government emerged as the national norm, the percentage of nonsouthern states with divided government increased dramatically. Prior to 1956 just less than a third of all

Figure 9-3 Democratic Representation in the Senate, 1868-1992

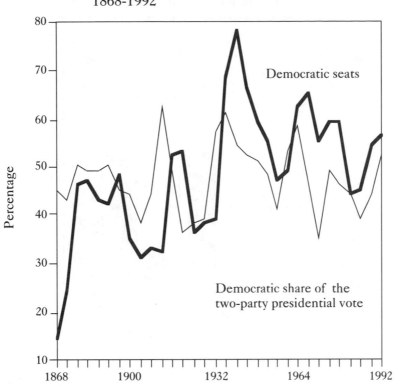

nonsouthern state governments were divided.[26] After 1956 more than 55 percent of state governments, on average, experienced divided government in any given year.

Taken together, this evidence points to a dramatic change in voter behavior. The partisan composition of American political institutions changed as well. Both shifts are enduring and pervasive. Divided government is more than an anomalous blip on the screen of American political history; it has become the dominant political regime. The pattern established in the mid-1950s suggests a significant break with previous patterns in American politics. Other major party eras were marked by a relatively high degree of united party government.[27] The era of divided government, in contrast, is marked by a very low degree of party government.

Patterns of Party Control

If the five political eras described above were marked by a high degree of united party government across institutions, the era of divided government is marked by a high degree of distinctive partisan control of

Figure 9-4   Percentage of Decade under Divided
Government, 1920s-1980s

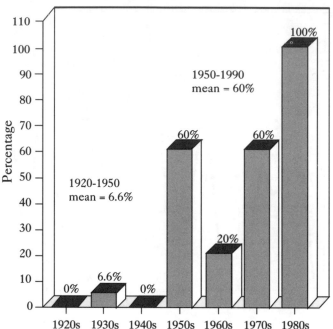

specific political institutions. The modal pattern has become Republican control of the executive branch and Democratic control of the legislature, at both the national and the state levels. This is a sharp departure from previous eras of American political history.[28]

The Democratic dominance of Congress has grown out of the New Deal realignment (see Figure 9-6). Prior to the 1930s the Democrats were effectively locked out of the control of Congress, while the Republicans controlled the Congress for the most part. Beginning with the New Deal realignment, Republican fortunes sagged. The GOP had unified control of the Congress for only four years between 1930 and 1990. Democrats surged, marking an ascendance that has characterized contemporary American political history.

By way of contrast, the Republican party has been successful at the presidential level, where GOP fortunes have remained fairly constant except for the New Deal period, when the Democrats maintained the White House from 1932 to 1952 (see Figure 9-7). Taken together, these figures illustrate the emergence of partisan control of political institutions that characterize the era of divided government. Sagging GOP fortunes in congressional elections were followed by a surge in electoral power at the presidential level.

Figure 9-5   Percentage of States with Divided
Government

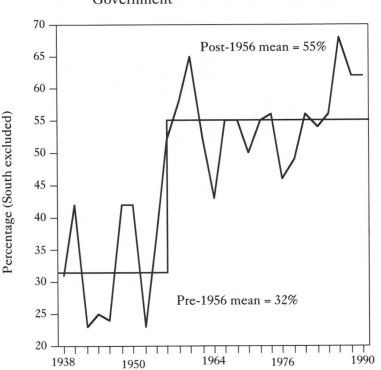

The era of divided government marks a break with the historical pattern of partisan control of both national and state-level political institutions. Beginning in the mid-1950s partisan control of state political institutions began to mirror partisan control of national political institutions. The Democratic party established itself as the dominant political party at the legislative level, and the Republican party began to dominate at the executive level.

Contrary to the conventional wisdom, Democratic dominance of state legislatures does not appear until well after the New Deal realignment (see Figure 9-8). During the early years of the realignment, many state legislatures were captured by the Democratic party, but this was only temporary. This initial success was followed by a period of decline in Democratic control of state legislatures into the early-1950s. Only in the mid-1950s did Democratic dominance of state legislatures increase, and the Democratic party firmly establish itself in the majority of nonsouthern state legislatures.

This finding leads one to reconsider the conventional wisdom about the New Deal realignment. Traditional interpretations of this period imply that a sizable portion of the electorate changed its party loyalty to the

Figure 9-6   Democratic Unified Congresses, 1870s-1980s

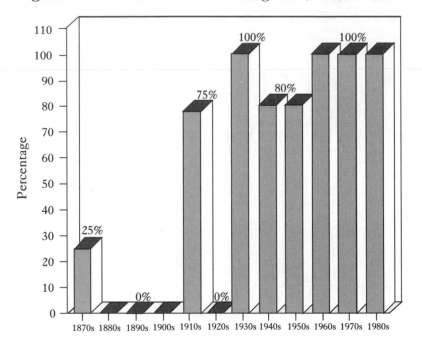

Democratic party, and thus the Democrats came to control state as well as national government following the New Deal realignment.[29] But this interpretation does not hold at the state level (see Figure 9-8). At the national level the Democrats were the dominant party, controlling both the White House and Congress between 1932 and 1946. At the state level the Republican party continued as a dominant force, controlling all or part of most statehouses throughout the 1940s and into the 1950s.[30] Voters seemingly turned to the Democratic party to solve a national crisis but continued to hold on to their Republican sympathies at the state level.

This Democratic dominance of state legislatures is matched over this period by a corresponding increase in the percentage of states with divided government led by Republican executives (see Figure 9-9). This general trend reveals the same change in control over political institutions in the states that is apparent at the national level.

The Dimensions of Divided Government

Divided partisan control of government, both state and national, has transformed American politics in a way not widely recognized by scholars. Prior to the mid-1950s America experienced divided government with a

Figure 9-7 Divided Government with Republican
President, 1870s-1980s

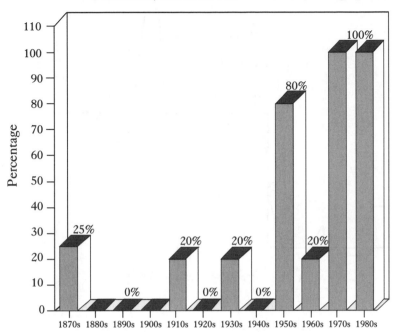

horizontal division between national and state government. After the 1950s America came to experience divided branches of government, a vertical division with different parties controlling the executive and the legislature (see Table 9-1).

From the New Deal realignment to the mid-1950s, the Democratic national government was pitted against state governments that were primarily controlled by the Republican party. Since the mid-1950s, however, Republican executives have largely faced-off against Democratic legislatures. The period following the New Deal realignment thus can be divided into two distinct eras: a period of *horizontal division* in party control of government from 1938 to 1956, and a period of *vertical division* in party control of government since 1958.

The horizontal division in American politics has developed into a vertical split both at the state and national levels. When divided government is present, the dominant pattern has the Republican party capturing the executive at the national and state levels, and the Democrats capturing the legislatures.

This division might be interpreted as a realignment of voters along the lines provided by political institutions; that is, an *institutionally based* alignment of voters at the national and state levels. Paradoxically, al-

Figure 9-8   Democratic Unified Legislatures, 1938-1990

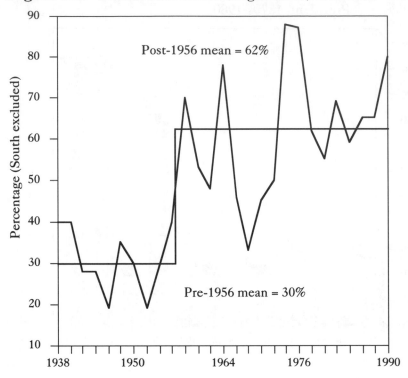

though the importance of parties as providers of integrative voting cues across institutions has declined, voters have retained a shared understanding of what the two political parties "stand for": the Democratic party dispenses public goods, and the Republican party represents fiscal restraint.[31]

Voters have changed in that they are now willing to ignore partisan loyalties as their exclusive cue in voting for national office, as witnessed by increased split-ticket voting, the decoupling of presidential and congressional elections, and so forth.[32] Equally as important, the voters' perception of political institutions has changed. In the early period following the New Deal, the national government was the focus for the provision of public goods and the state governments were the focus of fiscal constraint.[33] But as the national government began to engage in "creative federalism" in the 1950s, using state government to implement some programs, the voters' calculus shifted. On the one hand, the vote for the legislatures reflects the voters' underlying partisan sympathies with respect to social policy. The vote for the executive, on the other hand, is a vote to "govern" or control governmental "outputs." [34] This shift produced the transformation from the horizontal to the vertical dimension in party control of government.

Table 9-1   Dimensions of Divided Government

	Horizontal 1938-1956		Vertical 1958-1990	
	Executive	Legislature	Executive	Legislature
Federal	Democratic	Democratic	Republican	Democratic
State	Republican	Republican	Republican	Democratic

Since the mid-1950s the American political system has undergone a transformation. Before, political change was channeled by *parties* within a particular institutional context. Changes in voter behavior revolved around the parties, that is, changes in allegiance to one party or another. Policy change was the result of monopoly control of a single political party over the institutions of government. This was true of the five political eras described above.

In the era of divided government, political change has been channeled by institutions within a particular partisan context. Political parties

Figure 9-9   States with Divided Government, Republican Executive, 1938-1990

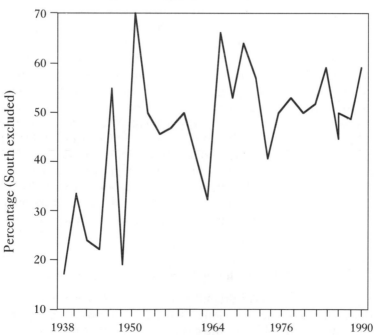

remain strong symbolic forces in American politics. Largely because of the Democrats' role as architects and defenders of the modern service state, voters perceive them as champions of social programs and liberal social policy. Historically opposed to extensive social services and government intervention, the Republican party is perceived to be economically and socially conservative and better able to manage foreign affairs. However, parties have declined as voting cues that link political institutions for voters. Control of the legislature reflects the aggregate demand for collective goods, and control of the executive reflects the degree of fiscal constraint that voters prefer. These choices are premised on the voters' understanding of contemporary political parties.

Within this electoral context, a politically relevant minority of voters chooses to divide control of political institutions based on their understanding of the "strengths" of each political party and the "roles" of political institutions. Democratic candidates, perceived as defenders of particularized benefits, thus have an advantage when vying for positions in the institutions best able to protect and expand social programs: the legislature. Similarly, Republican candidates, who are seen as fiscally conservative economic managers, have an advantage in contests for the institution best able to control governmental outputs: the executive.

The first criterion of punctuated change has therefore been met: individual voters have displayed an enduring change in their electoral behavior. Periods of punctuated change are also marked, however, by distinctive policy dynamics. I contend that the era of divided government has a unique policy dynamic. In the past, punctuated change resulted in a new and innovative policy agenda; political conflict centered on how these changes would be maintained or adjusted.[35] But the institutional conditions do not now exist for a focused and coherent policy agenda to emerge. Divided government cannot provide a coherent agenda for policy change because political parties are unable to function as the medium through which policy change may take place. Divided government intensifies conflict between Congress and the president, damaging prospects for policy agreement. In addition, divided government reduces the amount of important legislation, legislation that might address pressing political, social, and economic issues. Thus, the era of divided government has a unique policy dynamic of its own, but that dynamic diverges from previous patterns in American political history.

The Policy Consequences of Divided Government

In the American constitutional system there is a natural rivalry between Congress and the president. It divides the power to govern in a conscious attempt to debilitate the exercise of power at the national level. Most important, the Constitution divides the power to legislate between

Congress and the president, granting the power to legislate to the former, and to the latter the power to veto. The logic of "separate institutions sharing power" thrusts Congress and the presidency into an eternal struggle for institutional advantage and for predominance in the policy-making process.[36]

The conventional wisdom in political science, fashioned by authors such as Woodrow Wilson, E. E. Schattschneider, and others, holds that partisan control of distinct political institutions shapes the contours of the interbranch relationship.[37] According to the conventional wisdom, political parties bridge these institutional fissures, helping to hold together an otherwise hopelessly fragmented institutional system. Cooperation across institutional divides is encouraged by common programmatic interests, as well as shared political fortunes, when a single party controls both Congress and the presidency.

When the majority party in Congress faces a minority party president, natural institutional rivalries are exacerbated.[38] First, under divided government members of Congress and the president do not share a common electoral fate. Therefore, they feel no compunction to cooperate with one another on many issues. The majority party in Congress fears the president will benefit electorally from their cooperation and will therefore refuse to follow the lead of the president. Similarly, the president will not want the Congress to capitalize on its own successes, and will not cooperate with congressional initiatives. Second, institutional conflict will increase because the majority party in Congress controls the levers of congressional power: the committee system, the nature and flow of the legislative agenda, and so forth. The majority party will use these powers to pursue its own interests, which are often opposed to those of the minority party president. Although conflict is inherent and desirable in democratic political systems, divided government leads programmatically opposed parties to feud across institutional boundaries, resulting in institutional conflict, delay, and inaction.[39] Divided government, then, represents a qualitative shift in the relationship between Congress and the president.

Revisionist scholars argue that divided government does not qualitatively alter the relationship between the branches, largely dismissing the importance of political parties in contemporary American politics. They further contend that parties do not serve as mechanisms for overcoming the institutional rivalry between Congress and the president. Parties fail on this count because individual members of Congress have no incentive to adhere to their party's policy agenda. Given electorally weak political parties, members of Congress concerned with reelection must pursue party-neutral strategies for gaining reelection.[40] Thus, parties will be ineffective institutions for shaping the collective behavior of individual members of Congress.

Recent scholarship to the contrary suggests that congressional political parties have enjoyed a renaissance over the last two decades. David Rohde demonstrates that majority party leaders in the House have become increasingly influential over the last two decades, and that partisan voting patterns have become much more pronounced. Similarly, Barbara Sinclair argues that the House majority party leadership has become more willing to use its powers to shape the legislative agenda and influence legislative outcomes. According to David Price, "the congressional parties over the last twenty years have become more active and their operations more extensive than at any other time in American history [and] the parties retain a central role in the present functioning of the Congress." And Bond and Fleisher identify party as a central variable in predicting a member's support of presidential initiatives.[41]

Without question American political parties are relatively weak electoral organizations. In fact, weak political parties, I have argued, are a central cause of divided government. But this weakness in the electorate has not incapacitated the parties in government. If anything, the past two decades have been characterized by the continued, and perhaps increasing, importance of partisan loyalties in the Congress. This presents the analyst of American politics with an important paradox: in an era of weakening parties in the electorate, political parties remain important forces within government and play a strong role in shaping policy outcomes.

This paradox can be partly explained by the electoral dynamics of the era of divided government. The shift in the electoral context of the era of divided government has prompted office seekers to adopt new strategies within government that reinforce partisanship, in order to maintain electoral support.

Members of both parties have a primary interest in maintaining the symbolic importance of their party labels: the Democrats as the party of social and economic liberalism, and the Republicans as the party of social and economic conservatism. Within the electoral context of divided government, these symbolic positions impart to each party an electoral advantage, at the congressional level for the Democrats, and at the presidential level for the Republicans. Each party has an intense interest in maintaining the "value" of this label because of the electoral payoff it holds for members of each party.[42] This electoral incentive will lead members of the two parties to behave in a more partisan fashion than we would otherwise expect given electorally weak parties, and in turn help to shape policy outcomes and reinforce public perceptions of the two parties. Parties, then, may function in a manner that is consistent with the conventional wisdom and its expectations.

Thus, political parties can and do play a central role in shaping the relationship between Congress and the president. Unlike previous political eras, which were marked by united party government, however, political parties will be unable to provide a means for establishing a focused and coherent policy agenda. Programmatic differences between the parties and sustained institutional conflict will stifle policy innovation and prevent a coherent policy agenda from emerging.

Policy Agreement

The conventional wisdom suggests that divided government will lead, in part, to less institutional cooperation between the branches. Partisan competition laid on top of natural institutional rivalries will heighten conflict between the branches over matters of public policy. A simple way to test this hypothesis is to examine Congressional Quarterly's "presidential success" scores. These scores reflect the percentage of policy issues on which a majority in Congress supported the expressed policy position of the president, thus representing the level of policy agreement between the branches. Despite its flaws, the CQ system provides a fairly accurate measure of the "state of the relationship" between Congress and the president.[43]

Mean policy agreement scores are given in Table 9-2. The first thing to note is that mean policy agreement scores under united government hover around 82 percent in all three interbranch relationships, and between 57 percent and 66 percent under divided government. The difference between these means ranges from 15.6 percent for the Senate-president and 25.8 percent for the House-president data. These are important differences, which are dismissed by revisionist scholars Petracca and Thurber.[44]

Equally enlightening is an examination of the Eisenhower and Reagan administrations. The Republican party controlled the Congress during the first two years of the Eisenhower administration; it controlled the Senate for the first six years of the Reagan administration. The differences between policy agreement under united and divided government are truly striking under Eisenhower: 19.3 percent, 26.3 percent, and 17.3 percent, respectively. Under Reagan, the switch from a Republican to a Democratic Senate resulted in a drop of more than 20 percent in policy agreement between the Senate and the president.

These results lend some insight regarding the consequences of divided government for interbranch policy agreement, suggesting that the contentions of traditional scholars have empirical support. Divided government represents a qualitative shift in the relationship between Congress and the president.[45] Interbranch policy agreement is increased when a single party controls both Congress and the presidency; conversely, interbranch policy agreement declines during periods of divided government.

United government will not necessarily result in a harmonious relationship between the branches. Our last period of united government, 1977 to 1981, is illustrative. President Jimmy Carter often found himself at loggerheads with the Congress, and the public perception of his travails

Table 9-2   Policy Agreement in the Era of Divided Government

President	Congress-President Uni.	Div.	House-President Uni.	Div.	Senate-President Uni.	Div.
Eisenhower	86.00	67.70	91.20	64.95	87.80	70.53
Kennedy	84.67	—	83.73	—	85.27	—
Johnson	82.64	—	86.54	—	79.82	—
Nixon	—	68.68	—	73.70	—	64.80
Ford	—	56.67	—	51.00	—	64.20
Carter	76.40	—	73.15	—	78.90	—
Reagan	—	61.86	—	46.64	82.65	60.60
Bush	—	54.70	—	41.20	—	68.35
Mean	81.77	62.43	82.78	57.33	81.59	66.35

Source: Calculated by the author from Congressional Quarterly presidential success scores.

no doubt contributed to his unsuccessful bid for reelection in 1980. Nevertheless, the existence of united government creates the conditions under which cooperation between the branches may emerge. The level of policy agreement between President Carter and the Congress was higher than that of his Republican counterparts.

In the absence of united government the conditions for a stable, cooperative relationship between the branches are nonexistent. Persistent divided government may encourage the Democrats in Congress and the Republican president to engage in what Ginsberg and Shefter call "institutional combat." Attempting to gain institutional and electoral advantage, the parties will use the institution they control to attack the other institution and, thereby, the other party. As domestic and international concerns intensify, such behavior may ultimately subvert attempts to cope with pressing policy issues at home and abroad.[46]

Innovative Legislation

Although an examination of broad patterns of interbranch policy agreement can further our understanding of the institutional dynamics of divided government, our ultimate interest is in policymaking. Previous political eras provided a partisan and institutional context within which significant public policy could emerge. The conventional wisdom suggests that divided government hinders the ability of the American political system to respond to the pressing issues of the day through innovative legislation.[47]

Contrary to the conventional wisdom, Mayhew presents evidence that partisan control of government has little effect on the formulation of innovative legislation. His analysis of data collected from various primary and secondary sources leads him to conclude that innovative legislation is

Table 9-3   Mean Innovative Policy in the Era of Divided
Government

| | Mayhew Measure | | Kelly Measure | |
| | 1946-1990 | | 1946-1986 | |
	Uni.	Div.	Uni.	Div.
Mean	12.78	11.69	8.78	6.09
S.D.	4.60	5.48	3.83	2.84
N	9	13	9	11

more directly linked to timing (it is more likely to be enacted in the first two years of a presidential term) and the "public mood" (it is more likely to emerge when there is a public demand for an activist government). Mayhew concludes that "unified versus divided control has probably not made a notable difference during the postwar era." [48]

Mayhew fails to provide a framework for distinguishing innovative policies from ordinary legislation. Innovative legislation is both *timely* and *enduring*.[49] It addresses salient problems. For instance, New Deal programs were aimed at alleviating the burden of the Great Depression on the poor and the elderly, thus addressing a salient political need. Innovative legislation is enduring in that the impact of the policy remains evident across time and can be identified as having been successful in addressing a policy concern. New Deal programs such as Social Security and medical aid for the poor have endured; the public expects the government to continue them. Such legislation may therefore be considered innovative.

The most innovative pieces of legislation in Mayhew's database, then, are those viewed as innovative at the time of their passage and since judged to have been important. When taken as a group, these innovative policies comprise 147 of Mayhew's original 267 laws, or 55 percent of the original list of legislation.

The most straightforward test of the divided government hypothesis is to examine the mean number of innovative policies generated under divided and united government (see Table 9-3). When Mayhew's original data are used, divided government does not seem to hinder the passage of innovative legislation. Under united government, 12.8 pieces of innovative legislation were passed; under divided government, the figure is 11.7. Using a more stringent definition, however, a significant difference emerges. Periods of united government average 8.8 acts, with divided government producing about 6 acts. In more concrete terms, about 30 percent fewer innovative policies are passed in Congress under divided government than under a united one.

Of course a more sophisticated analysis of the data is in order so that alternative causes of this difference may be ruled out. Mayhew provides a model for a multivariate test.[50] He argues that there are three possible other causes, beyond partisan control of government, of variation in innovative policy. When Mayhew's model is applied to the more restrictive list of innovative policy, divided government has the significant negative impact that is expected. All other things being equal, under divided government two fewer innovative policies are passed in every Congress. In more substantive terms, over the twelve periods of divided government accounted for in this data, perhaps twenty-four innovative policies were not passed because of divided government. Reassessed in this way, Mayhew's data reveals that divided government *matters*.

Does the era of divided government have a unique policy dynamic? The evidence presented here suggests that it does; it increases policy conflict between the branches. Perhaps more important, divided government inhibits passage of innovative legislation, which in turn hampers the ability of policymakers to establish a coherent policy agenda aimed at addressing the country's ills. During previous periods of "punctuated change," persistent united government allowed a stable policy agenda to emerge; under persistent divided government we should have no such expectation.

Conclusion

Over the past four decades divided government has become the primary means for organizing national and state politics. At the national level Republicans have controlled the White House, and Democrats have controlled the Congress. Likewise, most states had Republican governors and Democratic legislatures. Although the 1992 elections maintained divided government in the states, united government returned at the national level for the first time in twelve years. With the inauguration of Bill Clinton as president and solid Democratic majorities in the House and the Senate, the question becomes, why the return to united government at this point in history?

We need to reexamine one of the central causes of divided government. In contemporary American politics the Republican party has become associated with economic management, command over foreign affairs, and fiscal conservatism. The Democratic party has become associated with the maintenance of the modern service state and social liberalism. Given unique historical and institutional conditions, a politically significant minority of voters makes electoral choices based on the symbolic roles of the parties.

The 1992 presidential election was the first post-Cold War election. Significant arms control agreements, engineered by Ronald Reagan and George Bush, with the Soviets in the late 1980s and early 1990s decreased the perceived military threat of a large-scale nuclear war with the

Soviets. The subsequent disintegration of the Soviet Union into the Commonwealth of Independent States further reduced the specter of Communist aggression around the world.

As the historically isolationist American electorate turned inward after an unprecedented, six-decade period of intense international involvement, one of the Republican party's major advantages in presidential politics was neutralized. Although foreign policy brushfires flared in the Balkans, East Africa, and elsewhere, they hardly rivaled the immediate dangers represented in the past by the Soviet Union. The new foreign policy map, although more complex—and for that reason perhaps more difficult to read—is not the bipolar map of the Cold War period. Without a powerful or well-defined enemy, U.S. foreign policy was eclipsed as an electoral concern, to the disadvantage of the Republican party. Paradoxically, then, Republican success in confronting and taming the Soviet threat undermined one of the party's primary electoral advantages.

When the American public focused on domestic concerns, it found a country in economic disarray. The economic dislocation prompted by the transition to a post-Cold War economy had spurred a recession; and the Republican president, seemingly preoccupied with foreign policy, appeared strangely out of touch with the widespread dissatisfaction of the American public. With the encouragement of independent candidate Ross Perot, domestic economic concerns focused more closely on the immense federal budget deficit and the national debt—all of which had emerged on the Republicans' watch.

Since the New Deal the American public has come to expect that the national government will take a proactive role in controlling the economy, especially during economic downturns, and will help to relieve the suffering of the economically disadvantaged. In particular, it has become the president's responsibility to respond to economic crises. The reliance of the contemporary Republican party on a philosophy of laissez-faire economics makes it ill-prepared to *actively* confront domestic economic concerns. Since the depression the Republican party has advanced a "ride it out" approach to the economy. This approach may have worked if the economy recovered before the presidential election, but a weak economy during the election undermined the electoral appeal of the Republican emphasis on economic conservatism.

National forces during 1992 thus favored the Democratic party at the presidential level. Republican successes abroad largely removed foreign policy from the national agenda, and the public subsequently focused on economic issues that the Republican president seemed reluctant to address. The Democratic party is symbolically and philosophically better prepared to offer programmatic solutions such as infrastructure development (roads, bridges, mass-transit, and so forth), development of a national health care reform, national service, and the like. As the public mood shifted to domestic social issues, Clinton was therefore better able to capitalize on the perceived social liberalism of the Democratic party, stressing its prochoice stance on abortion, and support of family medical leave, expanded voter registration, and so forth.[51]

What should we expect from this period of united government? Based on previous experience with united government in the post-World War II period, the Clinton administration should enjoy high levels of cooperation with the Congress. Clinton and the Democratic Congress seem especially sensitive to their majority party status and are consciously seeking to build a relationship of trust between the two institutions. Despite early press coverage to the contrary, congressional Democrats have exhibited a willingness to cooperate with Clinton, and the White House has taken great pains to coordinate its policy agenda with the leadership in both chambers. Based on the CQ measure of policy agreement, Clinton should experience an overall "success" rate of between 76 and 83 percent, well above the historical average of 62 percent under divided government (see Table 9-2).[52]

In addition, I suspect that united government will result in a flurry of innovative legislation aimed at turning back the Reagan-Bush social "revolution." Early in the Clinton administration Congress passed, and Clinton signed, the Family and Medical Leave Act and the National Voter Registration Act, both of which were vetoed by George Bush. Clinton and the Democrats in Congress will also seek to codify abortion rights through passage of the Freedom of Choice Act.

United government and the current political context suggest that the most promising area for significant progress is on the national budget deficit. As the public has focused on the domestic economy, it has demonstrated a new willingness to deal substantively with the deficit. President Clinton may be able to use his majority party status to raise taxes and cut spending in a manner that could not be conceived under divided government. Under divided government, Republican presidents resist tax increases and insist on spending cuts that impact traditional Democratic constituencies and hence meet congressional resistance.[53] The Democratic Congress insists on tax increases that impact traditional Republican constituencies and resist spending cuts. United party government provides a context in which balanced tax increases and spending cuts may be enacted as the majority party keeps one eye on its future electoral fortunes. That old chestnut "only Nixon could go to China" may develop a contemporary analogue: "only Clinton could cut the deficit."

Although united government is likely to continue for at least four years, the electoral context that undergirds the era of divided government is still present. Parties remain a weak force in the electorate, split-ticket voting is still prevalent, the institutional and symbolic expectations of the American electorate are intact, and so forth. Bill Clinton may very well represent the exception to the rule of divided government rather than a harbinger of a return to normalcy, to united government. There is little reason to believe that the election of Bill Clinton represents an enduring shift toward the Democratic party, or even that Clinton will be successful in securing a second term; recent history suggests that he will not.

Given that these underlying dynamics are still present, and that the 1992 election was not a realigning event that will return us to a pattern of united party government, this period of united government should only further encourage us to seek more refined approaches and answers to the puzzle that divided government offers students of American politics.

Notes

I would like to acknowledge the support of the Department of Political Science and the Center for the Study of American Politics at the University of Colorado, and the Department of Political Science at East Carolina University. Helpful comments and encouragement at various points in the evolution of this project came from Larry Dodd, Walter Dean Burnham, Mo Fiorina, Rodney Hero, Cal Jillson, Steve Majstorovic, David Mayhew, Vince McGuire, Will Moore, Sheen Rajmaira, Lee Chambers Schiller, Walt Stone, and Bob Thompson.

1. On the prevalence of united government see Walter Dean Burnham, *Critical Elections: The Mainsprings of American Politics* (New York: Norton, 1970), and James L. Sundquist, *Dynamics of the Party System: Alignment and Realignment of Political Parties in the United States* (Washington, D.C.: Brookings Institution, 1983). On policy agendas see David W. Brady, *Critical Elections and Congressional Policy Making* (Stanford, Calif.: Stanford University Press, 1988), and Barbara Sinclair, "Agenda and Alignment Change: The House of Representatives, 1925-1978," in *Congress Reconsidered*, 2d ed., ed. Lawrence C. Dodd and Bruce I. Oppenheimer (Washington, D.C.: CQ Press, 1981).

2. Critics of realignment theory are increasingly skeptical of its relevance to the study of American politics. See the excellent essays in *The End of Realignment?: Interpreting American Electoral Eras*, ed. Byron E. Sharer (Madison: University of Wisconsin Press, 1991).

3. Charles Stewart III, "Lessons from the Post-Civil War Era," in *The Politics of Divided Government*, ed. Gary W. Cox and Samuel Kernell (Boulder, Colo.: Westview, 1991).

4. That divided government in this period is the result of random forces is argued by James L. Sundquist. See, for example, "The Crisis of Competence in Our National Government," *Political Science Quarterly* 96 (1981):183-208; and, "Needed: A Political Theory for the New Era of Coalition Government in the United States" *Political Science Quarterly* 103 (1988): 613-635.

5. Morris P. Fiorina, *Divided Government* (New York: Macmillan, 1987); see also, Sean Q Kelly, "Dimensions of Divided Government," *Legislative Studies Newsletter* 15 (1992): 6-8.

6. Gary C. Jacobson, *The Electoral Origins of Divided Government: Competition in U.S. House Elections, 1946-1988* (Boulder, Colo.: Westview, 1990).

7. John Petrocik, "Divided Government: Is It All in the Campaigns?" in *Politics of Divided Government*, ed. Cox and Kernell. See also Byron Sharer. "The Notion of an Electoral Order: The Structure of Electoral Politics at the Accession of George Bush," in *The End of Realignment?*, ed. Shafer.

8. Martin Wattenberg, "The Republican Presidential Advantage in the Age of Partisan Disunity," in *Politics of Divided Government*, ed. Cox and Kernell.

9. Fiorina, *Divided Government*.

10. Walter Dean Burnham, "Critical Realignment: Dead or Alive?" in *End of Realignment?*, ed. Shafer; for a similar approach see Peter Gourevitch, *Politics in Hard Times: Comparative Responses to International Economic Crises* (Ithaca, N.Y.: Cornell University Press, 1986).

11. Niles Eldredge and Stephen Jay Gould, "Punctuated Equilibria: An Alternative to Phyletic Gradualism," in *Models in Paleobiology*, ed. Thomas Schopf (San Francisco: Freeman, Cooper, 1972), 84. See also Niles Eldredge, *Time Frames: The Evolution of Punctuated Equilibria* (Princeton, N.J.: Princeton University Press, 1989). Useful discussion of this theory may also be found in Stephen Jay Gould, *Wonderful Life: The Burgess Shale and the Nature of History* (New York: Norton, 1989).

12. Eldredge and Gould, "Punctuated Equilibria," 89.

13. Ibid., 84.

14. Walter Dean Burnham introduces punctuated equilibria in his essay "Critical Realignment." Burnham previously discussed critical realignments in *Critical Elections*. For the "party system" perspective see James L. Sundquist, *Dynamics of the Party System*, and John Clubb, William Flanagan, and Nancy Zingale, *Partisan Realignment* (Beverly Hills, Calif.: Sage, 1980). Constitutional eras are suggested by Theodore J. Lowi, *The End of Liberalism: The Second Republic of the United States* (New York: Norton, 1979). Mood cycles are suggested in the works of Samuel J. Huntington, *American Politics: The Promise of Disharmony* (Cambridge: Harvard University Press, 1981); Arthur Schlesinger, Jr., *The Cycles of American History* (Boston: Houghton Mifflin, 1986); David R. Mayhew, *Divided We Govern: Party Control, Lawmaking, and Investigations, 1946-1990* (New Haven: Yale University Press, 1991); and James Stimson, *Public Opinion in America: Moods, Cycles, and Swings* (Boulder, Colo.: Westview, 1991).

15. See Walter Dean Burnham, "Pattern Recognition: Art, Science, or Bootless Enterprise?" in *The Dynamics of American Politics*, ed. Lawrence C. Dodd and Calvin Jillson (Boulder, Colo.: Westview, 1993); also, for an exhaustive review of the timing of these periods, see Calvin Jillson, "Patterns of American Political Change," in *Dynamics of American Politics*, ed. Dodd and Jillson.

16. Burnham, "Critical Realignment," 110, 115-116, 116.

17. Lawrence C. Dodd, "Political Leaning and Political Change: Understanding Development Across Time," *Dynamics of American Politics*, ed. Dodd and Jillson; and Gould, *Wonderful Life*, 14.

18. See, for instance, Lawrence C. Dodd, "Congress, the President, and the American Experience: A Transformational Perspective," in *Divided Democracy: Cooperation and Conflict Between the President and Congress*, ed. James A. Thurber (Washington, D.C.: CQ Press, 1991).

19. Years indicate the inception date of the period. See William Nisbet, *Chambers, Political Parties in a New Nation: The American Experience* (London: Oxford University Press, 1963); James Sterling Young, *The Washington Community, 1800-1828* (New York: Columbia University Press, 1966); and Joel Silbey, "Beyond Realignment and Realignment Theory: American Political Eras, 1789-1989," in *End of Realignment?*, ed. Sharer.

20. Nelson W. Polsby, "The Institutionalization of the U.S. House of Representatives," *American Political Science Review* 62 (1968): 144-168; and Lawrence C. Dodd, "Congress, the Constitution, and the Crisis of Legitimation," in *Congress Reconsidered*, 2d ed., ed. Dodd and Oppenheimer.

21. Philip E. Converse, "Change in the American Electorate," in *The Human Meaning of Social Change*, ed. Angus Campbell and Philip E. Converse (New York: Russell Sage, 1972).

22. For example, the Budget Act of 1920 transferred one of the most powerful tools that the Congress possessed, power over the fiscal agenda, to the executive

branch. See Lawrence C. Dodd and Richard Schott, *Congress and the Administrative State* (New York: Wiley, 1979); Burnham, *Critical Realignment*.

23. Silbey, "Beyond Realignment."

24. This interpretation rests heavily on the work of Theodore J. Lowi, *The Personal President: Power Invested, Promise Unfulfilled* (Ithaca, N.Y.: Cornell University Press, 1985).

25. The 1920s constituted the first full decade in which Senate elections were popularly contested in all states.

26. For the sake of simplicity I discuss only the nonsouthern states here. The inclusion of the southern states does not alter the substantive conclusions, although it does add a layer of complexity that cannot be addressed in this chapter.

27. For a more detailed treatment see Charles Stewart III, "Lessons from the Post-Civil War Era."

28. I must emphasize that this is the dominant, not the only, pattern. The frequency and complexion of divided government varies from state to state.

29. Sundquist, *Dynamics.*

30. Burnham, "Critical Realignment," 134.

31. Jacobson, *Electoral Origins;* Petrocik, "Divided Government."

32. For an excellent summary of the decline of political parties see Martin Wattenberg, *The Decline of American Political Parties, 1952-1988* (Cambridge: Harvard University Press, 1990).

33. See, for instance, Lowi, *End of Liberalism,* and Timothy Conlan, *New Federalism: Inter-Governmental From Nixon to Reagan* (Washington, D.C.: Brookings Institution, 1988).

34. Of course, this voting calculus applies to only a small, but significant, politically relevant minority of voters.

35. Political conflict within such an era revolves around an established political agenda, and change is within the bounds of this established agenda; political conflict thus represents "turbulence," or "normal politics," rather than conflict over fundamental principles. See Lowi, *End of Liberalism.*

36. The phrase is borrowed from Richard E. Neustadt, *Presidential Power: The Politics of Leadership* (New York: Wiley, 1960).

37. Woodrow Wilson, *Congressional Government* (1885; reprint, Baltimore: Johns Hopkins University Press, 1981); E. E. Schattschneider, *Party Government* (New York: Rinehart, 1942).

38. A nicely argued summary of the president's bargaining strategy under divided government is Samuel Kernell, "The President's Strategic Circumstance," in *Politics of Divided Government,* ed. Cox and Kernell.

39. See Sundquist, "Needed: A Political Theory."

40. Revisionist arguments appear in David Menefee-Libey, "Divided Government as Scapegoat," *PS: Political Science and Politics* 24 (December 1991); Mark Petracca, "Divided Government and the Risks of Constitutional Reform," *PS: Political Science and Politics* 24 (December 1991); and David Mayhew, *Divided We Govern,* and his article in this volume. Mayhew identifies party-neutral strategies as advertising, credit claiming, and position taking. See his *Congress: The Electoral Connection* (New Haven: Yale University Press, 1974). More generally party-neutral strategies include building electoral support based on the personal characteristics of an individual member of Congress. See, for instance, Richard Fenno, Jr., *Home Style: House Members in Their Districts* (Boston: Little, Brown, 1978); Bruce Cain, John Ferejohn, and Morris Fiorina, *The Personal Vote: Constituency Service and Electoral Independence* (Cambridge: Harvard University Press, 1987).

41. David Rohde, *Parties and Leaders in the Postreform House* (Chicago: University of Chicago Press, 1991); Barbara Sinclair, "The Emergence of Strong Leadership in the 1980s House of Representatives," *Journal of Politics* 54 (August 1992): **657-**

190 Sean Q Kelly

684; Barbara Sinclair, "The Congressional Party: Evolving Organizational, Agenda-Setting, and Policy Roles," in *The Parties Respond: Changes in the American Party System*, ed. L. Sandy Maisel (Boulder, Colo.: Westview, 1990), 227-248; David E. Price, *The Congressional Experience: A View From the Hill* (Boulder, Colo.: Westview, 1992), 73; Jon Bond and Richard Fleisher, *The President in the Legislative Arena* (Chicago: University of Chicago Press, 1990).

42. Similar arguments are made in D. Roderick Kiewiel and Mathew D. McCubbins, *The Logic of Delegation: Congressional Parties and the Appropriations Process* (Chicago: University of Chicago Press, 1991), 39-47; and in Sharer, "Notion of an Electoral Order," 39. After all, partisan identification remains the single best predictor of an individual voter's choice in congressional elections. See Gary Jacobson, *The Politics of Congressional Elections*, 2d ed. (Boston: Little, Brown, 1991).

43. See Norman Ornstein, Thomas Mann, and Michael Malbin, *Vital Statistics on Congress* (Washington, D.C.: CQ Press, 1991). For a more comprehensive discussion of this measure see Sean Q Kelly, "Divided Government and Seat Aggregation: Exploring the Foundations of Inter-Branch Conflict in the Era of Divided Government" (Paper presented at the Southern Political Science Association meetings Atlanta, November 1992).

44. See Mark Petracca, Lonce Bailey, and Pamela Smith, "Proposals for Constitutional Reform: An Evaluation of the Committee on the Constitutional System," *Presidential Studies Quarterly* 20 (Summer 1990); and James A. Thurber, "Representation, Accountability, and Efficiency in Divided Party Control of Government," *PS: Political Science and Politics* 24 (December 1991).

45. This qualitative shift is addressed in Kelly, "Divided Government and Seat Aggregation."

46. Benjamin Ginsberg and Martin Shefter, *Politics by Other Means* (New York: Basic Books, 1990). See also Sean Q Kelly, "Divided We Fall: Punctuated Change in the Era of Divided Government," Ph.D. diss., University of Colorado, 1992, 160-164.

47. For instance, see Lloyd N. Cutler, "To Form a Government," *Foreign Affairs* 59 (Fall 1980), and "Some Reflections about Divided Government," *Presidential Studies Quarterly* 18 (Summer 1988).

48. See Mayhew, *Divided We Govern*, 179.

49. See Kelly, "Divided We Govern?: A Reassessment," *Polity* 25 (1993): 474-484; and "Let's Stick with the Larger Question," *Polity* 25 (1993): 489-490.

50. Mayhew, *Divided We Govern*, 175-177.

51. On changes in the "public mood" over time, see Stimson, *Public Opinion in America*.

52. Estimate is based on a forecast of the CQ data. See Kelly, "Divided We Fall," 95.

53. For a discussion of the general logic behind divided government and budget priorities see Mathew D. McCubbins, "Government on Lay-Away: Federal Spending and Deficits under Divided Party Control," in *Politics of Divided Government*, ed. Cox and Kernell.

10

Explaining Deadlock: Domestic Policymaking in the Bush Presidency

Paul J. Quirk and Bruce Nesmith

B y the end of George Bush's presidency, Democrats and Republicans, liberals and conservatives, commentators and the public found themselves in rare unity on one point: they were dissatisfied with the performance of the federal government. They complained that government was in "gridlock," unable to make decisions or deal effectively with the nation's problems. In a poll taken during the 1992 presidential campaign, only 36 percent of the respondents expressed satisfaction with "the way democracy is working in this country." [1]

This frustration with government, although unusually severe, had much precedent in American politics. For years critics have charged that U.S. political institutions are prone to inaction and ineffectiveness.[2] In almost the current terminology, they have often lamented governmental "stalemate" or "deadlock." During the Bush administration most commentary linked government inaction to divided party control of the presidency and Congress. In earlier periods it blamed other features of American politics, such as the organizational weakness of the political parties, the decentralization of authority in Congress, or the constitutional scheme of separation of powers.

This chapter explores the problem of deadlock in American government, with special attention to the Bush presidency. To set the terms of the discussion, we first suggest a rough definition of the concept of "deadlock." Next we review several distinct explanations for deadlock in American government. Then we examine the record of domestic policymaking during the Bush presidency. Did deadlock actually occur? If so, what caused it? In the concluding section, we draw together our findings and discuss their significance for a general analysis of the sources of deadlock and the need for change in American government.

The Concept of Deadlock

The term *deadlock* refers to a pathological inability of government to act; or, in a broader sense, to an inability to act decisively, effectively, or responsively. In either sense, the concept of deadlock is subject to a great deal of ambiguity. In particular, theories of democratic government disagree on how and when government should act; they therefore disagree on when a failure to act is pathological.

Two influential conceptions of democratic politics point toward very different definitions of deadlock.[3] A strict majoritarianism, such as the doctrine of party government, argues that elections should install an effective governing majority, such as the "government" in a parliamentary system. That majority should be able to work its will on any issue. So the government should fail to act on an issue only if the governing majority is satisfied with the status quo. For the United States, the majoritarian doctrine implies that the president and an effective majority of Congress should act in concert.[4] If policy change is stymied because the president and Congress are in conflict, or because one or the other institution cannot overcome internal divisions, the failure to act is considered pathological and can therefore be called deadlock.

In contrast, a consensualist theory of democratic government, articulated by James Madison in *The Federalist Papers*,[5] tolerates considerable disagreement and inaction. The Madisonian view calls for multiple independent policy-making bodies that are explicitly intended to oppose each other in many circumstances and are each capable of blocking policy change. By design, government will often be unable to act, and there will be a bias toward maintaining the status quo. Nevertheless, even a Madisonian will expect government to act in some circumstances and will employ some concept of deadlock. As the Founders demonstrated in their critique of the Articles of Confederation, a Madisonian perspective will expect government to accomplish policy change when, by some criteria, such change is needed to respond to broadly based public demands or to address genuinely important national problems.[6] Such a view will define deadlock as failure to act in such circumstances. So defined, deadlock does not imply any particular cause of inaction, such as institutional conflict. It is simply a failure to act, for whatever the reason, in the face of a pressing need or demand for action.

Although the application of such a concept will often be controversial, the Madisonian theory will distinguish different cases of inaction. On the one hand, for example, if opposing political forces are fairly evenly divided over whether to increase or reduce government spending, this view will expect an inconclusive struggle; it will find virtue in the maintenance of the status quo. On the other hand, if most policymakers recognize a need to reduce budget deficits to avoid serious harm to the economy, we find the Madisonian theory will expect the president and Congress to reach the necessary agreement to effect that reduction. It will define a prolonged failure to do so as deadlock.

In this essay we will rely on the restrictive, Madisonian notion of deadlock. It is more compatible than the majoritarian notion with the original design and rationale of the Constitution. It also seems to fit the main complaints about government during the Bush presidency—namely, that it failed to address major problems such as the economy, the deficit, and health care. Finally, although the issues are too complex to develop in this essay, we find the Madisonian conception more persuasive. The reason is not only that it affords greater protection against rash or exploitive government action. In view of the barriers to effective, responsive government in any large democracy, it is reasonable to worry mainly about whether political institutions cause widespread dissatisfaction or clear-cut substantial harm, and not about whether they are somewhat sluggish in reflecting small changes in majority preferences.

Explanations of Deadlock

Observers of American politics have suggested various explanations of deadlock. In this section, we try to set out the leading proposed explanations and comment briefly on their likely validity.

Institutional Fragmentation

An important category of explanation for deadlock blames various forms of institutional fragmentation. Considerable fragmentation is, of course, permanently built into the American constitutional system. Yet many analysts have argued that additional forms of fragmentation, present mainly in recent periods, have sharply increased the difficulty of policy-making.

Legislative Decentralization. In the early and mid-1970s, Congress adopted a series of reforms that substantially decentralized its decision-making structures. Pushed by activist liberal Democrats, the reforms reduced the power of the full committees and committee chairs and increased that of subcommittees and rank-and-file committee members. The reforms also gave greater opportunity to individual legislators to overturn committee recommendations on the House or Senate floor.[7]

Many argue that this diffusion of power undermines Congress's ability to make policy. They claim that decentralization makes it hard for Congress to develop a coherent program. It gives advantages to parochial interests, reducing Congress's ability to respond to broad national interests. Moreover, because it forces presidents to deal with multiple independent decision makers, it increases the difficulties of presidential leadership.[8]

This view of the effect of legislative decentralization is plausible. Yet there are some grounds for discounting it. Although the diffusion of authority clearly complicates coordination and leadership, it also creates more potential sources of initiative. In fact, the decentralized Congress of the 1970s showed considerable capability for policy innovation.[9] In any event, a significant recentralization has occurred, with increasingly active party leadership, in the so-called postreform Congress of the 1980s and 1990s.[10]

Divided Government. For twenty of the twenty-four years from 1969 to 1992, opposite parties controlled the presidency and Congress. It is widely assumed that divided government leads to deadlock. And there are several reasons for the assumption: Divided government increases policy disagreement between the president and the congressional majority; it gives leaders of the two branches electoral incentives to oppose each other; and it blurs responsibility, undermining accountability to the public.[11] According to a 1992 election day exit poll, most of the public has come to see divided government as undesirable.[12]

In this case too, however, there are reasons for discounting the adverse effects. Members of Congress are presumably more concerned to win reelection themselves than to help out their party in a collective struggle with the opposing party. Given the choice either to make trouble for an opposite-party president or to satisfy their own constituencies, they will choose the latter. Divided government should not prevent the adoption of a proposal that is broadly popular or promises benefits to constituencies of both parties.

The best available evidence supports this reasoning. In his careful study of legislative productivity from 1949 to 1990, David Mayhew has found that unified and divided party government produced important laws with almost identical frequency.[13] He also disputes claims that divided government diminishes other aspects of governmental performance, such as coherence or responsibility. It is still possible, however, that divided government obstructs policy change or undermines performance in some circumstances. For example, it may cause difficulty mainly on issues that are subject to highly salient partisan conflict, or with a president who is intensely partisan or ideological.[14]

Constituency Pressure

A second category of explanation finds the source of deadlock in excessive responsiveness to pressure from constituencies. In one version of this account, the main pressures come from the mass public; in another, from organized interest groups. In either case, the argument is that such pressures prevent useful or necessary actions that policymakers would otherwise take.

Mass Opinion. The Founding Fathers designed the Constitution to guard against an "excess of democracy," or undue response to public sentiment. As popular participation expanded over the nineteenth and twentieth centuries, such distrust of the citizenry went out of fashion, with only an occasional conservative expressing reservations about mass democracy.[15] This concern has recently regained currency, however, as a number of academic observers have pointed to adverse effects of mass opinion on policymaking.[16]

Such critics note that two kinds of trends have converged during the past two decades to make public opinion a more powerful force in policy-making. On the one hand, decision making has become more open and exposed to public observation. Since the mid-1970s Congress has opened most committee hearings and markup sessions to the public, permitted television coverage of committee meetings and floor debate, and recorded most votes on the House and Senate floor. Presidents have increasingly "gone public" with their policy positions.[17] On the other hand, the public has become more prone to react to policymakers' actions and statements on particular issues. Citizens have become more educated, less attached to political parties, and more inclined to vote on the basis of issues.[18] Political candidates have increasingly used negative issue-oriented advertising and other issue appeals in their campaigns. Some groups of voters, such as the elderly, have become highly organized. And citizens at large have acquired more opportunity to express their views through opinion polls and radio and television talk shows. Because of this convergence of increased exposure and wider attention, critics claim, mass opinion imposes increasing constraint on policymaking; and these constraints often prevent effective or responsible policymaking.

We find this analysis generally persuasive. From the standpoint of some theories of democracy, of course, strong constraints of mass opinion are desirable. In many cases, however, such constraints cause serious difficulties. The reason is simple: the public tends not to be well-informed about the consequences of policies and often has distorted perceptions or unbalanced awareness of those consequences.[19] The pressures of uninformed public opinion may impel irresponsible policy change or cause deadlock when important interests call for action.

Interest Group Demands. As with every other large-scale democracy, American government accords disproportionate influence to narrow, well-organized groups—industries, labor unions, agricultural commodity groups, and professional associations, among others. It is often suggested that such groups gain influence from the fragmented structure of American political institutions.[20] Some analysts, such as Mancur Olson, have even argued that interest-group influence has been increasing.[21] They point to the proliferation of groups, the expansion of their lobbying activities, and their increasing financial contributions to political campaigns. All the major candidates in the 1992 presidential campaign lamented the supposedly growing power of "special interests."

A more plausible view, however, is that interest-group power has generally been diminishing. The increasing pressure of mass opinion creates a counterweight to the interest groups. Indeed, the proliferation of groups makes special interest lobbying more competitive and, paradoxically, gives policymakers more leeway. In fact, in such areas as taxation, economic regulation, trade, and agriculture, interest groups in recent years have often lost major battles with broadly based forces.[22] Interest-group benefits account for a declining share of the federal budget.[23] Certainly interest groups can still dominate policymaking on issues of limited salience, but it is unlikely that group pressure has been the major cause of deadlock in recent years.

Leadership Failure

Another explanation for deadlock, often emphasized in journalistic accounts, points to failure of leadership, especially on the president's part.[24] This explanation may claim, for example, that the president made strategic mistakes, that he lacked skills needed for policy promotion, or that he was not committed to achieving policy change. Jimmy Carter and George Bush were both criticized as lacking a clear agenda; Ronald Reagan as refusing to recognize the budget deficit.

Because one can always find something to blame in every leader's performance, some skepticism about claims of leadership failure is warranted. There is evidence on one aspect of presidential leadership—influencing roll-call votes in Congress—that the role of skill is modest.[25] Nevertheless, the loose linkages among institutions in the American political system suggest a great deal of potential for ineffective leadership to produce deadlock.

Each of the above explanations in some way concerns the performance of political institutions. We will call any case of deadlock that fits these explanations "institutional" deadlock. Another sort of explanation points to constraints that arise, even for well-functioning institutions, primarily from the difficulties of particular issues or from other political or economic circumstances. We will call deadlock that results from such difficulties "circumstantial" deadlock.[26]

Conflicts, Resources, and Issues

The most important circumstantial explanations of deadlock assign blame to the severity of conflicts, the scarcity of resources, or the complexity of issues. E. J. Dionne, Jr., argues that American politics has been polarized, embroiled in a "cultural civil war" between liberal and conservative activists, in the aftermath of the Vietnam War and the New Left rebellion of the 1960s.[27] This polarization has often set up a series of "false choices" between extreme alternatives, drowned out the moderate views of most of the public, and precluded agreement on balanced, workable solutions to policy problems.

More simply, many have attributed deadlock to economic and budgetary constraints. On this view, policymakers have often been unable to address important problems in the 1980s and 1990s because of unacceptably large budget deficits. In turn, these budget deficits are attributed partly to the slow growth of economic productivity since the early 1970s. Much commentary on the Bush presidency observed that economic and budgetary conditions virtually precluded policy innovations that would require substantial new federal expenditures.[28]

Finally, analysts of particular cases sometimes argue that policy change is obstructed by the sheer uncertainty or complexity of the issues. It was far more difficult and took much longer to deregulate the massively complex telecommunications industry, for example, than to do so with the relatively simple airline industry.[29] The barriers of uncertainty or complexity should prevent rapid action; but in the absence of institutional failure, they should not block change indefinitely.

Domestic Policy in the Bush Administration

The record of domestic policymaking during the Bush presidency should provide fertile ground for examining the causes of deadlock. Indeed, the lack of policy movement became so widely acknowledged that the term "gridlock" entered into everyday language to describe the state of national policymaking. To the extent that the sources of deadlock can be inferred from a brief examination of policymaking during one presidential term, we will attempt to do so.

Successes and Failures

The pattern of Bush's successes and failures in domestic policy suggests that the constraints posed by the issues themselves played a major role in blocking action.[30] Much of the difficulty was budgetary. Indeed, the 101st and 102d Congresses passed several important laws in areas that did not require large commitments of federal funds: a 1990 measure on budget procedures, a long-overdue revision of the Clean Air Act, a civil rights bill, and a sweeping measure on the rights of the disabled. In areas where direct expenditure was required, however, action was cautious or nonexistent. Congress passed a modest expansion of the child-care tax credit and limited spending increases for AIDS research and drug abuse treatment and prevention. After a lengthy internal study, the Bush administration refrained from making a proposal on welfare reform, and it mostly confined itself to jawboning the states on education.

Much of the *appearance* of deadlock, though not necessarily the reality of it, resulted from polarized ideological conflict on symbolically charged "veto issues." These included abortion, flag burning, funding for the arts, gun control, the exclusionary rule, family and medical laws, and school choice, among others. In all, Bush vetoed thirty-six bills, including nine on abortion alone. Most of these issues, however, did not reflect broad demands or generally recognized needs for policy change. They arose instead from efforts by Bush or the Democrats to serve their party constituencies, or just to make a political statement. Under the Madisonian conception, the failure to act on such issues did not constitute deadlock.

The main source of the perception of deadlock, however, was that the government failed to act effectively on several crucial issues, each of which arose from widespread public demands or manifestly important national problems. Despite the 1990 budget agreement, the federal budget deficit was not reduced to a manageable size. Virtually nothing was done to address the sluggish economy and high unemployment of 1990-1992. Government did not respond to a rash of bank failures and sweeping technological change in the banking industry. Despite widespread dissatisfaction with the health care system, no health care plan was even brought to the stage of floor consideration. To further explore the causes of deadlock in the Bush presidency, we will briefly review each of these cases. After recounting the events of the four cases, in the concluding section we will draw the inferences that seem warranted.[31]

The Budget Deficit

Debate about how to control the federal budget deficit absorbed a great deal of governmental energy in the 1980s and early 1990s. In the view of economists, persisting large deficits threatened the long-term health of the economy. Yet during the Bush administration, the deficit, instead of shrinking, actually grew, from $153 billion in FY 1989 to $290 billion in FY 1992. Most of the increase reflected developments that federal policymakers could not control, especially the savings and loans bailout, a recession that began in summer 1990, and rising entitlement payments for health care. But the president and Congress also missed opportunities to attack the deficit during the strong economy of 1989 and early 1990.

President Bush came to office in 1989 determined to keep his categorical 1988 campaign promise not to raise taxes.[32] An antitax posture had helped to elect Ronald Reagan in 1980 and 1984, and Bush's "read my lips" rhetoric had boosted his candidacy in 1988. However, because the Democrats were unwilling to accept domestic spending cuts unless the Republicans reciprocated by accepting a tax increase, Bush's position virtually precluded significant deficit reduction.

Bush's FY 1990 budget, submitted in February 1989, projected a deficit within the targets set by the Gramm-Rudman-Hollings Act of 1985. But it did so only through accounting gimmicks, highly optimistic economic projections, and unspecified spending cuts under a "flexible freeze" on total nondefense spending. In fact, the proposal added to the deficit through increased spending on education and childcare and a cut in the capital gains tax.

The Bush budget was designed for political advantage, not deficit cutting. It adhered to Bush's antitax campaign pledge. The capital gains tax cut benefited the wealthy, a Republican constituency. And the flexible freeze left the task of finding spending cuts to the Congress. "He picks the increases and lets us make the cuts," complained a Democrat on the House Budget Committee.[33]

In the absence of a spirit of mutual sacrifice, Bush and Congress in the spring negotiated a budget that contained little genuine deficit reduction. The summit agreement met the Gramm-Rudman targets through heavy reliance on vagueness, accounting gimmickery, and economic optimism. In the fall the administration tried to bypass the Democratic leadership and secure the capital gains tax cut by working with a coalition of Republicans and conservative Democrats. Although this coalition managed to push the measure through the House, a Democratic filibuster killed it in the Senate, and the two branches agreed to a budget without a capital gains measure. Despite favorable economic conditions, the FY 1990 budget failed to achieve significant deficit reduction. Only unrealistic predictions kept the projected deficit under the Gramm-Rudman target of $100 billion; the actual figure at year-end was $220 billion.

For FY 1991, Bush sent another low-political-risk budget to Capitol Hill, relying on high economic hopes and previously rejected proposals to project a deficit of $100 billion. This time, however, the escalating costs of the savings and loan bailout made facile optimism untenable. The Democrats refused to join the White House in summit meetings until Bush stipulated that he would impose no "preconditions" on the negotiations—in effect renouncing his pledge not to raise taxes. In a May statement that became a defining episode of Bush's presidency, he did so. In response, eighteen Senate Republicans reiterated their opposition to any new tax plan, while more than one hundred House Republicans signed a pledge to oppose new taxes.

Partly because Bush tried once again to renew his demands on capital gains, agreement was not reached until September 30, the eve of the new fiscal year. The summit budget called for increases in excise taxes and cuts in Medicare and other domestic programs. Most of the Congress, however, refused to go along. Conservatives, led by Rep. Newt Gingrich (R-Ga.), objected to the tax increases; liberals rejected the spending cuts; and the agreement was defeated in the House on October 6.

After a month of chaos without a budget, a new agreement emerged in late October. Because the president and the Republicans were suffering most of the political damage from the budget fiasco, the Democrats had more leverage to shape the new agreement than they had had with the original one. The final budget contained a $146 billion tax increase, spread over five years, with much of the burden falling on high-income families. It also included substantial cuts in Medicare, Medicaid, and other domestic programs. In a climate of budgetary emergency, it cut the deficit by a substantial $500 billion over five years.

Significantly, the 1990 budget measure also replaced the discredited Gramm-Rudman-Hollings deficit targets with separate limits on spending for defense, domestic programs, and international affairs over the following three fiscal years. By walling off each set of programs from incursions on behalf of the others, the spending caps reduced partisan conflict over budget priorities, but they did not require further deficit reduction.

Budgeting for fiscal years 1992 and 1993 was less eventful. The budget walls helped the Republicans block Democratic efforts to use post-Cold War defense cuts to begin new domestic initiatives. More important, by the spring of 1991 attention had shifted from reducing the deficit to lifting the economy out of recession. To avoid the risk of sending a weak economy spiraling downward, the administration and Congress put deficit reduction on the back burner for the duration of Bush's presidency.

The Recession

The most important cause of the public perception of gridlock during the Bush presidency was the lack of governmental response to the economic slump that began in 1990 and lasted through most of the 1992 election year. Despite a variety of proposals from both parties and increasing public impatience with the failure to act, no substantial economic package was adopted.

An economic slowdown became apparent during the second half of 1990. The economy grew at an annual rate of only 0.4 percent in the second quarter, and one million jobs were lost from July to December. Slow to recognize these trends, President Bush waited until January to acknowledge the recession. But even after everyone in government agreed that a recession was under way, they had difficulty agreeing on what to do about it.

Most economists counseled patience.[34] They opposed fiscal stimulation because it would increase an already excessive federal deficit, and because violating the hard-won agreement on spending caps would undermine confidence in the nation's resolve to reduce deficits in the long term. In view of the already high levels of public and private debt, many economists also cautioned against monetary stimulus, although the Federal Reserve Board still cut the discount rate to a twenty-seven-year low in December 1991. A Washington economist observed, "We're in a recession with no tools to get out." [35] Furthermore, most forecasters believed the economy would soon recover on its own.

In early 1991 leaders of both parties were willing to refrain from combating the recession with new spending. Although the 1990 budget agreement allowed the president to declare a recession and suspend the budget caps, Bush declined to do so. The leadership of the House Budget Committee, Chair Leon Panetta (D-Calif.), and ranking member Bill Gradison (R-Ohio), also opposed countercyclical spending, and the Senate overwhelmingly rejected two proposals to set aside the spending caps.

As the economy remained stagnant, the pressure to act increased and the consensus for restraint eroded. But no new consensus formed. Rather, there were divisions on the proper course of action both between the two parties and within them. President Bush and some congressional leaders of both parties continued to heed economists' warnings against any kind of economic stimulus. But some congressional Republicans advocated tax cuts for businesses and investors. And many Democrats called for tax cuts for lower- and middle-income groups, the extension of unemployment benefits, new public-works spending, or even a tax increase for the wealthy.

These cross-cutting disagreements led to a confused, inconclusive policy debate. Democratic leaders in May presented an antirecession package with middle-class tax relief, expanded unemployment benefits, and funds for highway construction. The Bush administration, arguing that the economy was improving, opposed these proposals. It got help in delaying them from Chair Dan Rostenkowski (D-Ill.) of the Ways and Means Committee and Bill Gradison (R-Ohio) of the Budget Committee, even though Gradison worried that "inaction is perceived as a lack of concern." [36] Congress passed a Democratic bill authorizing the president to extend unemployment benefits, and later another bill mandating that he do so. But Bush declined to act on the first bill and vetoed the second, arguing that the Democratic strategy "might make the situation worse." [37] With congressional Republicans becoming restive, Gingrich revived discussion of the capital gains tax cut. But senior administration officials—including Richard Darman, director of the Office of Managment and Budget, Treasury secretary Nicholas Brady, and chief of staff John Sununu—continued to oppose a major tax cut to stimulate the economy.

By late 1991 Bush began to accede to the pressure for action. He accepted an extension of unemployment benefits and gave qualified support to the congressional Republicans' tax cut package. Finally, in his 1992 State of the Union address, Bush broke with most economic advice and presented an antirecession plan based on the congressional Republicans' strategy.

Even though Bush, congressional Republicans, and the Democrats all had proposed economic stimulus measures, however, they made little effort to come to terms and pass a bill. Adopting a combative posture, Bush gave Congress a March 20 deadline to pass his stimulus package. Uncowed, congressional Democrats instead passed a bill that closely resembled their own plan. The president issued an angry veto announcement, and neither side sought negotiations to work out a compromise plan. In a presidential election year, Bush and the Democratic leadership may each have doubted that the other would negotiate in good faith. Probably more important, the fact that both parties remained divided or uncertain about whether any stimulus package was even advisable militated against their compromising party positions to get one.

Health Care

Apart from the economy, the area of domestic policy that elicited the most complaints of deadlock was health care. Criticism of the nation's health care system had reached a crescendo in the late 1980s and early 1990s. Yet the Bush administration and Congress took no significant steps toward achieving reform.

Two problems in the American health care system created a sense of crisis. First, a rapidly growing number of Americans lacked health insurance and thus affordable access to health care; thirty-seven million were uninsured in 1986, up nearly 25 percent from 1980. Second, the costs of medical care were rising at about twice the rate of inflation. In 1992 they accounted for more than 12 percent of the GNP, and the proportion of the federal budget devoted to health care had nearly doubled in a decade. In a February 1989 poll, 89 percent of respondents said that the American health care system needed fundamental change.[38]

Nevertheless, health care reform did not become a leading item on the policy agenda until 1991. Congress created a fifteen-member bipartisan commission in 1988 to study universal access and long-term care. But Democratic presidential candidate Michael Dukakis had only slight success in his effort to make universal coverage a major issue in the 1988 election campaign. The Bush administration sought to avoid a substantial expansion of the government's role in health care. As a White House policy adviser explained in 1989, "the candidate who made universal access to health care a central theme of his campaign did not win the 1988 election." [39] Moreover, the embarrassing repeal, a year after enactment, of a 1988 bill on catastrophic medical coverage convinced many in Congress that the public was unwilling to pay higher taxes for increased health coverage. The catalyst for the health care issue was Harris Wofford's stunning, come-from-behind victory over Richard Thornburgh, who had been Bush's attorney general and was thought to have been a shoo-in, in the special Pennsylvania race in 1991 for the U.S. Senate. Wofford, a Democrat, campaigned on health care, and his victory was widely interpreted as proof that the public finally wanted action on the issue.

Reforming the health care system, however, was a task of enormous complexity and political difficulty. Expanding access would require restructuring relationships among government, business, insurance companies, and health care providers. To control costs—an essential step in any long-term strategy for expanding access—health care services would have to be rationed, and the incomes of providers reduced.

Faced with such challenges, the president and Congress did not even begin to reach agreement on a solution in the remaining months of Bush's term; indeed, neither party reached such agreement. There were two different Democratic plans. Following the bipartisan commission's recommendations, Senate majority leader George Mitchell advocated broadening insurance coverage through mandates for insurance companies, tax incentives and subsidies for businesses, and a "play or pay" plan for businesses that did not participate. Rep. Pete Stark (D-Calif.) introduced a similar bill for debate in the House Ways and Means Committee. But the leading Democrats in the House Energy and Commerce Committee, Henry Waxman (D-Calif.) and John Dingell (D-Mich.), criticized play-or-pay for not guaranteeing coverage for the jobless and promoted a single-payer system to be financed by a national value-added tax. The Democrats did not coalesce behind a single plan in 1992.

Republican proposals were generally more restrained but equally varied. Although Bush spoke out against the Democratic plans, until mid-1991 he left health care reform in the hands of Health and Human Services secretary Louis Sullivan, who offered no proposals. In February 1992 Bush presented a package that sought to reduce the cost of malpractice suits and offered tax incentives to help lower-income and self-employed people purchase health insurance. Finding Bush's ideas too cautious, however, congressional Republicans put together their own proposals. In the Senate John Chafee (R-R.I.) introduced a plan that gave employers incentives to provide health insurance. In the House Republicans proposed to expand community health centers and require small businesses to make affordable insurance available to their employees. Campaigning for reelection in July, Bush claimed that the Republicans had reached agreement on a health care plan. But in fact he withheld an endorsement of the Chafee bill and called for changes in the House Republican package.

Thus by the time of the 1992 election, both parties had acknowledged the need for health care reform but neither had resolved even the fundamental issues about the nature of that reform. Apart from Bush's suggestions on the peripheral issue of malpractice suits, neither party had addressed the problem of costs. And no major health care bill had come close to passage in either house.

Banking Deregulation

A final case of deadlock during the Bush presidency was the failure of efforts to reform regulation of the banking industry. Most banking analysts in the 1980s and early 1990s saw an urgent need to loosen controls on the banking industry to recognize changes in the financial world, especially the rise of international competition in financial services, and to reverse a steady decline of American banking. President Bush proposed a major deregulation bill. Congress debated the issue extensively. But in the end, it failed to act.

The problems in the banking industry were unquestionably serious. More than one thousand banks failed between 1985 and 1991, and many others were insolvent or operating on thin margins. The industry's weakness threatened to disrupt the economy and, as in the collapse of the savings and loan industry, to create huge governmental obligations to insured depositors.[40]

In early 1991 Bush sent Congress a major banking bill. To make American banks more competitive, the bill authorized interstate branch banking, permitted firms in other industries to own banks, and allowed banks to undertake nonbanking commercial activities. To prevent abuses, it limited federal deposit insurance and provided for closer supervision of banks with weak capital balances. It also brought all banking regulation under a single agency in the Treasury Department.[41]

The Bush bill was applauded by economists, banking regulators, and large banks. But it was opposed by a powerful coalition of interest groups. Small banks, which were well organized and represented in every congressional district, feared that interstate branch banking would enable large banks to drive them out of business. Insurance agents and securities firms sought to prevent bank inroads into their markets. Some consumer groups argued that allowing banks to enter other financial services markets would increase instability in the industry. And state governments defended their role in banking regulation.[42] Perhaps crucial in the bill's defeat was that banking reform had little apparent support from the general public. Indeed, for reasons that are easy to understand, no one tried very hard to elicit such support. Banks and bankers have been unpopular in America for at least 150 years, and the public would undoubtedly have given a lukewarm response to a measure giving more freedom to big banks.

In this political environment, Congress was divided and hesitant; and even the Bush administration failed to follow through with a vigorous effort on its behalf. The House Banking Committee, which had strong ties to the large banks, easily approved the Bush bill. But there was heavy resistance from other committees and the full House. Four other committees claimed jurisdiction over the bill, including the Energy and Commerce Committee headed by John Dingell, who was an ally of the securities industry. Significantly, the House leadership did not help the reformers. Speaker Thomas Foley (D-Wash.) agreed to let the four rival committees share jurisdiction. They proceeded to delete or water down the bill's central provisions, sending a very weak bill to the House floor.

There was less conflict in the Senate. The Banking Committee, which had broader jurisdiction and a more diverse constituency than the House Banking Committee, was more responsive to the nonbanking interests that opposed reform. Accordingly, it produced a compromise bill. The Senate committee bill accommodated the opponents by keeping the existing ban on conglomerate ownership of banks. But it also provided for considerable deregulation, allowing some interstate branching and bank participation in other commercial activities. The compromise apparently helped the reform effort: In contrast with the revolt against the committee bill in the House, the Senate passed its committee bill without major amendments.

Quite possibly, the president could have used the Senate action for leverage to extract a moderate reform bill from the House floor. But even though secretary Brady had initially called the banking bill "an enormously high priority," the administration largely absented itself from the critical stages of the debate. "At some time, I'd like the administration's support for its own bill," a senior Republican member of the Senate Banking Committee said in April.[43] Bush met with congressional leaders on the bill in June but then went more than three months without mentioning it. It is unclear whether the Bush administration chose to avoid further alienating the interest group opposition, anticipated defeat and decided to cut its losses, or simply turned its attention to other issues.

In the absence of a major lobbying effort by the administration, the House passed a severely weakened version of the banking bill. The conference committee, rather than reporting a very weak bill that would compromise between the Senate and House versions, decided to leave the major issues unresolved. It reported a routine banking bill, dealing with several peripheral issues, which Congress passed. After the disappointing result with the 1991 bill, Bush and the Congress set aside the issue of banking reform during 1992.

Explaining Deadlock and Restructuring Government

In the remainder of this essay, we will attempt to draw out the lessons of our brief survey of domestic policymaking during Bush's presidency and consider their implications for the task of restructuring American government.

The evidence appears to support three principal points about deadlock during this period. First, some of the conflicts that created the appearance of deadlock did not represent deadlock in the restricted, Madisonian sense. Bush and the Democrats fought pitched battles on several cultural and social issues—such as abortion, the flag, pornography, and family leave. But the demands for policy change in each of these disputes came entirely from one or the other of the parties' ideological constituencies. The public was sharply divided. From the Madisonian perspective, government inaction was an appropriate response.

Second, where government did fail to respond to broad national interests, the sources of deadlock were often circumstantial rather than institutional. In the case of the recession, the budget deficit severely compromised the fiscal tools normally available for stimulating the economy. The deficit also discouraged the administration from undertaking a significant initiative on welfare reform and dictated a hortatory strategy on education. The enormous complexity of the health care issue made it unlikely that the president and Congress could come up with a feasible, mutually satisfactory reform plan in only two years of serious debate. In our terms, only the failures to act on banking and the budget deficit were clear cases of institutional deadlock.

Third, although several of the sources of institutional deadlock hindered policymaking in one or more of the four cases, the influence of mass opinion was most important. The decentralization of Congress was not a manifest, critical hindrance in any of the cases. It is true that the rank-and-file members of Congress killed the original 1990 budget agreement. But the resistance of Republican members, at least, reflected the inconsistency of the president's position. Many Republicans, following Bush's lead and counting on his support, had also campaigned on a pledge not to raise taxes; when the president changed his mind, they could not easily keep in step. In any case, the rank-and-file did accept the final 1990 budget, which contained even more deficit reduction than the original agreement. On banking, conflicts among several House committees played a role in blocking adoption of a reform bill. But only a single, unrepresentative committee, the Banking Committee, favored reform; the leadership helped the opponents with an important jurisdictional ruling; and the president dropped out of the picture during the crucial stages of the debate. It is by no means clear that a more centralized Congress, or one more responsive to presidential leadership, would have produced a stronger bill.

Nor did the cases indicate obstruction that resulted primarily from divided government. The two parties failed to agree on stimulative measures to combat the recession. In all likelihood, they failed largely because members of each party, including the president, doubted the utility of such measures. The conflicts on banking and, in part, on health care took place within each party, rather than between them. Party conflict was apparent in the 1989 and 1990 debates on the budget deficit. But neither the president nor Democrats in Congress made budget proposals separately that called for significantly more deficit reduction than they ultimately adopted. There is no evidence that either party would have enacted more deficit reduction if it had controlled both branches.[44]

The influence of organized interest groups was central to one case of deadlock—that of banking reform. Yet this case does not refute our argument that the power of interest groups has been declining. The banking reform bill was blocked by a coalition of opposing interest groups and a lack of popular support that could easily have stymied a reform effort in any period of American history.

The leadership of President Bush appears to have contributed in some cases to deadlock. His "read-my-lips" campaign promise not to raise taxes, repeated frequently during his first year in office, was a major obstacle to deficit reduction. To some extent antitax rhetoric merely reflected the Republican party strategy of the period rather than a choice specific to President Bush. Yet he certainly could have left himself more discretion or refrained from reinforcing the promise after the election. More generally, Bush's partisan, confrontational strategy on many domestic issues may have distracted attention from opportunities for cooperative policy change on welfare, education, or health care; certainly his unrelenting attempts to push a capital gains tax cut opposed by the Democratic leadership was a further obstacle to deficit reduction. The confrontational strategy was also apparently avoidable; for reasons that are not entirely clear, Bush seemed to place inordinate emphasis on satisfying the conservative wing of the Republican party. Finally, Bush's preference for foreign policy led him to neglect domestic issues, which may help to explain his slow start on health care and lack of follow-through on banking.

Judging from the cases, the most general, fundamental, and significant source of deadlock was the influence of mass opinion.[45] The principal obstacle to deficit reduction was public resistance both to tax increases and to cuts in popular spending programs, especially Medicare. Republicans and Democrats had both promised to oppose such measures, thus reinforcing public resistance, in their election campaigns. The main reason that neither party seriously addressed health care costs was probably the expectation of public resistance to any form of rationing of services.

Even though other obstacles prevented action on banking and the recession, some of the difficulties with mass opinion were also evident in those cases. Public antipathy toward large banks probably played a significant role in allowing small banks, insurance companies, and other narrow groups to defeat banking reform and protect their interests in the status quo. In dealing with the recession, the president and Congress resisted public pressure to stimulate the economy. But they were willing to do so only because they expected, incorrectly, that the economy would rebound before the election. They did not demonstrate a willingness to resist such pressure if the benefits would appear after the election. Indeed, in the aftermath of the recession episode and Bush's failure to win reelection in 1992, it seems unlikely that either Republicans or Democrats will show much resistance to stimulating the economy in another recession in the foreseeable future.

It is possible that another set of cases in another presidential term would lead to a different analysis of the causes of deadlock. It is also possible that another kind of investigation, such as one based on comparisons among presidencies or among countries, would have different results.[46] But if our analysis is broadly correct, it has implications for the task of "restructuring government," which was often discussed during the 1992 election campaign and appears to be an important item on President Bill Clinton's agenda.

The critical task in reforming government to avoid deadlock and improve policymaking is not to reduce the influence of organized groups or "special interests," as politicians like to suggest. Nor is it to overcome institutional fragmentation by strengthening political party organization or centralizing policymaking under the president or congressional party leaders, as journalists and academic commentators often argue.[47] Rather, the main task is to reduce the influence of uninformed mass opinion. Unfortunately, this is even more difficult than weakening interest groups or curing fragmentation.

Broadly speaking, there are two approaches for pursuing that objective. One is to limit the scope and immediacy of mass influence and thus give more autonomy to officeholders. By such means as reducing the visibility of some decision processes, this approach would seek to refocus the public's involvement on the values, priorities, and accomplishments of government, rather than on specific policies. In a sense, this approach would make democracy, in its representative form, safe from the people.[48] The other approach is to enhance the public's ability to reach reasonably balanced and realistic judgments about policy. By improving the depth and integrity of policy debate in political campaigns, for example, this strategy would make it less harmful or dangerous for policymakers to defer to mass opinion. It would make the people safe for democracy.[49]

But any effort to mitigate the excesses of democracy in contemporary American politics will face formidable obstacles. Unlike in the founding period, the very notion of such excesses has long been virtually absent from our national discourse. Yet several developments in the early 1990s have caused this concern to reemerge: among others, the degeneration of some Senate confirmation hearings into something like trials judged by a national television audience; Colorado's sharp swing from a supportive to a hostile environment for gay rights as the result of a referendum; the near financial collapse of California government, widely blamed on a series of referenda; and several episodes in which public debate in the peculiar and unrepresentative forum of radio talk shows sharply altered government decisions. After two hundred years during which the public has acquired an increasingly direct role in policymaking, the time may be approaching for a new national debate on the nature and limits of that role.

Notes

1. Larry Huglick, "Dissatisfied with the State of the Nation," *Polling Report* 8 (July 6, 1992): 1-2.
2. James McGregor Burns, *The Deadlock of Democracy* (New York: Prentice-Hall, 1963); James Sundquist, *Constitutional Reform and Effective Government* (Washington, D.C.: Brookings Institution, 1986); and Gary Mucciaroni, *The Political Failure of Employment Policy, 1945-1982* (Pittsburgh: University of Pittsburgh Press, 1990).
3. For a review of the alternative theories, see J. Roland Pennock, *Democratic Political Theory* (Princeton, N.J.: Princeton University Press, 1979).
4. James L. Sundquist, "Needed: A Political Theory for a New Era of Coalition Government in the United States," *Political Science Quarterly* 103 (Winter 1988-1989): 613-635; Michael L. Mezey, *Congress, the President, and Public Policy*

(Boulder, Colo.: Westview, 1989).

5. Alexander Hamilton, James Madison, and John Jay, *The Federalist Papers* (New York: Mentor Books, 1961), see esp. nos. 10 and 51.

6. To be more precise, a proviso is needed: that no countervailing demands or interests of comparable magnitude are served by the status quo. There is of course room for disagreement in weighing public demands and interests.

7. James L. Sundquist, *The Decline and Resurgence of Congress* (Washington, D.C.: Brookings Institution, 1981).

8. Ibid.; Charles O. Jones, "Presidential Negotiation With Congress," in *Both Ends of the Avenue*, ed. Anthony King (Washington, D.C.: American Enterprise Institute, 1983), 96-130.

9. See Martha Derthick and Paul J. Quirk, *The Politics of Deregulation* (Washington, D.C.: Brookings Institution, 1985); Richard A. Harris and Sidney M. Milkis, *The Politics of Regulatory Change: A Tale of Two Agencies* (New York: Oxford University Press, 1989).

10. Roger A. Davidson, ed., *The Postreform Congress* (New York: St. Martin's, 1991).

11. For a strong statement of this view, see Sundquist, "Needed: A Political Theory;" see also, James P. Pfiffner, "Divided Government and the Problem of Governance," in *Divided Democracy*, ed. James A. Thurber (Washington, D.C.: CQ Press, 1991), 39-60.

12. Voter Research and Surveys, *General Election Poll*, November 3, 1992.

13. David R. Mayhew, *Divided We Govern* (New Haven: Yale University Press, 1991).

14. See also Gary W. Cox and Samuel Kernell, *The Politics of Divided Government* (Boulder, Colo.: Westview, 1991); Morris P. Fiorina, *Divided Government* (New York: Macmillan, 1992).

15. See for example, Samuel P. Huntington, "The United States," in *The Crisis of Democracy*, ed. Michael Crozier, Samuel P. Huntington, and Joji Watanuki (New York: New York University Press, 1975).

16. Jeffrey Tulis, *The Rhetorical Presidency* (Princeton, N.J.: Princeton University Press, 1987); Anthony King and Giles Austin, "Good Government and the Politics of High Exposure," in *The Bush Presidency: First Appraisals*, ed. Colin Campbell and Bert A. Rockman (Chatham, N.J.: Chatham House, 1991), 249-286; Joseph Bessette, *The Mild Voice of Reason* (Chicago: University of Chicago Press, forthcoming).

17. Samuel Kernell, *Going Public: New Strategies of Presidential Leadership* (Washington, D.C.: CQ Press, 1986).

18. Herbert Asher, *Presidential Elections and American Politics*, 3d. ed. (Chicago: Dorsey Press, 1992).

19. Moreover, these deficiencies are readily understood: members of very large groups like the general public normally have little incentive to invest effort, individually, in understanding issues that affect their collective interests; see Mancur Olson, *The Logic of Collective Action* (Cambridge: Harvard University Press, 1965). As a result, public opinion about policy is exceptionally subject to the general biases and limitations of human judgment; see Daniel Kahneman, Paul Slovic, and Amos Tversky, eds., *Judgment Under Uncertainty: Heuristics and Biases* (New York: Cambridge University Press, 1982).

20. Grant McConnell, *Private Power and American Democracy* (New York: Knopf, 1966); Mark P. Petracca, "The Rediscovery of Interest Group Politics," in *The Politics of Interests*, ed. Mark P. Petracca (Boulder, Colo.: Westview, 1992), 3-31. Compare Graham Wilson, "American Interest Groups in Comparative Perspective," in *Politics of Interests*, ed. Petracca, 80-95.

21. Mancur Olson, *The Rise and Decline of Nations* (New Haven: Yale University Press, 1982).

22. Gary Mucciaroni, *Private Interests and Public Policies* (Washington, D.C.: Brookings Institution, forthcoming).
23. Paul E. Peterson, "The Rise and Fall of Special Interest Politics," in *Politics of Interests*, ed. Petracca, 326-342.
24. Robert Shogun, *The Riddle of Power: Presidential Leadership From Truman to Bush* (New York: Penguin, 1992); Barbara Kellerman, *The Political Presidency* (New York: Oxford University Press, 1984).
25. George Edwards, *At the Margins: Presidential Leadership of Congress* (New Haven: Yale University Press, 1989); Jon R. Bond and Richard Fleischer, *The President in the Legislative Arena* (Chicago: University of Chicago Press, 1990); for contrasting views, see Kellerman, *Political Presidency*, and Mayhew, *Divided We Govern*. For discussion, see Paul J. Quirk, "What Do We Know and How Do We Know It? Research on the Presidency," in *American Institutions*, ed. William Crotty (Evanston, Ill.: Northwestern University Press, 1991), 37-66. Presidents probably make serious efforts to change votes on only a handful of roll calls per year; the effect of presidential skill in such efforts would be hard to detect in a statistical analysis.
26. Because we have defined deadlock as inaction in the face of significant need or demand, one could argue that perfectly functioning institutions would always respond, and circumstantial deadlock cannot exist. By allowing for circumstantial deadlock, we recognize that no institutions function perfectly, and some circumstances present challenges that exceed the capabilities even of reasonably well functioning institutions.
27. E. J. Dionne, Jr., *Why Americans Hate Politics* (New York: Simon and Schuster, 1991).
28. Of course resource constraints are not absolute. The source of deadlock in this case is the political difficulty of transferring resources from other uses in the absence of budgetary or economic growth.
29. See Derthick and Quirk, *Politics of Deregulation.*
30. Most of our account of policymaking in the Bush administration is based on reporting in the *Congressional Quarterly Almanac*, *Congressional Quarterly Weekly Report*, *Challenge*, the *New York Times*, and the *Wall Street Journal*. To save space, we do not cite the individual articles, except to document quotations and some other specific information. For a general treatment of the early part of the Bush presidency, see Colin Campbell and Bert A. Rockman, eds., *The Bush Presidency: First Appraisals* (Chatham. N.J.: Chatham House, 1991). See also Ryan J. Barilleaux and Mary E. Stuckey, eds., *Leadership and the Bush Presidency: Prudence or Drift in an Era of Change?* (Westport, Conn.: Praeger, 1992).
31. The sources of deadlock can be difficult to track in the events of particular cases so that we can easily sort out their separate effects. But those events nevertheless provide useful evidence. If divided government obstructs a decision, for example, we should find sharp conflict between the parties. If legislative decentralization does so, we should find conflict between party leaders and committees or subcommittees, or conflict among such units. Pressure from mass or interest-group constituencies and failures of leadership also leave observable evidence. A general difficulty is that if policymakers adjust their behavior to anticipated obstacles, we may not find evidence of the obstacles. Usually, however, policymakers do enough struggling with their constraints to reveal a good deal about them. Ultimately, the results of such inquiries must be combined with other kinds of observation, such as Mayhew's comparisons of performance in different periods, to make the most reliable judgments possible.
32. On the politics of the deficit in the Bush administration, see Paul J. Quirk, "Domestic Policy: Divided Government and Cooperative Presidential Leadership," in Campbell and Rockman, *Bush Presidency*, 69-92; Barbara Sinclair, "Governing Unheroically (and Sometimes Unappetizingly): Bush and the 101st Congress," in

Bush Presidency, ed. Campbell and Rockman, 155-189; Howard E. Shuman, *Politics and the Budget: The Struggle Between the President and Congress*, 3d ed. (Englewood Cliffs, N.J.: Prentice-Hall, 1992); Daniel P. Franklin, *Making Ends Meet: Congressional Budgeting in the Age of Deficits* (Washington, D.C.: CQ Press, 1993).

33. The member was Rep. Charles Schumer (D-NY): *Congressional Quarterly Weekly Report*, February 11, 1989, 280.

34. Peter Passell, "Spurning Fine-Tuning," *New York Times*, December 11, 1991, A1, C4.

35. The economist was C. Fred Bergsten of the Institute for International Economics, quoted in Peter Passell, "Does Government Have the Stuff to End a Recession?" *New York Times*, February 11, 1991, A13.

36. John R. Cranford, "Hill's Response to Recession Defies Economists' Advice," *Congressional Quarterly Weekly Report*, January 25, 1992, 160-163.

37. David S. Cloud, "Fear of Veto, Controversy Kills Possibility of Cut," *Congressional Quarterly Weekly Report*, November 2, 1991, 3190.

38. Barbara L. Wolfe, "Changing the U.S. Health Care System: How Difficult Will It Be?" *Focus* 14 (Summer 1992): 16-20; Dennis Hevesi, "Polls Show Discontent With Health Care," *New York Times*, February 15, 1989, A16.

39. Julie Rovner, "Congress Feels the Pressure of Health Care Squeeze," *Congressional Quarterly Weekly Report*, February 16, 1991, 418.

40. R. Dan Brumbaugh, Jr., and Robert E. Litan, "The Banks Are Worse Off Than You Think," *Challenge* 33 (January-February, 1990): 4-12; James R. Barth, Jr., R. Dan Brumbaugh, Jr., and Robert E. Litan, "Bank Failures are Sinking the FDIC," *Challenge* 34 (March-April, 1991): 4-15.

41. Kenneth H. Bacon, "Big Banks Would Get Vastly Broader Powers Under Treasury's Plan," *Wall Street Journal*, February 6, 1991, A1, 6.

42. John R. Cranford, "Walls Around Banking System May Face Congress," *Congressional Quarterly Weekly Report*, June 15, 1991, 1560-1566.

43. Paulette Thomas, "Bush Introduces Bill to Overhaul Bank Industry," *Wall Street Journal*, March 21, 1991, A2; "Wake-Up Call," *Wall Street Journal*, April 19, 1991, A1. The senator was Jake Garn (R-Utah).

44. It is possible that a party with control of both branches would produce smaller deficits than it is willing to propose under divided government. Casting doubt on that possibility, however, Mayhew observes in *Divided We Govern* that if one sets aside the Reagan-Bush era, divided government has not produced larger budget deficits than unified government.

45. For a similar view of the failures of the Bush administration, see King and Alston, "Good Government and High Exposure."

46. As we have noted above (31), case study evidence needs to be supplemented with comparative analyses. Of course, comparative approaches have difficulties of their own. For an ambitious, useful attempt at international comparison, see Bert A. Rockman and Kent Weaver, *Do Institutions Make a Difference?* (Washington, D.C.: Brookings Institution, 1993).

47. Donald L. Robinson, ed., *Reforming American Government: The Bicentennial Papers of the Committee on the Constitutional System* (Boulder, Colo.: Westview, 1990).

48. For a study that emphasizes leaders' efforts to control the exposure of decision making, see R. Douglas Arnold, *The Logic of Congressional Action* (New Haven: Yale University Press, 1990).

49. See James Fishkin, *Deliberative Democracy* (New Haven: Yale University Press, 1991).

IV. IDEAS, AGENDAS, AND PUBLIC POLICY

11

Agendas, Ideas, and Policy Change
John W. Kingdon

I t seems fitting that changes in agendas and ideas should be considered in a work on the dynamics of American politics. Changes in public policy or dominant national moods do not take place simply by shifts on constant dimensions. The country does not change, for instance, only as a result of oscillations between liberal and conservative positions along a basically constant dimension concerning the appropriate extent of government intervention in the economy and the society. Rather, new issues come to the fore, old issues recede, new dimensions emerge, and policy agendas change. This chapter discusses how and why these changes take place, considers some approaches for studying such changes, and suggests the strengths and weaknesses of these approaches.

In this chapter, I will concentrate on governmental agendas, not agendas in public opinion or in the media. A governmental agenda is a list of subjects or problems to which government officials and those close to them are paying serious attention. Over time, a given issue (for example, health care) rises and falls on the agenda, receiving more attention at some times than at others. We're talking here about how issues come to be issues in the first place, not about how they get decided, nor about how decisions are implemented and what impacts they have.

This chapter has two major parts. First I discuss some of the major conclusions that emerged from my study of agenda setting in the federal government, including some of the strengths and weaknesses of the approach I used.[1] I will not present a comprehensive overview of the conclusions; rather, I will concentrate on a few particularly instructive aspects. Second I consider the place of ideas (as opposed to things like interest group pressure or career election incentives) in public policy formation. Along the way, I say some things about both theoretical and methodological issues.

Agendas and Alternatives

It is common to think of public policy as changing slowly or incrementally. But policy agendas, in contrast to many government activities, do not change gradually. Instead, issues "hit" suddenly. There is a tremendous burst of activity, and government policy changes in major ways all at once. The New Deal, the Great Society, and the Reagan revolution all illustrate this phenomenon. After such an intense period of change, people fall exhausted, the system adjusts to a new status quo, and a period of rest sets in.

A satisfying model of agenda change needs to comprehend these sudden changes, to tolerate the enormous complexity that is clearly a major feature of this world, and to model these extraordinarily messy processes in orderly ways. In my work on agenda setting, I have used such a model, a revised version of the Cohen-March-Olsen "garbage can" model of "organized anarchies." [2] In my revised model, three streams— problems, proposals, and politics—flow through and around the federal government, each stream with a life of its own and largely unrelated to the others. First, people in and around government concentrate on certain problems rather than others at any given time. Second, policy proposals are initiated and refined. Third, political events like changes of adminis- tration, party realignments, or interest group campaigns occur. These three streams develop largely independently of one another. Proposals are generated whether or not they are solving a problem, problems are recog- nized whether or not there is a solution, and political events move along according to their own dynamics.

Some policy change can be explained by the dynamics within each stream. With the political stream, for instance, party realignments, changes of administration, and the power of social movements all contrib- ute to major changes. But the greatest agenda change occurs when the three streams join, which accounts for the sometimes sudden, dramatic changes we observe. A problem is recognized, a proposal is available that can be related to that problem, and the political conditions are right. Advocates of proposals (policy entrepreneurs) seize on those times of opportunity (open policy windows) to hook their solutions to problems that seem pressing or to take advantage of such propitious political hap- penings as changes of administration. Something is done when the win- dow is open, or the opportunity is lost, and entrepreneurs must wait for the next window to open. Thus Lyndon Johnson told his major advisors that the election of 1964 opened a window for Great Society proposals that would last only two years, and a tremendous amount of major legisla- tion passed before it closed. Conversely, the stock market crash of Octo- ber 1987 created a golden opportunity to work on the federal budget deficit, but the opportunity was not seized and was lost.

Methods and Data

Obviously, one needs data that track changes in government agendas over time. It is impractical, and probably theoretically wrong-headed, to think of a given item as being either "on" or "off" an agenda at any particular time. Instead, items rise or fall over time, and agenda status is a continuum of attention rather than a dichotomy.

Various publicly available indicators are used by scholars to track agenda status from one time to another and through different venues. One can follow the appearance and disappearance of subjects in the media, for instance, such as the index to the *New York Times* or similar indexes to more specialized publications. One can track mentions of a given subject in government documents, such as the *Congressional Record* or the *Federal Register*. One can follow the contents of congressional hearings, noticing which subjects are highlighted by hearings and when. The content of such standard documents as State of the Union messages can also be analyzed.

I used these sources but relied mostly on interviews with knowledgeable informants concerned with two federal policy areas, health and transportation. In comparing agenda status as reflected in the interviews and status accorded by media and hearings, I found that the publicly available sources often highlighted a subject to which my informants were paying scant attention, and they sometimes overlooked a subject on which others were spending a lot of time and energy. I concluded that the publicly available sources were making mistakes both of omission and commission. For my purpose of ascertaining which subjects were occupying the time, energy, and attention of important people in and around government, there was no substitute for asking them directly.

What the interviews lack, however, is the ability to take in a considerable sweep of history. In principle, one can follow developments in sources like congressional documents or large-circulation newspapers for a long time. I followed my informants for four years, a short time compared to the use of publicly available sources, but quite a long time as interviewing studies go.

Case studies can combine both types of data. I supplemented my interviews with an analysis of cases of policy initiation stretching over a period of about three decades. The obvious trade-off is that, in exchange for the variety of data, the historical sweep, and the depth of investigation possible with case studies, one sacrifices some ability to generalize to policy events beyond the case under study.

It should be apparent that no one research strategy serves the scholarly community perfectly. Some combination of strategies, however, is gradually building a set of understandings about these processes.

Problem Recognition

One would think that government officials pay attention to subjects when a problem becomes pressing. Indeed, government does routinely monitor the performance of systems through standard indicators like highway deaths, Medicare costs, commuter ridership, or disease rates. Sudden shifts in these indicators of performance contrary to expectation does focus attention on the problem. Disasters or crises (such as plane crashes) also bring attention to a subject.

The puzzle, however, is that governmental attention does not always track on some objective indicator of a problem, or even on focusing events. Walker discovered, for example, that government attended to highway safety some time *after* highway deaths started a long-term decline.[3] In such instances, obviously something beyond straightforward problem solving is going on. In the case of highway safety, Walker makes clear that attention to the problem was driven as much by the development of a solution in the technical literature (making the automobile safer, rather than educating the driver) as by the urgency of the problem.

Government recognition of a problem often involves interpretation and perception, not simply observing objective conditions. There is a difference between a problem and a condition. As one of my respondents said, "If you have only four fingers on one hand, that's not a problem; that's a situation." So how do we transform conditions into problems? Conditions become problems when we feel we should and can do something to change them. Uneven access to health care is or is not a problem, for instance, depending on whether one views health care as a right. The categories into which issues get placed also affect their treatment. If transportation of the handicapped is treated as a transportation problem, for example, then inexpensive and effective solutions like dial-a-ride or subsidized taxi service are appropriate. But if it gets placed in the category of civil rights, then retrofitting subways for elevators and providing bus lifts are appropriate.

How Proposals Are Generated

There is a community of specialists in health, transportation, or any other area: researchers, congressional staffers, bureaucrats, academics, and lobbyists. Ideas float around in such communities. Specialists try out and revise their ideas by attending conferences, circulating papers, holding hearings, presenting testimony, publishing articles, and drafting legislative proposals. Many, many ideas are considered at some point in the evolution of an issue.

The process by which proposals are selected from this very large set of ideas resembles biological natural selection. Much as molecules floated around in the "primeval soup" before life came into being, ideas float around in a "policy primeval soup" in these communities of specialists. Both molecules and ideas bump into one another and combine in various ways. In each type of evolution, new elements are sometimes introduced (mutation), and others are formed from previously existing elements (recombination). In the process of policy evolution, some ideas fall away, others survive and prosper, and some are selected to become serious contenders for adoption.

There are several advantages to thinking of the formation of policy proposals as a sort of evolutionary selection process. First, it frees us from the shackles of determinism. I wasted a lot of time on drawing out decision trees, trying to specify necessary and sufficient conditions, and figuring out laws of causation. Unlike my experience with congressmen's voting decisions,[4] here it just was not working. There were too many exceptions, and taking account of them was making the specifications unduly ornate, one might even say baroque. A probabilistic rather than deterministic model fits the world better. Second, despite Charles Darwin's title, *The Origin of Species*, one does not have to follow the origins of proposals back in an infinite regress. Concentration on selection focuses scholarly attention, not on where ideas came from, but on what made them catch on in certain communities at certain times, which is a much more productive preoccupation. Third, we are not obliged to look for equilibria. These systems evolve; they do not necessarily settle into equilibria. They may resemble *punctuated* equilibrium, particularly in the sense that they exhibit dramatic change in short bursts followed by periods of rest. But they may not seek equilibria at all. Fourth, concentrating on recombination solves the puzzle presented by sudden and substantial change occurring when there is "no new thing under the sun." Change is there, but it is in the recombination of familiar elements. In many ways, a turn to evolutionary thinking proves liberating. It has the additional virtue of fitting the world we want to understand.

Some Reflections on This Kind of Modeling

Evolutionary models have the advantages just discussed. The garbage can model can accommodate great complexity, comprehend sudden and dramatic change, recognize the fluidity that inheres in the process, and yet impose an appropriate degree of order. In this section, I reflect on four issues.

First, critics of the garbage can model often argue that it is not sufficiently structured. In my view, this model has quite a bit of structure, while leaving room for residual randomness, as is true of the real world. It is not true that outcomes are essentially "fortuitous," "random," or "chaotic"—words used a lot to describe this style of theorizing. Everything does not have an equal chance to be thrown together with everything else. For instance, which participants are invited to a decisive meeting is not random; which solutions are in the queue with what timing is not; nor is a solution randomly available when a problem is pressing. I discuss the various kinds of structure in the model in greater detail elsewhere.[5] The model is also constrained in a variety of ways—by political culture, budget constraints, class biases, national mood, partisan dominance, and so forth. The problem is that, although structure is present, it is not the orthodox type to which we are accustomed. The fact that the model is not a Marxist-style class analysis, or a bureaucratic hierarchy, or a rational choice-maximizing model that seeks equilibrium does not mean that it has no pattern or structure; it is just an unorthodox type of structure.

A second question in the literature on agenda setting is the issue of state autonomy. One of Cobb and Elder's fundamental notions is that issues flow from a systemic agenda to a formal agenda.[6] Issues first get attention in the political system at large through such processes as the mass media and social movements, and are then transferred to the government agenda. Writers like Theda Skocpol would object that government is more autonomous than that.[7] The state is more than the creature of the interest group structure or a reflection of class interests. People in government are not blank slates, but instead have their own interests and adopt their own goals and strategies. One need not reify the state to see that people in government are at least somewhat autonomous.

Examples of both state autonomy and the state as a reflection of society can be found in cases of agenda setting. On the one hand, government really does generate its own agenda. Ralph Nader, for instance, had Senate patrons as he launched his crusade for consumer protection. On the other hand, as with the taxpayer revolt, social movements come along and overwhelm everything in their path, including government. The trick for scholars is not to opt for one or the other picture, it seems to me, but to specify the conditions under which and the ways in which policymaking works from the top down or from the bottom up.

A third issue is the degree to which the streams in a garbage can model flow along independently of each other. It does seem likely, contrary to this supposed independence, that the streams get linked in various ways before the critical time of open windows and coupling. Among the criteria by which some proposals survive and others fall by the wayside in the policy stream, for instance, is the anticipation by policy specialists of likely support or opposition in the political stream, which indicates that the policy and political streams are related. My own view is that, in the main, the policy and political streams do flow along largely on their own, each according to dynamics not much related to the other, and that the critical thing to understand is how these largely independent streams come together. One way of capturing the complexity of this issue might be to say that the streams get joined at times other than the final, decisive moments when opportunities for real action present themselves. But more work does need to be done on this critical feature of the model.

Fourth and finally, one nice property of this picture of agenda change involving entrepreneurial activity is that it makes some sense of "great man" theories of history. It is common among biographers and journalists to attribute outcomes to the activities of titanic individuals like Lyndon Johnson, Abraham Lincoln, or Franklin Roosevelt. To a social scientist, this concentration on individuals is uncomfortably idiosyncratic and atheoretical, and neglects the pattern and regularity in social, economic, and political events. Our treatment of policy entrepreneurs shows a way out. In that treatment, much of the process is governed by large events not under any individual's control. But entrepreneurs take advantage of their opportunities (the "large events") and play a part in the joining of the streams. One of my respondents articulated that process beautifully by describing policy entrepreneurs as "surfers waiting for the big wave." Individuals don't control the waves, but they can ride them. Policy entrepreneurs do not control events, but they can anticipate them and bend events to their purposes to some degree.

Ideas and Politics

As the foregoing discussion of agenda setting makes clear, policy formation is not simply driven by such conventional political forces as reelection incentives, interest group pressure, and marshaling votes and power. Argumentation, persuasion, and marshaling evidence and information are also important. In other words, participants traffic in the world of ideas. "Ideas" are either goals or motivations other than self-interested pursuits, or theories that individuals hold about how the world works (e.g., about cause-and-effect relationships) that can be used to further self-interest as well as other goals.[8]

Political scientists are accustomed to self-interested explanations for behavior, public policy, and collective outcomes. We usually see parties and candidates as seeking power, incumbents pursuing reelection, interest groups competing for government benefits (policy outcomes being the results of such struggles), bureaucrats protecting their turf and maximizing their budgets, and voters looking after their economic well-being.

Our traditional dependence on self-interest as a motive for behavior has been given a tremendous push lately by rational choice modeling. Rational choice approaches need not assume self-interest, only purposive or goal-oriented behavior. Politicians, for instance, can rationally pursue their conception of good public policy or their understanding of the national interest. But most rational choice work does assume that actors are self-interested. Thus politicians, to continue our example, are assumed to be seekers of election and reelection, and more generally promoters of their own careers.

Of course, self-interest does motivate a good deal of political behavior and does affect governmental outcomes. But the content of ideas also seems to be as important as the things political scientists conventionally study. Argumentation, persuasion, the construction of effective appeals, and the evocation of values and ideology seem as important as interest group pressure, reelection, career advantage, and the pursuit of power. Voters behave according to judgments about governmental performance and traditional party loyalties as much as they behave according to calculations of their own individual self-interest or group benefits. Congressional representatives pursue good public policy as much as they pursue reelection. Bureaucrats are as interested in the mission of their agencies as they are in maximizing job stability or salaries. Finally, it is difficult to understand the origins, attractions to adherents, and tremendous power of such movements as abolition, civil rights, environmental protection, and consumerism without resort to the power of ideas. Indeed, the histories of public policy formation resulting from such movements suggest that powerful interests often lose when confronted by such tides in social movements or in general climate of the times.

Let me be clear about what I am *not* arguing. First, I do not argue that self-interest is unimportant. Politicians are clearly interested in their careers, as voters are in jobs, interest groups in hustling benefits for their members, and bureaucrats in protecting turf. I only wish to argue that explanations for behaviors and political outcomes that rely solely on self-interest are incomplete, and that political scientists need to turn some of their attention to the world of ideas at this stage in the discipline's development. Second, I also do not argue that pursuit of "the good" is normatively superior to the pursuit of self-interest. Indeed, a lot of harm has been done through history in the name of some "good." Third, I do not wish to bash rational choice modeling. Indeed, I believe rational choice is a powerful way to build theory; not the only way, but an extremely productive way. We have made a lot of progress by constructing highly simplified deductive theories that clarify the logic of the argument, show explicitly what follows from what, and, if mathematical, make the math tractable. Fourth and finally, I do not wish to posit a necessary conflict between self-interest and ideas. As I argue presently, the two are inextricably intertwined both empirically and theoretically.

Ideas vs. Self-Interest?

Scholars might be tempted to devise ways to distinguish the effects of ideas from self-interest and thereby to compare the weights of the two in accounting for behaviors and outcomes. If we could clearly separate ideas from self-interest and make contrary predictions of behaviors or policy outcomes based on the two, we could then test which explanation (ideas or self-interest) holds over a set of empirical cases, how frequently, and under what conditions. Much of current writing in this area takes the posture that ideas are quite different from self-interest and that the two run at counterpurposes.

Unfortunately, ideas and self-interest probably cannot be disentangled, either empirically or theoretically. Empirically, the two work together. A reelection-maximizing member of Congress, for example, also believes in certain principles of good public policy. The nomination and election processes that select incumbents from among the pool of eligibles tend heavily to bring politicians to office whose views are roughly similar to constituency views. So it is usually impossible to distinguish the cases in which representatives vote according to their own policy preferences from those in which they vote to maximize their chances of reelection. Most of the time, reelection and good public policy point them in the same direction. Most of the time, they take both the expedient and principled course at once. The same point applies to others. Bureaucrats take positions both to maximize budgets and to promote their agency's mission. Interest group leaders promote both the policy goals of the group and their own reputation for power.

The same problem is found at a macro level. Ideas are tightly linked with more conventional political forces in setting governmental agendas. One account of the movement in the 1970s and 1980s toward deregulation, for example, emphasizes the sheer power of the idea.[9] Economists' work on natural monopoly, capture, and regulation, together with conservative ideology, powerfully affected public policy and extended into transportation, communication, banking, retailing, and many other areas. My discussion of agenda setting, while certainly emphasizing the importance of such ideas, also stresses the importance of joining those ideas in the policy stream with events in the political stream such as the taxpayer revolt, the rebellion against "big government" and "tax-and-spend liberals" (as represented by some aspects of the Great Society programs), the election first of Jimmy Carter and then of Ronald Reagan, and the political impulse to "get government off our backs." The ideas are themselves important, but their combination with other forces is critical.

Neither can ideas and self-interest be successfully disentangled theoretically. People need to attach meaning to their behavior, even if that behavior is motivated by self-interest. That need for meaning does not simply involve rationalization for base motives, although there certainly is an abundance of ex post rationalization. Nor is it merely cloaking self-interested motives in symbolic politics, although again there is plenty of manipulation of symbols to go around. The point is that without meaning, people do not behave in the same way as they do if they can find meaning in their actions. In persuading others and in explaining her votes, for example, a politician also persuades herself and her explanations affect her decisions.

So people often find it impossible to pursue only their "raw" self-interest. They cannot arrive at positions without both self-interest and principle. The intimate connection between ideas and self-interest, both empirically and theoretically, implies that we cannot separate the two and assess their relative strengths or independent effects.

Self-Interest and Ideas as Guides to Action

We are accustomed to thinking of self-interest as quite a sure guide to action. We think that individuals can figure out how to maximize their economic wealth, politicians know how to maximize votes, and interest groups know what they want to achieve and how to pursue their own aggrandizement.

Actually, self-interest is not self-evident and may not be nearly as sure a guide to action as we customarily think. Interest groups, for example, spend a lot of time and energy trying to define their interests. Curiously, self-interest may not be as sure a guide to action as ideas. Even if incumbent members of Congress want to maximize their chance of reelection, for instance, it is often not at all clear how to do so. Their constituencies often do not give them clear signals, because many people have no opinion, different people have different opinions, intensities must be taken into account as much as direction of preferences, and the effects of current constituency opinions (even when well known) on future elections are unclear. So a legislator uses decision criteria like ideology and party, and takes cues from committee members who share his or her party and ideology. If the world sorts itself roughly into liberal vs. conservative and Republican vs. Democrat, then it is easier to decide most things by those cues than to divine the preferences of constituents.

The Importance of Ideas Revisited

Our difficulty in distinguishing between ideas and self-interest does not mean ideas are unimportant or simply a cover or rationalization for self-interest. It also does not mean we should abandon a study of ideas and politics and concentrate on self-interest; quite the reverse. But it does mean that we need to construct models that include interactions between ideas and self-interest, rather than pitting them against each other.

At this point in the discipline's development, there are several reasons for devoting greater scholarly attention to ideas than they have gotten recently. First, people in and around government spend a lot of time, money, and energy on ideas. They hire analysts; they marshal arguments and collect evidence in support of those arguments; they attempt to persuade. One reason they devote resources to ideas is that part of building a coalition involves persuading other groups to join, and an appeal to the persuader's own interest is not sufficient. On the assumption that the behavior of these practitioners reveals something of their motivations, one must conclude that ideas are important. If they were not, then smart people wouldn't invest so much in them. At this juncture, political scientists might well devote as much energy to studying the ways in which practitioners marshal arguments and evidence in persuasive efforts as continuing to study the ways in which they marshal votes, campaign contributions, and interest group endorsements.

Second, study of the world of talk gives us clues about the world around the talker. Assume for the sake of argument that politicians never reveal what is "truly" driving their behavior. They must couch what they want, not in terms of their own advantage, but in terms of some larger theme that others will find attractive. They choose some words rather than others because they find those words have some appeal to larger publics, to undecided fellow legislators, to constituents, or to whomever is important to them in that situation. Thus a study of their words indicates something about the context within which the politicians work—the culture surrounding them, the nature of the times, the coalitions they try to build, the kinds of justifications that would appeal to constituents or other important people—whether or not it taps their motivations or the causes of their behavior.

Third, ideas are important whether or not they affect decisions. A bill that is signed into law, for instance, even if entirely the result of the push and pull of interest groups, electoral considerations, or other self-interested forces, nevertheless embodies ideas that have consequences. So it makes sense to study the content of ideas in authoritative decisions, whether or not they drive the policy-making process. One reason for the importance of this content in authoritative decisions is that people worry about precedent. Even when a given change is not very important in itself, people ask whether that change would set a precedent. Beyond judicial meanings of stare decisis and beyond the symbolic value of small changes, a principle of equity demands that one does in future cases what one did in the instant case, and practical pressures therefore build to argue for similar treatment.

Studying Ideas and Politics

Empirical research and theory building on ideas and politics could take a number of directions. In this section, I discuss examples of current work in this area, suggest some future directions, and sketch one direction I have been pursuing.

Some of the most interesting work on ideas and public policy concentrates on diffusion across governmental units. A good literature has developed, for instance, on the spread of Keynesian economics from one country to another, with its obvious consequences for the shape of public policy in those countries.[10] Alt demonstrates the importance of dominant economic theories for public policy formation in a fascinating cross-national comparison.[11] To go to a more micro level, there is an excellent literature on how voting behavior is driven by evaluations of the overall performance of the economy and the incumbent administration, rather than voters' own economic circumstances;[12] by preferences over collective goods rather than distributive benefits;[13] and by racial symbols rather than actual impact on neighborhoods.[14] I have mentioned above current or recent research on legislative behavior and public policy formation. In short, without an extensive literature review, I simply want to argue that good research on ideas and politics is possible and important.

Research could take a number of directions. More cross-national comparisons could be undertaken or, for that matter, more cross-state or cross-locality comparisons within the United States. We could investigate how citizens use ideas in reasoning about political matters. If they evoke principles in concrete situations instead of reasoning deductively from principles, for example, we could investigate which principles are evoked under what circumstances, which are neglected, how ideas and action are connected, and how such reasoning differs from elite to mass levels. Finally, we might want to know more about the actual content of the ideas people use inside and outside government, how that content varies from one issue area to another, and how it is used in arguments to persuade and in strategies to build coalitions.

One area of research on ideas and politics that is directly related to the theme of this volume is changes in dominant ideas over time. Different scholars have argued that there is a periodicity in American politics and public policy. Theories of party realignment are well known, and the connections between realignments and public policy have been well established.[15] Some authors have posited that American politics runs in cycles that alternate between periods of public activism and private interest, and have propounded various theories to account for the oscillations.[16] It is not entirely clear whether American politics is best seen as cyclical, or, if it is cyclical, what the alternations are and how they can be explained.[17] But, at least, the ideas that come to dominate our politics change from one time to another.[18]

How do dominant ideas change? What drives those changes? What public policy consequences ensue? As a first step in undertaking research on these topics, I have been reading the *Congressional Record* from several different historical periods to see whether change in language can be documented from one time to another. My preliminary research indicates that there are in fact very clear differences. Consider, for instance, some quotations from the debate over the renewal of the poverty program on the House floor on July 21, 1965:

> We should no longer be debating whether we need a massive federal program attacking the root causes of poverty. Congress faced up to this moral imperative last year. . . . We have a compassionate concern for the underprivileged of this nation. (James Scheuer, D-N.Y.)
>
> [Lyndon Johnson has] won the excited admiration of millions throughout this country. (Michael Feighan, D-Ohio)
>
> It is incumbent on all of us to reaffirm and rededicate ourselves to this great national commitment in order to assure its success. [Leonard Farbstein, D-N.Y.)
>
> The Economic Opportunity Act of 1964 is one of the boldest pieces of legislation in our history. . . . [It is an] idealistic, yet practical,

attempt to bridge the gap between the haves and have-nots. (William Hathaway, D-Maine)

[These are] broad, imaginative programs which seek to get at the heart of the problems of the poor. (Patsy Mink, D-Hawaii)

We cannot stumble now. We cannot lose sight of that magnificent vision outlined for us by our President. This can, and will, be a land where every person shares in our great prosperity. (James Roosevelt, D-Calif.)

Of course, there were contrary voices, especially from Republicans, concerning the effectiveness of the poverty program and the political fallout from the program even as it was then operating in its early days. Still the words quoted above were on the prevailing side.

The striking feature of such rhetoric in July 1965 is that one could not even imagine such fulsome liberal language in congressional debates on any subject during, say, the first year of the Reagan administration. Indeed, an inspection of the House debates on July 22, 1981, reveals a dramatically different tone. Rep. Sidney Yates (D-Ill.), managing an appropriations bill, repeatedly expresses his sympathy with amendments to add spending, but pleads that he cannot bust the budget. His position is repeatedly sustained. Rep. Christopher Smith (R-N.J.) refers to the current period as "a time that we are trying to practice fiscal austerity." Language has so clearly taken a more conservative turn.

This comparison between comparable dates in 1965 and 1981 provides no answers but raises a multitude of interesting questions. Are the changes the result of differences in the governmental agenda between the two periods, or has there been a shift along a common dimension (such as the desirability of government spending)? How do these clear changes square with suggestions that common themes have been running through American political thought from colonial days to the present? What has brought about the change in rhetoric? Is it leaner times for the economy, a party realignment, a different administration, a reaction to the perceived excesses of the Great Society, a shift in dominant national values, some sort of demographic change, a natural swing of the political pendulum, or what? Finally, what consequences ensue? Is this rhetoric merely window dressing, or does it have some policy consequence? How might one go about answering these sorts of questions? Could a more systematic study over many historical periods produce similar changes in language? If so, what would they mean?

This chapter is plainly not the place to provide answers. But I hope it does pique the curiosity of readers. Such dramatic changes over time seem important, and could be studied to provide valuable information about political and policy change. Different ideas do seem to dominate our political system at different times, and we need to understand more fully why they do.

Change and the Clinton Administration

It is quite common in writing on the American political system to observe that change is infrequent and difficult. The institutions of government are sluggish, and interest groups that benefit from government programs mobilize their supporters in the bureaucracy and in the Congress to prevent substantial change. Both the academic literature and practical experience are replete with examples of fresh ideas that ran afoul of institutional or political barriers.

Much of this chapter provides a different emphasis. There are conditions under which we observe quite sudden and dramatic changes in public policy. Opportunities (open windows) arise for entrepreneurial advocates to push their policies. Most of these ideas are not new. They have been developed, revised, and resubmitted many times, in many venues, over a period of many years. Sometimes after a long incubation, conditions come to be right for "new ideas" to be seriously considered and even adopted.

Nowhere is that process more evident than in the first days of a new administration. The Reagan administration, for instance, seized the moment and pushed through Congress a substantial reordering of budgetary priorities in the first ten months of 1981. That reordering has fundamentally affected the government, the economy, and the political system to the present day. As of this writing (April 1993), it is impossible to state with much confidence whether the Clinton administration will produce such dramatic changes. But new directions in issues related to abortion, new taxes (which—wonder of wonders—the American public seems to be accepting), a renewed determination to tackle the federal budget deficit, and a promised fundamental restructuring of health care financing and delivery all suggest that change is possible. Indeed, I would argue that change is as much a systematic and regular feature of our political system as is stasis, and that we know much less about why change occurs than we know about why it does not.

Conclusion

To return to the topic of the dynamics of American politics, we have learned a good deal about agenda change. The importance of ideas has been revealed along the way. This chapter does not question the considerable body of empirical research or the theoretical understandings that have been generated about political change in the United States in recent decades. I only suggest some new directions for future scholarly attention. I hope scholars will sense the potential for exciting research along these lines and will work on some of these problems.

Notes

1. John W. Kingdon, *Agendas, Alternatives, and Public Policies* (Boston: Little, Brown, 1984).
2. Michael Cohen, James March, and Johan Olsen, "A Garbage Can Model of Organizational Choice," *Administrative Science Quarterly* 17 (March 1972): 1-25.
3. Jack L. Walker, "Setting the Agenda in the U.S. Senate," *British Journal of Political Science* 7 (October 1977): 423-445.
4. John W. Kingdon, *Congressmen's Voting Decisions*, 3d ed. (Ann Arbor: University of Michigan Press, 1989).
5. Kingdon, *Agendas*, 216-218.
6. Roger Cobb and Charles Elder, *Participation in American Politics: The Dynamics of Agenda-Building* (Boston: Allyn and Bacon, 1972).
7. Peter Evans, Dietrich Rueschemeyer, and Theda Skocpol, *Bringing the State Back In* (New York: Cambridge University Press, 1985).
8. For a more complete statement of my thinking on ideas and politics, see John W. Kingdon, "Ideas, Politics, and Public Policies" (Paper delivered at the 1988 Annual Meeting of the American Political Science Association). A revised version of that paper appears in *Reconsidering the Democratic Public*, ed. George Marcus and Russell Hanson (State College: Pennsylvania State University Press, 1993).
9. Martha Derthick and Paul Quirk, *The Politics of Deregulation* (Washington, D.C.: Brookings Institution, 1985).
10. Peter A. Hall, ed., *The Political Power of Economic Ideas: Keynesianism Across Nations* (Princeton, N.J.: Princeton University Press, 1989).
11. James E. Alt, "Crude Politics: Oil and the Political Economy of Unemployment in Britain and Norway," *British Journal of Political Science* 17 (1987): 149-199.
12. Donald Kinder and Roderick Kiewiet, "Economic Discontent and Political Behavior: The Role of Personal Grievances and Collective Economic Judgments in Congressional Voting," *American Journal of Political Science* 23 (August 1981): 495-527.
13. Michael Hawthorne and John E. Jackson, "The Individual Political Economy of Federal Tax Policy," *American Political Science Review* 81 (1987): 757-774; and John E. Jackson and David C. King, "Public Goods, Private Interests, and Representation," *American Political Science Review* 83 (December 1989): 1143-1164.
14. David O. Sears, Carl P. Hensler, and Leslie K. Spear, "Whites' Opposition to Busing: Self-Interest or Symbolic Racism?" *American Political Science Review* 73 (1979): 369-384; and David O. Sears, Richard R. Lau, Tom R. Tyler, and Harris M. Allen, "Self-Interest Versus Symbolic Politics in Policy Attitudes and Presidential Voting," *American Political Science Review* 74 (1980): 670-684.
15. David W. Brady, *Critical Elections and Congressional Policy Making* (Stanford, Calif.: Stanford University Press, 1988).
16. Albert O. Hirschman, *Shifting Involvements: Private Interest and Public Action* (Princeton, N.J.: Princeton University Press, 1982); and Arthur M. Schlesinger, Jr., *The Cycles of American History*, 3d ed. (Boston: Little, Brown, 1986).
17. Andrew McFarland, "Interest Groups and Political Time: Cycles in America," *British Journal of Political Science* 21 (July 1991): 257-284.
18. James Stimson, *Public Opinion in America* (Boulder, Colo.: Westview, 1991).

12

Competition, Emulation, and Policy Innovation
Virginia Gray

Introduction

W here do policy ideas come from? . . . [They are] something you can steal from everybody." At least that is what Governor Lawton Chiles told a college class in the summer of 1991. The Florida governor exemplifies the twin pressures of emulation and competition facing the states. State governments act as policy laboratories experimenting with new ideas. Experiments that succeed are passed on to other states or to the federal government; those that fail do so without great cost. States compete with one another to be first in some areas, and they emulate other states' actions so as not to be last in others. The sharing of ideas among governments is "one of the happy incidents of the federal system," as Justice Louis Brandeis put it. Emulation and cue taking among the states largely determine the pace and direction of social and political change, according to Jack Walker, a noted scholar of policy innovation.[1]

The study of the diffusion of innovations, then, deserves a prominent place in the federalism literature. This essay will describe and critique the policy innovation literature and evaluate its overall contribution. But federalism is also concerned with the distribution of power between the national and state levels and among the fifty states. The Founders envisioned the creation of "opposite and rival" interests among governments; these opposing interests would lead the governments to behave differently. In other words, the distribution of power would set up a competition among governments that would have a salutary effect on the scope of governmental power.

Thomas Dye's recent book expounds the virtues of this competition. Drawing on the work of public choice economists, Dye outlines the "competitive federalism model." This model assumes that subnational governments offer a range of goods, services, and tax rates in a marketplace; that citizens have information about governmental performance; and that citizens can (and do) express their dissatisfactions by voice and or exit. Dye argues that, by and large, these conditions are fulfilled in America today.[2]

The driving force behind policy innovation, according to Dye, is the competition among governments to satisfy their citizens. It motivates public officials to come up with new ideas, just as competition in the private sector motivates entrepreneurs to improve their products and to invent new ones. Thus, Dye's work is valuable in linking interstate competition to the innovation process. We will return to this theme below, arguing that many policy competitions can be conceptualized as diffusion processes.

Most of the diffusion literature reviewed here concerns the transmission of ideas from one state to another (horizontal diffusion). Very little has been written on vertical diffusion: the transmission of ideas from the states to the national government. In one of the few pieces on vertical diffusion, Keith Boeckelman finds that in a four-year period Congress emulated the states in only three cases, welfare reform, child care, and homeless aid.[3] More often, it ignored state successes or adopted programs that had already failed in the states. States were most important as laboratories when expensive social programs were involved and when state officials pressed vigorously for federal action.

We can assume that with former governor Bill Clinton in the White House, state experiments will be considered more seriously. During the 1992 presidential campaign Clinton frequently spoke of experimental programs in Arkansas and in other states, and he had been the National Governors' Association's chief lobbyist for the welfare reform Congress enacted in 1988. Political conditions are therefore ripe for more vertical diffusion.

Definitions

The study of policy diffusion proceeds from certain shared understandings. One is that a policy innovation is an idea or practice *perceived* as new to the unit adopting it. Thus, a program or policy that is new to one state is labeled an innovation there even though other states may already have adopted it. Second, new ideas are communicated in a process called diffusion, which simply means that ideas spread from one unit to another. Diffusion researchers typically focus on the rate of adoption, that is, the relative speed by which new ideas travel and are adopted. Analysts distinguish between innovative states and laggard states, for example, by calculating the elapsed time between invention of the idea and its adoption by a particular state.

The diffusion literature has its intellectual roots, appropriately enough, in communications theory, which scholars use to analyze the diffusion of new ideas as a special type of communication. These scholars typically focus on the individual level of analysis, investigating the innovation decision process, attributes of innovations, characteristics of adopters (early vs. late), and the role of change agents, opinion leaders, and communication networks. They report an important empirical regularity: the adoption of an innovation follows a normal, bell-shaped curve when the frequency of adoptions is plotted over time. When the cumulative number of adopters is plotted, the result is an S-shaped curve.[4] This distribution characterizes diverse innovations, from farmers' adoption of new crops in India to consumers' adoption of household products in the United States.

The field of sociology has focused on the diffusion of innovations at the organizational level. By investigating innovative firms, scholars have found that organizations with "slack resources" such as size and wealth are the first to adopt innovations. They also found some influence from the organization's environment: a disturbance in the environment is likely to lead to innovation. Lawrence Mohr was among the first to apply these theories to public agencies, thereby introducing sociological ideas to political scientists.[5]

Political scientists have concentrated on the system level, investigating how policy innovations are diffused across cities, states, and nations. They have closely relied on the individual- and organizational-level theories in their work. For example, they found that the S-curve describes the cumulative adoption pattern and that slack resources (such as wealth) determine the rate of adoption of state laws.[6]

Most of the political science work has been what Mohr calls "variance" studies, that is, a set of independent (or causal) variables is used to explain statistically the rate of adoption.[7] Few diffusion studies have been in the other mode—what Mohr terms "process studies"—where a time-ordered sequence of events is analyzed to determine the final cause of the adoption.

Yet political scientists do study the sequence of events leading to the adoption of new laws, but they call this the "policy process model" or approach. John Kingdon used this approach in his study of agenda setting in Congress, as did Nelson Polsby in his study of eight national policy innovations. Hugh Heclo used a similar approach in a comparative context in his work on political learning in Sweden and Britain, as did a variety of authors studying "lesson drawing" among foreign nations. All of these works are process studies in Mohr's sense: they look at discrete events in a time-ordered sequence and search for a final cause. Because the events are unique, they cannot be measured quantitatively and explained variance cannot be computed.[8]

Variance studies and process studies could learn from one another; thus, one is disappointed to see a work on innovation such as Polsby's proceed without acknowledging the diffusion literature (aside from a footnote to Everett M. Rogers). Similarly, the quantitative analyses of diffusion could profit from knowledge about policy entrepreneurs and agenda formation. I will return to this point later.

Theories of Diffusion of Policy Innovations

Political scientists have found two sets of explanations helpful in explaining why some states adopt new ideas first and why others lag behind. First, a set of *internal determinants* is often critical—that is, factors within the adopting unit can aid or deter adoption of innovations. Political, economic, and social factors are typically included in such a model. Second, a set of *external determinants* often influences the adoption of new ideas. Regional diffusion models are the most popular, although federal incentives and professional associations are sometimes important factors as well. A few scholars have incorporated both sets of factors into their explanation of adoption rates.

Internal Determinants

Internal determinants models have been tested in two ways. For some researchers the dependent variable is the proportion of elapsed time between the first state's adoption and a particular state's adoption. Often a number of innovations are combined so that the resulting score is an index of average innovativeness. For other researchers the dependent variable is the date (or age) of a single adoption. Thus, the older the adoption, the more innovative the state.[9]

Internal determinants models are typically tested using a cross-sectional design, a problematic procedure because the adoptions may have spanned several decades. The internal characteristics are measured at a single time point that may be either too early or too late to influence a given state's adoption. Where a composite innovation index extends over a hundred years or so, researchers have subdivided the index into shorter time spans and then measured the explanatory variables at different, more relevant points. Still, the causal variables are not measured immediately before the adoption event.

Scholars have accumulated a body of knowledge about the economic, political, and social characteristics that predispose states to innovate. The impact of economic resources on the probability of adoption has been consistently identified as important. For example, Walker in his study of eighty-eight program innovations found that larger, wealthier states adopted programs faster than smaller and poorer states. He reasoned that such states (e.g., New York and California) had more slack resources to devote to policy experimentation than did poorer states like Mississippi. I reported a similar finding in my study of twelve innovations.[10]

Thus, the idea of "slack resources" derived from organizational theory was found to be valid for the fifty states. But organizational theories based on environmental disturbances have also proved valid. Berry and Berry found that as a state's fiscal health declines, it is more likely to adopt a lottery.[11] This explanation seems to be more relevant for tax policy than for expenditure policy.

In addition, researchers have focused on the political conditions in the state at the time of the adoption decision. Typical political variables include political culture, electoral competition, turnover, and measures of legislative and bureaucratic professionalism. Moralistic states engage in the most innovation, traditionalistic states the least. Politically competitive states tend to be the most innovative as do those with higher turnover in office. The capacity of governmental institutions makes a difference in innovativeness, as well. States with fairly apportioned, professional legislatures (that is, with longer sessions, higher pay, more staff) adopt new policies faster than do other states. Similarly, bureaucratic professionalism is a key factor. Bureaucrats initiating a variety of model innovations were found to be more educated, more experienced, and more active in professional organizations than the typical state employee.[12]

Social factors hypothesized to affect innovation include education, illiteracy, urbanism, diversity, and religion. Of these, education and urbanism seem to be more important. Religion is critical for some innovations such as the lottery, where the presence of fundamentalists reduces the likelihood of adoption.[13]

Overall, like state expenditures, policy innovation is most influenced by economic variables, followed by political factors. Social factors are more mixed in their effects.

Diffusion Models

Diffusion models capture the influence of external actions on adoption decisions. Although a variety of external factors could be considered in such a model, the most popular is the regional diffusion model, in which a state is assumed to be influenced by its neighbors' actions. That is, a new program is more likely to be adopted if neighboring states have already done so. Four strategies have been used to evaluate regional diffusion models. First, Walker and others employed factor analysis to isolate clusters of states that adopted policies in similar orders. Then they examined the clusters (that is, the factor scores) to see if these groupings appeared to be regional. This procedure, however, yields a description rather than an explanation of the diffusion process.

Second, researchers have ascertained whether a state is more likely to adopt a particular policy if its neighbor has already adopted it.[14] If neighboring states have similar adoption patterns, the researchers assume it is because they emulate one another. But they might have similar internal characteristics, which lead them to make the same adoption decision. This assumption about emulation is an analytic shortcoming in this approach as well as in the one using factor analysis.

Third, investigators have conducted surveys of public officials to find out who contacts whom. This approach identifies actual diffusion patterns, both regional and national. But it is impractical for large-scale studies of innovation; thus, it is usually done on a single policy at one point in time, which limits generalizability. A fourth strategy is to include a dummy variable for region in the model. This approach assumes that diffusion occurs within preexisting census regions, which is not necessarily true.[15]

Using these methods, a number of scholars have documented regional diffusion effects. They reason that state leaders look to other nearby states for ideas and solutions to policy problems rather than searching within their own boundaries. If the neighboring state has adopted a program that successfully solved the problem, then the first state is more likely to adopt the same solution. Walker's study was the first to find a regional clustering pattern, indicating that states in the same geographic region adopted programs in a similar order. Canon and Baum found a regional effect for tort law diffusion but to a lesser extent than did Walker. The diffusion of the lottery also evinced a clear regional pattern, as did the spread of the gasoline tax and even the individual income tax. Presumably, the possibility of citizens traveling across state lines to gamble or buy gas motivates states to start their own lotteries and to institute the gasoline tax.[16]

But two caveats must be mentioned. One is that regionalism in cue taking seems to have declined over time. Lutz found that innovations that diffused early in this century displayed more of a regional pattern than those that diffused in the second half. Nevertheless, the results of Berry and Berry for recent tax policies show that regional diffusion still occurs. A second caveat is that the studies based on survey data report mixed findings: some policies diffuse regionally and some through national networks. Technology transfer is accomplished more through national professional associations and federal incentives than through regional emulation. But in energy policy, cue-taking emanates most often from neighboring states and secondarily from national leaders in the field. Light suggests that the degree of consensus about policy leaders is the key: in policy areas where bureaucrats share a consensus about which states are leaders, national leaders get consulted first. In other policy areas there is less consensus about agency prestige, and consequently, more copying goes on.[17]

It is important to heed these mixed results from survey-based studies because, presumably, the surveys are better at detecting who contacts whom. Analyses based on aggregate data (that is, factor analysis or dummy variables) are less reliable because one can't be sure that the correlation between neighbors is a true indication of regional emulation. The correlation may be due to similar internal characteristics of neighboring states. Moreover, it is reasonable to assume that over time more national diffusion is occurring because of emerging policy networks, active professional associations, and federal governmental incentives. Thus, diffusion need no longer be purely regional; it may be more of a top-down, vertical process. Such a process has not been explicitly modeled, although several studies document the role of incentives and professional networks in speeding up diffusion.[18]

Combined Models

Although many scholars have considered internal determinants and diffusion models separately in a single article, very few have combined both models into a single integrated explanation. Berry and Berry have done this and have also offered a new methodology for testing the integrated model.[19] They use event history analysis (EHA), borrowed from biostatistics, to predict the probability that a state will adopt a policy in a single year, given that it has not already adopted it. Such models are estimated using a pooled cross-sectional time series technique in which the data consist of one observation per state for each year the state might adopt. The independent variables include both internal characteristics that vary over time and the number of neighboring states that have already adopted. Compared to the cross-sectional design, this procedure has the advantage of including timely measures of the independent variables. The major estimation problem is the low variance in the dependent variable because so few states adopt in any one year. But that seems to have posed no difficulty for Berry and Berry's analysis of the lottery, the gasoline tax, or the income tax.

In the unified model, internal determinants, both economic and political, and regional diffusion are significant. The lottery is likely to be adopted when a state's fiscal health is poor, during an election year, when party control is split, when per capita income is high, where fundamentalism is absent, and when neighboring states have already adopted it. Basically, Berry and Berry find that when the internal characteristics of a state are favorable for innovation, then the actions of neighboring states have a stronger impact. Note that several of their significant variables must be measured immediately—such as election year and party control—so that time series data must be used.

Their 1992 study of the adoption of the gasoline tax and individual income tax yields similar conclusions.[20] The chances of tax innovation are greatest when political and economic conditions within a state converge with favorable actions of neighboring states. Specifically, the existence of a fiscal crisis, distance from the next election, and the presence of neighboring states that have adopted all increase the likelihood of tax innovation.

Several articles had demonstrated the operation of both internal characteristics and regional diffusion, but Berry and Berry's articles are notable in their testing of both explanations in a single model. The EHA technique allowed them to include time-varying independent variables. EHA can be used in many other applications when the purpose is to predict exactly when a particular adoption will take place. It is not needed when the researcher wants to explain average innovativeness for a set of policies.

Historical Applications of Diffusion Theory

Tort Law Reform

Diffusion theories can be used to explain many historical changes in public policy. First, we will look outside the legislative realm to the judiciary. A major change in the state judiciary is its expanded policymaking role; the tort law revolution is a good example of such policymaking. Tort law has undergone tremendous changes in the past hundred years, moving from being defendant-oriented (protecting business) to being plaintiff-oriented (protecting consumers and workers). This shift has been accomplished without federal court guidance or without much state legislative intervention. How did it happen?

Canon and Baum examined this question, formulating it as a diffusion process extending from 1876 to 1975.[21] They calculated the relative speed of adoption of twenty-three tort doctrines that expanded the rights of the plaintiff. This produced an index of innovativeness similar to Walker's, but with Minnesota at the top and Wyoming at the bottom. They found some regional pattern but less than Walker did. Like him, they found that diffusion has speeded up in the second half of the twentieth century.

The authors also tested for the effect of internal characteristics of states and found that population size was important, as were manufacturing and urbanization (but only in the postwar period). Political variables were not significant in their model, but because judges are supposed to be nonpolitical, this finding is not surprising. Then Canon and Baum looked at traits of the courts, discovering that innovative courts were highly professional and staffed by judges with prior metropolitan legal practices. Thus, they provide an explanation for the transmission of new legal doctrines that rests primarily on aspects of the judiciary, and to a lesser extent on regionalism and on the states' social aspects.

The primacy of internal judicial traits makes sense when one considers how judges make decisions: they cite other authorities, state and federal constitutions, state statutes, and precedents from other cases in the state and outside the state. Thus, citing a case from another state is the mechanism by which new tort doctrines are diffused. We can anticipate that other doctrinal revolutions might proceed along the same lines: new legal doctrines diffuse from the large, liberal states with professionalized judicial systems to the rest of the states. Significant policy change can and does occur in this fashion.

The Progressive Movement

Diffusion theory can also be applied to broad historical eras. During the period 1865 to 1900, state governments expanded their scope: by the turn of the century, 25 states had commissions regulating railroads, 30 had boards regulating health, and 25 had labor bureaus. Many had boards regulating the private charities that constituted the nineteenth century's welfare system. This "expansion of public responsibility," as historian William Brock called it, occurred well before expansion at the national level. Legislatures in Michigan, Ohio, Minnesota, Wisconsin, Illinois, and New York were considered to be leaders in state policymaking. There was some evidence of regional diffusion even then. Albert Shaw, writing about the Minnesota legislature in 1887, said that "laws find their way verbatim" from one state to another, and argued that "the spirit, aims, and methods" of statutes are the same throughout a group of neighboring states.[22]

In the early twentieth century the Progressive movement brought more policy innovation. Child labor laws were reformed; workers' compensation laws were enacted in forty-three states; aid to the blind was provided in ten; minimum wage legislation was passed in several states. How can we understand these innovations?

In one of the first quantitative studies of state policy innovation, Edgar McVoy considered twelve laws adopted between 1869 and 1931. He included women's suffrage, old age pensions, and workers' compensation and then ranked the states according to whether they were early or late adopters. Using maps, he located the centers of social innovation in New York, Wisconsin, California, and Michigan and traced diffusion paths in concentric circles beyond these points. The diffusion paths, he argued, are modified by several factors: the presence of transportation and communication facilities, urbanization, cultural opportunities, and wealth. These factors all correlated positively with McVoy's innovation index. Thus, it appears that regional diffusion networks were already operating early in this century.[23]

A recent study by Skocpol, Howard, Lehmann, and Abend-Wein focuses on one of these innovations, mothers' pensions. Its diffusion pattern is strikingly different from those identified by Walker and Gray: mothers' aid originated in smaller, nonindustrial states and spread very rapidly. The authors found that the support of women's social movements was the most critical factor explaining early enactments, followed by state capacity and labor force composition. Their results suggest that finer-grained analyses incorporating imaginative measures may allow variance studies to be used historically.[24]

A Broadening of Diffusion Theory

Policy Process Models

Diffusion studies, as outlined above, have typically been variance studies; that is, they have used a set of independent variables to explain statistically the rate of adoption of a law. Few have been process studies, qualitative analyses of the sequence of events leading up to an adoption. Yet process studies conducted elsewhere are relevant to innovation. Let us consider a few of the central findings from the agenda formation literature and their relation to diffusion studies.

The first is Kingdon's concept of the "policy window." [25] After a new presidential administration comes in (or a new party seizes control in Congress), it is looking for new ideas to incorporate into a legislative program. This is a window of opportunity for anyone who has a new idea to peddle. Later on in the administration fewer new ideas will be accepted. This finding helps to explain why Walker found that states with high office turnover were more innovative; the policy window opened up more often. Presumably the policy window is wide open as the Clinton administration begins.

The second key concept is that of the policy entrepreneur. Kingdon says that one can nearly always pinpoint a specific person (or persons) who was central in moving a subject up on the agenda. Such persons are crucial because the agenda is always crowded, and new ideas are resisted. These people are called policy entrepreneurs (or policy champions). Advocates for particular policy solutions, they are experts located inside or outside of government, in universities, think tanks, interest groups, or consulting firms. They take advantage of policy windows to get their pet ideas onto the agenda. We would assume that the more innovative states are blessed with a larger number of policy entrepreneurs.

Recently a few case studies of policy entrepreneurship at the state level have emerged. Paula King focused on their role in initiating the open school enrollment plan in Minnesota. [26] This was the first school "choice" plan in the nation, and variants of it have now been adopted in several states. King found that a group of nine policy entrepreneurs met regularly to discuss ways to improve Minnesota's educational performance. Of the nine people, only one was in government at the time; none was in the educational establishment.

Another study of policy entrepreneurs in a state legislative setting was conducted by Carol Weissert. [27] She equated entrepreneurship with persistence. In her study of North Carolina, she found that persistent legislators were rated more effective by their peers than were new sponsors or other legislators. A willingness to do one's homework and to wait for a policy window, she reasoned, brings respect from North Carolina legislators.

What the agenda formation literature needs is a systematic empirical study of policy entrepreneurship across states. Just as states differ in the number of venture capitalists and private entrepreneurs, surely they differ in the amount of "social capital" (that is, the stock of new ideas) and in the number of policy entrepreneurs peddling new ideas. The availability of social capital might be measured by the number of think tanks, public affairs organizations, policy journals, research universities, public affairs media, and consulting firms in the state. Exposure to new ideas might also be measured by the amount of resources in the legislature and bureaucracy devoted to the purchase of journals, the establishment of reference services, attendance at professional conferences, and so forth. These measures in turn should be related to innovation at the state level. Such a study could add a lot to the little we know about fostering a culture of innovation in states.

Policy entrepreneurship also affects how ideas diffuse across the country. As mentioned earlier, innovations are diffusing more rapidly now, and their spread is less regionally based. Probably this is the result of policy networks that cross governmental boundaries. These are loose collections of governmental and nongovernmental participants in a particular policy area. They include policy entrepreneurs in a variety of settings: government, mass media, professional associations, interest groups, universities, and so forth. Numerous case studies have documented how a professional association or a particular policy network quickly disseminated information about a new idea. For instance, Kirst, Meister, and Rowley examined the rapid diffusion of educational innovations and attributed it to an active policy network.[28] But no variance study of diffusion has measured this effect; usually they measure regional diffusion and attribute any departures from it to other sources.

What is needed is a survey of state legislators and their staff members to ascertain the multiple sources of information they use. We would expect to find that the information network is much wider than just knowing what neighboring states are doing. Also we should find differences in the search strategies used in professional and less professional legislatures. Sabatier and Whiteman found that in the California legislature (and presumably other professionalized bodies) the flow of policy information is a three-stage process: from outsiders to committee staff, from staff to specialist legislator, from specialist to ordinary legislator.[29] In legislative bodies with fewer staff the flow of information is probably in two stages (or even one). Outsiders talk directly to legislators about new ideas. These nonspecialist legislators may depend on blindly copying another state's laws or on carrying bills for interest groups. Their states tend to be the followers, not the leaders, in policy innovation.

Basically, I am advocating a melding of quantitative diffusion studies and qualitative process studies. Perhaps the best example of what I have in mind is Herbert Jacob's *Silent Revolution*.[30] It explains the rapid diffusion of no-fault divorce law. New York and California adopted this concept in 1966 and 1970, respectively; by 1974 forty-five states had followed suit; and in 1985 the lone holdout (South Dakota) joined in. Jacob uses mostly qualitative information to assess the standard explanations for diffusion. He found no evidence that the idea was propagated by the usual sources: social movements or interest groups, policy networks, bureaucrats, the governor, or legislators. Basically, because no-fault divorce was kept nonconflictual it spread rather easily, aided by its policy sponsors, its cost-free character, and states' desire to keep up with others already adopting it. Moving beyond his case study, Jacob argues that many other noncontroversial laws spread in a similar routine fashion. He warns against generalizing from the conflictual policymaking that we so often study.

Economic Development Policy

As argued in the beginning of this chapter, competition among the states is fundamental to federalism. States today compete in many areas: to lower their tax rates, to deter welfare clients, to attract business, and so on. Following the recession of 1981-1982, the economy was the fiercest area of competition as states experimented with industrial policies and high tech development and dabbled in venture capitalism. There is no doubt that economic development concerns came to occupy a central place on the state policy agenda. A body of scholarly literature has developed on the initiation of economic development policies and on the impact of such policies. Typically the case studies focus on the governor's role in initiating development programs, while the quantitative studies focus on internal characteristics that facilitate adoption. For example, Gray and Lowery found that states that had adopted more industrial policies by 1986 had experienced severe economic stress, had balanced interest systems (that is, business did not dominate), competitive political parties, and high government capacity.[31]

Oddly enough, although many have noted the proliferation of economic development tools, no one has conceptualized their spread as a diffusion process. Only Boeckelman, Hanson and Berkman, and Hanson have even noted the regional dimension in the adoption pattern. Yet plenty of evidence points to a contagion process. For example, Peter Eisinger, in the most extensive study to date, reports that location incentive programs increased from 840 in 1966, to 1,213 in 1976, to 1,633 in 1985. The average number of programs per state doubled in the twenty-year time period. Surely this rapid spread of location incentives did not happen because state governments independently reached the same conclusion about their desirability.[32]

Another example lies in the competition to lure automobile manufacturers to one's state. In the early 1980s bidding wars broke out among states seeking plants to be built by General Motors, Toyota, Nissan, and so forth. State officials promised all sorts of inducements from land purchases, site renovations, transportation improvements, worker training subsidies, and Saturday school for the children of Japanese workers. The winning states were geographically contiguous states under a lot of economic pressure. States that lost the first competition redoubled their efforts in the next round. The cost per worker escalated each time, rising from $11,000 per worker in 1980 to $50,580 by 1986.[33] Surely this escalation of costs is a product of a diffusion process and could be modeled as such.

Instead of cross-sectional analysis predicting the number of states using a particular economic development instrument, one should do a time series analysis of the spread of instruments based on the state's own characteristics and on the actions of neighboring states. Then, I believe, the analyst would find regional diffusion. Probably factor scores should be used as the dependent variables instead of specific policies because the individual economic development programs are usually small. The focus of interest is whether a state's overall strategy changes in response to what its neighbors are doing. In this way studies of interstate economic competition could be profitably linked to studies of diffusion.

Welfare Policy

At the same time that interstate competition stimulates states to spend more on economic development, it also pressures them to do less in other areas, most notably welfare. Competition exerts a downward pressure on a state to stay in line lest it become a "welfare magnet"—a haven for undesirable citizens. Recent experience in Wisconsin illustrates this situation. Given the difference in Wisconsin's and Illinois's welfare benefits, a welfare client's move from Chicago to Kenosha (about fifty miles north) could increase the family's income by about one-fourth. The perception that generous benefits were drawing poor people from Chicago (and elsewhere) became an issue in the 1986 gubernatorial campaign and led to Republican Tommy Thompson's defeat of incumbent Democrat Tony Earl. As Wisconsin's economic climate deteriorated, concern about welfare migrants mounted.

Peterson and Rom in *Welfare Magnets* illuminate this debate by a careful statistical analysis of welfare benefit levels, poverty rates, and state-level explanatory variables.[34] They find that the poor move in response to benefit levels (and to employment opportunities). But they also find that state policymakers are sensitive to the size of the poor population and to the possibility of welfare migration, and they reduce benefits accordingly. In their time series analysis the states with high benefit levels (such as Wisconsin) cut them by the period's end. This action produces a convergence effect pushing benefit levels downward. Peterson and Rom do not model this as a diffusion process, but they could have done so. They could have included information about a state's neighbors and estimated its effect on a state's benefit levels.

In summary, we have argued that various competitions among the states could usefully be conceptualized as diffusion processes. Both economic development and welfare policy are areas where states imitate one another and where the actions of one's immediate neighbors are quite relevant.

Evaluation of Diffusion Studies

At their introduction to political science in the late 1960s, diffusion studies were hailed because they offered an alternative to expenditure studies. The subfield of comparative state politics had just begun but had suffered a setback when economic variables were continually shown to be more important than political variables in explaining expenditure differences among states. Scholars felt that economic explanations might not apply when predicting policy innovations, especially because many of them did not cost much money. Thus, analyzing the diffusion of innovations seemed to offer a useful antidote to studying the monetary dimensions of public policy.

Another noteworthy aspect of the early studies was their intellectual linkage to diffusion studies in other social sciences. The same basic diffusion model, the S-curve, was confirmed in many disciplines—anthropology, public health and medical sociology, rural sociology, political science, education, communications, marketing, and geography. Diffusion research itself diffused: Everett M. Rogers reports that when the first edition of his classic *Diffusion of Innovations* was published in 1962, 405 publications were available.[35] When his second edition came out in 1971, there were 1,500. By 1983 he had found 3,085. The early diffusion studies in political science paid close attention to studies in other fields, whereas contemporary political science seems to have forgotten this heritage.

Perhaps political scientists lost their interest in generalizability because they discovered so much variability in their own findings. The extant results differ by policy area (some diffusion relies on regional networks, others on national networks), by time period (diffusion is speeding up), and so forth. Mohr, Downs, and others have expressed pessimism about variance models capturing the complexity of the diffusion process, and they have urged process models instead. But Rogers is able to assemble a collection of generalizations about diffusion that are supported by 60 to 80 percent of the studies done on each point. Thus, he finds it possible to generalize across a range of social phenomenon. My own position is somewhere in the middle: we should continue classic diffusion studies but also add the literature on policy entrepreneurship.[36]

With regard to instability of findings, it is worth noting that in the late 1800s Michigan, Ohio, Minnesota, Wisconsin, Illinois, and New York were identified as leaders in various policy areas. In 1940 McVoy produced the first systematic ranking of the states: his top ten innovators were New York, Wisconsin, California, Michigan, Illinois, Minnesota, Colorado, Ohio, Massachusetts, and Pennsylvania. In 1969 Walker furnished the first modern ranking of the states: all of the states listed above were in his first thirteen states. The consistency of state rankings over time is quite remarkable.[37]

Why have diffusion studies been so popular? I believe it is because getting a new idea accepted is so difficult, whether it is persuading another individual, an organization, or a government to try something new. Thus, analyzing innovation, and what factors facilitate or retard it, is intrinsically valuable. At the state level the increasing competition among the states lends added significance to understanding innovation.

Diffusion studies in political science have identified factors at the local, state, and national levels that affect the rate of adoption and hence the spread of innovations. Economic resources, political opportunities, and the professionalism of governmental institutions are the major internal determinants. Wealthier jurisdictions with capable legislators and bureaucrats tend to be the first to try new ideas. The timing of innovation also depends on turnover in office, political competition levels, and a political culture that values change. The governments that consistently lead in innovation are blessed with an abundance of these factors.

Governments and their leaders are also influenced by forces outside their boundaries, especially if the internal conditions already favor innovation. State policymakers—legislators, governors, and bureaucrats—often turn to neighboring states for answers to their problems. Or they use their professional networks and associations as information-gathering mechanisms. Over time, cue taking from national leaders has increased so that innovations diffuse more rapidly than in the past, and their spread is less tied to regional boundaries. These trends mean that states' exposure to new ideas will become more similar and that the lag time between the first and last adopters will shrink.

State innovation studies highlight the states as policy laboratories; they portray the activism in states that is so often ignored. These "laboratories of democracy" serve a valuable role in the federal system, perhaps moving it in a different normative direction from what we expect. Economic development offers just one example: during the 1980s while official Washington took a hands-off stance on a national industrial policy, the states became entrepreneurs with equity in various businesses they financed. As one observer quipped, "That's called socialism in other countries, but not here." [38]

Richard Nathan is one of the few federalism scholars who has taken the state innovation literature seriously, arguing that the states have frequently counterbalanced the national government, ideologically speaking.[39] He observes that states have often undertaken liberal initiatives when the national government is captured by conservatives; then later when liberals capture Washington, they bring along policies already tested. Noting that state initiatives in the 1920s were the models for federal New Deal programs in the 1930s, Nathan finds it unsurprising that the opposite situation obtained in the 1980s: conservatives controlled Washington while liberals turned to the states. This is part of an equilibrating tendency in our federal system wherein interests not satisfied at one level turn to another. As such, it counters the centralizing trend most observers see in American federalism and lends credence to Madison's claim that "opposite and rival" interests could be accommodated in a federal system.

The equilibrating tendency identified by Nathan offers the strong possibility of more vertical diffusion, that is, state innovations trickling up to the national level. Many instances of vertical diffusion can be observed in the early months of the Clinton administration, most notably in health and welfare but in many other policy areas as well. As a former governor, a former leader of the National Governors' Association (NGA), and a self-described "policy wonk," President Bill Clinton is naturally inclined to rely on ideas already tested in the states.

Health care was the first domestic problem on Clinton's agenda, and the effort gained instant visibility when he appointed Hillary Rodham Clinton to head his task force on health care reform. As the twin problems of bettering access for the uninsured and controlling costs were considered, national policymakers turned to those states that had already tackled these issues—Florida, Minnesota, Vermont, Massachusetts, Oregon, Washington, and Hawaii. Minnesota, Washington, and Florida by 1993 had adopted health plans similar to the reforms under consideration in Washington, combining managed competition with governmental regulation of costs. These states are simultaneously broadening access to the citizenry and attempting to reduce cost growth. Their experiences in the early stages of implementation will help guide the design of national health care legislation.

In the welfare area states initiated a number of experiments that were the basis for the Family Support Act of 1988, an act that Bill Clinton helped guide through Congress for the NGA. The act's basic purpose was to require more of welfare recipients but to offer them more assistance so that they might become self-sufficient. Since 1988 several states have tried even more stringent approaches, for example, cutting a family's welfare benefits if children skip school too often or if single women have more children. These second-round reforms are being closely studied in Washington, and President Clinton plans to turn to welfare as soon as he finishes the health care agenda. Thus, horizontal diffusion is being complemented by vertical diffusion.

Notes

The author wishes to thank William Berry and Frances Berry, both of Florida State University, for their helpful comments on an earlier draft of this paper.

1. Tim Golden, "Florida Governor Aims to Reinvent Ailing State," *New York Times*, August 11, 1991, A10; Justice Brandeis's remarks in *New State Ice Company* v. *Liebmann*, 285 U.S. 262 (1932); Jack L. Walker, "The Diffusion of Innovations Among the American States," *American Political Science Review* 63 (September 1969): 880-899.

2. Thomas R. Dye, *American Federalism: Competition Among Governments* (Lexington, Mass.: Lexington Books, 1990).

3. Keith Boeckelman, "The Influence of States on Federal Policy Adoptions," *Policy Studies Journal* 20 (1992): 365-375.

4. See the literature review in Everett M. Rogers and F. Floyd Shoemaker, *Communication of Innovations*, 2d ed. (New York: Free Press, 1971).

5. Lawrence B. Mohr, "Determinants of Innovation in Organizations," *American Political Science Review* 63 (March 1969): 111-126.

6. Virginia Gray, "Innovation in the States: A Diffusion Study," *American Political Science Review* 67 (December 1973): 1174-1185; and Walker, "The Diffusion of Innovations."

7. Lawrence B. Mohr, "Process Theory and Variance Theory in Innovation Research," in *The Diffusion of Innovations: An Assessment*, ed. Michael Radnor, Irwin Feller, and Everett Rogers (Washington, D.C.: A report prepared for the National Science Foundation, 1978): 315-342.

8. John W. Kingdon, *Agendas, Alternatives, and Public Policies* (Boston: Little, Brown, 1984); Nelson W. Polsby, *Political Innovation in America: The Politics of Policy Initiation* (New Haven: Yale University Press, 1984); also see John Kingdon's chapter in this volume; Hugh Heclo, *Modern Social Politics in Britain and Sweden* (New Haven: Yale University Press, 1974); see special issue of *Journal of Public Policy* 11, no. 1 (1991).

9. Here I rely on the literature summary in Frances Stokes Berry and William D. Berry, "State Lottery Adoptions as Policy Innovations: An Event History Analysis," *American Political Science Review* 84 (June 1990): 395-416; Walker, "The Diffusion of Innovations"; Bradley C. Canon and Lawrence Baum, "Patterns of Adoption of Tort Law Innovations: An Application of Diffusion Theory to Judicial Doctrines," *American Political Science Review* 75 (December 1981): 975-987; and Henry R. Glick, "Innovation in State Judicial Administration," *American Politics Quarterly* 9 (January 1981): 49-69; John E. Filer, Donald L. Moak, and Barry Uze, "Why Some States Adopt Lotteries and Others Don't," *Public Finance Quarterly* 16 (July 1988): 259-283.

10. Walker, "Diffusion of Innovations"; Gray, "Innovation in the States."

11. Berry and Berry, "State Lottery Adoptions."

12. David R. Morgan and Sheilah S. Watson, "Political Culture, Political System Characteristics, and Public Policies Among the American States," *Publius* 21 (Spring 1991): 31-48; Walker, "Diffusion of Innovations"; Gray, "Innovation in the States"; Lee Sigelman and Roland E. Smith, "Consumer Legislation in the American States: An Attempt at Explanation," *Social Science Quarterly* 61 (June 1980): 58-70; Lee Sigelman, Phillip W. Roeder, and Carol K. Sigelman, "Social Service Innovation in the American States: Deinstitutionalization of the Mentally Retarded," *Social Science Quarterly* 62 (September 1981): 503-515; Keon Chi and Dennis O. Grady, "Innovators in State Government: Their Organizational and Professional Environment," in *The Book of the States: 1990-91* (Lexington, Ky.: Council of State Governments, 1990), vol. 28, 382-404.

13. Berry and Berry, "State Lottery Adoptions."

14. James M. Lutz, "Regional Leadership Patterns in the Diffusion of Public Policies," *American Politics Quarterly* 15 (July 1987): 387-398; Filer, Moak, and Uze, "Lotteries."

15. Donald C. Menzel and Irwin Feller, "Leadership and Interaction Patterns in the

Diffusion of Innovations Among the American States," *Western Political Quarterly* 30 (December 1977): 528-536; Patricia K. Freeman, "Interstate Communication Among State Legislators Regarding Energy Policy Innovation," *Publius* 15 (Fall 1985): 99-111; Fred W. Grupp, Jr., and Alan R. Richards, "Variations in Elite Perceptions of American States as Referents for Public Policy Making," *American Political Science Review* 69 (September 1975): 850-858; Chi and Grady, "Innovators in State Government"; Lee Sigelman, David Lowery, and Roland Smith, "The Tax Revolt: A Comparative State Analysis," *Western Political Quarterly* 36 (March 1983): 30-51.

16. Walker, "Diffusion of Innovations"; Canon and Baum, "Patterns of Adoption"; Berry and Berry, "State Lottery Adoptions"; Frances Stokes Berry and William D. Berry, "Tax Innovation by American States: Capitalizing on Political Opportunity," *American Journal of Political Science* 36 (August 1992): 715-742.

17. Lutz, "Regional Leadership Patterns"; Menzel and Feller, "Leadership and Interaction Patterns"; Freeman, "Interstate Communication"; Alfred Light, "Intergovernmental Sources of Innovation in State Administration," *American Politics Quarterly* 6 (April 1978): 147-166.

18. For example, Susan Welch and Kay Thompson, "The Impact of Federal Incentives on State Policy Innovation," *American Journal of Political Science* 24 (November 1980): 715-729.

19. Berry and Berry, "State Lottery Adoptions," and "Tax Innovation"; for an explanation of event history analysis see, Paul D. Allison, *Event History Analysis* (Beverly Hills: Sage, 1984).

20. Berry and Berry, "Tax Innovation."

21. Canon and Baum, "Patterns of Adoption."

22. William R. Brock, *Investigation and Responsibility: Public Responsibility in the United States, 1865-1900* (Cambridge: Cambridge University Press, 1984); Albert Shaw, "The American State and the American Man," *Contemporary Review* 51 (May 1887): 695-711.

23. Edgar C. McVoy, "Patterns of Diffusion in the United States," *American Sociological Review* 5 (April 1940): 219-227.

24. Theda Skocpol, Christopher Howard, Susan Goodrich Lehmann, and Marjorie Abend-Wein, "Women's Associations and the Enactment of Mothers' Pensions in the United States," *American Political Science Review* 87 (September 1993): 686-701; also see Theda Skocpol's chapter in this volume.

25. Kingdon, *Agendas.*

26. Paula King, "Policy Entrepreneurs: Catalysts in the Policy Innovation Process," Ph.D. dissertation, University of Minnesota, 1989.

27. Carol S. Weissert, "Policy Entrepreneurs, Policy Opportunists, and Legislative Effectiveness," *American Politics Quarterly* 19 (April 1991): 262-274.

28. Michael Kirst, Gail Meister, and Stephen Rowley, "Policy Issue Networks: Their Influence on State Policymaking," *Policy Studies Journal* 13 (December 1984): 247-264.

29. Paul Sabatier and David Whiteman, "Legislative Decision Making and Substantive Policy Information: Models of Information Flow," *Legislative Studies Quarterly* 10 (August 1985): 395-421.

30. Herbert Jacob, *Silent Revolution: The Transformation of Divorce Law in the United States* (Chicago: University of Chicago Press, 1990).

31. Virginia Gray and David Lowery, "The Corporatist Foundations of State Industrial Policy," *Social Science Quarterly* 71 (March 1990): 3-24.

32. Keith Boeckelman, "Political Culture and State Development Policy," *Publius* 21 (Spring 1991): 49-62; Russell L. Hanson and Michael B. Berkman, "Gauging the Rainmakers: Toward a Meteorology of State Legislative Climates," *Economic Development Quarterly* 5 (August 1991): 213-228; Russell L. Hanson, "Bidding

for Business: A Second War Between the States?" *Economic Development Quarterly* 7 (May 1993): 183-148; Peter K. Eisinger, *The Rise of the Entrepreneurial State* (Madison: University of Wisconsin Press, 1988), 19.

33. H. Brinton Milward and Heidi Hosbach Newman, "State Incentive Packages and the Industrial Location Decision," *Economic Development Quarterly* 3 (August 1989): 203-222.

34. Paul E. Peterson and Mark C. Rom, *Welfare Magnets* (Washington, D.C.: Brookings Institution, 1990).

35. Everett M. Rogers, *Diffusion of Innovations*, 3d ed. (New York: Free Press, 1983).

36. Mohr, "Process Theory"; George Downs, "Complexity and Innovation Research," in *The Diffusion of Innovations: An Assessment*, ed. Michael Radnor, Irwin Feller, and Everett Rogers (Washington, D.C.: A report prepared for the National Science Foundation, 1978): 293-314. Rogers, *Diffusion of Innovations*, 3d ed.

37. McVoy, "Patterns of Diffusion"; Walker, "Diffusion of Innovations."

38. Jonathan Rauch, "Stateside Strategizing," *National Journal*, May 27, 1989, 1294.

39. Richard Nathan, "The Role of the States in American Federalism," in *The State of the States*, ed. Carl E. Van Horn (Washington, D.C.: CQ Press, 1989), 15-32.

13

Public Opinion and Public Policy:
A View from the States

John P. McIver, Robert S. Erikson, Gerald C. Wright

There is hardly anywhere a work in political science that does not, when it examines the phenomena of public opinion, either indulge in some wise and vague observations, or else make a frank admission of ignorance. And yet what can there possibly be to a political science with the very breath of its life left out? He who writes of the state, of law, or of politics without first coming to close quarters with public opinion is simply evading the very central structure of his study.

—*Arthur F. Bentley*, The Process of Government, *1908.*[1]

Introduction: Public Opinion and Democracy

Some degree of responsiveness to the preferences of the public by governmental leaders is often considered a necessary condition for democratic rule. Bentley's claim about the centrality of public preferences to political science is matched by Key's assertion that "unless mass views have some place in the shaping of public policy, all the talk about democracy is nonsense."[2] Yet ascertaining the extent of governmental responsiveness is a surprisingly difficult task that has troubled empirical political researchers for many years. One needs to measure public opinion and policy output, and to describe (if not measure) plausible mechanisms for the translation of opinion into policy. Despite all attempts to examine the representational abilities of the American national government, a more fruitful location for research may be the state governments. Often referred to as "laboratories of democracy," it is in the states that we see a range of publics and policies that provide the variation needed to assess theories of democratic accountability and to make empirically based assertions about the quality of the American experiment.

The study of state politics also involves a series of research problems that must be overcome. For the past decade, the authors of this chapter have been involved in a research project that examines the relationship between public opinion and policy in the American states. Reported elsewhere in greater detail, we find conclusive evidence of state-government responsiveness to public opinion.[3] In this chapter, we offer a brief summary of this work and speculate on its implications and future research directions.

Linking Public Opinion and Policy: A Research Program

Measuring Public Opinion

Attempts to link public preferences with public policies must address the difficult issue of measurement. National public opinion surveys have served to identify the policy preferences of the American electorate. Yet similar surveys of fifty state electorates have not been available.[4] In view of these limitations, researchers have sought alternative ways to estimate the opinions of state electorates. Pioneering work by Pool, Abelson, and Popkin simulating the policy preferences of the national electorate in the 1960 presidential campaign was extended to the states by Weber and his colleagues.[5] This methodology attempted to recreate state publics by weighting the opinions of groups in national polls by their presence in each state electorate. This approach, however, failed to capture all of the elements of state publics.

Recently, we offered an alternative methodology for estimating the opinions of state publics.[6] By aggregating the national polls conducted by CBS News and the *New York Times,* we have been able to compile state sample sizes in the smallest states comparable to those of most state polls.

This approach has a number of strengths. It is cost effective relative to fielding fifty simultaneous state polls. Absent fifty state surveys, it may be the only reasonable way to estimate basic characteristics of the opinions of state publics. Over time, large numbers of state respondents can be accumulated, leading to estimates of stable state characteristics with smaller standard errors than the typical state poll. Public opinions that are not stable can, in larger states, be examined over time for systematic changes.[7] By concentrating on the multiple surveys conducted by one organization, "house effects"—differences between the polling operations of the variety of national survey firms—are minimized.

In pooling estimates of state opinion from the cumulative CBS News/*New York Times* national surveys, we are limited to questions that are repeatedly asked of the public. With polls conducted by news organizations, few issue items will be repeated often enough to produce enough respondents per state to generate accurate state estimates. Thus, despite popular interest in policy issues such as abortion, gun control, and capital punishment, we cannot directly measure state differences in preferences.

Fortunately, the extensive collection of CBS News/*New York Times* surveys does include repeated measures of one important summary measure of political preferences. This is self-identification of the respondent as liberal, moderate, or conservative.[8] We convert survey responses to this question into a measure of mean state opinion. From 141,798 individual responses to 118 surveys conducted between 1976 and 1988, we operationalize state opinion as the net difference between the proportion of the state's electorate who respond "liberal" and the proportion who respond "conservative." Thus, our key measure is an estimate of the net ideological preference or ideological taste of state publics. As a second measure, we utilize a similar index of state party identification, the percentage of Democrats minus the percentage of Republicans. This measure of partisanship plays a peripheral but interesting role in our analysis of the linkage between opinion and policy. State positions on the liberal-conservative and Democratic-Republican continuums are often quite different from one another, for reasons we explore below.

As we measure them, the mean positions of state electorates on the liberal-conservative scale conform to popular stereotypes. The most conservative states tend to be in the South and interior West. Liberal states are found mainly on the West Coast and in the Northeast, plus the upper Midwest. The most conservative state is Utah, where conservatives outnumber liberals 44.1 percent to 16.1 percent. The most liberal state is Massachusetts, where conservatives exceed liberals by only 28.3 percent to 27.3 percent. The average liberal-conservative gap is about 12 percentage points.

Conservative identifiers outnumber liberal identifiers even in seemingly "liberal" states. Self-identifications have leaned conservatively ever since the late 1960s and have not become appreciably more conservative during the period of our analysis (1976-1988). From the public's perspective, the center of political gravity is slightly to the right of "moderate." For example, National Election Studies show that, on average, the electorate rates itself slightly right of center with the Democratic and Republican parties about equally distant from this mean voter position, but with the Democrats closer to the moderate position (although left of center) than are the Republicans.

The Origins of State Differences in Opinion

Where do state differences in ideological preferences come from? In part, state differences stem from the group compositions of the states. States with the kinds of people who tend to call themselves liberal should naturally tend toward the liberal end of the spectrum; states populated by conservative types will be at the conservative end. Thus, states with disproportionate numbers of big-city residents, highly educated people, blacks, Jews, and Catholics tend to be relatively liberal. Similarly, states with disproportionate numbers of rural people, the less educated, whites, and fundamentalist Protestants tend to be relatively conservative.

But group demographics account for only a small part of state differences in ideological preference. States with similar demographic profiles are often quite different in terms of ideological preference. A good example is provided by Wisconsin and Indiana. These states are similar demographically, and both are located in the Midwest. Yet, consistent with state stereotypes commonly reported in the political press, Wisconsin has a relatively liberal population and Indiana is relatively conservative. Many other state electorates manifest ideological preferences that appear very real but that cannot be explained by the state's group composition. We account for these differences as contextual effects due to the differences in the state political culture. According to our estimates, for example, the effect on ideological preference of living in Wisconsin versus Indiana is a difference equal to the difference in ideological preference between living in a big city and living in the countryside.[9]

Does Opinion Predict Public Policy?

Public policies enacted by governments range from local regulations governing the upkeep of one's yard and sidewalks to the nuclear defense of our nation's borders. While the policies of state governments are restricted somewhat, they nonetheless vary greatly in the range of programs offered and the generosity with which they are funded. Given the limitations of our public opinion measures, we collected information on a number of policies that reflect the fundamental distinctions between liberals and conservatives on current social and domestic policy. We created measures that tap aspects of liberalism-conservatism in eight separate policy arenas. These quantitative indices measure state differences in:

- Support for primary and secondary education
- Expansiveness of AFDC benefits
- Expansiveness of Medicaid benefits
- Consumer protection legislation
- Criminal justice legislation
- Legal support for gambling
- Support for women's rights
- Tax progressivity

These eight indices each reflect one common dimension of liberal-conservative policy. A single-factor model explains 60 percent of the common variance among them. We consequently combined the eight indices into a composite state policy index by standardizing and then averaging the eight individual scores. The resulting composite policy index serves as a measure of the state's propensity toward liberal policies versus conservative policies.[10] The state with the most liberal policies by our measure is New York. The state with the most conservative

Table 13-1   Relationship between Public Opinion
and Public Policy

	r	Beta
Legalized gaming	.70	.68
ERA support	.55	.59
Medicaid	.64	.54
Education (expenditures per pupil)	.72	.49
Aid to Families with Dependent Children	.65	.43
Consumer policy	.55	.41
Criminal justice policy	.49	.39
Tax progressivity	.46	.39
Composite Opinion Liberalism	.82	.70

Notes: N = 47. Alaska, Hawaii, and Nevada are not included. All correlations and standardized regression coefficients are significant at .05. The standardized regression coefficients, B, are calculated by controlling for state wealth (median family income), education (percentage of state residents twenty-five and older with a high school degree), and urbanism (percentage of state population residing in metropolitan areas).

policies by our measure is, ironically, Arkansas, but the policies examined here had largely been determined before Bill Clinton began his reign as governor of Arkansas.

Linking Public Opinion and Public Policy

Evidence can be marshalled to support the proposition that state policies are correlated with and responsive to public preferences. Table 13-1 presents a simple correlational summary of this link for eight state policies as well as a measure of the strength of the relationship between opinion and policy once socioeconomic determinants of state policies are controlled.[11]

Table 13-1, above, shows that public policy is in some cases strongly related to public preferences and in other cases only moderately so. In each case, however, the relationship between public opinion and public policy remains once state socioeconomic variables are controlled. These findings reflect the responsiveness of state policymakers to public preferences.

Our key result comes, however, when we consider the relationship between state ideological preferences and the composite index of policy liberalism. The correlation is 0.82, meaning that the ideology of state electorates accounts for almost two-thirds of the variance in the ideological character of states' policies. This relationship is illustrated dramatically as shown in Figure 13-1 on page 254. With both measures appropri-

Figure 13-1 Public Opinion and State Policy Liberalism

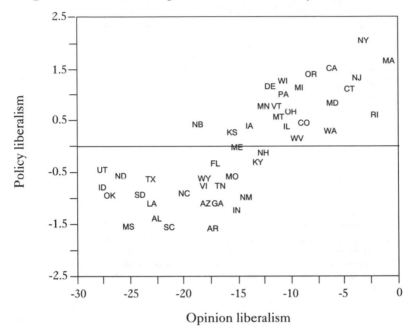

Source: Adapted from Robert S. Erikson, Gerald C. Wright, and John P. McIver, *State-house Democracy* (New York: Cambridge University Press, 1993).

ately corrected for reliability, the estimated correlation is even higher: 0.91.

The connection we identify is not between opinion and policy on specific issues but rather between ideological preference and the ideological nature of a state's policy propensity. To some observers it may seem highly surprising, or even implausible, that we should obtain evidence of such a strong linkage between two broad ideological measures of opinion and policy. After all, many years of electoral research have seemed to demonstrate that average members of the electorate are relatively inattentive to matters of public policy. This would seem to be particularly true regarding arcane aspects of state policy, which few people are in a position to follow closely. Why did we find such a strong opinion-policy connection?

The answer to this question has several aspects, each of which involves the process of aggregation. Each policy measure involves the aggregation of policies over years and decades. These policies, which only partially reflect state liberalism-conservatism, are then aggregated into our composite measure. In the process all intrastate variance is squeezed out of the measure except that which is due to ideology. Each contribut-

ing state policy decision involves several inputs, with ideological considerations among them. Idiosyncratic factors cancel out, leaving ideology.

Another aspect of aggregation involves the combination of individual
preferences to generate aggregate state ideological tendencies. Differences in public opinion that are trivial if measured at the individual level
become major when aggregated to state or national electorates. This phenomenon is easy to understand in the context of, let us say, public opinions about the economy. Most individuals at any one time are uninformed
regarding the most recent upturns or downturns in the national or state
economy. However, their aggregated perceptions of economic conditions
can have powerful effects on political trends and even on the strength of
the economy itself.

The combined effect of aggregating across individuals, across policies, and across time eliminates the individual variations in opinion and
policy, leaving relatively pure measures of the ideological preferences of
state electorates and the ideological component of state legislation. Absent individual and temporal variation, liberal policies are enacted in liberal states and conservative policies are legislated in conservative states.

How Does State Opinion Influence Policy?

Ultimately, we must ask what drives the connection between state
ideology and state policy. Is it simply the benign desire of state officials to
enact polices that satisfy public needs? Obviously more must be involved.

The force behind the ideological linkage between state opinion and
policy is that of democratic elections. Over time, state electorates tend to
elect politicians who share their ideological views. In turn, politicians (and
parties) respond to state ideological opinion out of a desire to get or stay
elected.[12]

Responsiveness to state public opinion means that state parties from
Mississippi to Massachusetts will differ significantly because their constituents differ significantly. Everywhere the Democratic party occupies a
more liberal position than the Republican party. Yet Democrats in Mississippi are more conservative than their counterparts in Massachusetts.
Similarly, Republicans in Mississippi are more conservative than their
counterparts in Massachusetts.

Simply to say that state Democratic parties are more liberal than
their Republican competitors does not explain how either party achieves
electoral success within a state. Parties that wish to remain competitive
must move toward the center of the ideological spectrum *within their*
state. Each party starts out by appealing to its core activists—Democrats
on the left and Republicans on the right. But neither would be successful
as a strictly ideological party. Democrats win by becoming more conservative. Republicans win by becoming more liberal. The Republican party
can be found to the right of the Democratic party in every state. But by

how much and where, relative to the state's median voter, is the relevant question regarding electoral success.

To assess the responsiveness of state parties to state opinion, we needed to measure the ideological positions of state parties. We did so by combining four measures of the ideological leanings of state political elites:

- State parties' congressional candidates
- State parties' delegates to presidential nominating conventions
- County chairs affiliated with the state parties
- State parties' state legislators[13]

The electoral connection can be seen in the pattern of the parties' relative success in terms of party identification and ultimately in achieving electoral office in the state. Closeness to the center of the state electorate largely determines the parties' relative success in the state.[14] The Democratic party tends to thrive not when a state is particularly liberal but rather when the state Democratic party elite is closer ideologically to the median voter. Similarly, the Republicans do best not in conservative states but where the Republican party elite is closer to the middle of the state's electorate than the Democratic party. As is well known, Democratic parties are most conservative in the conservative South and Border States where they face even more stridently conservative Republican parties. It is in these states that the Democrats have been most successful both in terms of party identification and state elections. What is less well known is that Republicans are most successful in terms of party identification and state elections in states where the Republican party is relatively liberal, such as New York or Connecticut.

To summarize the electoral connection for ideological representation involves several steps. First, parties respond to state opinion out of a desire to win elections, but they do not converge on the center of the state's spectrum because they are constrained by ideological interests. Second, the more representative the parties, the greater their success will be. They will be more successful in attracting party followers and enjoy, on average, a greater number of victories at the ballot box. The relative strength of the parties in the state legislature reflects the sum of these electoral triumphs. Third, we find statistical evidence that party strength in the legislators in turn affects policy independently of the preferences of legislators and the electorate. This effect is negative in sign, so that, everything else being equal, Democrats trim to the right and Republicans to the left. This is somewhat counterintuitive but logical. If a Democrat and a Republican politician hold the same personal ideological preferences and represent ideologically similar constituencies, the Democrat would be more pressured to move to the right out of electoral considerations and the Republican more likely to be pressured to move left.

The net result of these causal connections is the strong correlation

Figure 13-2 A Representational Model of the State Policy
Process

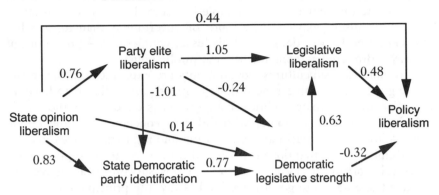

Source: Adapted from Robert S. Erikson, Gerald C. Wright, and John P. McIver, *Statehouse Democracy* (New York: Cambridge University Press, 1993).

Note: Coefficients are standardized regression coefficients (beta weights). All variables are scored in a liberal or Democratic direction.

between state ideological preferences and state policy. These connections are shown statistically in the causal model presented in Figure 13-2. The model shows the many ways in which the electorate affects public policy. Party elites respond to the wishes of the public out of desire to win office. The public's partisan attachments, a function of party elite positions relative to public policy preferences, and party positions determine the partisan balance of the legislature. State legislators in turn respond to the policy preferences of the electorate. And the public has an impact on policy independent of the kinds of legislators they elect.

The Role of Political Culture

Despite our findings that parties are important intermediaries, our model remains incomplete. Party competition occurs within political cultures that may encourage citizen involvement in government or may treat citizens as wards of the state. At the same time, cultural variations may or may not spur attentiveness to public preferences. Consequently, responsiveness to public opinion can be expected to vary across political cultures as a function of the roles adopted by citizens and government officials.

Political culture summarizes as well as imparts the assumptions, values, and expectations that citizens and elites bring to the structure and operation of the polity. Daniel Elazar, an observer of state politics, has identified three political subcultures in the United States: moralistic, traditionalistic, individualistic. Within each state one of these subcultures dominates and thus serves to organize how politics and governance operate.[15]

In Elazar's view, an individualistic subculture sees the polity as a "marketplace" in which goals and ideals compete. Government is seen as responsive to the demands of the people it was explicitly created to serve. Such a subculture expects little more of government than to do what Chrysler's Lee Iacocca demands of his lesser competitors—"to get out of the way." Brokered agreements become public policy.

In moralistic subcultures, governments are expected to advance the public good. At the same time ordinary citizens are believed to have an obligation to participate. Political competition is expected as the public and elites engage one another with different conceptions of the public good. Political parties facilitate competition and regularize discussion.

Members of a traditionalistic subculture, in contrast, support a hierarchically organized social structure. In this subculture an active but restricted orientation to governance holds sway: the principal role of government is maintenance of the status quo, which means stabilizing the existing social order. The subculture is paternalistic in the sense that government advocates traditional values and elitist in that only certain groups are perceived to be able to fulfill the mission. Elazar believes that parties are "of minimal importance" in a traditionalistic style of politics because they encourage openness and competition.[16]

We view culture as a contextual variable, that is, as one that affects the relationship between public opinion and governmental policies. Subcultures affect the *process* of representation as well as shifting policy outcomes in one direction or another. Elazar's characterization of these subcultures suggests that moralistic states should exhibit the greatest degree of responsiveness to public opinion and traditionalistic states the least, with individualistic states exhibiting greater responsiveness only for policies mandating government nonintervention.

As they affect the process of representation, subcultures may also affect policy levels. Traditionalistic states can be expected to enact the most conservative policies and moralistic states the most liberal.

A simple analysis of the subcultural differences in the representation of public opinion in state policymaking is presented in Table 13-2. The results are consistent with expectations, although they are not statistically significant in all instances. Moralistic states enact more liberal policies, whereas traditionalistic states enact more conservative ones. Political subcultures affect the representation process as evidenced in the variations in slope coefficients, as explained in the note to Table 13-2. Traditionalistic states are relatively unresponsive, moralistic states slightly more responsive, and individualistic states most responsive to public opinion.

Space limitations preclude more than this brief introduction to the effects of political culture on state governance. A more extensive examination of the consequences of political culture on the party representation model described above and the causal status of political culture can be found in our recent work.[17]

Table 13-2 Representation under Three Political Subcultures

(State policy $= b_0 + b_1$ public opinion)	Parameter estimates[a]	
	b_0	b_1
Overall	.029	.101
(adj. $R^2 = .633$)		
Subcultures		
(adj. $R^2 = .830$)		
Moralistic	.443	.076
Individualistic	−.213	.148
Traditionalistic	−.654	.059

[a] Alaska, Hawaii, and Nevada are excluded from the analysis.

Note: In a statistical framework, political culture expands the simple regression equation [1] into a second equation [2]:

[1] Policy$=b_0 + b_1$ Opinion
[2] Policy$=b_0 + b_1$ Opinion$+ b_2$ TC$+ b_3$ MC
        $+ b_4$ (Opinion$\times$TC)$+ b_5$ (Opinion$\times$MC)

where TC is a dummy variable coded 1 if a state's political culture is predominantly traditionalistic and zero otherwise and MC is a dummy variable coded 1 if a state's political culture is predominantly moralistic and zero otherwise. Equation 2 predicts the relationship between public opinion and public policy under each of the three political subcultures:

Individualistic: [2a] Policy$=b_0 + b_1$ Opinion;
Traditionalistic: [2b] Policy$= (b_0 + b_2) + (b_1 + b_4)$ Opinion;
Moralistic: [2c] Policy$= (b_0 + b_3) + (b_1 + b_5)$ Opinion.

Coefficients b_2 and b_4 represent the direction in which traditionalistic and moralistic subcultures shift policy outcomes relative to individualistic states. Coefficients b_3 and b_5 reflect the change in the representational process. Positive coefficients denote more responsive legislatures in traditionalistic and moralistic states relative to individualistic ones.

A Research Agenda

We do not argue that public opinion is decisive in all policy debates. Indeed, we have not conducted an exhaustive study of the link between all public opinion and all state policies.[18] But the literature on state politics is quickly filling in the voids. The degree of liberalism of public opinion has been used by many state policy researchers to try to predict state policies. In some cases, these attempts have been successful. In others, they have not.[19]

The pattern of successes and failures raises a number of questions about the study of representation in individual policy arenas:

- Is the policy tied to a liberal-conservative dimension?
- Is the measurement of opinion flawed?
- Is the measurement of policy flawed?
- Is this a new policy question? (Have all states had the opportunity to respond to public preferences? Has public opinion on this policy "crystallized"?)
- Is representation of public opinion in this policy arena impor-

tant? (Do legislators act as trustees rather than delegates?)
• Do elites and interest groups dominate in the policy arena?

Answers to these questions will be provided by investigation of constituencies, governing institutions, and policy characteristics. In this way, future research will specify the conditions under which public input influences the policy decisions of state governments. Examination of these conditions awaits theoretical advances as well as funding for data collection efforts. Because the theoretical developments are primary, we focus attention on these areas and offer considerations for the future work.

Institutional Structure

If institutions matter, how they operate is critical to the translation of public preferences into policies. Across the states, legislative and executive powers vary, thereby providing the opportunity for citizens to influence the policy process in diverse ways. Legislatures differ in their committee structures, staff support, professional membership, election frequency, tenure, and control of interest group activity, to name a few dimensions. Governors vary in everything from their appointment powers to their veto powers. How each of these institutional variations affects government responsiveness to public preferences remains to be investigated.

Not only do the formal institutions of government vary in ways that may influence the way public inputs become official outputs but so do the institutional means that permit citizens to establish public policy directly. With the initiative and referendum, citizens in recent years have changed the face of state governments by establishing policies ranging from taxing and spending limits to the regulation of civil rights of gays and lesbians. Ballot issues have even been used to establish the maximum length of service of elected officials to ensure that such officials remain responsive to their electorate. Do the initiative and referendum increase governmental responsiveness to the public by creating an atmosphere of anticipatory actions? Do ballot issues correct for the failures of formal governmental structures? Or are ballot issues mere symbolic politics, an exercise that keeps the public engaged but allows little real input into the operation of state government? As the number and variety of ballot issues placed before voters increases, the consequences of direct democracy should be high on the agendas of state politics researchers.

Characteristics of Policy

Most policy research focuses on single substantive-issue areas. The litany includes: air, water, and general environmental quality; public safety; national defense; criminal and civil justice; public welfare; housing and urban affairs; health care; primary, secondary, and higher education; energy; urban growth and decay; land and housing; national and local infrastructure (a euphemism for roads and bridges); public utilities; business regulation; and economic development. Each policy area is of interest to practitioners but the value of these studies to political scientists lies in what they can tell us about the process of governance generally. A successful aggregation of these policy studies requires some theoretical overview of the ways in which representation works across the variety of policies.

Various theoretical distinctions between political issues and public policies are presented in the literature. Carmines and Stimson offer a simple typology of issue types that might bear fruit in a classification of problems as more or less likely to promote the translation of constituent preferences into public policies. They distinguish "easy" issues from "hard" issues: Easy issues are those that are readily accessible to an electorate that devotes little cognitive energy to politics, whereas hard issues require an investment in understanding the policy alternatives.[20] Easy issues exhibit at least the following three characteristics:

1. They are largely symbolic rather than technical in nature.
2. They deal primarily with policy ends rather than means.
3. They are issues long on the political agenda.

Additional characteristics are necessary for the representation of interests. The issue must be salient to voters and it must be of concern to large numbers of the public and not just a selected subset. Intensity and numbers increase the probability that elected officials will respond to citizen policy preferences. Furthermore, it is not enough that voters be able to understand and vote on the issues. Representatives must be able to hear them.

Issues become easy or hard depending on how they are presented to and viewed by the public. Carmines and Stimson acknowledge as much in citing racial desegregation as an example of an easy issue and Vietnam as a prototypical hard issue:

> Our classification of desegregation and Vietnam into theoretical categories rests, in the end, on empirical knowledge. Racial desegregation could be complex and Vietnam simple if the issues had evolved that way in the political system *and if voters saw them that way*. All issues have intrinsically simple and complex facets.[21]

The ability to structure debate on an issue by defining it properly is a critical skill for politicians of all persuasions. Hard issues can be made easy and easy issues hard by the way they are presented. The environmental agenda can be established in terms of air and water quality standards, the competing impacts of jobs versus endangered species, or the orphaning of bear cubs by trapping their mothers with jelly donuts. The agenda is changed by expanding the scope of conflict (bringing jobs into the equation) or redefining the conflict (policies for managing the wilderness can become a dispute over the killing of bear cubs).

Can we offer a typology of state policies based upon the degree of public input? At first glance, the easy/hard distinction looks useful. Easy issues are those that motivate active electorates and attentive representatives, whereas hard issues remain the focus of special interest groups and elite negotiation. Unfortunately, most policies cannot be identified *a priori* as easy or hard. If issues can be redefined in political debate, a stable issue typology may not be possible. What makes the task of state policy researchers particularly difficult is that an issue may be easy in one state and hard elsewhere. If enough temporal stability in issue debates exists to classify issues as easy or hard for periods of political history and if issues can be consistently classified as easy or hard across states, perhaps this distinction will prove useful. At this point, we are uncertain whether this simple issue typology or any other existing classification scheme will provide the theoretical leverage we need to cumulate the many single policy studies that have been conducted. We hope that future research will synthesize these case studies. Policy researchers and political scientists need to establish the importance of these policy case studies in understanding the process of state governance.

Characteristics of the Constituency

If linkage varies with the policy, that relationship is likely a function of the characteristics of the citizenry and its abilities to organize and express its preferences to government officials. Miller, Fiorina, Erikson and his collaborators, Uslaner and Weber, Fenno, and Clausen and his coauthors are among those who have speculated on characteristics that affect constituency influence.[22]

Citizen understanding and evaluation of government policies is first and foremost a function of their education and information levels. What do voters know about each policy? Does this information influence their feelings about it? Indeed, do they have any feelings about the policy? Do they communicate their opinions? Are communications organized? How homogeneous are citizen preferences? How many citizens have preferences on the policy?

Communication is a two way street. Do representatives hear what citizens have to say? Does a cacophony of voices preclude any general sense of constituency preference? Can representatives distinguish between the vocal minority and a more silent majority? The flow of information at the state level remains to be explored. Again, individual case studies exist but cross-state comparison will proceed most fruitfully with the standardization of state polling or the simultaneous fielding of multiple state polls.

Discussion

The subfield of state politics has been especially active in recent years, a step forward from its status as "neglected subfield." Weissert identifies almost 300 state politics articles in six of the major national and regional journals. Yet closer examination of her data suggests that these articles are predominantly found in regional journals; state politics research is less visible in the national journals.[23]

The subfield of state politics is no longer the crazy aunt hidden away in the discipline's attic. Yet its considerable potential largely remains to be realized. Although advances have been made since Jewell expressed his concern that the subfield was theoretically barren, the audience may not yet be convinced.

Conclusion

Our work in state politics and democratic representation emphasizes the connection between public policy preferences and state policy in terms of general ideological direction. In the broad context of liberal versus conservative political competition, representation works well in the American states.

Depending on the perspective from which it is viewed, this conclusion may appear surprising or it may seem no more than verification of the obvious. It is most surprising from the perspective of contemporary research on public opinion and voting, which portrays the average American voter as having limited interest in and knowledge about government activities, and as being unfocused on policy matters when casting a ballot. In contrast, our claim of ideological representation at work in the states may seem matter-of-fact from a consideration of the aggregative process that results from the cumulative scoring of a state on a liberal-conservative basis. Consider what else could cause the ideological direction of government policies, other than ideological inputs? Any one policy could be the result of many forces, but in aggregation, a composite policy measure is a function of what its components share in common. That shared component is ideology.

This chapter has also emphasized that for understanding specific policies, the contribution of public opinion remains uncertain. Public ideology, as we measure it, often appears to matter, but sometimes it does not. Where it does, the mechanism by which it works is not clear. One general consideration is that policies reflect the people who make them. Through elections, citizens determine who serves in legislatures and other state offices, and ideology is important here. The personal ideologies of government officials in turn will affect the specific policies they sponsor or enforce. In this mundane way, we often see a connection between public opinion and specific policies, even if the public shows little direct concern about government activity.

Notes

1. Arthur F. Bentley, *The Process of Government* (Bloomington, Ind.: Principia Press, 1908), 163.
2. V. O. Key, *Public Opinion and American Democracy* (New York: Knopf, 1961), 7.
3. Robert S. Erikson, Gerald C. Wright, and John P. McIver, *Statehouse Democracy* (New York: Cambridge University Press, 1993).
4. We move closer and closer to fielding fifty simultaneous state surveys. The consortium of national media who have joined together to conduct exit polling during presidential elections will likely provide the first such set of polls to state political researchers. Yet the methodology summarized here and described in greater detail in Gerald C. Wright, Robert S. Erickson, and John P. McIver, "Measuring State Partisanship and Ideology with Survey Data," *Journal of Politics* 47 (1985): 469-489, and in Erikson et al., *Statehouse Democracy*, remains the only available method for historical public opinion research at the state level.
5. Ithiel de Sola Pool, Robert P. Abelson, and Samuel Popkin, *Candidates, Issues, and Strategies* (Cambridge, Mass.: MIT Press, 1964-1965); Ronald E. Weber, Anne H. Hopkins, Michael L. Mezey, and Frank Munger, "Computer Simulation of State Electorates," *Public Opinion Quarterly* 36 (1972): 49-65; Ronald E. Weber and William R. Shaffer, "Public Opinion and American State Policy Making," *Midwest Journal of Political Science* 16 (1972): 633-699.
6. Wright, Erikson, and McIver, "Measuring State Partisanship."
7. John P. McIver, "Presidents and the States: Public Opinion of Presidential Performance" (Paper delivered to the Annual Meeting of the Midwest Political Science Association, 1992).
8. Repeatedly asked, with minor variations in the early years, by CBS News/*New York Times* interviewers is the question: "How would you describe your views on most political matters? Generally, do you think of yourself as liberal, moderate, or conservative?"
9. Ideally, we should be able to explain why some states have liberal political cultures while others have conservative cultures. Some of the differences are regional, particularly the difference between the conservative southern culture and the more liberal political culture of the North. But considerable variation also exists within regions. The complete explanation probably would refer to variations in state political histories and unique political events or political personalities. For the most part, we must accept these differences as exogenous (in statistical parlance), that is, as aspects of state differences that are simply givens.
10. Our measure of policy liberalism is highly reliable: Cronbach's alpha equals .89 for the composite index.
11. We do not examine "congruence" of opinion and policy per se, as we are unable to measure both opinion and policy on a common scale. Rather our focus is on "responsiveness": policy changes in the same direction as changes in public preferences.
12. Anthony Downs, *An Economic Theory of Democracy* (New York: Harper, 1957).
13. Warren E. Miller and M. Kent Jennings, *Parties in Transition: A Longitudinal Study of Party Elites and Supporters* (New York: Russell Sage Foundation, 1986); Cornelius Cotter, James Gibson, John Bibby, and Robert Huckshorn, *Party Organizations in American Politics* (New York: Praeger, 1984); Eric Uslaner and Ronald E. Weber, *Patterns of Decision Making in State Legislatures* (New York: Praeger, 1977).
14. One thing we cannot do, without making major assumptions, is calibrate the elite scores and the public's ideological preferences on the same scale. That is, because we are stuck with different sets of relative scores we cannot say for sure whether a particular party elite is more liberal or more conservative than the state public.

Our solution to this problem is to assume that the two parties are equally representative on average for each level of state ideological preference.

15. Daniel J. Elazar, *American Federalism: A View from the States* (New York: Crowell, 1966).

16. Ibid., 93.

17. Erikson et al., *Statehouse Democracy*.

18. Ibid. In our work, we have made little of interpolicy variations. We quite deliberately chose policies with what we believed to be some unidimensional (liberal-conservative) content. Other policies we ignored. Yet of the policies we studied some interpolicy variation exists in the relationship between opinion and policy (Table 13-1). Some of this variation could be due to the level of aggregation of opinion—it may not be policy-specific but rather reflect a general orientation to "normal" politics. Some policies, more closely aligned with a generally agreed upon liberal-conservative continuum, correlate more highly with ideology than other policies less well connected.

19. Wright et al., "Measuring State Partisanship"; Ronald J. Berger, Lawrence Neuman, and Patricia Searles, "The Social and Political Context of Rape Law Reform: An Aggregate Analysis," *Social Science Quarterly* 72 (1991): 221-238; Michael B. Berkman and Robert E. O'Connor, "Do Women Legislators Matter? Female Legislators and State Abortion Policy," *American Politics Quarterly* 21 (1993): 102-124; David R. Berman and Lawrence L. Martin, "The New Approach to Economic Development: An Analysis of Innovativeness in the States," *Policy Studies Journal* 20 (1992): 10-21; Paul Burstein, "Attacking Sex Discrimination in the Labor Market: A Study of Law and Politics," *Social Forces* 67 (1989): 641-665; Jack E. Call, David Nice, and Susette M. Talarico, "An Analysis of Rape Shield Laws," *Social Science Quarterly* 72 (1991): 774-788; Cathy Marie Johnson and Kenneth J. Meier, "The Wages of Sin: Taxing America's Legal Vices," *Western Political Quarterly* 43 (1990): 577-595; David Lowery, Virginia Gray, and Gregory Hager, "Public Opinion and Policy Change in the American States," *American Politics Quarterly* 17 (1989): 3-31; David C. Nice, "State-Financed Property Tax Relief to Individuals: A Research Note," *Western Political Quarterly* 40 (1987): 179-185; David C. Nice, "State Deregulation of Intimate Behavior," *Social Science Quarterly* 69 (1988): 203-211; David C. Nice, "Abortion Clinic Bombings as Political Violence," *American Journal of Political Science* 32 (1988): 178-195; David C. Nice, "State Programs for Crime Victims," *Policy Studies Journal* 17 (1988): 25-41; David C. Nice, "Service Distribution on a National Scale," *Polity* 23 (1991): 487-503; James L. Regens and Margaret Reams, "State Strategies for Regulating Groundwater Quality," *Social Science Quarterly* 69 (1988): 53-69.

20. Edward G. Carmines and James A. Stimson, *Issue Evolution* (Princeton: Princeton University Press, 1989); Edward G. Carmines and James A. Stimson, "The Two Faces of Issue Voting," *American Political Science Review* 74 (1980): 78-91.

21. Carmines and Stimson, "Two Faces," 81.

22. Warren E. Miller, "Majority Rule and the Representative System of Government," in *Mass Politics*, ed. Eric Allardt and Stein Rokkan (New York: Free Press, 1970); Morris P. Fiorina, *Representatives, Roll Calls, and Constituencies* (Lexington, Mass.: D. C. Heath, 1974); Robert S. Erikson, Norman R. Luttbeg, and William V. Holloway, "Knowing One's District: How Legislators Predict Referendum Voting," *American Journal of Political Science* 19 (1975): 231-246; Uslaner and Weber, *Patterns of Decision Making*; Richard Fenno, *Home Style: House Members in Their Districts* (Boston: Little, Brown, 1978); Aage R. Clausen, Soren Holmberg, and Lance deHaven-Smith, "Contextual Factors in the Accuracy of Leader Perceptions of Constituents' Views," *Journal of Politics* 45 (1983): 449-472.

23. Malcolm Jewell, "The Neglected World of State Politics," *Journal of Politics* 44 (1982): 638-657; Carol S. Weissert, "The Neglected World of State Politics Revisited" (Paper delivered to the Annual Meeting of the American Political Science Association, Washington, D.C., August 29-September 1, 1991).

14

Early U.S. Social Policies:
A Challenge to Theories of the Welfare State

Theda Skocpol

M odern welfare states grew up in successive phases in parts of the industrializing Western world. Around the turn of the twentieth century, many Western nations launched the labor regulations, old age pensions, and social insurance programs that have come to be considered at the core of modern welfare states. At first, social expenditures were devoted to "workingmen's insurance," or to keep respectable old people, usually former workers and their spouses, out of demeaning local poorhouses. From the 1920s onward, many of the early Western welfare states for workers (as we might call them) evolved into comprehensive welfare states for all citizens.[1]

The United States did not take this road; it did not move from early social policies for workingmen toward a comprehensive national welfare state. But this fact has not kept scholars from measuring U.S. social policy developments against an ideal-typical conception of "the development of the welfare state." Most scholars take it for granted that the United States did virtually nothing to establish nationwide public social provision prior to the Great Depression and the New Deal of the 1930s—at which point, supposedly, it started but did not "complete" a Western-style welfare state. The United States is thus treated as an extreme laggard on the universal path toward "the modern welfare state." Unfortunately, this is misleading for all phases of U.S. social policy development, especially for the period between the 1870s and the 1920s. Universal, evolutionary theories of welfare state development necessarily blind us to early patterns of U.S. social policy, patterns that challenge us to rework available theoretical frameworks.[2]

In some ways, the late nineteenth- and early twentieth-century United States was a precocious social spending regime.[3] By 1910 more than a quarter of all elderly American men—and more than a third of them in the North—were receiving regular old-age and disability pensions funded by the U.S. federal government under the rubric of military pensions for Union veterans of the Civil War. Many widows and orphans were receiving benefits as well. Civil War benefits cannot be set aside as minor expenditures, nor as mere unavoidable concomitants of the original military conflict of the 1860s. The broadest extension of these benefits came after claims directly due to wartime casualties had peaked and were in decline; and between 1880 and 1910 more than a quarter of all U.S. federal public expenditures were devoted to them. The extent and terms of these disability and old age benefits compared favorably with the coverage and terms of old age pensions and workingmen's social insurance then in place in other Western nations.

During the early twentieth century, many U.S. reformers tried to move from Civil War pensions directly to general old age pensions and workingmen's social insurance; but their efforts failed. Instead, new social policies for mothers, children, and working women were enacted in this period.[4]

Mothers' pensions were the United States' first publicly funded social benefits outside of military pensions. Laws passed in 40 states between 1911 and 1920 enabled localities to provide payments for needy widowed mothers (and occasionally others) in order to let them care for children at home. Protective labor regulations for women wageworkers understood as potential mothers also proliferated during this period. New or improved limits on women's working hours passed in thirteen states between 1900 and 1909, in thirty-nine states between 1909 and 1917, and in two more states prior to 1933. Minimum-wage laws for women workers were enacted by fifteen states between 1912 and 1923. In addition to state-level laws for women, in 1912 the U.S. federal government established the Children's Bureau, headed and staffed not by the usual male officials but by reformist professional women who aimed to look after the needs of all American mothers and children. Across the nation women's groups campaigned for the creation of the Children's Bureau, just as they pressed for the enactment of mothers' pensions and protective labor regulations. In the 1910s a national government bureau "run solely by women" was "without parallel elsewhere in the world."[5] By 1921 the bureau had successfully spearheaded a campaign for the first explicit federal social welfare program, one that offered grants-in-aid to the states. The Sheppard-Towner Infancy and Maternity Protection Act encouraged the creation of federally subsidized pre- and postnatal clinics to disseminate health care advice to mothers. It was hoped that such clinics would reduce the high infant mortality rates that the Children's Bureau had documented for the United States compared with other industrial nations.

In sum, U.S. social policies in the late nineteenth and early twentieth centuries cannot be understood merely in terms of the failure of the nation or the states to enact general old age pensions and regulations and benefits for workingmen. Often thought to have lagged behind other countries in providing for the welfare of its citizens, the United States actually pioneered certain policies to help honored groups of men and women. As certain other nations launched fledgling welfare states for workers between the 1880s and the 1920s, American federal and state governments created social policies for soldiers and mothers.

How can early U.S. social policies—protecting soldiers and mothers, but not workers—best be explained? In the remainder of this chapter, I shall first review major schools of thought about welfare state development, assessing how well they help us to understand and explain early U.S. patterns. Then I will introduce a polity-centered theoretical framework—one that "brings the state back in" *and* is sensitive to the gendered dimensions of policy and politics.[6] Only such a framework, I argue, can enable us to explain U.S. social policies in comparison to those that have emerged and developed in other nations.

The Limits of Existing Comparative Theories

Thoughtful scholars have endeavored for many years to make sense of the origins and development of modern social policies in the United States. Until the mid-1970s debates oscillated between two perspectives. The *logic of industrialism* approach held sway among social scientists who did research on large numbers of nations, using statistical techniques and highly aggregated data for restricted slices of time. Meanwhile, the *national values* approach found special favor among scholars who preferred to use historical methods. Then a sea change occurred. From the middle of the 1970s onward, a third approach, *the social democratic model*, became dominant in comparative studies of welfare states. This approach gained favor as scholars focused on qualitative and quantitative comparisons of six to eighteen advanced industrial countries. Finally, during the past few years, various feminist scholars have started to invoke ideas about patriarchical domination and women's politics to interpret aspects of modern social policies in the United States and elsewhere.

Are Modern Social Policies a By-Product of Industrialization?

"Economic growth is the ultimate cause of welfare state development." [7] This has been the guiding assumption for those who understand modern social policies as rooted in a universal logic of industrialism. As countries develop economically, the reasoning goes, industries emerge, labor forces shift out of agriculture, and cities grow. Regardless of ideologies or political regimes, the populations of economically developing nations face broadly similar problems and dislocations. Once families are off the land and dependent on wages and salaries, they cannot rely only on their own resources or local community help to cope with injuries at work, with episodes of illness and unemployment, or with the upkeep of elderly relatives no longer able to be economically productive. Social demands for pensions and social insurance thus inevitably grow with industrialization and urbanization. At the same time, improved economic productivity makes it possible for government to respond to the new needs with appropriate programs.[8]

U.S. patterns do not accord well with the expectations of the logic-of-industrialism perspective. Prior to the 1930s the United States was one of the world's industrial leaders yet lagged far behind other nations—even those much less urban and industrial—when instituting nationwide pensions or social insurance.[9] Perhaps the picture could be improved by counting Civil War pensions as modern social policies, for such pensions certainly expanded with American industries and cities in the decades following the war. Civil War pensions, however, did not chiefly benefit the denizens of the greatest U.S. industrial centers; they were more likely to help farmers and townsmen in turn-of-the-century America.[10] Nor can a logic-of-industrialism perspective explain why early industrializing U.S. states such as Massachusetts failed to enact British-style proposals for old age pensions and social insurance, proposals that were debated in such states during the early 1900s.[11]

In the final analysis, socioeconomic modernization is a poor predictor of social policies—either what they will be or when they might be enacted. It also says little about specific national- or state-level policy profiles, ignoring the particularities of program constituencies and the public rhetoric used to legitimate them. Why did so many other Western nations launch paternalist welfare states between the 1880s and the 1920s while the United States primarily enacted maternalist regulations and social benefits? This perspective doesn't tell us. What is needed is an approach that is more alert to the political causes and the substantive contents of social policies.

Can National Values Explain the Making of Social Policies?

Rather than assimilate the U.S. case into a worldwide logic of industrialism, some have sought to highlight "American exceptionalism," tracing it to the country's extraordinarily strong liberal values. In a classic formulation, Louis Hartz argued that the United States—born of rebellion against British rule and innocent of class divisions and feudal heritage—developed an all-encompassing liberal culture in which individual rights are sacred, private property is honored, and state authority is distrusted.[12] Since Hartz, others have pointed to the hegemony of liberal values to account more specifically for American social politics in contrast to the development of European welfare states.[13]

Scholars of the national values school point convincingly to overall correlations between major cultural traditions and the forms and rationales of social policies. The arguments are especially plausible when countries at the opposite poles of authoritarianism vs. liberalism are contrasted, as they often are by these scholars; Germany vs. the United States is a favorite comparison.[14] Nevertheless, proponents of this approach have so far failed to pinpoint exactly how cultural values, intellectual traditions, and ideological outlooks concretely influenced processes of political conflict and policy debate. Nor have these scholars addressed the most difficult puzzles about political culture and the development of U.S. social policies.

Why did public education spread early and very extensively in the United States, but not social insurance?[15] National values theorist Anthony King answers, simply, that access to public education is more congruent with American values about equal opportunity and individual initiative.[16] Perhaps. But, then, why have public policies to support full employment opportunities and employment training not been much more readily instituted in the United States than straightforward public benefits for the elderly and the poor? Throughout U.S. history, American citizens have preferred public help to get jobs over other kinds of public assistance. Proposed employment policies have been accompanied by compelling rhetoric about the need to help citizens help themselves, but only sometimes have such policies been enacted.[17] Obviously, the mere value-content of arguments made on behalf of policy proposals is not enough to explain their fate.

Nor is the value-content of arguments made against proposed policies sufficient to explain legislative outcomes. Perhaps the clearest example of ideologically imbued opposition to a U.S. social policy innovation was the strong resistance of most charity organizations during the 1910s to the enactment of pensions for poor mothers and children. Eloquent appeals were made to fundamental liberal values of voluntarism and individual responsibility, as charity spokespersons argued that private help was best for the poor, who should not become "dependent" on governmental hand-outs.[18] Despite such appeals, mothers' pensions were enacted anyway.

Early welfare state measures could in fact be intellectually justified and morally valued through internal reworkings of liberalism itself. Liberal values were in many respects just as hegemonic in nineteenth-century Britain as they were in the nineteenth-century United States. Yet before World War I, Britain enacted a full range of social protective measures, including workers' compensation (1906), old age pensions (1908), and unemployment and health insurance (1911). These innovations came under the auspices of the British Liberal party, and they were intellectually and politically justified by appeals to "new liberal" values of the sort that were also making progress among educated Americans around the turn of the century.[19] Under modern urban-industrial conditions, the "new liberals" argued, the government must act to support individual security; and this can be accomplished without undermining individuals' liberty or making them dependent on the state. If British Liberals could use such ideas to justify both state-funded pensions and contributory social insurance in the second decade of the twentieth century, why couldn't American Progressives do the same? In both Britain and the United States by the turn of the twentieth century, sufficient cultural transformation within liberalism had occurred to legitimate fledgling welfare states without resort either to conservative-paternalist or socialist justifications.[20] Eventually, indeed, U.S. New Dealers used just such new-liberal arguments to justify the nationwide Social Security policies they successfully launched during the 1930s.

We can retain the salutary emphasis on historical process that scholars of the national values school have introduced in response to logic of industrialism arguments. Yet general deductions from national values simply cannot supply answers to many crucial questions about the making of public policy. We must also investigate how the changing institutional configurations of national polities benefit some strategies and ideological outlooks and hamper others. Too often, national values explanations one-sidedly derive political outcomes from values, without revealing that experiences with governmental institutions and political processes profoundly affect the way people understand and evaluate alternative policy possibilities within a given cultural frame.

Working Class Weakness?
The United States and the Social Democratic Model

Recently, debates among scholars doing cross-national studies of six to eighteen Western industrial nations have converged on what Michael Shalev calls the "social democratic model" of welfare state development.[21] According to the boldest form of this model put forward by such theorists as Walter Korpi and John Stephens, a fully developed welfare state is the historical construction of

> a highly centralized trade union movement with a class-wide membership base, operating in close coordination with a unified reformist-socialist party which, primarily on the basis of massive working class support, is able to achieve hegemonic status in the party system. To the extent that these criteria are met, it is hypothesized that the welfare state will emerge earlier, grow faster, and be structured in ways which systematically favor the interests of labor over those of capital.[22]

For the adherents of this approach, public social provision in the United States commenced later and was less generous than Europe's because U.S. industrial unions were weak and labor-based political parties are nonexistent.

Plausible as the social democratic model may seem, it is misleading or insufficient in several ways if our intention is to explain the *overall* trajectory and specific patterns of U.S. social provision since the nineteenth century. In the first place, the social democratic model does not adequately illuminate historical events and sequences prior to the 1940s for either the United States or Europe. In the late-nineteenth-century United States, the expansion of Civil War pensions owed little to trade unions or working-class-based politicians; the benefits that fully enfranchised American workers gained from nineteenth-century politics are not captured by the social democratic model. Meanwhile, between the 1880s and 1920s in Germany, Sweden, Britain, and other nations that launched pioneering paternalist welfare states, social insurance programs were devised by conservative or liberal politicians and bureaucrats, not by trade unions and social democratic political parties.[23]

Additional problems with the social democratic model flow from its overemphasis on political conflicts between capitalists and industrial workers. This deflects our attention from other social classes and from cross-class coalitions that have played major roles in creating modern social provision. Cross-class coalitions between professionals and popular groups have been crucial to the enactment of all modern social policies in every nation. Agrarian parties and agrarian-urban alliances were important in launching and expanding social provision in Europe; and in the United States regionally differentiated agrarian interests have always been crucial arbiters of the extension and limitation of public social provision.[24]

Social identities and conflicts based on ethnicity, race, and gender also tend to be overlooked in the social democratic perspective, with its primary focus on working-class organization. Along with other theorists of modern welfare states to date, proponents of the social democratic model have tended to assume that all significant social policies are targeted on wageworkers or employees (or perhaps "citizens" in general, with a tacit assumption that they are employees or economic dependents of employees). But this conception of the policies to be explained is misleading. Certain major phases and sectors of U.S. social provision, such as Civil War pensions and workingmen's benefits, have been constructed around male roles—including the nonclass role of the soldier-veteran, as well as that of wage-earning family breadwinner—while others have been focused on the female roles of mother and working woman understood as a potential mother.

When accounting for policy developments in Europe and the United States, social democratic theorists prefer to treat racial, ethnic, or gender factors simply as potential "divisions" that may undercut the unified class organization of wageworkers and salary earners. Of course, these social differences do often function to subdivide workers but they are not sufficient for the analysis of any country's policy history, and especially not for understanding the United States, where political forces grounded in ethnic and gender identities positively shaped early patterns of public social provision. Competing political parties rooted in regional and ethnic differences, and in white male fraternalism, fueled the expansion of Civil War benefits. Federated women's clubs, expressing a certain kind of gender ideology, agitated for maternalist social policies during the early 1900s. To make sense of all of this, we must have a theoretical frame of reference that sensitizes us to the full range of identities and relationships, including class but not restricted to it, that may figure in a nation's social politics.

How Should Gender Enter the Analysis?

Until very recently, all theoretical perspectives on modern social policies ignored gendered dimensions of politics, as well as the roles that women's organizations may have played in bringing about particular sorts of measures. In the welfare state literature, as in standard U.S. welfare historiography, "public" life has been typically presumed to be an exclusively male sphere, with women regarded as "private" actors confined to homes and charitable associations. Debates have centered on the relative contributions of male-dominated unions, political parties, and bureaucracies to the shaping of labor regulations and social benefits designed to help male breadwinners and their dependents. Established approaches have overlooked social policies targeted on mothers and working women. And they have failed to notice the contributions of female-dominated modes of politics, some of which are not dependent on action through parties, elections, trade unions, or official bureaucracies.

Serious scholarship on gender and welfare states is so new that much of it is either historically descriptive or devoted to alerting readers to matters previously overlooked. Interpretive essays abound in a very recent, lively literature about women and welfare, but it is difficult to find straightfoward causal propositions about gender and social policies. Nevertheless, a few things can be said about theoretical frames of reference and tentative arguments already in the literature.

Much as the early neo-Marxist debates about "the capitalist state" found myriad ways to repeat the insight that all kinds of governmental actions could express capitalist class interests or reproduce capitalist class relationships, so many of today's fledgling feminist theories of the welfare state argue that modern social policies express dominant male interests and reproduce "patriarchal" relations between the genders in ever-changing ways. The focus may be on gendered relations of domination in families, in paid workforces, or (most often) on shifts in the linkages between the two spheres of patriarchal domination. Regardless, governmental actions, including social policies, are portrayed as functioning to reinforce or rework male domination of women. In a characteristic formulation, Eileen Boris and Peter Bardaglio argue in "The Transformation of State Patriarchy" that the

> nineteenth and early twentieth centuries . . . saw not the decline of
> patriarchy but its transformation from a familial to a state form. . . .
> The emergence of the welfare state did not erode the family as such,
> but it did begin to undermine the patriarchal structure of relations
> between men and women within many families. . . . Laws and public
> policies—as well as governmental institutions and professional supervi-
> sion by doctors, educators, social workers, and other so-called family
> experts—developed as part of a larger support system that reproduced
> patriarchal social relations. Consequently, male-dominated—even

male-headed—families became less important to the maintenance of male domination in the social arena outside the family. . . . Increasingly egalitarian legal relations in families were counterbalanced by the continued economic exploitation of women at home and in the workplace.[25]

Patriarchal domination perspectives have been used to interpret various kinds of U.S. social legislation in the early twentieth century. Protective labor laws for working women have been presented as devices to keep women from competing equally in labor markets with male wage earners.[26] Mothers' pensions have been presented as devices to keep women at home and away from well-paid wage labor.[27] We do not learn from patriarchal domination accounts, however, that prior to the enactment of mothers' pensions, poor widows usually faced worse options, including more repressive forms of low-wage toil and government intervention to take away their children.[28] Nor do we learn that many women's groups, including trade unions as well as elite and middle-class clubs, mobilized politically to press for the enactment of protective labor laws and mothers' pensions—even if these laws, once implemented, eventually belied the hopes of many of their original supporters. We do not learn of that era's celebration of the universal civic value of mothering—by mothers of all classes and races—a core value of the women's movements for mothers' pensions and protective labor legislation in the early 1900s.[29]

Theories highlighting patriarchal domination have also tended to obscure crucial variations among early national social policies. Many scholars have insightfully argued that most (although not all) early social policies in Europe, Australasia, and the Americas idealized the "family wage," that is, the notion that male wage earners should earn enough to sustain their families. Empirically speaking, adequate family wages were rarely actually earned by working-class males during industrialization. But professional reformers as well as male trade unionists in many nations—including the United States and Britain—did tend to believe in the male-earned family wage as an ideal. Along with many other forces, this ideal devalued women's wage work and played up the value of their unwaged roles as housewives and mothers. When applied to early modern labor regulations and social spending policies, the family wage ideal encouraged measures that would, on the one hand, increase male wages and, on the other, sustain women and children who lacked "male breadwinners."

Nevertheless, we should not allow an insight about the similar breadwinner-led family norms on which most modern social policies were based to obscure crucial differences between what I call "paternalist" and "maternalist" versions of such policies. Besides being devised by male politicians, bureaucrats, and trade unionists, paternalist measures—such as those that dominated British social policy during the early 1900s—attempted to shore up the working condition of all workers in ways that reinforced male trade unions and attempted to channel public benefits to women and children through male wage-earning capacities. Thus, British wives gained rights to maternity benefits under the 1911 National Insurance law if they were married to wage-earners who "contributed" to the system; and the same was true for survivors of British male breadwinners under the 1925 Widows, Orphans, and Old Age Contributory Pensions Act. In contrast, early U.S. labor regulations were not only devised and implemented primarily by female professionals and women's groups, but they also applied directly to women. U.S. labor regulations covered women workers. U.S. mothers' pensions went directly to widowed mothers (and occasionally to nonwidowed mothers) regardless of the previous wage-earning status of their dead or departed husbands. And the educational services of Sheppard-Towner clinics went directly to all mothers, including many who were not tied to wage earners. All of these are properly understood as "maternalist" versions of policies that presumed breadwinner ideals. These measures reached broader categories of women than if the measures had been oriented more exclusively to the dependents of wage-earning men. There are, in short, policy variations within "patriarchy" that need to be fully understood and analyzed, along with variations in the timing and geographical spread of legislative enactments.

Interpretations highlighting patriarchal domination are not the only way feminist scholars are seeking to understand early modern social policies. Historians of middle-class women's activities and outlooks in the industrializing United States have produced a rich literature. This body of work highlights not patriarchal oppression, but American women's political agency, and what historian Paula Baker calls the "domestication" of U.S. politics.[30] It probes the ways in which many elite and middle-class women, mostly Protestant and white, but also including some others, created organizations infused with aspirations to extend women's domestic values into civic and national life.

Unfortunately, most historiography of women and early twentieth-century U.S. policymaking remains very insular, relying on archival sources about particular individuals or organizations—usually intellectuals based in New York, Massachusetts, Illinois, and Washington, D.C.—and not making use of systematic comparisons. Yet a few fully comparative studies have appeared, analyzing the place of gender relationships and women's agency in the social politics of various U.S. states, and in the launching of different national systems of social provision within the Western world.[31]

An example of this valuable new comparative scholarship is Seth Koven and Sonya Michel's " 'Womanly Duties': Maternalist Politics and the Origins of Welfare States in France, Germany, Great Britain, and the United States, 1880-1920," a synthetic article that draws on a range of historical studies by its authors as well as others.[32] Koven and Michel stress that women's voluntary groups developed models and proposals for early welfare state policies across all these Western nations. Women's groups were often "maternalist" in orientation—that is, devoted to extending domestic ideals into public life—and they demanded benefits and services especially targeted on mothers and children. In Koven and Michel's view, maternalist women's politics was strongest in the nations with the "weakest," least bureaucratic states. Thus they group Britain and the United States together in contrast to France and Germany, where "strong" bureaucratic states tended to crowd out women's politics. Yet Koven and Michel also point to a supreme irony in early welfare state formation. They argue that the countries that had stronger women's movements ended up with less generous social benefits for mothers and children as their national systems of public social provision matured.

I do not fully agree with Koven and Michel's analysis. Their juxtaposition of "weak" and "strong" states is too crude and one-dimensional to get at the differences among national political systems that affect how likely women are to become politically active and (a separate issue) in what ways women can have an impact on policy decisions. In particular, Koven and Michel fail to analyze crucial differences between the ways class and gender identities figured in the social politics of Britain and the United States between the 1880s and the 1920s. Although both of these nations had "weak states" in Koven and Michel's terms, they actually had very different governmental institutions, administrative systems, and electoral and political party systems. The different patterns of British and U.S. political organizations encouraged class-oriented social policies for workingmen in the former nation, and gender-oriented social policies, from Civil War pensions to maternalist regulations and social benefits, in the United States.[33]

Still, along with recent U.S. women's history, the comparative historical approach used by Koven and Michel suggests analytical possibilities that students of gender and social policies need to keep in mind. For one thing, gender is not just a relation of social domination or social inequality, as the patriarchal theorists assert. Female gender identities—which are not all the same, and which change over time—can also be sources of social solidarity, organization, and moral purpose. The nineteenth-century social identity of the domestically oriented wife and mother functioned in this way for the maternalist women's groups that figured so prominently in turn-of-the-century social politics in the United States and elsewhere. Male gender identities also sustain solidarities and outlooks, as they did in nineteenth-century U.S. political parties and election rituals and in the politics of Civil War pensions; and as they did for many trade unionists who advocated early workingmen's social benefits as a way to buttress the wage-earning role of the male family breadwinner.

Like other social identities, gender identities are not only historically changing and cross-nationally variable; they are always defined and expressed in relation to various social structures, economies, and political institutions. As Desley Deacon has argued, "the struggle between the sexes over the construction of the gender order" may be "universal and ongoing," yet we must direct our "attention to what might be called intermediate structures, that is to institutions specific to certain times and places through which the particular gender order of that time and place is shaped." [34] Systematic comparisons across nations and states, moreover, can help us to find regularities in the ways that institutional arrangements influence and respond to gendered forces that aim to shape public policy outcomes.

Historical and comparative historical studies sensitive to gender concerns suggest that the results of policies cannot be read back historically into their causes. Women's groups, for example, may achieve legislative victories but then be unable to control the implementation of social policies, so that they end up doing harm rather than good to many women. Or social policies may be supported by bureaucrats, or parties, or unions, or upper social classes, with the intention of "controlling" women, but then end up having beneficial primary or secondary effects on the situations of mothers or working women. Indeed, policies pursued for very different purposes, such as increasing national population or integrating workers into the polity, may end up having beneficial effects for women within the bounds of given gender relationships. [35] In sum, explorations of gender and social policies must be historically grounded, institutionally contextualized, and allow for the possibility of unintended outcomes and changing configurations of causally relevant processes over time.

A Gender-Sensitive, Polity-Oriented Perspective

This brings me to the approach I favor: a polity-oriented theoretical framework that incorporates the analysis of gender roles, identities, and relationships. [36] In several basic ways, my approach departs from presumptions shared by virtually all previous approaches to the explanation of welfare state development. First, I see long-term change not only as industrialization and urbanization (or capitalist development) but also as geopolitics and the formation of various sorts of national states through wars, revolutions, and constitutional transformations. Changes in the structures and activities of states matter just as much as socioeconomic development. Second, I see political parties (and systems of political parties) as organizational realities in their own right, not just as transmitters of the interests or values of groups in society.

Finally, I analyze the political processes through which public policies are made and remade in a way that differs from the society-centered theories that have heretofore dominated scholarship about the development of modern welfare states. Because states and political parties are central to my theoretical approach, I look for the ways in which governmental officials and politicians may actively shape policies to further their own organizational and career interests. At the same time, I attend to the institutional arrangements of government, along with the rules of electoral and party politics, and how these affect the possibilities for various social groups to gain political consciousness, to organize, and to ally with other groups. Historically formed governmental institutions and political party systems, I maintain, afford different sorts of advantages and disadvantages, leverage or its absence, to various groups in society—such as business, labor, farmers, women, and racial or ethnic minorities. Thus we cannot explain the making of public policy simply in terms of the values or interests of the social groups themselves. We must take into account the institutional contexts within which groups find themselves and must operate.

How can the analytical pointers offered by a polity-oriented frame of reference help us to make sense of early U.S. social policies? Let me briefly illustrate the kinds of insights the approach can offer.

The making of social policy in America must be understood against the backdrop of the historical geopolitical situation of the U.S. national state and its distinctive institutional formation. The United States was born of an anticolonial revolution against British parliamentary rule, a revolution that culminated in the creation of a federal state with internally divided legislative, executive, and judicial powers.[37] By the 1830s this state had evolved into the world's first mass electoral democracy for white males. The national polity was knit together throughout the nineteenth century by pairs of intensely electorally competitive political parties. No standing military, and no civil service bureaucracies held sway in the United States. Instead, powerful courts adjudicated property rights and patronage-oriented parties used government offices and legislation to reward particular individuals and local groups of followers within the cross-class male electorate.[38] Electoral contests were incessant, as the major parties vied for votes and control over the sources of governmental patronage.

The Civil War of 1861-1865 temporarily rent apart this federal, patronage-oriented democratic polity. This was the greatest war that the United States has ever fought, a war about itself. The ultimately victorious North mobilized hundreds of thousands of men to put down the Confederate rebellion, legislating in the process generous pension benefits for disabled veterans and the survivors of dead soldiers. By the mid-1870s it looked as if the numbers of Union pensioners and government expenditures on disability pensions had reached their peak. But then pension benefits became caught up in competitive party politics. This happened once the South returned to the Union, making national elections extremely competitive between the Republicans and the Democrats from the mid-1870s through the mid-1890s. The Republican party, especially, became the champion of pension generosity, and Republican politicians learned to target pensions on hard-fought states like Indiana, Ohio, and

New York, for example by sending in officials to sign veterans up just before crucial elections.[39] The social identity of the "Union veteran" was visibly politicized in late nineteenth-century America, and veterans' organizations such as the Grand Army of the Republic flourished as powerful associations enjoying a lot of political leverage.

In 1890 the triumphant Republicans enacted the Dependent Pension Act, which made all who had served ninety days or more in the Union military eligible for pensions that were quite generous by international standards of the day. Soon old age alone became a qualification for a veteran's pension. By 1910 many hundreds of thousands of pensions were being paid to elderly Union veterans, and to the widows, orphans, and other survivors of dead soldiers. Because of the operations of its patronage-oriented and electorally competitive nineteenth-century political system, the United States had evolved into a precocious social-spending regime for many of its elderly and disabled citizens.

Even as patronage-oriented democratic politics encouraged veterans' political consciousness and organization in the United States, wage-earning industrial workers found it much harder to achieve political consciousness or leverage as a class. U.S. political parties were rooted in cross-class and cross-regional electoral alliances based on ethnic identities; they had no need to court workers or their unions as a class-based constituency.[40] Moreover, U.S. governments at the state and national levels lacked strong professional bureaucracies. In early-twentieth-century Britain, civil servants, professional reformers, and political parties seeking to court votes from unionized workers were the actors who promoted paternalist social policies such as old age pensions, unemployment insurance, and health insurance. But analogous forces did not exist, or else were very weak, in the nonbureaucratic federal polity of the United States, where sovereign courts were determined to obstruct new kinds of labor regulations that might interfere with "free contracts" between businesses and male wage earners.[41] Thus, proposals for general old age pensions and workingmen's social insurance, and proposals for protective regulations for male workers, all failed to be enacted into law during the early twentieth century in the United States.

Yet associations led by middle-class married women became highly politically mobilized—and surprisingly politically effective—during the same turn-of-the-century period that witnessed many impediments to class-conscious workingmen's politics in the United States. Excluded from formal participation in America's nineteenth-century state of courts and parties, women developed an alternative kind of political capacity rooted in federated voluntary associations.[42]

During the nineteenth century, American women were excluded on a sharply gendered basis from the world's first mass electoral democracy for males of all classes. Culturally, women were relegated to the idealized domestic role of wife and mother. Yet the United States was a predominately Protestant nation, with no established church; so women had much opportunity to get involved in community religious and charitable activities. Furthermore, the United States developed during the nineteenth century a huge system of primary and secondary schools, and many public and private colleges. Schools needed teachers and employed unmarried females; and U.S. colleges and universities admitted many thousands of women to higher education, at a time in world history when very few women were allowed access to higher education in other nations (including Britain).

As a result of the combination of opportunities and exclusions that they faced in nineteenth-century U.S. politics and society, American women—particularly middle- and upper-class women—became civically involved via the creation of huge, nation-spanning voluntary associations. The Women's Christian Temperance Union, the National Congress of Mothers, and the General Federation of Women's Clubs (which had one to two million members by the 1910s) were rooted in thousands of local clubs of married women, knit together into state and federal associations that held regular conventions and decided on goals for women's groups to pursue in society and politics. By the early twentieth century, all of these women's associations were advocating new social policies for mothers and children, arguing that mothers should extend their maternal "caring" from private homes into communities and the nation as a whole. Women's associations wanted to help all American families, and particularly those of the less economically privileged, by shielding women from wage-exploitation and by honoring and supporting the role of housewife-mother.

Prior to 1920, of course, U.S. women did not yet have the right to vote in most state or national elections. Yet their widespread voluntary associations, aroused by maternalist ideology, could rapidly spread the word about social problems and policy priorities. Women's groups could shape public discussion, and put pressure on forty-eight state legislatures simultaneously—at a time, in the early twentieth century, when the male-dominated patronage parties were somewhat weakened and less able than previously to control what went on in legislatures. Women's associations were able to encourage state legislatures to enact maternalist laws, such as hours laws for working women and mothers' pensions, in snowballing waves of imitation during the 1910s. These associations also put pressure on the national U.S. Congress to create the Children's Bureau in 1912 and to expand its mission through the Sheppard-Towner Act of 1921.

Ultimately, the United States stopped short of becoming a full-fledged maternalist welfare state. Still, during the 1910s and the early 1920s, at the height of American women's political mobilization along maternalist ideological and organizational lines, the United States did establish many new social policies targeted on actual or potential mothers, some of which have endured to the present day. U.S. maternalist policy-making was most pronounced in the 1910s and 1920s, when Civil War pensions were fading along with the generation of men who had fought for the Union; and it happened at a time when bureaucratic and working-class forces that might have favored paternalist policies of workingmen's social insurance were especially weak, or completely absent, in the United States.

We cannot understand the distinctive maternalist, rather than paternalist, bent of early modern U.S. social policies without taking account of how sharply gender-differentiated U.S. patronage-oriented politics was during the nineteenth century. We also need to understand the special leverage that widespread voluntary associations of civically mobilized women could attain in early-twentieth-century U.S. federalism, at a time when the nineteenth-century parties were weakened, but when the stronger bureaucracies and interest groups characteristic of later New Deal politics had not yet crystalized. In the absence of class-conscious unions and strong political parties or bureaucracies, U.S. women's federations of the early twentieth century were uniquely—although only temporarily—positioned to shape an emerging public social welfare sphere along maternalist lines.

Conclusion

Let me conclude by commenting on the broader implications for political science of the points made in this essay.

Important social policies—for soldiers and mothers, but not workers—were enacted by the U.S. federal government and the states in the half-century prior to the New Deal. Existing theories about the development of the modern welfare state have failed to notice these early U.S. policy developments. Available theories must therefore be reoriented in order to encompass and explain the American experience.

I have argued that a polity-centered theoretical framework enriches the explanations we can offer for national variations in social policies. This framework examines geopolitics and the historical formation of government institutions and political parties. It focuses on politicians and officials as actors who initiate and shape policies and political coalitions. In addition, the polity-oriented perspective highlights the ways that changing governmental institutions and electoral arrangements influence the capacities of various social groups to become politically conscious and effective. A polity-oriented theoretical perspective can help us to understand why working-class identities and movements have been central in the development of some national systems of social provision, such as most European welfare states, while the activities and identities of women's groups, old people's groups, or racial or ethnic groups have been much more important in the development of other national systems of social provision, including the U.S. system.

In this essay, I have especially tried to illustrate concretely the value of looking at gender—not only through the lens of patriarchal domination, but also through the lens of male and female identities that can become politically relevant in various ways, depending on social and institutional contexts. This approach has value and application well beyond the empirical subject matter discussed here. For example, research on U.S. social policies in the contemporary period—since the 1930s and 1940s—must take into account the identities and experiences of American men both as wage earners and salaried workers, and as soldiers and veterans of World War II. For the World War II generation of men and their families, the GI Bill was as much a central part of "public social provision" as Civil War pensions were for an earlier generation of men and their families. At the same time, new challenges and dilemmas have been thrown up for makers of U.S. social policy by the changing mix of women's roles in families and workplaces, and of course by the rise of modern feminist movements since the 1960s.

In contrast to the maternalist movements of the late nineteenth and early twentieth century, contemporary feminist movements in the United States (and elsewhere) have placed the emphasis on equal and shared gender roles, rather than on "separate spheres" for women and men. Greater, but partial, incorporation of women into the paid labor force, along with changing patterns of marriage and childbearing, created new social conditions for feminist movements to emerge. U.S. political institutions also afforded such movements unusual space and leverage—especially for such activities as legislative lobbying and pressures on courts and administrative agencies.

It is interesting, however, to reflect on the question of whether U.S. feminist movements today have as much influence on politics and policy-making as did maternalist movements in the 1910s and early 1920s. Feminist movements today face greater difficulties than did maternalist forces in the 1910s in forging alliances between professional women operating at the national level and women who live and work in local communities across the United States. Feminists cannot invoke "motherhood" as a universally recognizable, moral category for purposes of moral solidarity and political argument. Instead, feminist movements often face outright opposition from other kinds of women's and conservative movements that invoke "family values" as reasons to oppose the public policy goals of gender equality in workplaces and homes. Moreover, U.S. politics itself has become more bureaucratic and media-driven, making it arguably more difficult for any popular or women's movement to have a sustained impact.

Further research and theorizing needs to be done on these and many more questions about contemporary U.S. politics and public policies. Gender identities and relationships, no matter how theorized, are unlikely ever to explain everything that we want to understand about such matters. But any adequate understanding of the varied ways that nations have made and remade social policies touching men and women—as workers and parents, as soldiers and citizens—must bring gender fully into the picture. And gender must be understood in terms of valued identities and effective forms of political agency, not simply in terms of the domination of women by men.

Notes

1. Peter Flora and Jens Alber, "Modernization, Democratization and the Development of Welfare States in Western Europe," in *The Development of Welfare States in Europe and America*, ed. P. Flora and A. Heidenheimer (New Brunswick, N.J.: Transaction Press, 1981), 37-80.
2. Further elaboration of this point appears in Edwin Amenta and Theda Skocpol, "Taking Exception: Explaining the Distinctiveness of American Public Policies in the Last Century," in *The Comparative History of Public Policy*, ed. Francis G. Castles (Oxford: Polity Press, 1989), 292-333.
3. Documentation for the arguments made here appears in Theda Skocpol, *Protecting Soldiers and Mothers: The Political Origins of Social Policy in the United States* (Cambridge: Belknap Press of Harvard University Press, 1992), chap. 2.
4. Ibid., pts. 2 and 3.
5. Kathryn Kish Sklar, "Florence Kelley and the Integration of 'Women's Sphere' into American Politics, 1890-1921" (Paper presented at the Annual Meeting of the Organization of American Historians, New York City, April 1986), 17.
6. Theda Skocpol, "Bringing the State Back In: Strategies of Analysis in Current Research," in *Bringing the State Back In*, ed. Peter B. Evans, Dietrich Rueschemeyer, and Theda Skocpol (New York: Cambridge University Press, 1985), 3-37.
7. Harold Wilensky, *The Welfare State and Equality* (Berkeley and Los Angeles: University of California Press, 1975), 24, echoing Harold Wilensky and Charles N. Lebeaux, *Industrial Society and Social Welfare* (New York: Russell Sage Foundation, 1958), 230.
8. For additional examples of logic of industrialism arguments, see Phillips Cutright, "Political Structure, Economic Development, and National Social Security Programs," *American Journal of Sociology* 70 (1965): 537-550; and Robert W. Jackman, *Politics and Social Equality: A Comparative Analysis* (New York: Wiley, 1975).
9. David Collier and Richard Messick, "Prerequisites versus Diffusion: Testing Alternative Explanations of Social Security Adoption," *American Political Science Review* 69 (1975): 1309.
10. The best evidence we have on who received pensions comes from the analysis of county-level data for Ohio, 1886-1890, by Heywood Sanders, "Paying for the 'Bloody Shirt': The Politics of Civil War Pensions," in *Political Benefits*, ed. Barry Rundquist (Lexington, Mass.: D. C. Heath, 1980), 150-154.
11. This argument is developed and documented in Ann Shola Orloff and Theda Skocpol, "Why Not Equal Protection?: Explaining the Politics of Public Social Spending in Britain, 1900-1911, and the United States, 1880s-1920," *American Sociological Review* 49 (December 1984): 732-733, 736, 743-744.
12. Louis Hartz, *The Liberal Tradition in America* (New York: Harcourt Brace, 1955).
13. For examples, see Gaston Rimlinger, *Welfare Policy and Industrialization in Europe, America, and Russia* (New York: Wiley, 1971); Daniel Levine, *Poverty and Society: The Growth of the American Welfare State in International Comparison* (New Brunswick, N.J.: Rutgers University Press, 1988); Roy Lubove, *The Struggle for*

Social Security, 1900-1935, 2d ed. (Pittsburgh, Penn.: University of Pittsburgh Press, 1986; originally 1968); and Anthony King, "Ideas, Institutions, and the Policies of Governments: A Comparative Analysis: Parts I and II," *British Journal of Political Science* 3(4) (1973): 418; emphasis in the original removed. The entire article spans 3(3): 291-313 and 3(4): 409-423.

14. Both Rimlinger, *Welfare Policy and Industrialization*, and Levine, *Poverty and Society*, emphasize this comparison.

15. Arnold J. Heidenheimer, "The Politics of Public Education, Health and Welfare in the USA and Western Europe: How Growth and Reform Potentials Have Differed," *British Journal of Political Science* 3(3) (July 1973): 315-340.

16. King, "Ideas and Policies," 419-420.

17. For futher discussion and documentation see Theda Skocpol, "Brother, Can You Spare a Job?: Work and Welfare in the United States," in *The Nature of Work*, ed. Kai Erikson and Steven Peter Vallas (New Haven: Yale University Press, 1990), 192-213.

18. Overviews of the arguments of the charitable societies appear in Lubove, *Struggle for Social Security*, 101-106. For telling examples, see Mary Richmond, "Motherhood and Pensions," *Survey* 29(22) (March 1, 1913): 774-780; and Edward T. Devine, "Pensions for Mothers," *American Labor Legislation Review* 3(2) (June 1913): 191-201.

19. Michael Freeden, *The New Liberalism: An Ideology of Social Reform* (Oxford: Clarendon Press, 1978).

20. On parallel developments in Britain and the United States, see Kenneth O. Morgan, "The Future at Work: Anglo-American Progressivism, 1870-1917," in *Contrast and Connection: Bicentennial Essays in Anglo-American History*, ed. by H. C. Allen and Roger Thompson (Columbus: Ohio University Press, 1976), 245-271; and Charles L. Mowat, "Social Legislation in Britain and the United States in the Early Twentieth Century: A Problem in the History of Ideas," in *Historical Studies: Papers Read Before the Irish Conference of Historians*, ed. J. C. Beckett (New York: Barnes and Noble, 1969), 7:81-96. See also the recent major study by James T. Kloppenberg, *Uncertain Victory: Social Democracy and Progressivism in European and American Thought, 1870-1920* (New York: Oxford University Press, 1986).

21. Michael Shalev, "The Social Democratic Model and Beyond: Two Generations of Comparative Research on the Welfare State," *Comparative Social Research* 6 (1983): 315-351. Examples of recent research in this tradition include Francis Castles, *The Social Democratic Image of Society* (London: Routledge & Kegan Paul, 1978); Gosta Esping-Andersen, *Politics Against Markets: The Social Democratic Road to Power* (Princeton, N.J.: Princeton University Press, 1985); Gosta Esping-Andersen, *The Three Worlds of Welfare Capitalism* (Princeton, N.J.: Princeton University Press, 1990); Bruce Headey, *Housing Policy in the Developed Economy: The United Kingdom, Sweden, and the United States* (London: Croom Helm, 1978); Walter Korpi, *The Democratic Class Struggle* (Boston: Routledge & Kegan Paul, 1983); John Myles, *Old Age in the Welfare State* (Boston: Little, Brown, 1984); and John Stephens, *The Transition from Capitalism to Socialism* (London: Macmillan, 1979).

22. Stephens, *From Capitalism to Socialism*, 89. See also Korpi, *Democratic Class Struggle*.

23. Jens Alber, "Governmental Responses to the Challenge of Unemployment: The Development of Unemployment Insurance in Western Europe," in *The Development of Welfare States in Europe and America*, ed. Peter Flora and Arnold J. Heidenheimer (New Brunswick, N.J.: Transaction Books, 1981), 151-183; and Flora and Alber, "Modernization, Democratization, and the Development of Welfare States."

24. Castles, *Social Democratic Image of Society*; Esping-Andersen, *Politics Against Markets*, chaps. 2-3; Margaret Weir and Theda Skocpol, "State Structures and Possibilities for 'Keynesian' Responses to the Great Depression in Sweden, Britain, and the United States," in *Bringing the State Back In*, ed. Evans, Rueschemeyer, and Skocpol, esp. 141-148; and Jill Quadagno, *The Transformation of Old Age Security: Class and Politics in the American Welfare State* (Chicago: University of Chicago Press, 1988).

25. Eileen Boris and Peter Bardaglio, "The Transformation of Patriarchy: The Historic Role of the State," in *Families, Politics, and Public Policy: A Feminist Dialogue on Women and the State*, ed. Irene Diamond (New York: Longman, 1983), 72-73. For a somewhat different patriarchal approach, see Mimi Abramovitz, *Regulating the Lives of Women: Social Welfare Policy from Colonial Times to the Present* (Boston: South End Press, 1988).

26. See Alice Kessler-Harris, *Out to Work: A History of Wage-Earning Women in the United States* (Oxford: Oxford University Press, 1981), chap. 5.

27. See Carol Brown, "Mothers, Fathers, and Children: From Private to Public Patriarchy," in *Women and Revolution: A Discussion of the Unhappy Marriage of Marxism and Feminism*, ed. by Lydia Sargent (Boston: South End Press, 1981), 239-267; Nancy Folbre, "The Pauperization of Motherhood: Patriarchy and Public Policy in the United States," *Review of Radical Political Economics* 16 (Winter): 72-88; Janet Marie Wedel, "The Origins of State Patriarchy During the Progressive Era: A Sociological Study of the Mothers' Aid Movement" (Ph.D. diss., Washington University, St. Louis, 1975), chap. 9; Libba Gage Moore, "Mothers' Pensions: The Origins of the Relationship Between Women and the Welfare State" (Ph.D. diss., University of Massachusetts, 1986); and Barbara Nelson, "The Gender, Race, and Class Origins of Early Welfare Policy and the Welfare State: A Comparison of Workmen's Compensation and Mothers' Aid," in *Women, Politics, and Change*, ed. Louise A. Tilly and Patricia Gurin (New York: Russell Sage Foundation, 1990), 413-435.

28. Ann Vandepol, "Dependent Children, Child Custody, and the Mothers' Pensions: The Transformation of State-Family Relations in the Early 20th Century," *Social Problems* 29(3) (February 1982): 221-235.

29. Paula Baker, "The Domestication of Politics: Women and American Political Society, 1780-1920," *American Historical Review* 89 (June 1984): 620-647.

30. Ibid. See also Kathryn Kish Sklar, "The Historical Foundations of Women's Power in the Creation of the American Welfare State, 1830-1930," in *Mothers of a New World: Maternalist Politics and the Origins of Welfare State*, ed. Seth D. Koven and Sonya Michel (New York: Routledge, 1993).

31. For examples, see Jane Jenson, "Gender and Reproduction: Or, Babies and the State," *Studies in Political Economy* 20 (Summer 1986): 9-46; Desley Deacon, "Politicizing Gender," *Genders* 6 (Fall 1989): 1-19; Susan Pedersen, "Social Policy and the Reconstruction of the Family in Britain and France, 1900-1945" (Ph.D. diss., Harvard University, 1989); and Elisabeth Clemens, "Redefining the Public Realm: Progressive Coalitions and Political Culture in the American States, 1890-1915" (Ph.D. diss., University of Chicago, 1990).

32. This article is published in the *American Historical Review* 95(4) (October 1990): 1067-1108.

33. This argument is elaborated in Skocpol, *Protecting Soldiers and Mothers*, pts. 2 and 3; and in Theda Skocpol and Gretchen Ritter, "Gender and the Origins of Modern Social Policies in Britain and the United States," *Studies in American Political Development* 5(1) (Spring 1991): 36-93. Koven and Michel are more inclined to stress similarities between the United States and Britain in part because they primarily focus on explaining local public health policies, whereas I place more emphasis on labor regulations and social spending policies.

34. Desley Deacon, "Reply to 'Re-Politicizing Gender,' " *Genders* 11 (Summer 1991).
35. Jenson, "Babies and the State"; and Mary Ruggie, *The State and Working Women: A Comparative Study of Britain and Sweden* (Princeton, N.J.: Princeton University Press, 1984).
36. See the introduction, *Protecting Soldiers and Mothers*, for a full explanation of my polity-oriented perspective.
37. On U.S. state formation in contrast to European, see J. Rogers Hollingsworth, "The United States," in *Crises of Political Development in Europe and the United States*, ed. Raymond Grew (Princeton, N.J.: Princeton University Press, 1978), 163-196; Samuel P. Huntington, *Political Order in Changing Societies* (New Haven: Yale University Press, 1968), chap. 2; and Stephen Skowronek, *Building a New American State: The Expansion of National Administrative Capacities, 1877-1920* (New York: Cambridge University Press, 1982), pt. 1.
38. Richard L. McCormick, "The Party Period and Public Policy: An Exploratory Hypothesis," *Journal of American History* 66 (1979): 279-298.
39. Sanders, "Paying for the 'Bloody Shirt' " and Donald McMurry, "The Political Significance of the Pension Question, 1885-1897," *Mississippi Valley Historical Review* 9 (1922): 19-36.
40. Martin Shefter, "Party and Patronage: Germany, England and Italy," *Politics and Society* 7 (1977): 403-451; Ira Katznelson, *City Trenches: Urban Politics and the Patterning of Class in the United States* (New York: Pantheon, 1981); and Richard Oestreicher, "Urban Working-Class Political Behavior and Theories of American Electoral Politics, 1870-1940," *Journal of American History* 74(4) (March 1988): 1269.
41. Willam E. Forbath, *Law and the Shaping of the American Labor Movement* (Cambridge: Harvard University Press, 1991); and Victoria Hattam, *Labor Visions and State Power* (Princeton, N.J.: Princeton University Press, 1993).
42. Full documentation appears in Skocpol, *Protecting Soldiers and Mothers*, pt. 3. For a supporting statistical analysis, see Theda Skocpol, Christopher Howard, Susan Goodrich Lehmann, and Marjorie Abend-Wein, "Women's Associations and the Enactment of Mothers' Pensions in the United States," *American Political Science Review* 87 (September 1993), 686-701.

V. CONCLUSION

15

Political Entrepreneurs, Governing Processes, and Political Change

Linda L. Fowler

Conventional wisdom about American politics fared badly in 1992. Voter turnout jumped five percentage points to reverse a thirty-year trend of declining electoral participation. A third-party candidate got more votes than at any time since Teddy Roosevelt campaigned on the Bull Moose ticket. An incumbent president, who enjoyed unprecedented approval ratings as a victorious commander-in-chief just a year prior to the election, suffered an ignominious defeat at the hands of a politically tarnished Arkansas governor. Turnover in the House of Representatives reached its highest level in nearly half a century. The perennial condition of divided party control of the federal government came to an abrupt end.

Political analysts not only failed to anticipate these changes, but also miscalculated their magnitude. They underestimated turnout, overestimated congressional turnover, and misjudged the final distribution of presidential votes. These mistakes were more than embarrassing lapses, for they raised troubling questions about the relevance of political science to contemporary American politics. Why did we fail to forecast the events of 1992 until they were almost over? How do we tell whether this election was an aberration or the harbinger of a new political era?

As often as I have tried to answer these questions for myself and for my scornful colleagues in more predictable disciplines, I am not persuaded that we did in fact do badly as analysts in 1992. With the benefit of hindsight, I still see nothing inevitable about the election of Bill Clinton, the apotheosis of Ross Perot, or the upheaval in the House, although in the latter case, heavy retirements were expected because of reapportionment and expiration of an obscure clause in the campaign finance laws that permitted senior members to retain surplus contributions for their personal use. Instead, I see the cumulative effect of many individual choices, some ill-advised and others strategically brilliant, a great deal of good and bad luck, and in the case of the Congress some fortuitous timing that launched the check writing scandal early enough to affect challenger recruitment. In short, it does not require much imagination to construct a different but plausible scenario for the second Bush administration, the perpetuation of gridlock in Washington, and the demise of the Perot movement.

In retrospect, moreover, it seems to me that we *did* predict the volatility of 1992—if not the particular events. Students of American politics have been writing for some time about the personalization of the presidency as an institution, the rise of candidate-centered campaigns, the internal contradictions within the Democratic and Republican coalitions, the dealignment of the electorate, the rise of single issue groups, and the decoupling of regional economies from national trends.[1] Any one of these could disrupt the historical regularities of U.S. politics, making the outcomes and patterns of the past less reliable indicators of future events. Thus, in a political environment dominated by personality and an issue-of-the-day mentality, such old standbys as partisanship, previous vote margins, public approval ratings, and economic indices lose some of their predictive value. In 1992 these possibilities came true—all at once. Our models performed poorly, yet in a curious way we did get it right.

The question now is whether we can live with our own prescience. Is there any point to a science of politics, when unpredictable and unstable outcomes are the expected result? In my view, the way to approach the current volatile state of American politics is by paying more attention to political entrepreneurs. When the parties and voters swing free from their traditional moorings, as they have done in recent years, opportunities abound for political activists who have the skill and the ambition to take advantage of a fluid situation.

A focus on entrepreneurs leads us to ask different questions about the 1992 election, however. Where did the Clintonites come from? How did the Perotistas get organized? And why did both groups choose 1992 to attempt a shift in the nation's political agenda? Equally important to the changes that eventually came about was the behavior of the established elites on the left and right. Why did prospective candidates, such as New York's Mario Cuomo or New Jersey's Bill Bradley, sit out the election? How did the fractures in the conservative Reagan coalition arise to undermine the Bush presidency in the spring primaries and sabotage the Republicans' August convention? It also is essential to understand why a record number of candidates, a historic proportion of whom were women and ethnic minorities, stood for Congress after a decade in which the supply of contenders for House seats dwindled steadily in both parties. In sum, 1992 was a year in which the activist public in American politics was in quiet ferment, drawing in new players, rearranging old alignments, and supporting causes as diverse as term limitations and neo-isolationism.

These entrepreneurs—the candidates, party activists and leaders, interest group participants, movement organizers, and the like—are interesting because they function at the grassroots and institutional levels but are distinctive from both realms. They are more involved and attentive to politics than the average citizen, yet lack formal responsibilities for governance, except in the case of party nominations of candidates. They give public voice to the private needs of ordinary citizens, they cast social and economic problems into political terms, and they provide resources and incentives to move government in new directions. Activists in the United States thus bridge the gap between the public and institutions usually filled by bureaucratized party organizations in other democracies.

Political scientists have not given much systematic attention to this middle layer of American politics, so we are in a weak position to explain its linking function. We need to figure out, therefore, how entrepreneurs emerge, what strategies they adopt for particular situations, and how the political environment favors one type of entrepreneurship over another. Most important, we need to consider how they bring about change. In this essay, I consider the role of entrepreneurs in contemporary American politics. I then address the theoretical underpinnings of entrepreneurial behavior. Finally, I offer some speculations about the implications of political entrepreneurs in shaping the Clinton presidency.

Entrepreneurs and the American Tradition

Entrepreneurship has been a hallmark of politics in the United States since the founding of the American Republic. The framers of the Constitution, themselves consummate entrepreneurs, anticipated a highly decentralized politics built around factions and rival loci of power. The constant competition among diverse interests provided maximum scope for politically ambitious people. The framers did little to channel their activism: they neither institutionalized the recruitment of a political class, as in Britain, nor established strong party organizations, as later in Europe, to channel and regulate the behavior of political activists. Accounts of early political life in Washington consequently stressed the dominance of skillful individuals rather than formal position holders.[2] Individual activism across the nation was evident in the voluntary associations and general "tumult" of American political life noted by Tocqueville in the 1830s.[3]

The activism implied by constitutional structure and enshrined in American tradition gained forceful expression during the twentieth century in the writings of Joseph Schumpeter. Schumpeter defined democracy as the competitive struggle for free votes in free elections, and he saw political entrepreneurs as the driving force behind that competition. In the process of bidding for ballots, candidates and party activists organized resources and packaged issues for political campaigns. Power, not profit, was the motivating force behind their actions, and policy, not product, was the means of satisfying citizen demand. Voters played a reactive role in this exchange, according to Schumpeter, by accepting or rejecting the planks and principles offered to them. But elites "wielded the initiative" by determining the alternatives from which citizens might choose.[4]

The party system in the United States has grown considerably weaker since Schumpeter's day, but this has simply heightened rather than diminished the importance of political entrepreneurs. The reasons, as Stone notes in this volume, lie in the mismatch of incentives between citizens and elected officials: ordinary individuals are too constrained to bring much pressure to bear on the government and elected officials have too much at stake in the status quo.[5] Hampered by inadequate resources; lack of time, interest, and information; and high transaction costs for engaging in collective action, citizens are at a significant disadvantage in bringing about change. In Nagel's words: "While spontaneous popular action warms the heart of any good democrat . . . people initiate little of what we normally call participation. . . . Acts of participation are stimulated by elites—if not by the government, then by parties, interest groups, agitators, and organizers." [6]

Conversely, elective officials command disproportionate political resources and information, but they tend to be wedded to current policies—in part because they have real difficulty in discovering their constituents' interests, in part because they tend to pursue political strategies that worked for them in the past, and in part because they develop vested interests in governmental programs. The incentives for different approaches to governance, therefore, are most likely to come from political elites who are dissatisfied with their current position and have the resources to attempt a redistribution of political power. Although entrepreneurship occurs among incumbent officeholders, generally it is the "losers" in the political arena, to invoke Schattschneider, who endeavor to redefine the scope of conflict and to bring new players into the action.[7]

The influence of political entrepreneurs in bridging the gap between the mass public and governmental institutions has emerged in several puzzles in American political literature. Each puzzle involves an inconsistency between micro-level and macro-level modes of analysis in which individually based theories and longitudinal models confront the same phenomenon. Too often, the singular behaviors of political actors or organizations do not seem to fit with broad historical trends, and there seems to be no middle ground between the two.

A conspicuous example of this type of contradiction lies in the inconsistent results obtained from aggregate time-series data in House elections and public-opinion surveys. Repeatedly, scholars have demonstrated substantial regularities in congressional election outcomes with respect to the condition of the economy, the performance of the president, and the salient issues of the day, but they can find little impetus for such patterns in the individual choices of voters, which are heavily influenced by local factors, incumbency, and candidates' personal attributes.[8] Jacobson and Kernell resolved this incongruity between times-series analysis and voting behavior through the strategic calculations of ambitious politicians. By demonstrating that strong candidates time their decisions to run for Congress when national tides favor their party, they contended that voters were given an appealing district choice that added up to a favorable trend for one party, even though voters never made the connection between local candidates and national issues.[9]

At present, when national factors have lost influence in congressional elections, Jacobson's more recent work again identifies entrepreneurs as the causal link. This time, it is the unwillingness of strong challengers to run against incumbents under any circumstances and the failure of the Republican party to recruit a pool of quality candidates that are decisive in determining outcomes in House races.[10]

A related puzzle pertains to the long-term erosion of party identification in the electorate. Despite the decrease in party-line voting, the net results of presidential and congressional elections still add up to a referendum of sorts on the government's policy performance.[11] In this case scholars cannot agree whether or not voters are dealigning, realigning, responding to new issue cleavages, reacting to weak candidates, or engaging in a rational strategy to strike an ideological balance between the branches of the federal government.[12] Whatever the electorate's attitudes, one key element in this debate concerns the role of party elites in promoting one sort of policy over another. On the one hand, Shafer argues elsewhere that activists have reinforced issue cleavages inside each party that are inconsistent with attitudes in the electorate, thereby leading to divided party control of the presidency and Congress.[13] On the other hand, several scholars suggest that candidates are an indispensable element in partisan realignments because they frame the alternatives that match emerging cleavages within the electorate and reinforce this pattern in subsequent election campaigns.[14]

A comparable paradox emerges from the study of participation. Interest group activity has expanded dramatically in the United States since the 1960s, while voting declined by 13 percentage points over the same period.[15] The rising levels of education among the general population are quite consistent with the increase in interest group participation, but are contrary to the downward trend in voter turnout.[16] Rosenstone and Hansen attribute these disjunctures to political elites who affect the ebb and flow of civic participation through their efforts to mobilize particular segments of the public.[17]

These are the paradoxes I know best, and other scholars doubtless can supply additional ones. What interests me about such discontinuities between individual and aggregate phenomena in contemporary American politics is how prominent political entrepreneurs figure in their attempted resolution—just as Schumpeter might have predicted. The middlemen of politics seem to offer scholars one means of examining changes in the American system that extend well beyond the peculiar events of the 1992 election.

Entrepreneurs and Political Science

Despite the importance of entrepreneurs in American politics, political scientists are preoccupied with the mass public and formal institutions and therefore tend to overlook them. This disciplinary bias holds both for theory and for empirical observation. We thus have learned a great deal about voter attitudes and the behavior of incumbent officeholders, but much less about the middle layer of activists. To draw an analogy with biological science, political science typically examines the body politic by analyzing single cells or whole skeletons, while neglecting the nerves, muscles, veins, and organs that enable these components to function as a whole. For example, although we have good descriptive data about the socioeconomic status of elites, we have little information about the recruitment and derecruitment of eligible individuals to party activism, interest group participation, and candidacy. Nor do we have much sense of how activists network with each other within and across community and state borders; how they formulate and pursue their strategic objectives; and how they ultimately prevail in the political arena.

There are several reasons for this imbalance. First, ordinary citizens and public officials are visible and accessible to scholars in ways that activists are not. Because the pool of political entrepreneurs is fluid, varying in both size and composition in response to events and to activity by other entrepreneurs,[18] it is extremely difficult to observe systematically. Unlike the general public, its population parameters are essentially unknowable, and unlike the universe of elected officials, its boundaries for eligibility are undefined. Scholars must rely on specialized data sets, such as Stone and Rapoport's survey of party convention delegates, Mitchell's sample of environmental group members, or Norris and Darcy's recent survey of congressional primary contestants. Or they must resort to heroic feats such as the recent poll by Verba, Schlozman, Brady, and Nie of 15,000 respondents in order to generate an adequate subset of activists.[19] In short, the very nature of political entrepreneurs tends to frustrate our usual methods for reliably controlling and assessing statistical variation.

A focus on political activists also is at odds with the norms in our profession about what is important in democratic politics. For a discipline in which the legitimacy and accountability of governmental decisions are dominant values, the institutionalized interaction between the ruled and their rulers is paramount. Inevitably this leads us to elections and to formal arenas of decision making, such as legislatures and executive agencies. Because activists are self-starters, their motives are suspect; because their positions are never ratified through popular consent, their participation raises troubling questions of bias; and because they so often operate through informal channels outside the public view, their influence is undemocratic. To tout political elites as agents of change, then, raises the old spectre of pluralist ideology with all its many sins.[20]

Finally, many political scientists tend to define political entrepreneurship somewhat restrictively. One approach views political entrepreneurs as analogous to their economic counterparts. Under this rubric, the entrepreneur is one who shifts public resources toward a more optimal (or

Pareto-efficient) use and therefore typically operates inside governmental agencies.[21] Another approach is found in the literature on political leadership, in which entrepreneurs engage in agenda setting and the strategic manipulation of incentives.[22] Again, entrepreneurs occupy formal positions of power.

Given the fragmentation and permeability of the American system, as well as the diversity of resources employed in political competition, a far more inclusive definition of entrepreneurship seems appropriate. In effect, we might characterize political entrepreneurs as individuals who mobilize economic and human resources in order to alter existing policies, rules, or institutions. Broadly speaking, they traffic in a variety of currencies—votes, money, group memberships, volunteers—and they operate at all levels of government, within parties and interest groups, and at the grassroots.

Recently, researchers have begun focusing on political entrepreneurs broadly defined in a variety of contexts, including interest-group behavior, party activists and organizations, candidacy, and a wide range of non-voting participation.[23] This volume of essays also reflects the emerging interest in political elites, whether through the class struggles of the Progressive and New Deal eras analyzed by Manley or Ferguson, the behavior of activists and candidates in partisan alignments considered by Stone and Carmines, the force of political ideas outlined by Kingdon, Mayhew, and Gray, or the gendered interpretations of equality among reformers in American history traced by McDonagh—to mention several. What such diverse perspectives highlight in one fashion or another is the role of intermediate-level actors in effecting change in the American democracy.

Entrepreneurship and Political Processes

Generally, investigations of political entrepreneurship come under the rubric of political processes, a term that reflects the connective role elites perform in linking the mass public to governmental institutions. But it is a phrase that can be misleading on two counts. The first stems from the fact that current work on political elites is quite different from process-oriented studies of the past. The second arises from the process terminology's false implication that present research on political elites has a common intellectual framework.

In its earlier guise, process research drew directly from the pluralist tradition of group competition articulated by theorists Robert Dahl and David Truman.[24] It regarded elites as broadly distributed in the society, or at least constrained by the presence of latent activists in unrepresented groups. It usually depicted political processes as a series of stages, each operating in accordance with its own internal dynamic and loosely connected in some linear fashion. Examples of this mode of analysis included the *policy process* that began with interest articulation and proceeded through the phases of policy formulation, legitimation, implementation, and evaluation;[25] or the candidate *recruitment process* that began with individual socialization and progressed through phases of certification, apprenticeship, nomination, and eventual election.[26] Although movement occurred as actors progressed from stage to stage, the process itself was static because each stage occurred in its own stable institutional environment. Moreover, conflicts were resolved through bargaining, rather than redistribution of rules or resources, so that when change occurred it was incremental.

Generally, the process literature tended toward description rather than theory, toward emphasis on the present rather than historical pattern. At its best, process-oriented research provided solid classification schemes of relevant variables and richly textured depictions of a variety of political entrepreneurs and organizations, such as candidates, activists, parties, interest groups, social movements, committees, agencies, neighborhood associations, and the like. At its worst, however, the process approach that grew out of pluralist theory had all the features of bad systems analysis, including boxes (with contents often unspecified) labeled to represent individual stages and vaguely connected one to the other by arrows.

It is important to recognize, therefore, that when we talk about political processes today the term has a different meaning than in the past. To be sure, much of what passes for process-oriented research is descriptive—appropriately so, given the neglect of political elites until recently. But scholars who presently study political elites make no pretense, as earlier students of political processes did, that entrepreneurial activity is broadly representative of the general population or that it necessarily serves the public interest. They neither assert that mass democracy is at work in the processes they study nor embrace the pluralist value system that treats political consensus and stability as indications of the polity's well-being.

More important, present-day process researchers tend to see social structures and political institutions not as constants but as relatively fluid parameters that themselves are subject to entrepreneurial manipulation. Thus, where the old-style process research focused on the stability and incrementalism of political outcomes, the new-style research is likely to examine elite conflict over the very rules of the social and political order. It is this dynamic quality that transforms political entrepreneurs into potential catalysts for change.

The terminology of political process can be misleading in another way because it implies a common intellectual framework linking the present study of political entrepreneurs, whereas nothing could be further from the truth. Granted, contemporary research on processes captures entrepreneurs' connective or linking function between the mass public and governmental institutions, it has a strong behavioral orientation, and it rejects the highly aggregative approach to politics that has been the norm in the discipline. Yet in contrast to a previous generation of process-oriented researchers, new-style process research does not have a shared theoretical and normative system comparable to pluralism. Nor does it employ a similar conceptual scheme, such as the boxes and stages adopted by previous researchers. Instead, separate research agendas have developed in relative isolation from each other and bear the stamp of several different intellectual paradigms, such as feminism, economic determinism, neo-pluralism, and rational choice. Indeed, judging from the bibliographies of these works it is not clear that scholars studying various elite activities even see themselves as part of a broad research enterprise on political entrepreneurship.

The lack of a common theoretical focus is probably the major barrier to developing a fuller understanding of political entrepreneurship in American politics. The current sociologically based theories of elite behavior cannot differentiate the relative handful of activists from among the larger class of eligibles; nor can they account for the ebb and flow of recruits within the elite ranks. The present rational-choice models are even more problematic because the purpose of political entrepreneurs is the provision of collective goods for the rest of society, which in theory ought not to occur at all. But since activism clearly does take place, scholars usually assume its presence, as in formulations of ambition theory regarding candidacy, or give it an extrarational foundation, as in the notions of civic duty, efficacy, and purposive benefits found in interest group theory.

The previous generation of process-oriented scholars finessed the theoretical issues of political entrepreneurship that now confront their successors. They accepted political activism as a natural occurrence in American life and consequently did not need to account for the emergence of entrepreneurs. Although recognizing different propensities for political participation, which they attributed to variation in socialization and distribution of resources, they assumed individuals engaged freely in political action in order to compensate for their lack of personal power in the complex U.S. system and to prevent other individuals and groups from dominating political outcomes. These scholars also regarded the political system as operating in a state of equilibrium. They therefore did not feel obliged to examine how broad social and political arrangements—rules, norms, institutions, classes—constrained or stimulated entrepreneurial activity, except as sources of bias in the political process.

Neither assumption is acceptable for present-day students of political processes who are interested in the linking function of activists. Instead, they need to confront the issue of entrepreneurs' emergence, and they ultimately need to consider when entrepreneurs perpetuate the status quo and under what conditions they may transform American democracy.

Political Entrepreneurship and Political Theory

Political entrepreneurs pose two quite different theoretical problems for political scientists. The most obvious deals with the micro-level of individual activism and the seeming irrationality of engaging in collective action to benefit society as a whole. Although this issue is typically debated within the context of interest group politics, it also applies to a wider range of political activism, such as participation in parties and campaigns or candidacy. A less visible and probably less tractable theoretical question occurs at the macro level. Here it is important to explain not only how broad social and institutional structures affect the emergence of various elites, but also how the cumulative efforts of many different entrepreneurs move the polity in one direction or another.

Mancur Olson's telling demonstration that rational citizens would not voluntarily engage in collective action poses a serious challenge to the study of political entrepreneurs. Not only did Olson discredit the idea that groups were the natural outlet for political interests, his argument implied that many types of political participation should not occur. With the exception of small groups, where social pressures could be applied, or certain large groups, where coercion could be implemented, the logical imperative to be a "free rider" dominated other motivations.[27]

Olson conceded that political organizations could operate if they were able to coerce participation, for example, through compulsory union membership, or to offer material and "solidary," or social, incentives. Indeed, many successful parties and groups have provided material incentives to their members in the form of patronage, services, insurance, and publications, while others, such as the civil rights movement, have relied on solidary incentives. These activities beg the question of rational nonparticipation, however, because a group has to exist before it can offer members solidary benefits, and it must be fairly well established before it can provide the services necessary to induce people to join. Thus selective and solidary incentives might be an effective strategy for group survival, but they cannot account for group origin or for the entrepreneurship that created the first package of membership incentives.

By disputing the rationality of political activism, Olson pushed scholars toward extrarational explanations of participation. Many theorists, therefore, have attributed the emergence of political activists to "purposive benefits," the psychological rewards of engaging in collective action. Moe, for example, argued that many citizens overestimate the importance of their political contribution because of imperfect information and hence are not as subject to the free rider problem as Olson supposed. Educated and affluent citizens, in particular, have a high sense of political efficacy, which causes them to inflate their contribution to the provision of a collective good and to join organizations. Riker and Ordeshook suggested that a sense of civic duty provides the reward for engaging in voting.

Mansbridge, too, pointed to altruistic motives as a force in American politics.[28] But the most common explanation for group participation is the high value citizens place on the benefits they derive from the achievement of policy goals.[29] What all these approaches have in common is the separation of the goals of activism from the cost-benefit calculation of participation.

Similarly, rational choice theories of candidacy assumed that would-be officeholders were politically ambitious and that office-seeking behavior could be reduced to a simple cost-benefit equation about means without addressing the underlying problem of motivation.[30] In the equation, $U(O) = p(B) - (1-p)C$, U is the utility or value a candidate would receive from gaining a particular office, O. Using the equation, theorists predicted that a candidate would run for office if $U(O)$ was positive, which would occur when the estimated probability of winning (p) was high, when the perceived benefits of the office (B) were great, and/or when the costs of losing (C) were low.

Like all theories of expected utility, the rational-actor paradigm of candidacy treats office seeking as a preference whose origins are not relevant. It assumes that prospective candidates rank their desires for various offices vis-à-vis the status quo and concentrates on the selection of strategies to maximize attainment of the preferred position. Consequently, if the individual runs, then $p(B)$ must have been greater than $(1-p)C$. Unfortunately, this formulation provides no clues about why the calculation turned out positively for one prospective candidate and negatively for another. Such an approach, consequently, can tell us nothing about the emergence of entrepreneurial candidates generally or about the factors that facilitate their role as agents of change.[31]

However, there is ample room in rational-choice theory to accommodate political entrepreneurship; hence, it is not necessary to stretch the bounds of rationality or to ignore the collective action problem. Three strands of scholarship dealing with the logic of the free rider indicate how collective action is rational for political entrepreneurs. They include (1) the definition of collective goods; (2) the size of an individual's share of a collective good or collective bad; and (3) the iterative aspect of many Prisoner's Dilemma games, which are a particular form of Olson's free-rider problem.

Entrepreneurship and Rational Action

Olson's analysis depended heavily on the *nonconsummability* and *nonexcludability* of collective goods characteristic of national defense, lighthouses, and clean air.[32] Very few goods satisfy both properties, however; most fall short on one or both dimensions, being either partially consumable or partially excludable. Indeed, it makes sense to think of each property as ranging along a continuum, with the two forming a matrix in which a pure collective good comprises but a single cell.[33]

The technical properties of collective goods are important in Olson's analysis because they affect the calculation of an individual's share of the good that leads to the rational choice of free ridership. When assumptions about the nature of collective goods are relaxed, Chamberlain has demonstrated that the individual's costs and benefits work out differently and large groups become feasible. Smith also focused on the partial exclusivity of environmental goods as a prime factor in the existence of environmental organizations.[34] In cases of a less than pure public good, then, some participation to provide it will result, although the supply generated will be suboptimal.

Similarly, it is quite feasible to assume that many public goods have private goods associated with them. This is the line of reasoning that lies behind Frolich, Oppenheimer, and Young's theory of political leadership and, less formally, behind Salisbury's theory of exchange between group leaders and members.[35] In both cases, the entrepreneurs who organize a group not only receive the collective good, they also obtain the personal benefits of money and prestige that accrue to the position of group leader. Because they get both kinds of rewards—only one of which is subject to the Olson logic—they are willing to bear the transaction costs of creating a group and developing the selective and solidary incentives to keep it going.

In a recent article, Sabatier gives this approach a somewhat different twist with what he terms "commitment theory." [36] This variation on Salisbury's theory of exchange contains the important addition of purposive benefits associated with the public good. The political entrepreneurs who organize groups, Sabatier contends, have strong ideological beliefs about their group's mission and therefore cannot be analyzed as the purely self-interested entrepreneurs Salisbury postulates. In short, Sabatier attempts to combine rational egoism with psychological commitment to explain group entrepreneurship, although he does not make clear which of these conditions is necessary or sufficient for entrepreneurship to occur.

If the nature of collective goods does not seem to rule out rational activism, neither does the individual's share of the public good turn out to be as severe an obstacle to the provision of collective goods as Olson's analysis implied. Hardin noted that Olson's mathematics leaves the door open for rational participation if the individual providing the collective good gets a very large proportion of the benefit.[37] In short, the benefits of producing the good can exceed the costs, even if free riders also enjoy its use. Olson recognized this possibility (he termed it the exploitation of the great by the small[38]) but Hardin developed the logical implications to show that such situations could be relatively common in politics.

This perspective on an individual's share of a collective good also leads to the consideration of collective bads—negative outcomes people wish very strongly to avoid. Again, Hardin demonstrated that collective action is rational when individuals assign a high utility to avoiding a collective bad, especially when the properties of nonexcludability and nonconsummability assure that everyone must partake of it. This, of course, accounts for the emergence of group leaders who feel aggrieved by a particular condition in society and hence offers partial analytic support for Truman's "disturbance" theory of interest groups.[39]

Hansen has added some embellishments to the rational-choice theory of collective bads by stressing how information affects individuals' calculations of their expected benefits. Those who have low information costs because of education and wealth or because of personal experience with a collective bad will be more likely to place a high value on becoming politically active. However, Hansen also resorts to an extrarational element by postulating that negative collective goods change people's attitudes toward risks and therefore make them more inclined to act cooperatively.[40]

Finally, it is important to consider the theoretical work on the logic of collective action that derives from Prisoner's Dilemma games. In the Prisoner's Dilemma two rational defendants can avoid going to jail by agreeing not to confess in exchange for a lighter sentence. But in the absence of communication or trust, each will choose the noncooperative outcome of confession in order to avoid the worst case scenario of betrayal in which one player remains silent and the other engages in a plea bargain. Such failure of cooperation lands both in jail, albeit under a lighter sentence. This "minimax logic," Hardin proved, applies to collective goods.[41] It follows, then, that the research on cooperative solutions in Prisoner's Dilemma games is relevant to the emergence of political entrepreneurs. Like Olson's theory, the Prisoner's Dilemma suggests that even though political activism in the form of group participation is beneficial, rational individuals will not engage in it.

The experimental and theoretical work on such games reveals that iteration has a powerful effect in producing cooperative outcomes. After a succession of games, players learn to avoid the minimax outcome in favor of the cooperative solution and come to trust one another, even when they are not permitted to communicate.[42] Rational calculation, then, does not necessarily lead to noncooperation, if players have repeated opportunities to develop their strategies. Individuals will bear the costs of providing collective benefits for themselves and others if they can interact with other participants and if there is continuity in their involvement.

Taken together, the variations on the logic of collective action discussed in this section lead to several important conclusions about the feasibility of a theory of political entrepreneurship. First, the properties of collective goods are not wholly inimical to collective action. Second, an individual's share of a collective good contains several possible avenues toward cooperative action without doing violence to Olson's mathematics or abandoning his assumption of rational action. Third, the iterative process of providing collective goods in the political arena, when combined with stable institutions, has the potential to foster the collective enterprises of political entrepreneurs.

Although these solutions to the Olson problem do not seem appropriate for explaining the existence of large, mass-based political organizations, nevertheless they do seem applicable to the small cadre of political elites in American politics. They are important to the construction of a theory of entrepreneurship, in fact, because they rescue political activism from the realm of extrarational behavior. Altruistic or policy motives consequently are neither a necessary nor a sufficient condition for political entrepreneurs to emerge. To be sure, many political elites may have feelings of collective responsibility and that is all to the good, but analysts do not have to depend upon altruism or ideology in order to construct explanations of the behavior of candidates, interest group leaders, and party or movement activists.

The rationale for political entrepreneurship pieced together here suggests several conditions under which political entrepreneurs are likely to thrive. First, there must be material incentives, or some quasi-private benefits, that accrue to activists independent of the collective good. Second, there must be the opportunity for activists to claim a disproportionate share of the collective good or to avoid a large proportion of the collective bad. Third, there must be repeated opportunities for activists to interact with each other over time, not simply to build solidarity, but to generate learning and trust. Each of these conditions suggests that the presence of reward systems and the development of political networks are critical to the emergence of entrepreneurs in American politics.

Are all of these conditions necessary for political activism? Are some more important than others? Such questions are interesting as well as researchable, but they are seldom asked by scholars who study the processes of elite participation. Indeed, it is fair to say that since Joseph Schlesinger's classic study of opportunity structures leading to higher office in the American states, the question of incentives for political entrepreneurs has seldom been taken beyond the short-term strategic problem of winning or losing a particular office.[43] It is difficult to say, therefore, whether some would-be activists never make it into the political arena because of high personal costs or because of social and institutional barriers.[44] Similarly, the interaction *among* elites rarely gets the attention that scholars lavish on activists' attempts to influence elective officials.[45]

In short, developing micro-level theories of entrepreneurship will require that scholars examine a different set of processes associated with political activists. Instead of focusing solely on the outcomes of entrepreneurship, it is also important to consider the origins of entrepreneurs. Instead of concentrating on the agendas of governmental officials, scholars should consider why certain issues are stricken from the agenda. Instead of trying to prove which individuals or groups exercise the most influence over particular policies, researchers should ask how groups of political players happen to be in the political arena. In sum, the very nature of entrepreneurship in American politics suggests that process-based researchers shift from analyzing outputs to examining inputs.

Having outlined a set of conditions for the occurrence of political entrepreneurship, how do we reckon with its aggregate effects? Activists may be necessary for political change, but they are not sufficient to bring it about. Many politicians and groups have ideas for policy innovation or concepts of the good society that they would like to implement. Yet relatively few overcome the dual hurdles of public ignorance and institutional fragmentation to win elective office or enact an agenda. The American political system is rather paradoxical in that it is extraordinarily open to political entrepreneurship at all levels of government but extremely resistant to change.

Given the legacy of pluralist thought, it is customary in political science to view elites as promoting the status quo. Indeed, Dahl stressed the stabilizing influence of elites as essential to democratic governance. He concluded that:

> Without [elite] consensus no democratic system would long survive the endless irritations and frustration of elections and party competition. With such a consensus the disputes over policy alternatives are nearly always disputes over a set of alternatives that have already been winnowed down to those within the broad area of basic agreement.[46]

More difficult to conceptualize, however, is the transforming role of political entrepreneurs in the American democracy. How do candidates and agitators, party activists and interest group leaders, seize on shifts in popular preferences to move government in a different direction? How do they change the public's frame of reference with respect to broad issues? We know this happens—witness the election of 1992. We also have seen that the middle layer of political elites translates the demands of the mass public into aggregate trends through grassroots mobilization, electoral campaigns, and conflict over the rules of the game. Understanding such trends, however, requires two types of information that are generally missing from the current literature on entrepreneurial elites: (1) a sense of the historical context in which activists operate and (2) a longitudinal perspective on their efforts.

However, it hardly seems likely that at any given time political entrepreneurs should all be pushing in the same direction. It is also clear that coordination among like-minded activists encounters significant institutional barriers and rests heavily on informal, often personal, networks. Consequently, the impact of political entrepreneurs is likely to be episodic and haphazard, and political eras are not likely to have the neat boundaries and distinctive characteristics attributed to earlier periods in American politics.[47] Large shocks to the system, such as occurred in 1992, are not random, but they show few of the regularities political scientists associate with major political realignments. Indeed, if entrepreneurs continue to figure so prominently in contemporary political processes, realignment theory and its many cousins will undoubtedly become obsolete, if that is not the case already.[48]

Political Entrepreneurs and the Clinton Presidency

In the aftermath of the 1992 election a new conventional wisdom quickly emerged. Supposedly, the country had rejected the ideological polarization of the 1980s and returned to its more typical pattern of centrist politics. The voters had finally tired of divided party control of the federal government and put an end to gridlock. The Clinton era would be a period of pragmatic progressivism that would restore the public's confidence in its political institutions and leaders. When skeptics, citing the Carter years, warned that a Democrat in the White House and a Democratic Congress did not necessarily produce effective government, the stock reply was: "But Bill Clinton is a much more skillful politician than Jimmy Carter."

This is the great danger inherent in entrepreneurial politics: that every problem, every flaw in the American democracy can be remedied if we just put more skillful people in office. Such thinking is the inevitable end product of the personalized campaigns and party coalitions that dominate presidential and congressional elections. It fuels Ross Perot's bid for political power and diverts the shell-shocked Republicans from the lessons of defeat. It applauds President Clinton's 18-hour days and treats every dealing with Congress as a zero-sum test of strength. It ultimately may destroy the Clinton presidency as it brought down George Bush, Jimmy Carter, and even Ronald Reagan in his second term.

A volatile public that gives political entrepreneurs like Clinton their scope is easily wooed by other entrepreneurs. A fragmented party system that permits savvy politicians to create majority coalitions from essentially inharmonious parts is highly susceptible to strategic manipulation. These were the conditions that enabled Bill Clinton to win the White House; the same conditions invite his downfall.

The challenges will come from the left and the right, from inside Clinton's party, from the opposing Republicans, and, of course, from the "temperamental Texas tycoon," Ross Perot. Self-starters in the Congress, the states, the lobbying organizations, the think tanks, and the grassroots will add to the mix of competing objectives and tactics. Somehow the news media will endeavor to make sense of the multiple players and carry out their self-appointed task of deciding who is on top. Having misjudged the former governor of Arkansas, reporters will be at pains to avoid overlooking any promising newcomers. Having overrated Bush, they undoubtedly will be on the lookout for every potentially fatal misstep his successor might make.

What are the likely consequences for the Clinton presidency? First, it is important to recognize that skillful entrepreneurship may be necessary to move the country in new directions—probably more so than at any time in our history—but such skill does not guarantee successful government. In politics, as in business, effective entrepreneurs are those who instill a sense of shared mission in the people around them and who take the long view of what they want to accomplish. Entrepreneurs thus need more than clever manipulation of people and symbols: they need a clear vision. Second, it is easy for politicians and the public to get distracted by the spectacle of the entrepreneur at work. Twisting arms in Congress, producing blueprints for sweeping health care reform, and charming second-graders in televised town meetings are all part of the modern political entrepreneur's tool kit. But they are no substitute for responsible and thorough deliberation in the legislature, in the parties, and in local communities to produce consensus about deep-seated differences. Unfortunately, the environment that breeds entrepreneurial politics provides little support for such activities. Thus, if one is realistic about the underlying conditions that brought Clinton to the White House, it is difficult to be optimistic about what his administration can accomplish.

As we come to understand the full implications of entrepreneurship in American politics, scholars will be able to speak with more authority about the likely impact of particular events or actors. For now we should expect the unexpected, refrain from inferring trends where none exist, and educate our students and the public about the inherent volatility of a democracy grounded on the personal skill and vision of political entrepreneurs.

Notes

1. See, for example, Theodore J. Lowi, *The Personal President* (Ithaca, N.Y.: Cornell University Press, 1985); Martin P. Wattenberg, *The Rise of Candidate-Centered Politics: Presidential Elections of the 1980s* (Cambridge, Mass.: Harvard University Press, 1991); Linda L. Fowler and Robert D. McClure, *Political Ambition: Who Decides to Run for Congress* (New Haven, Conn.: Yale University Press, 1989); Byron E. Shafer, "The Notion of an Electoral Order: The Structure of Electoral Politics at the Accession of George Bush," in *The End of Realignment? Interpreting American Electoral Eras*, ed. Byron E. Shafer (Madison: University of Wisconsin Press, 1991); Paul Allen Beck, "The Dealignment Era in America," in *Electoral Change in Advanced Industrial Democracies*, ed. Russell J. Dalton (Princeton: Princeton University Press, 1984); John R. Petrocik, "Divided Government: Is It All in the Campaigns?" in *The Politics of Divided Government*, ed. Gary W. Cox and Samuel Kernell (Boulder, Colo.: Westview Press, 1991); Burdett A. Loomis and Allan J. Cigler, "The Changing Nature of Interest Group Politics," in *Interest Group Politics*, 3d ed., ed. Allan J. Cigler and Burdett A. Loomis (Washington, D.C.: CQ Press, 1991); John R. Owens and Edward C. Olson, "Economic Fluctuations and Congressional Elections," *American Journal of Political Science* 24 (August 1980): 469-493; Benjamin Radcliff, "Solving a Puzzle: Aggregate Analy-

sis and Economic Voting Revisited," *Journal of Politics* 50 (May 1988): 440-445.

2. James Sterling Young, *The Washington Community* (New York: Columbia University Press, 1966).

3. Alexis de Tocqueville, *Democracy in America*, vol. 1 (New York: Vintage Books, 1945), 259-260.

4. Joseph A. Schumpeter, *Capitalism, Socialism and Democracy* (New York: Harper & Brothers, 1942), 282.

5. See Walter Stone's contribution to this volume.

6. Jack Nagel, *Participation* (Englewood Cliffs, N.J.: Prentice-Hall, 1987), 3-4.

7. See, for example, the case study of Warren Magnuson's championship of consumer causes in the early 1970s as part of his effort to remake his political persona under electoral pressures. David E. Price, *Who Makes the Laws? Creativity and Power in Senate Committees* (Cambridge, Mass.: Schenckman, 1972); E. E. Schattschneider, *The Semi-Sovereign People* (Hinsdale, Ill.: Dryden Press, 1975), 37-40.

8. Gerald H. Kramer, "Short-Term Fluctuations in U.S. Voting Behavior, 1896-1964," *American Political Science Review* 65 (March 1971): 131-143; Edward Tufte, "Determinants of Outcomes of Midterm Congressional Elections," *American Political Science Review* 69 (September 1975): 812-826; Robert S. Erickson, "Economic Conditions and the Congressional Vote: A Review of the Macrolevel Evidence," *American Journal of Political Science* 34 (May 1990): 373-399.

9. Gary C. Jacobson and Samuel Kernell, *Strategy and Choice in Congressional Elections* (New Haven, Conn.: Yale University Press, 1981).

10. Gary C. Jacobson, *The Electoral Origins of Divided Government* (Boulder, Colo.: Westview Press, 1990).

11. Morris P. Fiorina, *Retrospective Voting in American National Elections* (New Haven, Conn.: Yale University Press, 1981); Benjamin I. Page and Robert Y. Shapiro, *The Rational Public* (Chicago: University of Chicago Press, 1992).

12. See, for example, Beck, "Dealignment Era"; Shafer, "Notion of an Electoral Order"; Edward G. Carmines and James A. Stimson, *Issue Evolution: Race and the Transformation of American Politics* (Princeton: Princeton University Press, 1989; Jacobson, *Electoral Origins;* Morris P. Fiorina, *Divided Government* (New York: Macmillan, 1991).

13. Shafer, "Notion of an Electoral Order."

14. See Edward G. Carmines's chapter in this volume. David T. Canon, "The Emergence of the Republican Party in the South from 1964 to 1988," in *The Atomistic Congress: An Interpretation of Congressional Change*, ed. Allen D. Hertzke and Ronald M. Peters, Jr. (Armonk, N.Y.: M.E. Sharpe, 1992); James E. Campbell, "Divided Government, Partisan Bias, and Turnout in Congressional Elections: Do Democrats Sit in the 'Cheap Seats'?" (Paper presented at the Annual Meeting of the American Political Science Association, Washington, D.C., September 1991).

15. Steven J. Rosenstone and John Mark Hansen, *Mobilization, Participation, and Democracy in America* (New York: Macmillan, 1993).

16. Richard A. Brody, "The Puzzle of Political Participation in America," in *The New American Political System*, ed. Anthony King (Washington, D.C.: American Enterprise Institute, 1978).

17. Rosenstone and Hansen, *Mobilization*, 5, 56-63.

18. Walter J. Stone, Lonna Rae Atkeson, and Ronald B. Rapoport, "Turning On"; Rosenstone and Hansen, *Mobilization*, chap. 6.

19. Stone, Atkeson, and Rapoport, "Turning On"; Robert Cameron Mitchell, "National Environmental Lobbies and the Apparent Illogic of Collective Action," in *Collective Decision-Making*, ed. Clifford Russell (Baltimore: Johns Hopkins University Press, 1979); Pippa Norris and Robert Darcy, "The American Candidate Study," manuscript, Edinburgh University and Oklahoma State University, 1992;

Sidney Verba, Kay Lehman Schlozman, Henry R. Brady, and Norman H. Nie, "Does Equal Participation Matter? Political Activity and the Dilemmas of Representation" (Paper presented at the Annual Meeting of the Midwest Political Science Association, Chicago, April 1992).

20. Among the many famous criticisms of pluralism are those of Walker and Lowi, who attacked pluralism's seeming indifference to injustice, and Parenti and Schattschneider, who pointed to the numerous unrepresented or underrepresented groups in society as evidence of pluralism's political bias toward the wealthy. See Jack L. Walker, "A Critique of the Elitist Theory of Democracy," *American Political Science Review* 6 (June 1966): 285-295; Theodore J. Lowi, *The End of Liberalism: The Second Republic of the United States,* 2d ed. (New York: Norton, 1979); Michael Parenti, *Democracy for the Few,* 5th ed. (New York: St. Martin's, 1988); Schattschneider, *Semi-Sovereign People.*

21. See, for example, Mark Schneider and Paul Teske, "Toward a Theory of the Political Entrepreneur: Evidence from Local Government," *American Political Science Review* 86 (September 1992): 737-747; and David Osborne and Ted Gaebler, *Reinventing Government: How the Entrepreneurial Spirit Is Transforming the Public Sector* (Reading, Mass.: Addison-Wesley, 1992).

22. See, for example, R. Douglas Arnold, *The Logic of Congressional Action* (New Haven: Yale University Press, 1990); and William Riker, *The Art of Political Manipulation* (New Haven: Yale University Press, 1986).

23. See, for example, Jack L. Walker, *Mobilizing Political Interests in America: Interest Groups, Patrons, and Representation* (Ann Arbor: University of Michigan Press, 1991); David Vogel, *Fluctuating Fortunes* (New York: Basic Books, 1989); Mark P. Petracca, ed., *The Politics of Interests: Interest Groups Transformed* (Boulder, Colo.: Westview Press, 1992); John Mark Hansen, *Gaining Access: Congress and the Farm Lobby,* 1919-1981 (Chicago: University of Chicago Press, 1991); David T. Canon, *Actors, Athletes, and Astronauts: Political Amateurs in the United States Congress* (Chicago: University of Chicago Press, 1990); Jeffrey M. Berry, Kent E. Portnoy, and Ken Thompson, *The Rebirth of Urban Democracy* (Washington, D.C.: Brookings Institution, 1993).

24. Robert Dahl, *A Preface to Democratic Theory* (Chicago: University of Chicago Press, 1956); David B. Truman, *The Governmental Process,* 2d ed. (New York: Knopf, 1971).

25. See, for example, Randall B. Ripley and Grace A. Franklin, *Congress, the Bureaucracy, and Public Policy,* 3d ed. (Homewood, Ill.: Dorsey Press, 1984).

26. Kenneth Prewitt, *The Recruitment of Political Leaders: A Study of Citizen Politicians* (Indianapolis: Bobbs-Merrill, 1970).

27. Mancur J. Olson, *The Logic of Collective Action* (Cambridge, Mass.: Harvard University Press, 1965).

28. Terry M. Moe, *The Organization of Interests* (Chicago: University of Chicago Press, 1980); William H. Riker and Peter C. Ordeshook, "A Theory of the Calculus of Voting," *American Political Science Review* 63 (March 1968): 25-43. See the introductory essay in Jane J. Mansbridge, ed., *Beyond Self-Interest* (Chicago: University of Chicago Press, 1991), 1-22.

29. Lawrence S. Rothenberg, "Organizational Maintenance and the Retention Decision," *American Political Science Review* 82 (December 1988): 1129-1152; Mitchell, "National Environmental Lobbies"; Moe, *Organization of Interests;* Paul A. Sabatier, "Interest Group Membership and Organization: Multiple Theories," in *Politics of Interests,* 99-129.

30. See, for example, Gordon S. Black, "A Theory of Political Ambition: Career Choices and the Role of Structural Incentives," *American Political Science Review* 66 (March 1972): 144-159; David W. Rohde, "Risk-Bearing and Progressive Ambition: The Case of Members of the United States House of Representatives,"

American Journal of Political Science 23 (February 1979): 1-26.

31. For a more detailed critique of theories of ambition, see Linda L. Fowler, *Candidates, Congress, and the American Democracy* (Ann Arbor: University of Michigan Press, 1993).

32. A pure collective good is nonconsumable in that one person's use of the good does not preclude others from consuming it; it is nonexclusive with respect to the fact that once it has been provided others may enjoy it whether or not they have contributed to its provision.

33. David L. Weimer and Aidan R. Vining, *Policy Analysis: Concepts and Practice*, 2d ed. (Englewood Cliffs, N.J.: Prentice-Hall, 1992), 46.

34. John Chamberlain, "Provision of Collective Goods as a Function of Group Size," *American Political Science Review* 68 (September 1974): 707-716. V. Kerry Smith, "A Theoretical Analysis of the 'Green Lobby,'" *American Political Science Review* 79 (March 1985): 132-147.

35. Norman J. Frolich, Joe A. Oppenheimer, and Oran R. Young, *Political Leadership and Collective Goods* (Princeton: Princeton University Press, 1971); Robert H. Salisbury, "An Exchange Theory of Interest Groups," *Midwest Journal of Political Science* 13 (February 1969): 1-32.

36. Sabatier, "Interest Group Membership," 99-129.

37. Russell Hardin, *Collective Action* (Baltimore: Resources for the Future, 1982).

38. Olson, *Logic*, 35.

39. Hardin, *Collective Action*, 61-66. Truman, *Governmental Process*, 88.

40. John Mark Hansen, "The Political Economy of Group Membership," *American Political Science Review* 79 (March 1985): 79-96.

41. Russell Hardin, "Collective Action as an Agreeable n-Prisoner's Dilemma," *Behavioral Science* 16 (September 1971): 472-481.

42. See Hardin, *Collective Action*, chaps. 8 and 9.

43. Joseph A. Schlesinger, *Ambition and Politics: Political Careers in the United States* (Chicago: Rand McNally, 1966).

44. This is clearly the case for prospective congressional candidates. See Fowler and McClure, *Political Ambition*.

45. An exception would be studies of coalition politics among interest groups, but these are largely directed at organizational rather than interpersonal connections. See, for example, Christopher J. Bosso, "Adaptation and Change in the Environmental Movement," in Cigler and Loomis, eds., *Interest Group Politics*, 151-176.

46. Dahl, *Democratic Theory*, 133.

47. Joel Silbey argues along these lines in disputing the validity of realignment theory as a concept of political change in the American party system. See Joel H. Silbey, "Beyond Realignment and Realignment Theory: American Political Eras," in Shafer, ed., *The End of Realignment?*, 3-23.

48. See Everett Carl Ladd, "Like Waiting for Godot: The Uselessness of 'Realignment' for Understanding Change in Contemporary American Politics," in Shafer, ed., *The End of Realignment?*, 24-36.

16

International Influences
on American Politics

Martin Shefter

Nation-states do not exist in isolation from one another. Consequently their politics are subject to influences from beyond their borders. Both the international state system and the international economy—war and trade—shape national politics. International influences are most obvious in nations that are subject to severe external restrictions from abroad. Thus scholars who studied the peripheral regions of the world were the first to recognize international impacts on national economic and political development. But when political science was being established in the United States as an independent discipline at the turn of the twentieth century, the United States was becoming one of the wealthiest and most powerful states in the world. U.S. political science has, as a result, slighted the role of international influences on American national politics.[1]

International Influences as Viewed in Political Science

Although few Americanists have analyzed international influences on national politics, some prominent students of comparative politics and international relations have written about it.[2] Most eminently, Alexis de Tocqueville writes in *Democracy in America* (in a chapter entitled "Principal Causes Which Tend to Maintain the Democratic Republic in the United States") that the absence of threats from powerful neighbors provides Americans with a unique advantage:

> The Americans have no neighbors and consequently they have no great wars, or financial crises, or inroads, or conquest, to dread; they require neither great taxes, nor large armies, nor great generals; and they have nothing to fear from a scourge which is more formidable to republics than all these evils combined: namely, military glory.[3]

A prominent scholar of international relations, Robert Keohane, discusses how various regions of the United States established ties with the international economy prior to 1860 and then analyzes how these international linkages contributed to the nation's political disintegration in the Civil War.[4]

The impact of war on U.S. politics has also drawn some attention from scholars with comparative interests. In particular, Theda Skocpol and her student, Edwin Amenta, have published an outstanding essay that analyzes why World War II fostered a less substantial expansion of social welfare policy in the United States than in Great Britain.[5]

Amenta and Skocpol analyze how Franklin D. Roosevelt, in order to mobilize the U.S. economy for war, found it necessary to make political concessions to business. By way of contrast, the British government was able to play a more directive role in that nation's wartime economy. Moreover, in Great Britain the major parties united in a coalition government, and elections were suspended for the duration of the war. But in the United States, electoral and party politics continued as usual. When the Beveridge Report was issued in Great Britain—proposing to expand the welfare state as part of the postwar settlement—it was supported by all major political forces in the country. The parallel report in the United States, prepared by a presidential task force, was roundly opposed by businessmen, Republican politicians, and bureaucrats. The autonomy and power of these political forces, Amenta and Skocpol note, were preserved rather than reduced by the American mode of mobilizing for war.

These writings are atypical, however. On the whole, political scientists have devoted little attention to analyzing how the international state system and the international economy have influenced domestic U.S. politics.

Dimensions of International Influence

Despite the general neglect of international influences in the literature on U.S. politics, it has been extremely important in American political development. As a nation like any other, the United States has crossborder flows of great concern to its government and citizens. These flows fall into five different categories:

The first category is the movement of armed forces across national borders and efforts to deter military invasion. For example, the political map of the world was redrawn as a result of World War II. Although the politics of the defeated nations were altered most profoundly by the war, the experience of mobilization and the need to anticipate future military conflicts transformed politics for the victors as well—including the United States. The Department of Defense became by far the largest agency of the national government in the 1940s, and the federal government acquired unprecedented powers. These effects have lasted into the 1990s.

A second cross-border flow—that of goods—has also had important consequences for U.S. domestic politics. Traditionally, tariff and foreign trade policy were among the chief issues dividing the Republican and Democratic parties, with the GOP generally advocating protectionism and the Democrats free trade. As the 1990s open, foreign trade is reasserting its importance in party competition, though now the Democrats have become the more protectionist of the two parties.

Third, the movement of people across national borders is another influential cross-border flow. The United States was populated by migrants, both voluntary immigrants from Europe and slaves from Africa. Immigration from Ireland, Italy, and Eastern Europe aided in the emergence of powerful, ethnicity-based political machines in nineteenth-century U.S. cities.[6] As the twentieth century draws to a close, immigration into the United States is again increasing, with profound consequences for Amerian politics. Flows of people from Latin America and Asia are already having a substantial impact on politics in Miami and Los Angeles. And advocates of "cultural diversity" are seeking legitimation from pure demographics—the notion that a substantial proportion of the U.S. population will be Hispanic and nonwhite in the twenty-first century.

A fourth kind of cross-border flow involves ideas. Louis Hartz argued that the basic character of American politics was established by the liberalism imported by English colonists in the eighteenth century.[7] That the United States became a liberal society in this way, Hartz argues, accounts for the historic weakness of socialism in the country. More concretely, the very idea of social policy was, in large measure, imported from Great Britain and continental Europe.[8] In particular, during the Progressive era the American Association for Labor Legislation borrowed many of its proposals from the British Liberals.[9]

Fifth and finally, cross-border flows of capital can affect domestic American politics. For example, British investment in the Confederate states prolonged the Civil War enough to turn it into a total war.[10] To deter British support for the Confederacy, the North adopted the abolition of slavery as one of its war aims, with enormous consequences for the future course of American politics. More recent efforts to attract capital from outside or to prevent its flight have affected government policies. Paul Peterson argues that U.S. city governments have been importantly influenced by the desire both to attract investments to the locality and to prevent capital flight.[11] On the national level, the Reagan and Bush administrations argued that boosting investment in the United States required the national government to avoid public policies and taxes that would burden investment at home and encourage the export of capital abroad.

The Early Peak of International Influence

International events had the greatest influence on American politics early in the nation's history, when America was neither rich nor powerful. Prior to 1776 the American colonies were subject to the authority of Europe; indeed, they owed their independence to a war between the Great Powers of the day—the Seven Years' War between Britain and

France. With the expulsion of France from the Atlantic coast of North America, the Anglo-Americans no longer had a stake in maintaining an active British presence. In addition, to cover some of the war's costs, Britain levied a number of new taxes that the Americans found burdensome, sparking their rebellion. When the rebelling colonies launched their war against England, France intervened on their side. The Americans were thus able to defeat the British and win their independence. The very birth of the United States as an independent nation, therefore, was conditioned by the first of the international influences mentioned above—the movement of armed forces across national borders.

Even after America won its independence, the government of the new nation was weak and American politics was overwhelmingly influenced from abroad. As Donald Robinson observes:

> The most striking feature of life under the national government during the early national period was the saliency of foreign affairs. After the First Congress (1789-1791) ... the leading events until the close of the War of 1812 were almost all related to foreign affairs. Washington's Neutrality Proclamation, Jay's Treaty, the XYZ affair and the "quasi-war" with France, the Louisiana Purchase, Jefferson's Embargo Act, and "Mr. Madison's War"—all these were directly in the field of foreign affairs.[12]

The first national political parties, the Federalists (pro-British) and Jeffersonian Republicans (pro-French), were essentially distinguished by their attitude toward the French Revolution and by whether they wanted the U.S. economy closely linked to Great Britain or preferred for American producers to be able to sell in world markets.[13] The Napoleonic Wars also affected the young nation, encouraging the Americans to believe the British could be expelled entirely from North America. Such hopes contributed to the outbreak of the War of 1812, a conflict that produced a major crisis in American politics: the new nation nearly disintegrated when the New England states opposed "Mr. Madison's war" and threatened to withdraw from the Union at the Hartford Convention of 1814.

It is noteworthy that during the first century of American independence, political forces that were unhappy with the policies of the national government—from Jefferson's Embargo, the Louisiana Purchase, and the War of 1812 to Abraham Lincoln's refusal to countenance the expansion of slavery—threatened to secede from the Union. Secession was regarded as a viable alternative only because no powerful neighbors existed on U.S. borders. Thus, American states could consider seceding from the Union without having to fear that they might be gobbled up by a hostile neighbor. This unique international setting explains why the United States repeatedly contended with threats of secession during its first century of independence. The fledgling democracies of nineteenth-century Europe did not encounter this problem, despite their considerable linguistic and religious heterogeneity. (The major exception to this rule was Norway's secession from Sweden in 1905. It should be noted, however, that the Norse were situated on the very northern edge of Europe—on the periphery of the continent—at a considerable distance from land-hungry neighbors and the major European military powers.[14])

The most serious political crisis in American history—the Civil War—involved secession and also had international dimensions. As Keohane notes in the essay mentioned above, the increasing profits that slaveholders made selling cotton in world markets during the second quarter of the nineteenth century strengthened the South's commitment to the institution of slavery.[15] The perceived threat of slavery's expansion into new U.S. territories sparked interregional conflicts over the South's "peculiar institution." Ultimately, of course, the South seceded and the Civil War erupted. President Lincoln issued the Emancipation Proclamation largely to make it politically impossible for Britain and France to recognize the Confederacy, for he feared that such recognition from abroad might enable the South to prevail. Thus the conduct and outcome, as well as the outbreak, of the worst political crisis in American history involved the first two kinds of international influence discussed in the section above—military intervention and foreign trade.

International Influences on Modern American Politics: Some Hypotheses

A number of questions and hypotheses are worth exploring with regard to international influences on modern American politics. For example, it would be fruitful to examine the effects of war and peace on the organization and conduct of American party politics. The balance of power in Europe following the Napoleonic Wars insulated the United States from the threat of invasion by the world's most powerful states. It can be hypothesized that nineteenth-century international politics enabled the United States to develop distinct forms of political organization that came to characterize American party politics. During the nineteenth century American parties controlled or were associated with military formations and political militia. (The most notorious such relationship was that between the Democratic party and the Ku Klux Klan in the South during Reconstruction.) By the late nineteenth century the major parties mobilized 80 percent or more of the adult male population for virtual combat in the electoral arena.[16]

With the advent of German and Soviet challenges to U.S. national security in the twentieth century, the country's political parties underwent a transformation. Progressive reformers undertook to disband party militia and to deprive party organizations of their capacity to mobilize enormous numbers of people. They sought to endow the state with a monopoly over mass mobilization and coercion and to limit the use of mobilization and military formations to warfare against foreign foes. These reforms largely succeeded as Europe and the United States were moving toward World War I. The implementation of these reforms is what chiefly distinguishes twentieth-century American politics from its nineteenth-century forms.

Another hypothesis worth exploring concerns the interrelation of war and U.S. domestic politics. Wars endow the national government with unprecedented powers. When hostilities end, political forces face the question of which war-acquired powers they will permit the government to retain. The coming of peace also raises the issue of precisely who will influence the government's use of its expanded powers. Thus the cessation of international conflict and warfare often coincides with an intensification of domestic political hostilities.[17]

Following the United States' involvement in wars, conservative political forces generally sought to deprive Washington of the power it had acquired over the economy during the war. After World War I conservatives sought to bring about a "return to normalcy," as President Warren Harding termed it. Sen. Robert Taft of Ohio led a similar crusade after World War II.

Recognizing that it might not be possible to deprive the national government of all its new authority, conservatives have also been concerned to see that the wrong people do not gain influence over how Washington uses its enhanced powers in the aftermath of wars. Thus World Wars I and II were followed by right-wing attacks on the Left—the Red Scare following World War I and McCarthyism following World War II.[18]

In the case of both world wars, the American Left had been energized in part by the war's effects abroad—the Russian Revolution in 1917 and the enhanced prestige that communism acquired from the Soviet Union's role in the defeat of Nazi Germany in 1945. In the absence of such foreign inspiration, socialism and communism held out no special allure among the American working classes following the Civil War. Conservatives, therefore, did not perceive the need for an anti-Communist crusade in the late 1860s and the early 1870s. But wartime mobilization in the 1860s did strengthen the Radical Republicans and lead them to press for full equality for the former slaves. Mobilization also inspired more strikes among the northern working classes. Upper-class Republicans feared workers might conclude from the abolition of slavery that property rights could legitimately be abrogated by the U.S. government. To forestall such a disaster, wealthy Republicans began to profess the ideology of liberalism. Liberal Republicans argued that the powers that the national government acquired in the Civil War should be sharply circumscribed and the government should accord the utmost respect to the rights of property.

World War II and the Cold War significantly altered domestic politics

Table 16-1   Party Vote on the 1990 Congressional
Resolution Authorizing the President
to Use Force Against Iraq in the
Persian Gulf Crisis

		Yes	No
Senate			
	Republicans	43	2
	Democrats	9	45
House			
	Republicans	164	3
	Democrats	86	179

in the United States. To mobilize support at home in response to foreign crises, Presidents Roosevelt and Truman brought prominent businessmen and lawyers into their administrations. Members of what became known as the American Establishment thereby came to dominate the conduct of U.S. foreign policy. In this way, the political bases of the New Deal and Fair Deal were expanded; the conservative campaign of Senator Taft was defeated; and the Democratic party's dominance of the presidency was secured.

The end of the Cold War is likely to bring about a similar transformation of U.S. politics. Although the precise nature of these changes cannot be foreseen, it is possible to anticipate some broad outlines. The collapse of the Soviet Union and the end of the Cold War will probably work to the disadvantage of the Republican party. The two major parties in the United States have become entrenched in different segments of the American state apparatus—the Republicans in the national security sector and the Democrats in the social services, in regulatory agencies, and in the domestic state apparatus more generally. In recent years, Republicans have lent greater support than Democrats to new weapons systems (such as the "Star Wars" antimissile system). Republican officials have also favored vigorous use of the American military in foreign interventions. As Table 16-1 indicates, Republicans in both houses of Congress almost unanimously supported the 1990 resolution authorizing President Bush to use military force to expel Iraq from Kuwait. By contrast, four out of every five Democrats in the Senate and more than two-thirds of the Democrats voting in the House opposed using the American military in the Persian Gulf crisis. On the other hand, Democrats in both the Senate and the House are considerably more likely than congressional Republicans to support the expansion of federal social service and regulatory programs.

From the 1920s through the 1950s, however, conservative Republicans opposed the strengthening and active use of the military, and were denounced by their opponents as isolationists. Mainstream liberal political forces were distinguished from the extreme Left by their support for hard-line Cold War policies. In the 1948 presidential election, for example, leftists backed the Progressive party candidacy of Henry Wallace against the Democratic standard-bearer Harry Truman. Wallace denounced Truman's policy overseas as "war mongering." Liberals saw Truman's foreign and military policies, however, as the defense of freedom against Communist tyranny.

Liberal hostility to the military dates from the Vietnam War. Liberal academics and political activists argued that the war detracted from President Lyndon B. Johnson's Great Society programs.[19] Abandoned by liberal Democrats, the military cultivated the support of conservatives and Republicans during the Vietnamese conflict and has done so ever since.

The men and women who work in the social service sector naturally support the programs they administer and consequently are more likely to be liberals than conservatives. The converse is true of the employees of defense agencies and firms. Because Democratic politicians can be counted on to back social programs more than Republicans, elites and workers in the social welfare and nonprofit sectors have reasons to favor Democratic electoral victories. In a parallel fashion, individuals with commitments to, and stakes in, national security agencies and programs have reasons to favor the Republicans. In this way, the fates of the two parties have become linked to different segments of the state.

The Republicans' link with the national security apparatus and the Democrats with the domestic state was reinforced by Reaganism. President Ronald Reagan pushed vigorously to expand defense programs and cut social spending. He also made taxes a central issue in American national politics. Reagan's placing the issue of taxation on the political agenda had important consequences for American politics.

By reducing government revenues, Reaganite tax policies led Democrats and Republicans to conclude that defense and social expenditures sharply competed with one another. Therefore, Republicans had reasons not only to press for increases in spending on the defense programs they favored but also to oppose spending on social programs. Conversely, Democrats had reasons to oppose defense programs as well as to support greater social spending. So long as taxes had not been on the political agenda—even though tax rates ranged up to 91 percent of personal income—the welfare and warfare states had been compatible with one another. By raising the issue of taxes, Ronald Reagan changed American politics.

It is in this sense that the two parties developed commitments to, and become entrenched in, competing segments of the American state. The end of the Cold War will provide Democrats with the opportunity to secure reductions in defense spending. These cuts in national security expenditures are likely to injure the GOP by reducing the number of communities with military bases and weapons plants that provide local elites and voters with a stake in Republican electoral success.

Some Democrats have also used the collapse of the Soviet Union to argue that the most serious international threat the United States now faces is economic, not military. To prevail in international economic competition, these political leaders argue, the United States must adopt the institutions and practices of "state capitalism" that, liberal analysts assert, explain the economic success of America's most important international rivals, notably Japan. Democrats are thus using the end of the Cold War to argue for greater government involvement in the economy.[20]

Although harming the Republicans, the end of the Cold War may not benefit the Democrats. In electing a president, voters need no longer select a candidate they judge capable of leading the nation in a war with a superpower. Voters thus may no longer consider prior government experience a critically important qualification for candidates. This may help explain the surprisingly strong performance of the independent candidate, Ross Perot, in the 1992 presidential election and may presage strong runs for the presidency by candidates without prior government experience in the future.

Finally, U.S. domestic policy and politics have been shaped by the effort to influence foreign affairs. One of the most significant examples of this involved civil rights legislation in the 1960s.[21] The proponents of the 1964 Civil Rights Act outlawing racial discrimination in public accommodations argued that the system of racial segregation in the South embarrassed the United States in its competition with the Soviet Union for the "hearts and minds" of the leaders and the populations of the newly independent states of Africa and Asia. To emphasize this point, while Congress was considering the bill, civil rights demonstrators organized sit-ins at roadside restaurants in Maryland frequented by Third World diplomats traveling between the United Nations in New York and their embassies in Washington, D.C. And the first Kennedy administration official who testified for the bill was the secretary of state, who discussed the foreign policy implications of the racial practices civil rights legislation would outlaw.

It is also worth exploring a number of hypotheses concerning how the second of the international influences mentioned above—the world economy—has shaped American domestic politics. During the nineteenth century a direct tie existed between protectionism and state building in the United States. The Whig and Republican parties advocated levying high tariffs and using the revenues generated thereby to finance and strengthen the national government. Henry Clay called this the "American system." In the twentieth century, however, advocates of a stronger government in Washington have generally been proponents of free trade. Franklin D. Roosevelt exemplified this twentieth-century pattern. The United States' growing economic and political power internationally explains how it became possible in the twentieth century for American nationalists and state-builders to be supporters of free trade.

During its first century, the United States was responsible for only a small fraction of the world's economic output. Consequently, it was able to depend on the world's economic leader, Great Britain, to provide it with many crucial services. For example, it could rely on the Bank of England to serve as a lender of last resort to bail out American firms that were in danger of collapsing during economic crises. The United States could thus get by without its own central bank—indeed, without much of a central state—through the end of the nineteenth century. By the twentieth century, however, the U.S. economy had grown so large relative to the rest of the world that the country could no longer call on other governments to perform these vital services. In particular, the demands of U.S. firms during the depression of 1907 threatened to overwhelm the Bank of England. This experience persuaded American bankers to support the creation of a U.S. central bank, the Federal Reserve, in 1913.[22] Thus, the change in the United States' standing in the world economy is one explanation for the country's ability to get by without a strong national state during its first hundred years and why the national government became stronger in the twentieth century.

In addition, during the country's first hundred years, its economy was small enough relative to the rest of the world so that it did not have to worry about the impact its policies might have abroad. For example, the United States could pursue protectionist trade policies without having to worry that the manufacturers of many products might be unable to sell everything they produced if the U.S. market were closed to them. By 1930, however, the United States had become such a major economic force that the ultraprotectionist Hawley-Smoot Tariff enacted that year impaired much of the world's trade and thus contributed significantly to the global Great Depression of the 1930s.

The Great Depression made U.S. officials realize that the United States could no longer fail to consider the effects of its policies on the world economy. Indeed, in conjunction with World War II and the Cold War, it persuaded U.S. officials that the country was now practically obliged to assume the responsibility of international leadership. The United States now provides the currency that facilitates world commerce and also serves as the guarantor of international trade. The United States took the lead in negotiating the General Agreement on Tariffs and Trade (GATT) in 1947-1948, and it has headed up the operation of GATT over the past half-century.

The standing of the United States in the international economy and state system enabled it to enjoy many triumphs abroad and to exercise world leadership in the 1940s and 1950s. These successes in foreign policy, in turn, had important consequences for its domestic politics. A record of victories in foreign affairs helped liberal and moderate internationalists, such as Harry Truman and Dwight Eisenhower, to defeat their conservative isolationist opponents and enabled them to secure the enactment of policies that greatly strengthened the American national state. In other words, the standing of the United States in the international economic and political systems very much influenced who prevailed in the American domestic political system, the policies the victors were able to enact, and the growing size and strength of the American national state that they led.

The international system also helped to bring about a transformation in the relationship among, and the relative power of, the major institutions of U.S. government. It is commonly observed that World War II and the Cold War strengthened the presidency relative to Congress.[23] This was precisely one of the objections that Republican conservatives, Senator Taft was one, raised to the foreign policies of the Roosevelt and Truman administrations. They argued that by diminishing the role of Congress and enhancing the strength of the executive, the policies pursued in the 1940s and 1950s would adversely affect the constitutional separation of powers and weaken the democratic character of the American regime.

Since the Vietnam War the shoe has been on the other foot, so to speak, in partisan and ideological terms.[24] Liberal congressional Democrats opposed almost every use of the American military by successive presidents from the 1960s to the 1990s—from the War in Vietnam to the Persian Gulf War. Under Ronald Reagan, in particular, Republican presidents became closely identified with the buildup and vigorous use of the American military. It is therefore likely that the reduction of U.S. military spending now accompanying the demise of the Soviet Union and the end of the Cold War will weaken the Republican party, as argued above, and also lead to a decline in the power of the presidency that the Republicans dominated for a quarter-century and with whose power they became identified.

It certainly is the case that with the end of the Cold War, liberals and Democrats are exhibiting an increased determination to use all the political institutions in which they enjoy influence to attack the policies and powers of the "imperial presidency." A case in point was the disagreement between the Bush administration and various liberal forces over how the United States should deal with a flood of refugees from Haiti following the military coup in that country in 1991.

The Bush administration claimed that the Haitians were fleeing poverty, not political persecution, and hence were not eligible for admission to the United States as political refugees. The administration also noted that many Haitians were perishing at sea. To dissuade more refugees from setting out for the United States in unseaworthy craft, the White House ordered the U.S. Coast Guard to intercept them at sea, hold them at the U.S. naval base in Guantanamo Bay, Cuba, and then return them to Haiti. Liberal advocacy groups concerned with the Haitian refugees asserted that the Haitians were fleeing persecution by the military dictatorship that had overthrown Haiti's newly elected government and charged that the Bush administration's refusal to admit the refugees to the United

States was racist. They found a sympathetic federal district court judge who ruled in their favor and enjoined the military from returning the refugees to Haiti. The Bush White House found it necessary to appeal to the U.S. Supreme Court to void the injunction.

Liberal political forces were able to use their command of legal talent and access to the federal judiciary to reverse a presidential use of the military with which they disagreed, and to compel the president to fight in their arena. This may be a foretaste of some of the institutional challenges that U.S. presidents may face in the post-Cold War era: opponents of the president need not fear that intervening in the command structure of the military might encourage a hostile foreign power to invade the United States.

Conclusion

In conclusion, then, the United States exists in a world of nations. U.S. borders are permeable to five flows of great concern to its citizens and its government. The efforts of various political forces and the government to reduce or regulate these flows have shaped U.S. politics in important ways. When America occupied a peripheral position in the international economy and state system, its domestic politics—indeed, its very birth as an independent state and survival as a single, unified nation—were open to overwhelming influences from abroad. Even after America's early vulnerability to domination by foreign powers passed, however, the politics of the United States continued to be subject to a number of substantial international influences.

It is possible to propose a number of hypotheses concerning the character, sources, and consequences of international influences on modern American politics. Although there is presently little in the literature of American politics that analyzes these influences, it is a promising area for future work. Americanists might approach this topic by addressing the questions raised above and conducting research that would serve either to confirm or disconfirm the various hypotheses this chapter has proposed.

Notes

I would like to thank Martha Derthick, Peter Katzenstein, Steven Kennedy, Ronald Rogowski, Richard Valelly, and especially Benjamin Ginsberg for helpful comments on drafts of this chapter and express my appreciation to Glenn Altschuler, Tim Borstelmann, and Elaine Swift for suggesting references.

1. Peter Gourevitch, "The Second Image Reversed: The International Sources of Domestic Politics," *International Organization* 32 (1978): 881-912; Alexander Gerschenkron, *Economic Backwardness in Historical Perspective* (Cambridge: Harvard University Press, 1963).
2. See, for example, Gabriel Almond, "Review Article: The International-National Connection," *British Journal of Political Science* 19 (1989): 237-259; Peter

Gourevitch, "The Second Image Reversed: The International Sources of Domestic Politics," *International Organization* 32 (1978): 881-912; Peter Katzenstein, *Small States in World Markets* (Ithaca, N.Y.: Cornell University Press, 1985); James Kurth, "The Political Consequences of the Product Cycle: Industrial History and Comparative Politics," *International Organization* 33 (1979): 1-34; David Lake, *Power, Protection, and Free Trade* (Ithaca, N.Y.: Cornell University Press, 1988); Ronald Rogowski, *Commerce and Coalitions: How Trade Affects Domestic Political Alignments* (Princeton, N.J.: Princeton University Press, 1989); Aristide Zolberg, "Troubled Hegemon: The Impact of Global Engagement on American Democracy" (Paper delivered at the Annual Meeting of the American Political Science Association, 1989, Atlanta, Georgia).

3. Alexis de Tocqueville, *Democracy in America* (New York: Vintage Books, 1945), 299. I am grateful to Elaine Swift for bringing this passage to my attention.

4. Robert Keohane, "Associative American Development, 1776-1860: Economic Growth and Political Disintegration," in *The Antinomies of Interdependence*, ed. John Gerard Ruggie (New York: Columbia University Press, 1983), 43-90.

5. Edwin Amenta and Theda Skocpol, "Redefining the New Deal: World War II and the Development of Social Provision in the United States," in *The Politics of Social Policy in the United States*, ed. Margaret Weir, Ann Shola Orloff, and Theda Skocpol (Princeton, N.J.: Princeton University Press, 1988), 81-122.

6. Edward Banfield and James Q. Wilson, *City Politics* (Cambridge: Harvard University Press, 1963).

7. Louis Hartz, *The Liberal Tradition in America* (New York: Harcourt, Brace, 1955).

8. I am indebted to Martha Derthick for suggesting the relevance of this observation to my argument here.

9. Theda Skocpol, *Protecting Soldiers and Mothers: The Political Origins of Social Policy in the United States* (Cambridge: Harvard University Press, 1992).

10. I am indebted to Richard Valelly for this point.

11. Paul Peterson, *City Limits* (Chicago: University of Chicago Press, 1981).

12. Donald Robinson, *Slavery in the Structure of American Politics, 1765-1820* (New York: Norton, 1979), 250.

13. Richard Ellis, *The Jeffersonian Crisis* (New York: Norton, 1971).

14. Belgium seceded from the Netherlands, but its independence was guaranteed by a conference of Great Powers, preventing any single power from absorbing the new nation. E. H. Kossmann, *The Low Countries, 1780-1940* (New York: Oxford University Press, 1978). I am grateful to Ronald Rogowski and Peter Katzenstein for discussing with me the European instances of national secession.

15. Keohane, "Associative American Development."

16. Richard Jensen, *The Winning of the Midwest: Social and Political Conflict, 1888-1896* (Chicago: University of Chicago Press, 1971), chap. 6.

17. Compare with Charles Maier, *Recasting Bourgeois Europe* (Princeton, N.J.: Princeton University Press, 1975).

18. Michael Paul Rogin, *The Intellectuals and McCarthy: The Radical Specter* (Cambridge: MIT Press, 1967).

19. Doris Kearns Goodwin, *Lyndon Johnson and the American Dream* (New York: Harper and Row, 1976), chaps. 10-11.

20. I am indebted to Benjamin Ginsberg for this observation.

21. I am grateful to Martha Derthick for reinforcing my conviction that foreign policy considerations played a significant role in the enactment of the 1960s civil rights legislation.

22. J. Lawrence Broz, "The Rise of the United States, International Monetary Instability, and the Origins of the Federal Reserve Act of 1913" (Paper delivered at the Annual Meeting of the American Political Science Association, 1989, Atlanta, Georgia).

23. Franz Schurman, *The Logic of World Power* (New York: Pantheon Books, 1974).
24. Benjamin Ginsberg and Martin Shefter, *Politics by Other Means* (New York: Basic Books, 1990).

17

U.S. Policy Waves in Comparative Context
David R. Mayhew

During the twentieth century, the United States has seen three waves of particularly ambitious lawmaking—the Progressive era, the New Deal era, and the 1960s-1970s.[1] (This ignores legislative activity during the two world wars.) The country has also seen a major retrenchment of state activity highlighted by Ronald Reagan's program of 1981.

Patterns of "public politics" have accompanied and largely caused, at least in a proximate sense, these lawmaking waves. By "public politics" I mean a wide range of activities through which people try to affect what governments do, that reach large audiences through media coverage, and that sometimes achieve their aims. Included are elections, strikes, riots, demonstrations, media muckraking, official investigations, and relevant actions by political movements, reformers, think-tank builders, parties, government commissions, and elected officeholders. This is a broad net.

During the same four twentieth-century periods, many other developed countries have experienced quite similar policy waves backgrounded by quite similar patterns of "public politics." The other countries' waves and patterns have not been identical to ours, but they have been intriguingly similar. This holds even for the U.S. Progressive era, which, of all the periods in question, has been studied least often in comparative perspective.

If the above is true, it is food for thought—not least about explanations of policymaking that go beyond the proximate ones supplied by the "public politics" of the United States or any other country. Why do policy-making thrusts and attendant styles of "public politics" appear in many places nearly simultaneously? Explanations based on "co-occurring conditions" and "contagion" come to mind.

Before considering these explanations, my argument will proceed through stylized accounts, for each of the four twentieth-century periods, of lawmaking and its associated "public politics" in the United States and elsewhere. Except for the United States in the 1960s-1970s, these accounts rely on standard secondary sources. I hope I do not do great injustice to them or the history they cover.

The United States in the Progressive Era

Because much of the pioneering lawmaking of the Progressive era occurred in individual states, it makes sense to examine the states as well as the nation as a whole. Legislative activity was at a high pitch in the states from roughly 1905 through 1914; on Capitol Hill the peak period was 1906 through 1916.[2] Major themes included government efficiency, regulation of industry, progressive taxation, social reform, and democratization of public processes and institutions. In the states, reformers enacted process innovations such as corrupt practices acts and the direct primary, recall, referendum, and initiative throughout the era. Substantively, the state-level agenda shifted from railroad regulation around 1905 to items such as workmen's compensation, child labor codes, mothers' pensions, and maximum-hour laws for women after about 1910. Massachusetts passed the country's first minimum wage law. At the national level, two enactments in 1906—Theodore Roosevelt's Hepburn Act regulating railroads and his Pure Food and Drug Act—keynoted the era. Congresses under Taft in 1909-1913 voted more railroad regulation, created the Department of Labor and the Children's Bureau, approved the Sixteenth Amendment authorizing a federal income tax and the Seventeenth to elect senators directly, and dismantled the conservative House leadership hierarchy developed by Speakers Reed and Cannon. Congresses under Wilson in 1913-1916 produced, among other things, the Federal Reserve Act, the Clayton Antitrust Act, the Federal Trade Commission, a progressive income tax code, and a variety of labor enactments—though not welfare-state transfer programs; mothers' pensions at the state level were the chief such U.S. initiative during the Progressive era.[3]

What was the era's "public politics" background? The presidential election of 1904, waged mainly over the tariff, seems to have had little to do with the onset of reform. Rather, analysts write of a "turning-point [in] the weight of opinion" or a "new political mood" of reform activism that set in rather abruptly in 1905-1906.[4] With journalistic muckraking serving as a prod, movement activity erupted. The American Federation of Labor, to name one organization, inserted itself into electoral politics with unprecedented energy in 1906-1909.[5] Much of the educated public came to enlist in Progressive causes that engendered laws throughout the era—for example, a women's movement that maneuvered the establishment of the Children's Bureau in 1912.[6] In controversy and intensity of public involvement in politics, Taft's years seem to have exceeded Roosevelt's: "The simmering discontents of the previous decade boiled over [in 1909] into full-blown political turmoil. At the same time the insurgencies and reform movements of the time spewed forth a welter of exciting, unsettling ideas and doctrines." [7] The International Workers of the World triggered some of the notable strikes of U.S. history—Los Angeles (printers) in 1911, Lawrence (textile workers) in 1912, and Paterson (textile workers) in 1913. The American Socialist party grew to its peak strength in 1912, electing many mayors after 1910.

In the early Progressive era particularly, elected executives pressed legislatures in the cause of reform. Chiefly, as with Robert La Follette in Wisconsin, Charles Evans Hughes in New York, and Theodore Roosevelt in Washington, D.C., that meant Republican executives confronting Republican legislatures. In general, the executive reformers came away dissatisfied—Congress in 1907-1909 stonewalled Theodore Roosevelt and his program, for example. Small surprise that the chief targets of the era's democratizing reforms, aside from party organizations, were the U.S. House and Senate and the state legislatures (which could be circumvented, it was hoped, through initiatives and referenda). After about 1910, cross-party coalitions of insurgent Republicans and Democrats came into their own as enacters of reform legislation—in Massachusetts, North Dakota, and New Jersey, for example, as well as under President Taft in 1911-1913. The Republican party self-destructed into Progressive and orthodox fragments in 1912. Wilson as president won his chance at "party government" starting in 1913 (though he had just governed New Jersey no less effectively in harness with a Republican state senate), as did new Democratic majorities in, for example, New York and Ohio and other states. Many of the last Progressive governments were Democratic party affairs.

Elsewhere, 1905 to 1913

In Europe as in the United States, 1905-1906 was a political watershed in governments' policy stances and actions. Outside Britain (and unlike the United States), one reason for this was strikes and demonstrations in the revolutionary year of 1905. Verdicts by the then small European electorates do not seem to have played a role. To judge by its issue content, for example, the British Liberals' sweeping election victory of 1906 did not provide any more of a mandate for reform than did Theodore Roosevelt's landslide of 1904.[8]

What were the new stances and actions? According to one account that also brings to mind Theodore Roosevelt, Europe's post-1905 governments "were very consciously 'technocratic,' for they intended to use the power of the State to eliminate social evils." "In most European countries, the years from 1906 to 1909 were self-consciously progressive; technocrats well to the fore."[9] During 1906 through 1909 or so, leaders of many governments announced eye-catching programs that featured some mix of increased central taxation, government efficiency, labor laws, social welfare instruments, and various democratizing moves. That was true, for example, of Clemenceau's 17-point program in 1906 in France, Giolitti's program in Italy, the Campbell-Bannerman then Asquith program in Britain, and also Deakin's 1906 program of welfare-state nationalism in Australia.

But also like Theodore Roosevelt's, most such programs failed or only partly succeeded. Government leaders could not put them through their legislative bodies. Clemenceau won only one of his 17 points. Giolitti encountered resistance. In Britain, Lloyd George's controversial 1909 budget foundered in the House of Lords. Bülow in Germany, in search of more revenue, ran up against the restrictive Prussian voter franchise that colored his parliament. In Britain, Germany, to some extent Italy, as in the United States, prominent democratizing moves that followed during 1908-1911 took aim at obstructive legislative bodies. (Lloyd George won out over the House of Lords through the Parliament Act of 1911, and Giolitti expanded the Italian suffrage, but Germany took no action.)[10]

But that was not all. As in the United States, strikes, demonstrations, and movement activity like that by women's suffragists increased in 1909-1910. Labor unrest produced a general strike in Sweden in 1909 and one major strike after another in France during 1909-1913 and Britain during 1910-1914.[11] "After 1909, almost all European countries went into a period of relative chaos." [12] It was against this background that governments enacted labor reforms and some of their major social-welfare instruments of the century—for example, Britain's National Insurance Act of 1911, a comprehensive German measure that same year (updating Bismarck's), and Sweden's Pension Act of 1913.[13] France also experienced a high tide of welfare-state action during these years, but as in the United States, that high tide was not very high.[14] In general, in Europe as well as the United States in 1906-1914, reforms percolated through governments in ways more complicated than theories of party government would suggest. It was not a great party age.

The New Deal Era in the United States

As a surge of lawmaking aimed at recovery or reform, the New Deal era arguably extended from 1932 through 1938. Under Hoover in 1932, a resuscitated coalition of Democrats and insurgent Republicans passed significant labor, relief, and progressive-tax initiatives. Franklin Roosevelt's "hundred days" in the spring of 1933 set a new standard for legislative productivity; that season's National Industrial Recovery Act (NRA) and Agricultural Adjustment Act (AAA) headed an enactment list that included relief, securities regulation, banking deposit insurance, and the Tennessee Valley Authority. Just as remarkable were the second hundred days of the summer of 1935; that season yielded arguably the New Deal's two most important measures—the Wagner Labor Relations Act and the Social Security Act—as well as a controversial tax-the-rich measure and a breakup of public utility holding companies. More disappointing to New

Dealers, but still notable, was a series of 1937-1938 measures that addressed public housing and farm tenancy, established a national minimum
wage, and primed the economy.[15]

The background to the 1932 and 1933 lawmaking was an overriding
sense of depression emergency that produced the 1932 Democratic election landslide and licensed Roosevelt's quasi-corporatist experiments with
the economy through the AAA and NRA. In general, the enactments of
the "First New Deal" had a reformist Democratic or Progressive edge;
nonetheless a problem-solving, "coalition of the whole" atmosphere per-
sisted through most of Roosevelt's first two years. Much different was the
environment of 1935-1937, which brought, in Schlesinger's phrase, a
"politics of upheaval." Great nationwide strikes occurred in 1934, evidently with consequence on Capitol Hill: "It is unlikely that the NLRA
[the Wagner Act] would have been passed without the labor upsurge of
1934-1935."[16] Talented competitors in a 1935-1936 contest to mobilize
the public included Huey Long (to whom the Wealth Tax Act of 1935
was said to owe, indirectly), the Townsend movement (whose pressure for
old age pensions was felt in Congress in 1935), the radio priest Father
Charles E. Coughlin, and the Communist party (working through, for
example, the incipient CIO). There was a uniquely powerful upwelling of
the Left, and Roosevelt shifted his coalitional base to encompass it—by
words and actions and through alliances with, for example, the CIO, the
Farm-Labor party in Minnesota, the Progressive party in Wisconsin, and
the American Labor party in New York. One result was a bitter ideological polarization of American politics that, starting in 1938, cast the House
Un-American Activities Committees against the New Deal Left. That
polarization stayed prominent until the late 1940s.

Elsewhere, 1932 to 1938

For policymaking in the 1930s, the first thing one notices across a
wide range of countries is *dis*similarity.[17] That does not help my case. To
be sure, the United States, in being open to deficits and demand stimulation, resembled Sweden under the Social Democrats and Germany under
the Nazis, but that scarcely exhausts the three-way comparison. The decade's politics seem to merit this generalization: Parties really did have
distinctive programs—or assembled them on the spot, as in the case of the
New Dealers—and it made a considerable difference which parties or
coalitions ruled. Britain and Australia, run by Conservative-dominated
"national governments" after 1931, stayed close to economic orthodoxy.
New Zealand experienced a burst of welfare-state reform when Labour
took power in 1935. Sweden had its well-known Social Democratic innovations. France achieved a historic labor-relations pact under Léon Blum's
1936 Popular Front. Belgium, run by a fresh Social Democratic government starting in 1935, enacted "a 'New Deal' type of emergency pro-

gram" that year and then a comprehensive labor program (emulating France's next door) in 1936. Even Canada fits in a perverse way: A 1935 Tory government, beset by demagoguery and discontent matching those in the United States, enacted all at once a vast program replicating most of the New Deal. But a new Liberal government killed nearly all of it a few months later.[18] One pattern, then, for the decade is: Distinctive party programs and action, but not cross-national policy commonality.

Still, one commonality involving the United States does appear. That is the widespread incidence of movement activity, strikes, and other direct action from 1934 onward accompanied by the upwelling of the Left. The second New Deal of 1935, though not the first of 1933, arguably belongs in a category with the 1936 Popular Front governments of France and Spain. Ideological commitment, strikes, and roiling movements supplied an atmosphere for those governments too.[19] Also, directly contemporaneous with the 1935-1936 New Deal were the ambitious Canadian Tory program (though not under Left-coalition auspices) and the New Zealand Labour and Belgian Social Democratic programs (though I have not come across evidence of underpinning strikes, mass action, or Popular Front enthusiasm in the latter two cases). In the West in general, as in the United States, the energizing of the Left in the mid-1930s produced a bitter ideological polarization that did much to frame domestic political discourse until the coming of the Cold War in 1947-1948.

The United States in the 1960s and 1970s

Elsewhere I have argued that a long surge of national lawmaking took place in the United States from 1963 through 1975 or 1976. Important statutes kept winning passage in unusually high volume, constituting a major, continuous thrust toward greater federal spending and regulation.[20] Robert J. Lampman identifies 1965 through 1976 as the years between which the country's postwar surge in social welfare spending took place—rising from 11.2 to a peak 19.3 percent of GNP.[21] Seventy-seven new social programs were established under Johnson in 1963-1968; forty-four under Nixon and Ford in 1969-1976.[22] Major items included Medicare, Medicaid, and housing, education, and antipoverty initiatives under Johnson, but also an ambitious expansion of entitlements under Nixon—for example, Supplemental Security Income (SSI) for the aged, disabled, and blind; greatly multiplied food-stamps assistance; publicly financed "CETA jobs" for the unemployed; and a 23 percent hike in social security benefits (controlling for inflation) in 1969-1972. Major civil rights acts passed in 1964, 1965, and 1968 under Johnson. Drives to regulate industry gained momentum under Johnson but peaked under Nixon. Fourteen statutes and two new agencies to that end accrued under Johnson; eighteen statutes and six new agencies under Nixon.[23] Instances in the consumer field were the Traffic Safety Act of 1966, the Fair Packaging and Labeling Act of 1966, and the Consumer Product Safety Act of 1972. Landmark environmental acts—all passed under Nixon—included the National Environmental Policy Act (NEPA) of 1969, the Clean Air Act of 1970, and the Water Pollution Control Act of 1972. Other regulatory instruments included the Occupational Safety and Health Act (OSHA) of 1970 and the Federal Election Campaign Act of 1974. This account could go on; the general point is that a great deal kept happening.

Under the heading of public politics, Johnson's leadership in the wake of John Kennedy's assassination counted heavily. That time, until November 1964, was probably the most productive legislative season since 1935; it yielded the Higher Education Act of 1963, the Wilderness Act of 1964, the Food Stamp Act of 1964, the (delayed) Kennedy tax cut, the Civil Rights Act of 1964, and the Economic Opportunity (antipoverty) Act of 1964. The landslide election of 1964, producing a rare two-to-one Democratic edge in the House, empowered that party to enact a program it had been preparing for a decade—including Medicare and the Elementary and Secondary Education Act (ESEA) of 1965. Beyond that, much lawmaking seems to have owed to movement activity, other direct political action, and events. Civil-rights demonstrations, the violence in Birmingham and Selma, and the assassination of the Rev. Martin Luther King, Jr., seem to have supplied necessary conditions for enacting the civil rights instruments of 1964 (public accommodations), 1965 (voting rights), and 1968 (open housing). All three acts were passed by large cross-party majorities. Anyone who lived through 1968-1974 will remember the extraordinarily political turmoil of that time. Its ingredients were an antiwar movement that pursued legislative and other courses of action; a consumer movement that provoked several statutes; an environmental movement that mushroomed around 1970 and contributed to several more statutes; and a new women's movement that lobbied Congress with great success in 1971-1972 (the Equal Rights Amendment won approval then, although the states would not ratify it).[24] In general, congressional liberals responding to various causes had good luck passing laws under Nixon. Often they had administration support, as on entitlements expansion and some of the major environmental moves.

Elsewhere, 1963 through 1976

I will not try to track the equivalent of "regulation" in other countries. But government spending is easier, and the story is familiar and more or less the same everywhere. Figures marshaled by standard sources echo the surge in U.S. social spending between 1965 and 1976: Japan's social spending rose especially sharply (from 14 to 19 percent of the budget) between 1965 and 1975; total British government spending rose from 33.6 to 45.1 percent of GNP between 1964 and 1975. In one study of eighteen countries, the mean social share of GDP rose from 13.7 to

26.5 percent between 1960 and 1981. In another study of eighteen countries, mean government revenue rose from 28.5 to 38.5 percent of GDP between 1960 and 1975.[25] In direction of change, at least, the United States during this era was just one of the pack.

What kinds of public politics accompanied these public sector surges? This subject can only be touched on here, but certain interesting patterns appear. In some countries, ambitious party programs of the early or mid-1960s, presented and carried through in the style of the Democrats' Great Society program, seem to have made the difference. That was true of the Canadian Liberals' pension, assistance, and medical insurance plans of 1965-1966; the Dutch confessional parties' "mid-sixties social policy surge"; and the Italian center-left coalition's move into education spending in 1963-1968.[26] But in later years, events and pressure seem to have figured more prominently in forcing government policy initiatives. Youth turmoil spread across Europe in 1967-1968; leftist assertiveness grew in the Socialist parties; Italy in particular entered "a most extraordinary period of social ferment" featuring labor unrest; strikes rocked British politics in the early 1970s.[27] In this atmosphere, the Italian public sector swelled haphazardly in the early 1970s as a response to pressure.[28] The Japanese government shifted to welfare expansion in the early 1970s in reaction to local election losses to the Left.[29] Edward Heath's Conservative government in Britain took measures between 1970 and 1974 that were not in the Tory tradition—wage controls, nationalization of a major company, a surrender to unions—at the same time the Nixon administration was making un-Republican moves.[30] But note that even in the mid-1960s there had not existed a clear relation of the classical kind between the left- or right-leaningness of parties or coalitions and their records in office. Recall that, for example, a confessional coalition spurred the Dutch welfare expansion of the mid-1960s (Labour was in opposition).[31]

The United States in the Age of Carter and Reagan

Among recent U.S. measures aimed at cutting taxes, trimming expenditures, fostering monetarism, or deregulating industry—today's family of conservative economic thrusts—Ronald Reagan's $750 billion tax cut and omnibus expenditure cut (OBRA, or Gramm-Latta II) unquestionably stand out. But those two major 1981 measures are not all. The legislative history of deregulation is instructive. Starting in 1975, federal acts to deregulate business affected securities (1975), state fair-trade laws (1975), railroads (1976 and 1980), natural gas (1978), airlines (1978), banking (1980 and 1982), and trucking (1980). A Democratic Congress passed a surprisingly business-oriented tax revision in 1978. California adopted its Proposition 13 tax cut in 1978. Helping along conservative causes in the late 1970s were the Sagebrush Rebellion, the newly prominent religious Right, the Business Roundtable, a new cluster of well-

funded think-tanks, and some aggressive right-wing political action committees. By the end of the Carter administration in 1980, the political
environment had been well softened up for Reagan. Much of the policy
turnaround associated with his presidency had already come to pass under
a Democratic party fast losing faith in its welfarism and Keynesianism.[32]

Elsewhere around 1980

Two commonalities stand out. Especially in the English-speaking
world, government policy shifts toward free markets took place at about
the same time as the one in the United States. And they were carried out,
though with nuances, by parties of both the Left and Right.[33] A British
Labour government unraveled in 1976-1979 rather as did Carter's:
Keynesianism and public spending were abandoned in a muddled and
demoralized lead-in to Thatcher's victory in 1979.[34] Mulroney's Tory government in Canada tried out some of the new ideas. In Australia and New
Zealand, Labour governments elected in 1983 and 1984 radically deregu-
lated their economies. The New Zealand government (although not Australia's, where unions remained stronger) let unemployment rise and
moved abruptly away from progressive taxation.[35] Elsewhere the trends
are cloudier, though in general the case for cross-national policy commonality, regardless of party, seems strong enough. France, for example,
after "deplanifying" in the late 1970s, experimented with socialist planning following Mitterrand's 1981 election, but then blended back, still
under Mitterrand, into what seems to have been a European thrust toward
freer markets in the 1980s.[36] One contribution to the policy commonality
is that virtually everywhere during these years, parties of the left moved to
the right.[37]

Explaining the Commonalities:
Coincidence, Contagion, and Public Politics

In each of the four eras, at least in some respects, a wave of policymaking and certain patterns of popular politics in America corresponded
to a similar wave and patterns in other countries. Here are some reflections about these accounts.

First, they address what and when, not why. If they are half-way
plausible, the question of why arises. Why the commonalities across borders? I will not pursue this question here except to suggest that both "co-
occurring conditions" and "contagion" explanations seem to figure in
varying mixes as answers. In some cases, it is easy to point to conditions
co-occurring across national boundaries that no doubt helped to spur governments into similar policy moves nearly simultaneously. The growth of
industrial labor forces and union movements in the early twentieth century probably underpinned, somehow, the labor and welfare initiatives

undertaken by many governments around 1910. Likewise the coming of age of baby boomers triggered higher-education spending in many countries in the 1960s. Those are slow-acting causes. At a faster level, simultaneous experience of phases of the international business cycle spurred similar actions—as with the depression of the 1930s and the oil shocks of the 1970s.

All this is commonplace, but note that social and economic problems do not announce themselves or their remedies unproblematically. Ideas need to intrude. The "contagion" of ideas across national boundaries can shape common responses in a context where conditions co-occur, as in the case of the distinctive and fairly unified response of members of the Organization for Economic Cooperation and Development to economic troubles around 1980. Belgium copied Blum's program in 1936; Canada evidently copied Franklin Roosevelt's in 1935.

More interesting, though, is the wide range of cross-national policy-making commonality where no very clear case for co-occurring conditions exists—at least nothing on the order of a depression or an oil shock. There, contagion explanations look like a particularly good bet. Take, for example, policymaking in the United States and elsewhere around 1910. Notwithstanding the parallel growth of industrial labor forces, it would be a tough assignment to anchor the policy-making commonality of that era in co-occurring conditions. A better idea might be shared impulses or aspirations commonly expressed. One critic of American exceptionalism has recently written of the United States during the Progressive era as the "scene of a cosmopolitan interchange" and "a prime site for the study of transnational ideologies." [38] Policy ideas evidently crossed the Atlantic fast both ways. Much U.S. policymaking in the twentieth century probably follows this model, although scholarship on the point is sparse.[39]

Contagion, moreover, can apply not just to policy initiatives but to the styles of public politics underpinning them. That is the most intriguing idea suggested by the four foregoing accounts: National leaders aggressively mobilizing publics behind ambitious programs after 1905; movement activity in 1905-1914; political strikes in 1909-1913; strikes and movements again in 1934-1937; the energizing of the Left in the mid-1930s; state-enhancing party programs in the mid-1960s; student protest in 1968; movements and strikes again in 1968-1973—all these were transnational phenomena. All of them shaped policymaking in the United States and elsewhere. The cross-national simultaneity of political styles, formations, and tactics strongly suggests idea contagion as an explanation, but, again, evidence needs to be assembled.

A second reflection is that political scientists tend to overrate parties and elections as engines of U.S. policymaking. Transfixed by election returns, realignment theories, and models of party government, we tend to ignore other features of public politics and to present an impoverished picture of relations between the public and the government. Much in the foregoing accounts backs up this view. Consider, for example, the policy-rich junctures of 1909-1913, 1935-1937, and 1969-1974 in the United States and elsewhere. To do justice to these times, one needs to give attention to direct action, political movements, ideological impulses, and general turmoil. To be sure, parties won elections during these years and sometimes passed programs. But beyond that, governments got caught up in the currents of ideologies and movements and assumed what looks like a propitiating role. Both the Nixon administration and the Italian government of around 1970, for example, beleaguered by angry elements of their publics, presided over surprising policy initiatives, possibly as a consequence. The expansion of entitlements, after all, can be a remedy for disorder. The same explanation may be applied to the years between 1909-1913.

Third, it seems to me that U.S. political parties have played rather different policy roles in different eras of the twentieth century, and political science's theoretical tradition has evolved accordingly. Herbert Croly, who gave short shrift to parties as public instruments—instead emphasizing executive leadership and direct democracy—was as suitable a spokesman as one could imagine for the Progressive era. He gave written form to the politics he witnessed. A generation later, E. E. Schattschneider captured the unique, Promethean promise of parties in the 1930s. Then, here and in Europe, parties exhibited great mobilizing potential and made programmatic commitments that seemed to be distinct and reliable. "Party government" seemed to be a way to reconstruct societies. Another generation later in the 1950s, 1960s, and 1970s, with Keynesian macroeconomics accepted by all sides and incremental state expansion permitted by economic growth, Anthony Downs's model worked well. Party "bidding" at the center for voter support, to use the British term, came to characterize politics. So far, there does not seem to exist a successor model for the 1980s and beyond.

As a last reflection, why have U.S. political scientists addressed this country's policymaking in a fashion largely innocent of international comparisons? The comparisons are there to be drawn, and not just during the twentieth century. To go back farther in time, the U.S. switch to conservatism and imperialism in the mid-1890s had European correlates—for example, the new Salisbury-Balfour regime in Britain: "Everywhere in Europe, there were governments of the right." [40] Wouldn't a good look at those turn-of-the-century settings elsewhere promise more payoff—for illuminating *this* country's politics—than yet another study of the McKinley-Bryan realignment of 1896? A bit earlier, American Populism had a striking counterpart in New Zealand—where works by Americans Edward Bellamy and Henry George served as ideological texts—during exactly that movement's high tide here in the early 1890s.[41] It was evidently an earlier transnational reform wave. Even the Civil War and Reconstruction era, which seem about as homegrown as anything can be, had similarities in Europe, where liberal reform enjoyed a continental surge: "This was a decade of reform, of political liberalization, even of some concession to what was called 'the forces of democracy.' " [42] The comparative question is a good one to ask, as, to go back yet farther, R.R. Palmer memorably did for the late eighteenth century in his *Age of the Democratic Revolution*. Why did X happen in many places? can sometimes give better traction than: Why did X happen in the United States?

The Clinton Presidency

As Bill Clinton begins his presidency, one might ask whether a comparative-policy-waves perspective offers clues about likely U.S. policymaking during the remainder of the 1990s. Is a new wave forming? Does the 1992 victory of Clinton and the Democrats foreshadow, as some analysts have suggested, a new surge of government activism in the United States and perhaps abroad?

Although such an outcome cannot be ruled out, as of mid-1993 it is hard to find support for the prospect in the political environments of Japan, North America, Western Europe, and Australasia. Nothing with the force and cope of early-twentieth-century reform, the leftist surge of the 1930s, the state expansionism of the 1960s and 1970s, or Thatcher-Reaganism seems to be in sight. In general, policymaking is in a doldrums. The traditional agendas of both Left and Right seem to be exhausted.

The one policy impulse of the early 1990s that does seem to have force and carrying power concerns political institutions. The impulse is to reform them—parties, electoral systems, and instruments of government. So far this is particularly evident in the moves to dismantle Italy's post-World War II governing arrangements, abolish New Zealand's traditional single-member-district electoral system, reconfigure Canada's federalism, and establish "term limits" for legislators in the United States. But we may see much more, given the current high levels of discontent with parties, politicians, and governments in so many first-world countries. This is an environment in which ideas can be contagious, and entrepreneurs like Ross Perot can test and spread them. For its surprising reforms of political institutions, the 1990s could come to resemble the Progressive era, though so far there is little sign of equivalent policy thrusts in social or economic areas.

Notes

For their thoughtful comments on an early draft of this work, I would like to thank John Aldrich, Robert Dahl, Eileen McDonagh, Herbert Kaufman, Joseph LaPalombara, Karen Orren, and David Stebenne.

1. See for example Theda Skocpol, "A Society without a 'State'? Political Organiza-

tion, Social Conflict, and Welfare Provision in the United States," *Journal of Public Policy* 7 (October-December 1987): 364-365; Richard A. Harris, "A Decade of Reform," in *Remaking American Politics*, ed. Richard A. Harris and Sidney A. Milkis (Boulder, Colo.: Westview, 1989), 5, 9; David R. Mayhew, *Divided We Govern: Party Control, Lawmaking, and Investigations, 1946-1990* (New Haven: Yale University Press, 1991), chap. 6.

2. General sources on the states are Richard L. McCormick, "The Discovery That Business Corrupts Politics: A Reappraisal of the Origins of Progressivism," *American Historical Review* 86 (April 1981): 266-268; George E. Mowry, *The Era of Theodore Roosevelt, 1900-1912* (New York: Harper, 1958), 71-84; and David Sarasohn, *The Party of Reform: Democrats in the Progressive Era* (Jackson: University Press of Mississippi, 1989), 112-118. General sources on the national government include Mowry, *Era of Theodore Roosevelt*, chaps. 7, 11-14; Sarasohn, *Party of Reform*, chaps. 1, 3, 4, 6; John Milton Cooper, Jr., *Pivotal Decades: The United States, 1900-1920* (New York: Norton, 1990), 46-48, 90-102, 109-121, 145-157, 162, 195-202, 212-219, 291, 298, 307-308; Lewis L. Gould, *Reform and Regulation: American Politics, 1900-1916* (New York: Wiley, 1978), 32-33, 51-73, 90-96, 105-106, 149-158, 168-175; Paolo E. Coletta, *The Presidency of William Howard Taft* (Lawrence: University Press of Kansas, 1973), chaps. 3, 5-7, 13; Arthur S. Link, *Woodrow Wilson and the Progressive Era, 1900-1917* (New York: Harper, 1954), chaps. 2, 3, 9; Howard W. Allen, "Geography and Politics: Voting on Reform Issues in the United States Senate, 1911-1916," *Journal of Southern History* 27 (1961): 218.

3. See Theda Skocpol, *Protecting Soldiers and Mothers: The Political Origins of Social Policy in the United States* (Cambridge: Harvard University Press, 1992). For sketches of lawmaking at state and national levels during the Progressive era, see Mayhew, *Divided We Govern*, 146-152.

4. McCormick, "The Discovery," 268; Gould, *Reform and Regulation*, 59. See also Mowry, *Era of Theodore Roosevelt*, chap. 4 and pp. 206-211; Cooper, *Pivotal Decades*, 80-89.

5. Julia Greene, " 'The Strike at the Ballot Box': The American Federation of Labor's Entrance into Election Politics, 1906-1909," *Labor History* 32 (Spring 1991): 165-192.

6. Skocpol, "Protecting Soldiers and Mothers," chap. 8.

7. Cooper, *Pivotal Decades*, 123.

8. See for example Derek Fraser, *The Evolution of the Modern British Welfare State* (London: Macmillan, 1973), 136.

9. Norman Stone, *Europe Transformed, 1878-1919* (Glasgow: Fontana, 1983), 129, 141.

10. This reference covers the preceding two paragraphs. On France: David Thomson, *Democracy in France since 1870* (New York: Oxford University Press, 1969), 173-176. On Italy: Denis Mack Smith, *Italy: A Modern History* (Ann Arbor: University of Michigan Press, 1959), section 7. On Britain: R. C. K. Ensor, *England, 1870-1914* (Oxford: Clarendon Press, 1960), chaps. 12, 13. On Australia: Russel Ward, *Australia* (Englewood Cliffs, N.J.: Prentice-Hall, 1965), 85-97. On Germany: A. J. Ryder, *Twentieth-Century Germany: From Bismarck to Brandt* (New York: Columbia Press, 1973), 78-80. In general: Stone, *Europe Transformed*, 141.

11. Franklin D. Scott, *Sweden: The Nation's History* (Minneapolis: University of Minnesota Press, 1977), 416-417; Thomson, *Democracy in France*, 174; Ensor, *England*, 438-441.

12. Stone, *Europe Transformed*, 144.

13. Ryder, *Twentieth-Century Germany*, 80; Hugh Heclo, *Modern Social Politics in Britain and Sweden* (New Haven: Yale University Press, 1974), chaps. 3, 4; David Thomson, *Europe since Napoleon* (New York: Knopf, 1962), 330; Ensor, *England*,

444-455.

14. Thomson, *Europe since Napoleon*, 329; Thomson, *Democracy in France*, 173-176.
15. See Jordan A. Schwarz, *The Interregnum of Despair: Hoover, Congress, and the Depression* (Urbana: University of Illinois Press, 1970), 78-90 and chaps. 5, 6, 8; William E. Leuchtenberg, *Franklin D. Roosevelt and the New Deal, 1932-1940* (New York: Harper and Row, 1963); Arthur M. Schlesinger, Jr., *The Coming of the New Deal* (Boston: Houghton Mifflin, 1958; Arthur M. Schlesinger, Jr., *The Politics of Upheaval* (Boston: Houghton Mifflin, 1960), 261, chaps. 16-18, and 381-384;. James T. Patterson, *Congressional Conservatism and the New Deal: The Growth of the Conservative Coalition in Congress, 1933-1939* (Lexington: University Press of Kentucky, 1967), chap. 2 and 77-80. For a sketch, see Mayhew, *Divided we Govern*, 34, 152-156.
16. David Plotke, "The Wagner Act, Again: Politics and Labor, 1935-37," in *Studies in American Political Development*, vol. 3 (New Haven: Yale University Press, 1989), 117.
17. See Peter A. Gourevitch, "Breaking with Orthodoxy: The Politics of Economic Policy Responses to the Depression of the 1930s," *International Organization* 38 (1984): 95-129; Kim Quayle Hill, *Democracies in Crisis: Public Policy Responses to the Great Depression* (Boulder, Colo.: Westview, 1988), chap. 4; Ekkart Zimmermann and Thomas Saalfeld, "Economic and Political Reactions to the World Economic Crisis of the 1930s in Six European Countries," *International Studies Quarterly* 32 (September 1988): 305-334. This is not a well-trodden subject: "There has been surprisingly little comparative study of the political forces that shaped the policy choices of different nations in the 1930s, and there are no general theories about these matters indicating a parsimonious way to explore this terrain." Hill, *Democracies in Crisis*, 103.
18. Adolf Sturmthal, *The Tragedy of European Labor, 1918-1939* (New York: Columbia University Press, 1943), chaps. 10, 11; David Thomson, *England in the Twentieth Century* (New York: Penguin, 1979), 147-162; Clive Turnbull, *A Concise History of Australia* (South Yarra, Victoria: Currey-O'Neil, 1983), 143-148; Keith Sinclair, *A History of New Zealand* (London: Allen Lane, 1980), 264-270; J. Bartlett Brebner, *Canada: A Modern History* (Ann Arbor: University of Michigan Press, 1970), chap. 28. On Belgium: Zimmerman and Saalfeld, "Economic and Political Reactions," quotations at 314.
19. Sturmthal, *Tragedy of European Labor*, chaps. 10, 11; H. Stuart Hughes, *Contemporary Europe: A History* (Englewood Cliffs, N.J.: Prentice-Hall, 1961), 238-243, 285-288; Raymond J. Sontag, *A Broken World: 1919-1939* (New York: Harper and Row, 1971), chaps. 10, 11.
20. Mayhew, *Divided We Govern*, chaps. 3, 4. Of the eight stylized presentations, this is the one not based on standard secondary sources. To compile, for *Divided We Govern*, a list of major U.S. federal statutes enacted from 1946 through 1990, I made two "sweeps" through materials for those decades. In the first sweep, I used accounts by contemporary witnesses, chiefly journalists, who sized up the importance of laws just passed as they reported on each of the twenty-two postwar Congresses. In the second sweep, I used recent works of policy history by specialists in forty-three areas, probing them for the authors' judgments about the importance of postwar statutes enacted in their areas. The final overall list includes 267 statutes. This is, strictly speaking, a study of motion—does the government do much at all?—rather than ideological direction, but there can be no doubt about the record of 1963 through 1975-1976: The period is characterized by a very high volume of legislation as well as a continuous regulatory and spending thrust.
21. Robert J. Lampman, *Social Welfare Spending: Accounting for Changes from 1950 to 1978* (New York: Academic Press, 1984), 8-9. The figures are for federal, state, and local governments combined, but the federal government took the lead dur-

ing these years.

22. Robert X. Browning, *Politics and Social Welfare Policy in the United States* (Knoxville: University of Tennessee Press, 1986), 79-83.

23. David Vogel, "The 'New' Social Regulation in Historical and Comparative Perspective," in *Regulation in Perspective: Historical Essays*, ed. Thomas K. McCraw (Cambridge: Harvard Univerity Press, 1981), 161; Murray L. Weidenbaum, *Business, Government, and the Public* (Englewood Cliffs, N.J.: Prentice-Hall, 1977), 5-10.

24. On the women's movement, see Jo Freeman, *The Politics of Women's Liberation: A Case Study of an Emerging Social Movement and Its Relation to the Policy Process* (New York: David McKay, 1975), 202.

25. Bradley M. Richardson and Scott C. Flanagan, *Politics in Japan* (Boston: Little Brown, 1984), 412; Richard Rose, *Do Parties Make a Difference?* (London: Macmillan, 1984), 121-122; Manfred G. Schmidt, "Learning from Catastrophes: West Germany's Public Policy," in *The Comparative History of Public Policy*, ed. Francis G. Castles (Oxford: Polity Press, 1989), 63; David R. Cameron, "The Expansion of the Public Economy: A Comparative Analysis," *American Political Science Review* 72 (1978): 1244.

26. Brebner, *Canada*, 547; Goren Therborn, " 'Pillarization' and 'Popular Movements': Two Variants of Welfare State Capitalism: The Netherlands and Sweden," in *Comparative History of Public Policy*, ed. Castles, 211; Roger Morgan, *West European Politics since 1945: The Shaping of the European Community* (London: B. T. Batsford, 1972), 188; Norman Kogan, *A Political History of Italy: The Postwar Years* (New York: Praeger, 1983), 216.

27. Morgan, *West European Politics*, 177-178, 193; Walter Laqueur, *Europe since Hitler: The Rebirth of Europe* (Baltimore: Penguin, 1970), 440-446; Peter Lane, *Europe since 1945: An Introduction* (London: Batsford Academic and Educational, 1985), 159-160; Derek W. Urwin, *Western Europe since 1945: A Short Political History* (New York: Longman, 1981), chap. 15; Paul Ginsborg, *A History of Contemporary Italy: Society and Politics 1943-1988* (New York: Longman, 1990), chap. 9, quotation at 298.

28. Kogan, *Political History of Italy*, chaps. 16-20; Ginsborg, *History of Contemporary Italy*, chaps. 9, 10.

29. Kent E. Calder, *Crisis and Compensation: Public Policy and Political Stability in Japan, 1949-1986* (Princeton, N.J.: Princeton University Press, 1988), 103-105, 215-218, 357-359, 372-374.

30. Geoffrey Alderman, *Modern Britain: A Domestic History* (London: Croon Helm, 1986), 277; Peter Jenkins, *Mrs. Thatcher's Revolution: The Ending of the Socialist Era* (Cambridge: Harvard University Press, 1988), 13-15.

31. On this general point, see Rose, *Do Parties Make a Difference?* 119-126; Cameron, "Expansion of the Public Economy," 1253-1254. In Cameron's study, having a leftist government explains a third of the variance in revenue expansion, but many specified countries work against that relation.

32. See Mayhew, *Divided We Govern*, 93-94, 166-169.

33. Frances G. Castles, "The Dynamics of Policy Change: What Happened to the English-Speaking Nations in the 1980s," *European Journal of Political Research* 18 (September 1990): 491-497.

34. Jenkins, *Mrs. Thatcher's Revolution*, 18-28.

35. Castles, "Dynamics of Policy Change," 494-496.

36. Peter Hall, *Governing the Economy: The Politics of State Intervention in Britain and France* (New York: Oxford University Press, 1986), 185-191 and chap. 8.

37. Seymour Martin Lipset, "The Death of the Third Way: Everywhere but Here, That Is," *The National Interest* (Summer 1990): 25-37.

38. Ian Tyrrell, "American Exceptionalism in an Age of International History," *Amer-*

ican Historical Review 96 (October 1991): 1052.

39. For a good concrete account of how a policy idea traveled from the United States to Britain recently, see Michael M. Atkinson and William D. Coleman, "Policy Networks, Policy Communities and the Problems of Governance," *Governance* 5 (April 1992): 154-180.

40. Stone, *Europe Transformed*, 96.

41. Sinclair, *A History of New Zealand*, chap. 2-II.

42. E. J. Hobsbawm, *The Age of Capital, 1848-1875* (New York: Charles Scribner's Sons, 1975), 71-72, 102-106, quotation at 71.

Index